Neil M. Gunn

NEIL M. GUNN
A HIGHLAND LIFE

F.R.Hart &
J.B.Pick

POLYGON

The publisher acknowledges the financial assistance
of the Scottish Arts Council
in the publication of this volume

First Published 1981 by
John Murray (Publishers) Ltd., London
Reissued 1985 by Polygon Books
1 Buccleuch Place Edinburgh

The publisher acknowledges the financial assistance
of the Scottish Arts Council
in the publication of this volume

ISBN 0 904919 95 1

Printed and bound in Great Britain by
Bell and Bain Ltd., Glasgow

Contents

Illustrations

ILLUSTRATION SOURCES

Grateful acknowledgement is given to the following for their permission for illustrations to be reproduced in this book: Title-page drawing: Keith Henderson and Faber & Faber Ltd, publishers of *Highland Pack* by Neil Gunn; 1, 2, 6–10, 14–16: Alasdair and Dairmid Gunn and the National Library of Scotland (Neil Gunn papers); 3: Gretta (Mrs Alexander) Gunn; 4: Russell D. Hart; 5: Ena (Mrs Peter John) Macleod; 11: Distillers Company Ltd; 12: Stuart Photography, Dingwall; 13: Ellie (Mrs George) Blake; 17: Dr Nan Shepherd; 18: Lady Mitchison; 19: Glasgow Art Gallery; 20: photograph by Lida Moser, reproduced from *Vogue* © The Condé Nast Publications Ltd; 21: Francis Russell Hart. The map of Scotland between pages 146/7 was drawn by Denys Baker. The illustration on p. 174 is reproduced by permission of George G. Harrap & Company Ltd, publishers of *Fishermen and Fishing Ways* by Peter Anson.

Foreword

Neil M. Gunn was a distinguished man of letters, who, when he died in 1973, left behind him a large number of works, mainly novels, which not only depicted life and scenes in the Highlands of Scotland but also hinted at something beyond all that—something that touched the hearts and aroused the interest of men and women all over the world. It was not a case of these people being attracted to his work by romantic notions of a land of mountains and mists—an interpretation of Scotland so dear to the hearts of those countless Scots living in exile in England or abroad. The attraction rested in the identification by him of an essence of life at once indefinable and alluring which many had experienced in both childhood and maturity. The chord that his work struck caused men from countries as far apart as Germany, Japan and the United States to write to him and about him. It is no accident, therefore, that his biography, so enthusiastically and lovingly written, is the work of an American and an Englishman.

Both the American Francis Hart and the Englishman John Pick became acquainted with Neil Gunn when Neil had made a name for himself as the successful author of *Morning Tide, Highland River* and *The Silver Darlings*. Their initial contacts with him were touched with feelings of admiration. My first contacts with the novelist were different; they were bound to be for he was my uncle.

My earliest memories of Neil were associated with Braefarm House near Dingwall, a small Highland town, where he spent the most creative part of his literary life. I can still see him ensconced in his deep and comfortable armchair—a chair which only he used—passing his hand through his abundant thatch of fine grey hair with a movement that was both lazy and elegant, and pontificating on points arising from the easy conversation that used to develop between my father and him. 'Well it's like this,' he would start and his magnificent analytical mind would come into play. For the use of the word 'pontificate' I make no apology as it always seemed to me that he was speaking *ex cathedra* with all the authority of an inspired intellect that had been tempered by the wisdom and good sense of a man who had learnt much from his observations of nature. His analyses were never long, were delivered easily and without pomposity and were more often than not punctuated by laughter—spontaneous, infectious and gurgling.

The atmosphere in that house, and in the others in which he lived, was conducive to conversation and quiet merriment and for this much of the credit must go to his devoted wife Daisy. For me, she symbolised the spirit of the house and indeed of the garden. She was a quiet woman, the perfect companion for a creative husband. The tasteful arrangement of household things and a garden that always appeared to be in bloom reflected her touch. Neil acknowledged the value to him of this lovely presence in the inscription he wrote in her copy of each new work. In *Second Sight* there is 'For the warmth of the House and her garden this early summer's day' and in *Wild Geese Overhead*—'To one who cultivates her garden, from her husband'. But perhaps even more revealing are the inscriptions in *The Key of the Chest*—'To Herself who keeps all the keys'—and in *The Shadow*—'For one who chases all the shadows away'. In all the houses in which they lived a warm, relaxing and tranquil atmosphere prevailed. After her death in 1963 there was an incompleteness about the atmosphere—and even all Neil's charm and warmth could not completely compensate for that absence.

Another early memory of my uncle was to see him armed with rod nimbly moving from stone to stone across the stream that flowed through his native parish, that stream of streams so wonderfully described in his allegorical work, *Highland River*. Despite his height his movements were graceful— those of the hunter, which indeed he was. I can also remember him standing on the deck of a small fishing vessel returning from a night at sea. Even on the unsteady deck of the boat he moved with the assurance of the seasoned seafarer used to that most capricious of all elements. To me he was always a man on a quest—on the river, the moor, the sea and in his inward life.

His brother, John, my father, occupied a special place in Neil's affections. In terms of age they were close. John's distinguished career in mathematics was a great source of interest for Neil, who had a remarkable flair for figures. But there was more than age and a shared interest in mathematics that linked the two brothers. A common admiration of the values of the Highland community in which they had been brought up, a shared love of the sea and the hunt and the same capacity for wonder bound them together. It was an important relationship and one which was of great help to my uncle and a source of happiness for my father. Indeed, the creation of *Highland River*, as the dedication in that book shows, owed much to this friendship of brothers. Other relatives had their influence too. Alick (or Alec), the other younger brother, was a great favourite of Neil's. Indeed, Hamish, Alick's son, was the prototype for the boy in that magical dialogue between youth and old age known as *Young Art and Old Hector*. My own brother Alasdair, who might have written this Foreword had he not been abroad, appeared in an article written during the Second World War years. Yet John Gunn remained the closest contact, the brother with whom ideas were discussed, the brother whose friendship was essential to him.

As I grew older I found Neil's company a great source of pleasure and wisdom. Talking to him led to a feeling of detachment from worldly matters and an adhesion to the significant. I felt that his reserved manner was a form of completeness within himself. With him silences were never embarrassing; they seemed to be gently charged with meaning. They were essential. Neil disliked being referred to as a mystic because for many the word meant someone whose thinking was obscure and incomprehensible. His form of mysticism was clarity of vision, the ability to understand the Truth. In that context he would allude to Aldous Huxley's genius for communicating ideas on the concept of the passivity or 'grace' required to gain perceptions of what could be described as Heaven. Perceptions of Heaven were certainly his. 'I have discovered the World! Today, this very day, in the hours that are passed just passed, for I still hear them blowing on the wind, the softest loveliest wind, with clouds coming up over the sky, and even as I write this, in the tail of my eye, just outside the small gable window, a long new branch of a climber—a white rose—not tied up, blows up and down. Oh, I wish I could tell you about it.' This magnificent opening to *The Shadow* is no more than a revelation of happiness—a happiness engendered by a new perception of things, simple things.

Neil Gunn's sense of manhood stemmed from an upbringing in which manhood was idolised. He himself was a fine figure of a man whose success as a sportsman was undisputed. A fit man, too, with the daily walk or walks being in the nature of a ritual. Yet he was able to write sensitively and delicately about how women felt. With his innate courtesy and charm he was a popular man with women, with whom he was sometimes flirtatious, gently teasing but never condescending. But there was more than that. He saw women as being the custodians of all that was precious in everyday existence and the providers of that essential link between the then and now. In *Morning Tide* he referred to the earth as the mother that is behind all mothers and to the sea as the father that is behind all fathers. This idea of the association of women with the earth, with rootedness is illustrated again in *Butcher's Broom*, the book about the Clearances, when the continuity enshrined in womanhood in the shape of Old Mairi is contrasted with the brutal enforced exodus of a people from their land to make way for sheep.

But perhaps the loveliest allusion to womanhood is to be found in *Highland River*, the book in which he searches for the source of life: 'God goes to the door and knocks. A voice calls him to come in. He enters. She is leaning with one hand on the dresser, waiting for Him. He meets her eyes. She is shy, her body therefore aloof a little, for she has the manners that would not be too familiar even with a little boy. To ask would not occur to her. To give is her instinct. With this thought for the stranger upon her, smiling, she looks deep into God's eyes and offers Him a glass of milk.'

For Neil the search for the source of life was an essential quest. His happy and comfortable home background in the idyllic surroundings of a Highland strath had helped him in this quest. I feel that his interest in Scottish Nationalism—so marked in the 1930s—stemmed from a concern to prevent the complete erosion of so many of the values to which he had been attached as a child and to preserve the heritage of a proud people. Politics were not really for him. He has been described as a benevolent anarchist—a description of him with which I would agree. His philosophy was contained in his own definition of the aim of life, which was the pursuit of the maximum amount of freedom commensurate with one's duty to the Community.

Throughout Neil's spiritual Odyssey the quest for freedom, happiness, completeness is always there—implicit in some books, explicit in others. When in *Doctor Zhivago* Boris Pasternak writes that the fabulous is never anything else but the commonplace touched by the hand of genius, he could be describing Neil Gunn's work. In *Morning Tide* Neil transforms the simple scene of a boy on a beach into something miraculous: '. . . the beach sloped in clean grey blue stones rounded and smooth, some no bigger than his fist, but some larger than his hand. As he stepped on them, they slithered and rolled with a sea noise. The noise rose up and roared upon the dusk like a wave. All around no life was to be seen, there was no movement but the sea's.'

There are other descriptions in Neil's books that are equally enchanting. In all of them there is the feeling of something beyond the tangible everyday world in which most of us live. The very titles of his books hint at this: *The Other Landscape, The Well at the World's End, The Shadow, Second Sight* and *The Atom of Delight* to name a few. In *The Well at the World's End* there is: 'Then all at once the queer feeling came over me that we were at the beginning of an adventure to find the something in life that is not there.' There is no doubt that his interest in Zen Buddhism, so clearly revealed in *The Atom of Delight*, was prompted by that religion's emphasis on the reintegration of the conscious and unconscious selves. In the book, a sort of spiritual autobiography, he describes certain revelatory experiences as both an end and a beginning—a description that brings to mind T.S. Eliot's famous beginning to 'Burnt Norton':

> Time present and time past
> are both perhaps present in time future.

This is perhaps not a coincidence. Neil Gunn valued his early contacts with Eliot and was a great admirer of the work of the poet, who was at once a revolutionary in terms of writing and a traditionalist in terms of belief. Edwin Muir's name joined Eliot's as the subject for many a conversation on poetry. There were other names but those of these two occupied a very important place in Neil Gunn's esteem. After all, all three were on a form of spiritual quest.

Neil Gunn was a warm man whose company was something to be treasured. So often meetings with him either began or ended with that tot of whisky, known in Scotland as a dram. In the parlance of the Highlands he poured a good dram—an expression with the connotation essentially of quantity. But as with his works there was quality there too. From his book *Whisky and Scotland* there is this allusion to whisky, which is pregnant with meaning: 'These generous whiskies with their individual flavours do recall the world of hills and glens, of raging elements, of shelter, of divine ease. The perfect moment for their reception is after arduous bodily stress—or mental stress, if the body be sound. The essential oils that wind in the glass uncurl their long fingers in lingering benediction and the nobler works of Creation are made manifest.' But what was almost as important was how he poured the dram. The pouring and the offering were a form of ritual and somehow the dram tasted better for it. In the same way, his presence enriched any gathering of men of goodwill. To explain the atmosphere created by him is as difficult as translating Dante or Pushkin without losing the bloom of a native tongue. For me, the next best thing to having enjoyed Neil Gunn's company is to read his works.

March 1980   DAIRMID GUNN

Preface

At one time Neil Gunn was troubled by the rumour that someone who hardly knew him intended to write his biography. He told each of us separately that if the job were ever to be done he would prefer us to do it. We avoided the responsibility with great diligence until 1978 when the opportunity of working in collaboration leapt up and stared us in the face, and we could hide no longer. The Scottish Arts Council were kind enough to allow us a research grant, and we are deeply grateful to them. We have enjoyed every minute of the job, even the most difficult ones.

Neil Gunn was born in a Caithness fishing village in 1891, and he died in Inverness in 1973. He came from a warm and traditional Highland world which during his lifetime was visibly dying. If it survives and grows that will be thanks to his own books as much as to the efforts of the Highlands & Islands Development Board. He lived in the Highlands, drew nourishment from his roots in the Highlands, yet wrote his books in the whole universe of man and the 'other landscape' of the mind.

His boyhood took him from Highland glen to Galloway strath, and then abruptly to the streets of Edwardian London and Edinburgh. At fifteen he joined the Civil Service as a clerk, and at nineteen became an officer of the Customs & Excise. From 1923 until 1937—when he resigned to be a full-time writer—he supervised a Highland distillery, and became an authority on whisky.

In the late 1920s and through the 1930s he was among the leaders of Scottish Nationalist politics. He began serious writing in 1922 when his close friend and fellow Excise officer Maurice Walsh returned to Ireland. His first novel was published in 1926 and his last in 1954; in addition to novels he published dozens of short stories, wrote several plays, countless articles and essays, a classic volume on whisky, and two elusively autobiographical books. Although he preferred not to see himself as a literary man, his abiding delight in fellowship and in writing as a ploy brought his life into touch with other literary lives—to mention just a few, those of George Blake, T. S. Eliot, C. M. Grieve (Hugh MacDiarmid), Eric Linklater, O. H. Mavor (James Bridie), Naomi Mitchison, Edwin Muir and Neil Paterson.

John Pick met him in 1946, and remained a friend until Neil's death. Francis Hart began writing about the Gunn novels in 1961, and corresponded with Neil and visited him during his last decade. In addition, Alasdair and Dairmid Gunn, the sons of Neil's late brother John, gave us access to and use of the thirty-three boxes of Neil's papers and photographs in the National Library of Scotland. We are grateful to them, to Stanley Simpson, Alan Bell and other members of the National Library staff for help far beyond the call of duty, and to officers of the Scottish Arts Council for their interest and encouragement.

Neil's brother John, always his closest friend, and his brother Alexander, survived him for a time; we were fortunate enough to know them and talk to them about Neil's life. In the past few years we have spoken and corresponded with many of his relatives and friends, and we are grateful for the reminiscences and letters they have shared with us. The responsibility for this reconstruction of his life remains ours.

We agreed on the plan of a book in four sections: Neil's life up to his marriage in 1921; the Inverness years, to 1937; the years at Braefarm House, where Neil did most of his writing, 1937–49; and the later years. Hart wrote the first two sections, and Pick the last two. Then we exchanged them for notes, comments and revision. We differ sometimes in viewpoint, approach and style, although we had to work hard to manage that. The sections remain individual. What unites them is the personality of Neil Gunn. His own words, however informal, seemed to us better than ours, however carefully meditated, so we have quoted liberally throughout from his letters, essays, conversations and books.

We could not have written such a book, or employed such a method, without the permission and trust of the Gunn family. They have understood our need to tell the truth as we see it. Neil meant a great deal to both of us, and to our wives Gene (Pick) and Lorena (Hart); the book expresses our affection and gratitude. We hope it is fair as well.

We would like specifically to acknowledge help with information or with permission to quote from correspondence from Arthur Ball; Mrs Ellie Blake, for permission to quote from letters by George Blake; George Bruce; J. B. Caird; Isabel Campbell; Sir Matthew Campbell; the Controller of HMSO, for permission to publish an excerpt from Neil's letter of resignation from the Customs & Excise; Valerie (Mrs T. S.) Eliot, for permission to quote from letters by T. S. Eliot; Lady Faber, for permission to quote from a letter by Sir Geoffrey Faber; Chrystine Frew, both for valuable information and for every sort of practical help; John Gray, for permission to quote from a letter by Sir Alexander Gray; Mrs Valda Grieve, for permission to quote from letters by C. M. Grieve; Ian Grimble; Dairmid Gunn, not only for his Foreword and for his unfailing courtesy, but for all the work he did on our behalf; Gretta (Mrs Alexander) Gunn; Keith Henderson; Lt-Colonel Stanley Hill; Faber & Faber Ltd, for permission to quote from a letter by Frank Morley; Long John International, for their kind assistance; John Looker, for permission to quote from a letter by Samuel J. Looker; Margaret (Mrs William) McCance; Mrs Margaret MacCormick, for permission to quote from letters by Dr John MacCormick; the children of Sir Alexander and Lady MacEwen—Margaret and Molly, David, Malcolm and Robin; the Trustees of Dr Agnes Mure Mackenzie, for permission to quote from her letters; D. A. C. McKillop; Duncan Maclennan; Ena (Mrs Peter John) Macleod; Mrs Fionna Macleod of Ullapool; Joseph Macleod; Helen Macmillan; Duncan McNeill; Eoin Macrae; Belle Maltman; Mrs Rhea Martin, for permission to quote from letters by J. Leslie Mitchell; Ronald Mavor, both for his help and for permission to quote from the letters of James Bridie; Naomi Mitchison; Mrs Mowat, for permission to quote from a letter by Arthur Mowat; Mary Muhr, for permission to quote from a letter by Douglas Muhr; Gavin Muir and the Hogarth Press Ltd for permission to quote a letter by Edwin Muir from *Selected Letters of Edwin Muir*, ed. P. H. Butter; Neil and Rose Paterson, for help of all kinds; Alastair Reid; Alexander Reid; Mrs Elizabeth Reid, for permission to quote from a letter by John Macnair Reid; Nan Shepherd; Lady Taylor for permission to quote from a letter by Sir Thomas Taylor; George Malcolm Thomson; Ronald Thomson; Rena Wilson; J. M. Wotherspoon; Frederick Whyte; Finlay McIntosh. Finally, we would like to thank Duncan McAra at John Murray for his unfailing encouragement and support.

The following publishers kindly allowed us to quote from books and journals: William Blackwood & Sons Ltd, pieces from *Neil M. Gunn: The Man and the Writer*, ed. Scott and Gifford; W. & R. Chambers Ltd, a passage from Maurice Walsh's introduction to *Scotch Whisky: A Guide*, by J. M. Robb; Faber & Faber Ltd, extracts from *The Silver Darlings* and a Keith Henderson drawing from *Highland Pack*; Souvenir Press Ltd, extracts from *Butcher's Broom, The Drinking Well, The Green Isle of the Great Deep, The Grey Coast, Morning Tide, The Serpent, Whisky and Scotland, Young Art and Old Hector*; D. C. Thomson & Co. Ltd and the *Scots Magazine*, quotations from that periodical; and to Jonathan Cape Ltd, Hamlyn Publishing Group Ltd, and Hodder & Stoughton Ltd, extracts from letters to Neil Gunn.

F. R. H.   J.B.P.

PART ONE

YOUTH

(1891–1921)

1   The Gunns of Caithness

'Caithness', wrote Neil Gunn, 'is a triangle whose base had to be glued on to the county of Sutherland by a range of mountains, but whose other two sides are open to the sea: at least they characteristically confront the sea with sheer contorted, battling cliffs.' The triangle has 685 square miles, and is two-thirds covered with peat. A wide and windswept interior moorland is framed to the south and west by a more Highland landscape commanded by the old hulk of Morven and the ridges of the Scarabens. On the east and north is a sculpted dramatic coastline of 'geos', stacks, and skerries. An arable coastal plain makes some observers think Caithness the Lowlands beyond the Highlands, but labels won't do, and Caithness remains intriguingly unique.

Harbours are few, small, and narrow, and sudden violent gales from the east and south-east make it risky to enter them. Thirty-seven men and forty-one boats were lost one morning in 1848 trying to enter Wick harbour in an onshore gale. 'Ah! but what a wind!' wrote Neil Gunn. 'I remember taking three hours twenty minutes all out to cycle the thirteen miles from Wick to Lybster and on coming to the last slope decided I might as well walk down it and did. Over the immense inland moors the wind sweeps like a scythe, with the noise of a scythe, low to the heather and rushing, for it has a long way to go to the horizon.'[1]

There were 37,000 people in Caithness when Neil Gunn was born in 1891, and when he published *Morning Tide* forty years later, there were only 25,000 left. The people, wrote John R. Allan, are 'different from any other people in Scotland. They are not Highland, not Celtic, not Scots. In the great days of the Norse people, Caithness was colonised from Scandinavia and that strain remains, unique.'[2] He didn't look back far enough.

Caithness was settled by nomads after the ice withdrew in the Middle Stone Age; in the Neolithic period, about 3000 B.C., settlers from the middle east brought agriculture, and left sixty-seven chambered tombs built on the surface and covered as cairns. The Beaker Folk had bronze and left their ceremonial standing stones. The next immigrants, when the climate changed to wetter and colder, came from north-west Europe, built a defensive architecture of forty-foot round towers called brochs, and left 110 broch ruins in Caithness. In Neil's youth the local people called them Picts' Houses, but the Picts didn't come until early A.D. when the brochs were already in ruins. Pictish Scotland was ruled from Inverness by Brude when Columba and his missionaries came up the Great Glen, and the Picts had long been Christian when the Norse colonising went on between 900 and 1200. Caithness had many nameless peoples in its past, and they left their traces.

Neil Gunn had his choice among ethnic ancestries, and he enjoyed the uncertainty. As a boy up his strath among the ruins, he found and relished the intimacy—the word is his—of remote ancestors, nameless and hidden. But the Picts were especially intriguing, for no one could agree on who they were. 'Now I happen to be one of those Scots who always wanted to know more about the Picts, a subtle and fascinating people.' And he often said with amusement, 'I'm something of a Pict myself.' He certainly thought himself a Celtic Highlander, and even tried briefly to learn some Gaelic, but he identified more with an ancient way of life, whatever its name. And he enjoyed the Caithness sense of being 'different'.

If you live in Caithness, it isn't remote; you are at the centre, linked by the sea and seafarers and emigration to the far corners of the earth. If you go there, it seems remote, at the top corner of Britain. Unless you come by sea you must come by Sutherland, and Neil emphasises the contrast. Coming from Sutherland's grandeur in the west he has us 'walk out upon Caithness, and at once experience an austerity in the flat clean windswept lands', know 'a movement of the spirit that finds in the austerity, because strength is there also, a final serenity'. And here is his unmistakable keynote: 'the wind of time has searched out even the flaws here and cleansed them'. It echoes on the white beach of John o'Groats, 'the crushed shells of whiteness from which all the sticky humours have been withdrawn . . . typical of this clean-swept county'. Light on the moor catches the mind in timelessness 'more intimate than life and death'. And finally the sea. Coming from Sutherland, 'alluring, beckoning, heedless, feminine', one finds the Caithness coast 'something simple, elemental, masculine', and a kind of masculine life grew there. 'A fine breed of men, too, these Caithness fishermen, daring, self-reliant, rarely hypocritical or sanctimonious, game for whatever life offered in the sea-storm or in the public house, and God-fearing over all . . . Few of the mean "safe" qualities found time to sprout.'[3] And 'if his mother was the earth, his father was the sea'.[4]

If you come from the south and take Neil's favourite route, you turn north inland from the Cromarty Firth across the Altnamain Moor past Struie Hill, and look down on his favourite view of the north-east, the inner stretches of the Dornoch Firth, and the north-west beyond. The 'well at the world's end' is nearby. Crossing Bonar Bridge, the road runs through Sutherland towns to the fishing village of Helmsdale, the outlet of the Strath of Kildonan. 'Thence,' writes Neil, 'it climbs steeply, in great hairpin loops round ravines, to the Ord of Caithness, where the sea-cliffs are over 600 feet high. From this elevated primeval moorland, where no habitation is, the coastline is seen as a continuous wall of rock to distant Clyth Ness.' Neil stopped here one day on his way home in the early 1920s and saw it and called it 'the grey coast'. And when a Caithness man, once on his way to Australia, made it over the Ord and down to Inverness, 'Thank goodness,' he reflected, 'that's the worse half of the trip over.'

'Then on to where the road drops down from danger signals for a whole mile to Berriedale in its strath of trees and up an equally steep mile, round the Devil's Elbow, to the high road once more.' From Berriedale, the two streams of Langwell and Berriedale reach up on each side of the Scaraben ridge 'that culminates in Morven, the lodestar of the fishermen. These glens are wilder and bleaker than the Strath of Dunbeath, six miles farther on, which is a quiet lovely strath of birch and hazel, insensibly fading away into the moors.'[5]

Coming down the steep brae into Dunbeath, you see the wide coastal fields of the big farm, Dunbeath Mains, and glimpse Dunbeath Castle on its headland. On the left is the Free Kirk, on the right the Kirk of Scotland, the post office, the old school (built in the 1870s) with its modern additions, and then a hairpin loop. As the road curves inland you see the old stone bridge, Dunbeath Water reaching up the wooded strath, and across the bridge a terrace of two-storey stone houses. A garage, a hotel, a shop—and the red stone house with slate roof and orange drainpipes, built by his father in the 1880s—the house where Neil was born.

Where had the Gunns come from to settle in Dunbeath? Centuries of historians have suggested Norse pedigrees. The clan historian, M. R. Gunn, adheres to the older view of a descent from one of the Gunnis of the saga, Gaelicised as Guin or Guinne, anglicised as Gun with a later 'n' to avoid confusion with a musket. He opts for a Gun who was grandson of Sweyn Asleifson and whose mother was a Manx chieftain's daughter. Gun's son built two castles near mid-Clyth on the coast. By the start of the thirteenth century the lands of the Gunns may have extended over much of Caithness, west into Strathnaver, south to Braemore at the foot of Morven.[6]

But already they were encircled. Ian Grimble says, 'When the Picts were overrun by the Gaelic Scots of Dalriada in the south, and by Vikings from the north, the survivors would naturally have taken refuge in inaccessible hinterlands behind the areas in which such substantial evidence of their presence remains. It is precisely here, in the heights of the Caithness-Sutherland border, that Clan Gunn is to be found.'[7] Throughout the Middle Ages their territories were gradually reduced, their survival as a distinct clan menaced. In the mid-fifteenth century their power remained, for their chief was now hereditary coroner or Crowner of Caithness, charged with keeping the peace and raising troops. But George Gunn had new and rising families to contend with. The Norman Sinclairs married into the earldom of Caithness and Orkney and became rivals to the Gordon earls of Sutherland. The Mackays became powerful in the west, and Keiths from Aberdeenshire in the north-east. There are legends of the bloody feuds of Gunns and Keiths, and the Gunns were often betrayed or outwitted—as at Girnigo, when a prearrangement numbered the horses on both sides and the Keiths came two men to a horse, and the Crowner and several of his sons were killed in the slaughter. And then there was the lovely Helen of Braemore; let Neil tell of her:

> It so happened that the chief of the Keiths passed through Braemore—hospitality had its high rites in those days—and saw the lovely Helen. The vision must have preyed on his mind, as Helen of yore preyed on more minds than one; and news of her imminent marriage to one of her own clan in Braemore did not help, we may conclude, to allay the Keith's interest, for on the night of her marriage he, with his picked, armed followers, swooped down on the festivities, and though the unarmed Gunns did what they could, they were slaughtered, the bridegroom among them, and Keith carried off the lovely one to his castle at Ackergill on the other side of the county. But there was nothing wanton about Helen of Braemore. From the top of the tower she threw herself to her death. Among the shades of the old immortals she may pass not unnoticed.[8]

Like the MacGregors, the Gunns had become a scapegoat tribe, struggling in vain to hold their lands against a new feudal system of charters. The chief's line—the MacHamish Gunns—became allies and border guards of the Sutherland earls and were settled in Strath Ullie, particularly the lovely thirty-mile strath called Kildonan after St Donnan, the Gunns' patron saint. Kildonan was known as Gleann nan Guinneach (Glen of the Gunns) and Killearnan was their prize for faithful service to the Sutherland—until the early nineteenth century, when they were among the first to be evicted—'cleared'—by the Countess, who found sheep more profitable and described the Gunns as a people who 'live by distilling whisky and are unwilling to quit that occupation for a life of industry of a different sort'.[9] And so after 350 years the *Leine* or 'shirt'—the bodyguard—of the Sutherland were burned out of their valley, burial place of their chiefs, place of their saint, and their lands were turned into sheep farms, inhabited only by a few sheepfarmers from the Borders of England. As a final insult the Countess found the clan a new chief and made him factor at Dunrobin, while his clansmen were being 'resettled' on patches of bog and moor and in coastal creeks, or emigrating to the Red River Colony in Canada.

What did all this mean to Neil? He knew little of it until, in the early 1930s, he did research for *Butcher's Broom*, his novel of the Sutherland Clearances. When Lewis Grassic Gibbon read *Butcher's Broom* he wrote of his astonishment at Neil's charity; little did he know what a close triumph the charity was, but that was Neil's way. Like his old hero Sandy in *Bloodhunt* he determined that the bitterness and violence must have an end, and he chose to be silent. His way of confronting the gloomy memories was learned early from his parents. He says in 1954 in *Radio Times*:

> As children we did not hear much about it though we were born within a score of miles of the glen that wandered up into the thick of the Sutherland Clearances. Presumably our parents did not care to warp growing minds with old wrongs. The picture of Highlanders as a gloomy people with sad or nostalgic memories is quite false. A story much nearer the truth is that told by the Rev. Kenneth Macleod of the schoolmaster on a Hebridean island who, on dismal days, would say 'My curse on gloom!' and then take out his fiddle and play it to his pupils . . . Yet stories of the evictions there were, vivid and personal . . . Little, however, was learned of the actual scope of the clearances, not to mention what brought them about. Perhaps they were not only too near in time for school lessons but also too near the bone. Besides, there were all these important dates in English history to memorise . . . Indeed I can remember my surprise when some years ago I found that no less than seventy-eight crofters had been 'removed' to make room for one big farm in a place I knew from boyhood.[10]

When Neil was a boy, the boats and men of his harbour were there to speak of Caithness's more recent history. As the evicted moved down from their straths to the coast, Caithness was ready for them, for it was entering on its 'boom century'.[11] At the end of the Napoleonic wars a change in government policy fostered a rapid growth in the herring fisheries. Coastal crofters learned to draw part of their livelihood from the sea. During the winter they mended nets, ploughed, prepared for root crops, sowed and set, cut peats, attended to lambing, and then with the better weather they went off in growing numbers to the 'silver darlings', and came home to harvest. The herring boom brought netmaking, ropemaking, coopering, shipping and carting. New houses were built. Communications improved. Growing prosperity and literacy brought newspapers in the 1830s. Thomas Telford had directed a road survey, and a new coastal road was built with new bridges. Gaelic returned from the Sutherland straths, and from the Hebrides hired Gaelic speakers arrived in summer to sail as crews on the fishing boats. By 1840 seventy-six boats were operating out of Dunbeath alone and ten times that number out of Wick—the stunned minister lamented that Wick drank 500 gallons of whisky in a day. When the fishing reached its peak in the 1860s, Latheron Parish had 1,321 fishermen, 106 coopers, 937 packers (women), 178 labourers and fifty curers.

'To say,' wrote Neil, 'in the conventional phrase that [Dunbeath] was a hive of industry is to give little idea of its multitudinous activity.'[12] Elsewhere he recalled:

> A fisherman, who has barely reached the allotted span [this was 1938], once gave me a remarkable picture of the herring fleet sailing out of a creek on the Caithness coast when he was a boy. Though the curing stations and cooperages are now in ruinous decay, about one hundred and fifty boats fished out of the creek during the summer seasons of his boyhood and indeed until he was a grown man. How lovely a sight from that river-mouth, from that small horse-shoe bay in the gaunt cliff-wall of Caithness, when the fleet, all under sail, left for the fishing grounds in the afternoon or early evening!

And when 'the crews of hundreds upon hundreds of boats at sea on a quiet evening, after their nets had been shot, [took] up, one after another, one of the Psalms of David, until it seemed the sea itself sang and the cliffs and cottages were held in wonder'. By the end of the century the hopes were dying, the people once more betrayed by history's utilitarian dogmas. But Neil came early enough to see the last of the exuberance:

> I can remember as a very small boy watching a woman gutter to see if I could follow how she did it and being baffled. There they were, row after row of them, in stiff rustling oilskins, well-booted and shawled, silver-scaled and blood-flecked, with faces all alive, quick-voiced in retort or laughter, working, as we said, 'like lightning'. And all of them local women or girls, making their little bit while the going was good. Any visitor got a fry of herring from the generous skipper, whether a black-hooded widow from the hills or the friendly policeman from beside the church.[13]

It was an image of women he would never lose. And the 'generous skipper' may well have been his father.

One of the new breed of crofter-fishermen in the 1840s and 1850s was a William Gunn, who, with his wife Mary Sutherland, lived in Dunbeath.[14] The pairing of names suggests that they might have come down from the Sutherland straths or from the high country of Braemore. James, a son of William Gunn and Mary Sutherland, was born in 1847. He went to school in Dunbeath in the 1850s (even though schooling would not be compulsory until 1872) and grew up to be a quick, witty, brave man, who followed his father as a crofter-fisherman, and by the 1870s was one of the most admired young skippers on the coast. Later, his son Neil heard from an old Dunbeath man who had seen Jimmy Gunn bring back the boat he had bought from the duke in Sutherland and put her through her paces in the bay to the cheers of the local boys. (See *Highland River*, Ch. 6.)

An old man, who had sailed with James Gunn north about through the Pentland Firth, to the fishing in the west, remembered the storm off the outer Hebrides when *Isabella*, already dismasted once, was in danger again —and 'we had to lash your father with a rope to the tillie [tiller] and leave him sitting there . . . I heard his voice cry above the storm: "You have cast one mast before, Bella my lassie; you can cast a second—and welcome!" '[15]

James was forty-four when his son Neil was born, and Neil remembered him as a gentle, kindly man, the skipper in *Morning Tide*, who met the little boy on the stone steps up from the harbour road, and asked, 'Is it yourself?' There was 'a smile on his face and kindness in his eyes as if he had come from a far place, like a stranger, back to his own. "Your hands are cold," said his father . . . and brought the small hands in among the thick hair on his head and warmed them there in a way that was new and strange.'[16] His father must indeed have seemed a stranger, for the boats had to sail greater and greater distances to compete with big steam and serve big ports. And then, abruptly, Neil was sent away in 1904 and was away in the south for the next few years. Jimmy Gunn had an infected arm, improperly diagnosed, and wore it in a sling; he liked his dram, tended his garden, and died in 1916.

But in the 1870s he was a local hero, like Roddie in *The Silver Darlings*. He lived with his first wife in the crofting hamlet of Balnabruich up on the Braemore road. They had children, and four granddaughters live still in Caithness. His first wife died. On 4 October 1878, aged thirty-one, James Gunn, crofter-fisherman, married Isabella Miller, spinster, aged twenty-three, domestic servant at Knockinnon on the way up to Latheronwheel. Isabella's father, Donald Miller, also a crofter-fisherman, was dead. Her mother was Janet Stewart. 'On my mother's side,' Neil teased once, 'I'm afraid we had a professor in America. She was a Miller, related to Hugh

Miller of Cromarty. She runs into the Stewarts, all rather brainy people.'
And he remembered Stewart cousins from his Edinburgh years, and red-
haired cousins from Latheronwheel. To one of them he boasted one day of
the beauties of Dunbeath: 'I remember a young cousin of my own age, an
equally youthful, red-haired, vivid cousin who lived in Latheronwheel.
"What!" she replied. "Dunbeath strath the most beautiful? Nonsense! As
everyone knows Latheronwheel strath is the most beautiful strath in the
whole of Caithness." '[17]

James and Isabella were married in the Church of Scotland, Dunbeath. In
Balcladach, south of the village, the first of their nine children was born.
But James did well as a skipper, and some time late in the 1880s he built the
slate-roofed, two-storey house on the village terrace. By late in the century
such houses, built often by communal labour, were becoming more
numerous and comfortable. A slate roof meant affluence. Cotton or paper
ceilings hid divots. Some houses had flagstone floors. The *Caithness Book*
gives a general picture:

> by the end of the nineteenth century the kitchen of a well-doing fisherman or
> crofter-fisherman, with a house-proud wife, was a pleasant and comely place.
> With its cheerful open fire, either a clock on the mantelpiece or a 'wag at the
> wa', a wooden rocking chair, a spinning wheel, three or four plain wooden
> chairs, a meal-kist, a table, a dresser, papered walls and some sort of picture or
> text on the walls, a rag mat in front of the fire, and, of course, a box-bed, it was
> an attractive home.[18]

There was a sloping garden in front, and a byre for the cow behind, but the
days of crofting were over, and the cow went daily to rented pasture. James
was a full-time fisherman with his own crew.

The first child, Janet, had been born in 1879. Later she was always
'Jessie', though her husband John George Sutherland called her 'Janet'.
Sutherland was head of the police at Invergordon, then retired to the large
house on the high road next to the old hall. The Sutherlands provided a
family home after the Gunn parents died. Sutherland gave Neil some of his
knowledge of Dunbeath antiquities, and to him *Butcher's Broom* is dedicated.
Following Janet or 'Jessie' came Mary in 1882. Mary worked in the south,
married a doctor named Keiller, and settled at St John's Town of Dalry,
Kirkcudbrightshire. They had no children, and in 1904 Neil went to live
with them. They moved to Glenelg, then to Edinburgh, where they died in
the 1960s. After Mary came seven sons: James in 1883, twins David and
Donald in 1885, Benjamin in 1888, Neil in 1891, John in 1897, and
Alexander in 1901. It was a fine family in which to learn about brotherhood!

Isabella Gunn was ambitious for her sons, and ambition combined with fear in her determination that they should not go to sea. Actually, they were born too late for the fishing boom. James led the way which Neil would go. He entered the Civil Service and was stationed in London when Neil went there in 1907. The twins David and Donald emigrated to Canada, and Ben, having fished with his father for a time, followed them. When the First World War began, all three came home to join the Army and then went to France. One twin died in the Army; the other was wounded and died in Canada. Ben's horrible death, stranded on barbed wire before the trenches, is recounted in *Highland River*, as is John's war experience, caught in the first German gas attack. John recovered and returned to Edinburgh where he graduated MA, BSc with honours in Mathematics and Natural Philosophy. Alec took his degree at Aberdeen. John became Inspector of Schools and later Chief Inspector, and Alec became schoolmaster in Castletown, near Thurso. The 'brainy' Stewarts had won over croft and sea. The bookish Isabella had sent her sons away to 'get on'. The pattern is familiar. The odd piece in the pattern was her fifth son, Neil Miller, born on 8 November 1891. For he grew to belong to all of these worlds—the sea, the croft, the professions, the world of books—and yet he 'belonged' to none of them. And Isabella lived just long enough to see him publish a first novel in 1926 dedicated to her.

2   The Boy at Home

We can recreate Neil's boyhood, but how can we know Neil as a boy? He has left numerous accounts, but how shall we use them to see beyond Neil's imaginative memory? Keith Henderson (painter, illustrator of *Highland Pack*, Neil's close friend and candid private critic) said that all of Neil's novels are 'autobiographical', and of course there is always a real face behind the masques of art, but the masques are as cunningly refractory as lights and shadows on a salmon pool. A perceptive *Glasgow Herald* reviewer wrote of *Highland River* that the ascetic pagan Kenn Sutherland 'is Neil Gunn', but the boys of *Highland River* and *Morning Tide* originated not with Neil but with the recollections of his younger brother John. Young Art of two novels came from Neil's observations of his nephews. 'I never made up anything extraordinary in my novels,' Neil said once; 'invention is too easy.' But simple identification of art and life is 'too easy' as well.

As the autobiographer of *The Atom of Delight* scrupulously seeks to recreate the boy he was, he comes early on the experience (not uncommon in autobiography) of discovering himself, of the birth of self-consciousness. To the boy it seems that there are two selves in him. Then the autobiographer of *The Atom of Delight*—let's call him 'Gunn' and call the boy 'Neil'—perceives a pattern of experience. Throughout Neil's encounters with what social scientists now call 'socialising forces', he managed in some part of his consciousness to remain doggedly inviolate, untouched. From the start of the book, Gunn associates this with the act of running, the ecstasy of running 'out of himself'. Hugh of *Morning Tide* runs at climactic moments, runs in delight and affirmation but also in self-protection. The boy Art of *The Green Isle of the Great Deep* becomes a legendary rebel in his running.

Gunn theorises that there were in Neil two selves—a 'first self' responsive and vulnerable to social and institutional influences, and a 'second self' that is free. The first he calls the 'social self', the second 'the inner core of himself', and the 'sheer tenacity' of this 'inner core' is 'remarkably strong in a boy, if not indeed imperishable'. The 'second self' is found whenever the boy 'races away' from or 'shuts out' the 'social complex that normally had him in its toils'. The realising that this self of freedom is his 'very self' is, Gunn thinks, the source of delight, and the source of delight is the autobiographer's elusive quarry. One thing more: this 'second self ' is autonomous and *given*—in the sense that an axiom in Euclid is given (the analogy is Gunn's). But it is verified because it is true to Neil's experiences as Gunn recalls them.[1]

Now the meaning of this central thesis is clear enough, and it fits the experiences of *The Atom of Delight* like a glove—or perhaps like the hand within the glove, for it is impossible to say which does more of the shaping. Those who find the book vague or elusive are not attending to this fit; and when they complain that the autobiography is too 'philosophical', they are forgetting what autobiographies usually are: philosophical exercises in recollection.

But the issue for us is how to know Neil's boyhood self. Was it dual? Did his essential ('atomic') experiences really derive from a non-social self? Did the external influences that may be called 'social' have no comparable effect? Or was his true or 'second' self in part a creation of such influences? Was Neil's boyhood personality generally true of boys (as he clearly believes) or was it unusual? There is no biography of Neil Gunn without the recognition that he was a distinctive individual who led a unique life, but how and when did he become so? If we go carefully, *The Atom of Delight* will suggest some possible answers.

It presents a vivid image of the boy he remembers being: an 'extra-ordinarily apt pupil', who learns well to cope with the conventional demands made on him, and who, *at the same time*, acts from that 'inner urge of self-protection', which sets all such demands at a considerable psychic distance. An extremely sensuous boy—one in whom touch and taste are particularly vivid—and, at the same time, a boy of unusual bodily chastity, secretive about his physical self. A child with a strong susceptibility to certain emotions—pride, fear—and to psychic intuitions of intangible presences, and at the same time particularly strong in 'arithmetical reason-ing'. He copes with extraordinary experiences (the salmon) in line with that kind of reasoning, and adapts to school in the same way: 'If school had to be endured, let it be in the guise of arithmetic, which a fellow could get dead right and so keep himself intact'[2]—one of the most suggestive statements Neil ever made about himself. The boy felt very much at home in his community and, in retrospect, felt it to be an 'earthly paradise', and yet his chief delights came 'when there was no interference from the others'.[3] If this was the boy Neil, then the boy was father to the man. For the man was one whom some found to be 'one of the most conventional men' and at the same time (as he and others perceived) an elusive anarchist.

First, we see the boy at home in Dunbeath village. The house was there, his room was upstairs, and outside were the steps leading down to the road and along to the harbour, or across the stone bridge and up the hill to school or church. The river was below.

> When the river, or burn—the map compromises with Water—came down in spate I was forbidden its dangerous banks. Yet, coming from school, we had to cross the old stone bridge, and the sight one afternoon of its rolling waters [when he wasn't over seven], the spume, the wild mid-stream crashing of boulders, the treacherous whirls and dark eddies snaring the eyes to a giddy insecurity, the spinning foam in dip and rush, the endless hypnotic sound filling the head, the senses . . . the river came upon me and possessed me, and, starting back from it, I dared its challenge . . . But the river remained. It has always remained . . . something, in loneliness, secretive and strong, like an irony whose roots are in laughter. ['Dane McNeil' in *Scots Magazine* before *Morning Tide*.][4]

His father was often away, but his mother was always there. Alec Gunn found accurate descriptions of their parents in Neil's books. The mother, Neil recalls, was 'at the centre of the world. . . Where she was everything else was about her, naturally, each in its own right and pleased to be there.' She 'never got excited; she was calm and wise'.[5] Neil the boy delighted in being her solitary protector, guiding her through the dark, caring for her in illness. (Which 'self ' is this?) Here in germ are those solitudes of mother and son that give the novels some of their central moments.

She is pictured most clearly in *Highland River*: 'Her eyes, grey and wide-spaced, are lifted towards the trees of the plantation. Her straight dark hair is parted smoothly midway over her pale smooth forehead, and caught back behind the ears, so that the ears, flat to the head and shapely, are seen. All her features are shapely; and the skin has that unlined fullness that suggests the word comely. Her heavy body is neither unshapely nor billowing, but is deep-bosomed and solid, and stands with quiet poise.'[6] Her face has the look of her son Alec, and evidently of Ben, too. For the mother in *Highland River* looks at Angus and sees her people in him:

> It was a great pity he did not like schooling. That was her secret regret. For she loved the heart of learning. To 'get on' in commerce or business, to become wealthy there, was fine enough, and many a well-doing lad was a credit to his parents but she would rather have a son a professor than a millionaire.[7]

Others remember Isabella as a great reader of books, not much of a housekeeper, but one who fed her family well. And Neil's account of boyhood is filled with the sensuous delights of tasting and smelling food.

'Food! Hot food! The burst jackets of potatoes steaming upward.'[8] Deep affections there were, but these were never openly sensuous. Neil has 'no memory of having been kissed by his mother', because it simply was not done.

The remembered family also includes the 'long brotherly sequence'. Mary and Jessie were ten and twelve years older than Neil, and their intermittent appearances as the sisters in *Morning Tide* suggest they were away. The twin older brothers are not mentioned. The oldest, James (perhaps Joe in *Highland River*), comes home on holiday—the 'grand poacher' now training to be a gamekeeper (or in fact an Excise officer). But Ben is there—the lover of music, the hater of school—as a good-humoured older counsellor. The younger brother John is old enough to take a furtive pandrop at church. Alec, as he says himself, is 'still in swaddling clothes' when Neil goes away in 1904. Ben is the one close to Neil in these years, and one can only guess—for Neil never spoke of it directly—the effect on Neil when John told him how Ben died painfully in the trenches of the First World War.

Dunbeath as a larger community is remembered for its characters and its haunting and nameless, black-shawled, older women. Hector the roadman, wise old ally to the boys, lives on variously transformed in the books. The older fishermen are important, for it is they who make the boy aware of his social self. To the men Hugh meets on the way home from the harbour in *Morning Tide* he is 'the skipper's son', proud of his father's position, and something of a 'solitary' who 'does not belong' to the boys from the fishing hamlet of 'Seabrae' or Portormin. But he is a ready if reluctant fighter and they respect him, 'a bee from another hive, a gull from another rock'. Neil insisted later that there was no class sense in his boyhood community, but there is evidence that he appreciated his more comfortable place up in the village. True, he ran errands for his mother, led the cow to pasture, because he was helping *her*; and he went out with his father in the boat and helped lay down the potatoes, but there was a feeling that he 'didn't have to'. Later on he helped nurture the myth that he was a poor fisherman's son, but at the time he knew better.

The boy in *The Atom of Delight* is a solitary, but in fact Neil had his close friends—one or two, and he preferred it that way. 'Two was perhaps the ideal number on such an expedition,' he says, 'for then the acting, the scoffing, the facetiousness, the latent rivalries, that assail boys' relationships simply fall away and two become themselves in a rare companionship. Now things can be said that could never be said with others there.'[9] Fortunately we know who the 'rare companion' was. He has his real nickname in

Highland River, Beel, and 'Beelag' wrote 'Neilag' a fine letter of reminiscence and support when *Morning Tide* was published. William Mowat
approaches the famous man respectfully but warms to his subject. He has
recognised 'Neilag' of boyhood days, and recalls

> when such scenes as depicted there were seen in reality, even by my humble
> self at Dunbeath harbour. Memories of school days pass before me. I still
> remember your first days there, when such confinement seemed irksome. On
> this particular day you tried to claim your liberty by making for the door on
> tiptoe, but I think your 'tacketies' made too much noise and you were noticed.
> Our teacher — poor old . . . —rises to mind. I think he fell on evil days. I
> remember still with a certain amount of glee how he used to miss Georgie
> Cunningham's hand while dealing out punishment, with unhappy results to
> himself. Yon black eyes of his didn't half spit sparks. Our days together—happy
> memories crowd my mind so quickly that I can hardly sort them out, how we
> raced to yon milestone, how we guddled in the 'waite', dooked in the sluice
> pool, swared birds at Gunn's back door, spent hours in the loft in Gunn's byre.
> Happy days, weren't they?[10]

Alas, we don't know what 'Beelag' thought of himself in *Highland River*.
But other old Dunbeath boys heard the book dramatised on the radio in
1962, and Willie Alex Sutherland wrote Neil to report in fine style what
was said the morning after at his son's garage. How they corrected his local
idioms, and 'I wonder will Neil be remembering some of the old landmarks?
1st Rocks, such as: the "Sniver Sny", the "Singing Rock", the "Cradle Stone"
and the "Boddach". Everlasting monuments. Then long ago when Dunbeath was thriving it had Ports within a Port. "Port-a-Castle", "Portormin"
and "Port-gorram". Lastly came the lovely names of some of the boats
belonging to the days of *Highland River: Stormy Petrel, Morning Dawn, Rose of
Shannon, Brothers, Fidelity*, and *Unity*.'[11]

They finished up with a dram and a hope that Neil would find time to
come and see them. They could not know that Neil and Daisy were ill at the
time. But Neil seldom came, and when he did, he and his wife camped at a
distance. The old boys felt he cared little for his town and was proud and
'didn't bother with them'. Perhaps he had never 'bothered with them'
much, had never belonged. Or perhaps being sent away when he was twelve
had shut them off. And perhaps the desolation of Dunbeath when Neil came
back in the 1920s was something against which he had to draw a tight
circle. In that peculiarly personal book *The Serpent* there is this: 'Like a
countryman gone back home to the companions and scenes of his youth, to
find he can no longer stay there, the bands of ancient custom irking him in a
place gone small and grey'.[12] John and Alec stayed longer, went back often,

felt at home in the village. Neil seemed 'different'. He shut things out.

He had managed to shut out much of school, even if his tacketies would not quite allow him to race away from it. The master was 'a powerfully built man, over six feet and straight as a board, with a tread on the floor that resounded'.[13] The thrashings of Kenn in *Highland River* 'freed him from his school life and any obligation to the master; made him whole and secret and hostile'.[14] This may be closer to fact than the sunnier view in *The Atom of Delight* that the master was a natural force to be reckoned with, that thrashings could be born because they didn't *touch* 'the inner citadel'. Perhaps the thrashings helped build that citadel, 'whole and secret and hostile'.

Of one curricular misery Neil often made significant jokes. 'The Scots are pretty good at history,' he comments in *Off in a Boat*, 'which, perhaps, is why most of them mistrust it. For it is full of facts, most of them ugly.'[15] Neil was not 'pretty good' at school history. It was English history, and it involved memorising battle dates and names of power-addicts. Here is his version of the ordeal from the *Glasgow Herald* of 24 December 1949:

> Of all subjects at school, history contrived to be the dullest. Kings and dates and battles; dynasties, genealogical trees, and politicians. Sheer will, fearing the worst, forced memory to its job. But if memory did its best, it was always a deceitful best. Memory is like a woman who, asked to give house-room to guests she doesn't like, appears to entertain the request while cogitating ways of refusing it.
>
> I have seen me able to remember who John of Gaunt was for perhaps a week, and what the Wars of the Roses were about for almost as long as the information served, if never quite.

Out of school real history was close by. And real history came to mean something beyond the feuds of male egoists, a legendary continuity of 'innumerable women whose suffering and endurance were like little black knots holding the web of history together'.[16]

Of the three parts of poetry he liked parsing and analysis for it 'was in a way like arithmetic', and arithmetic he was good at and was assigned to help others with.[17] He 'hated English Composition'—a recollection not uncommon among accomplished writers—and doesn't recall writing at all. It was after leaving school that he began one day writing an adventure yarn in an old school jotter.[18] The *real* literature of his boyhood, naturally, was in penny dreadfuls, Red Indians on the Warpath, Buffalo Bill, and a step up to *Deerslayer* on the way to Sir Walter Scott. 'I have heard it said,' wrote brother Alec, 'that at school he showed great promise. English V.G., Maths V.G.,

History very poor, Grammar Ex., Geography G plus.' In his last session [leaving was at thirteen] there were essays to be written, and the subjects were seldom imaginative, but one was 'A Sea Storm'. To quote Alec:

> Came the day of retribution. Taking his stance mid floor with exam papers in left hand the teacher in no uncertain voice told the class what he thought of their misuse of tenses, poor spelling etc etc and then gave out the marks (possible 25). Mary McKay 21, Jean Sinclair 20, George Sutherland 20 until finally only two papers were left. John—5. 'Take it home, John. Frame it and nail it to the wall where you and all may see. Neil Gunn—come out to the floor. Your choice, and you were the only one in the class to choose it, was 'The Sea Storm'. 24½ marks out of 25. Boy, that is the highest mark I have ever given for an essay. You are a credit to your teacher, your school, and your parents.' Forthwith he read the essay to the class, then taking Neil by the shoulder led him through the other classrooms reading the essay in each one.[19]

The prize-winning writer was thus in public view a quarter of a century before a short story called 'The Sea' won a contest and was then expanded into a triumphant second novel, *Morning Tide*. Perhaps he was too embarrassed to remember the first occasion. But he never lost his fascination with 'arithmetical reasoning' and otherwise was sure that school hadn't 'touched' him.

The same went for that other formidably authoritarian institution, the church. In church 'the boy drew his circle so closely around him that he could feel it. God wasn't going to get past that circle if he could help it.'[20] Neither was the minister. The Reverend Charles Gordon Ross was a 'white-bearded, tall, erect, square-shouldered figure in the pulpit—archetype of all patriarchs', and the man Neil never trusted patriarchs. The boy could look furtively out the window at the trees during a sermon of an hour and a half, but the man admired the minister in retrospect, for he was 'the son of a poor crofter, and as a lad had walked his 250-odd miles to Edinburgh University with a stone of oatmeal on his back, and, at the end of the session, had walked them back.'[21] Only once, it appears, did a sermon 'touch' Neil. That was when a famous hellfire visitor drew an image of falling into the bottomless depths of hell. For here Neil was touched in his one terrible weakness, the fear of heights: 'he had a poor head for great heights—his one and awful secret weakness, driving him to a courage or foolhardiness which it still makes him a little sick to think of.' When he had to rescue the family cow from a cliff-edge he felt sick, for 'the height of a cliff could get inside him'.[22] And it often would 'get inside' the writer, whose books are filled with precipices and the heroic youths and men who scale them. Neil knew the meaning of *abyss* as a vivid and demonic image.

Religion had a quieter place at home. Were his parents orthodox? 'They were very broad-minded people,' John Gunn recalled, 'but they had to live in the community.'[23] Kenn's mother in *Highland River* 'rarely went to church'[24] and never sat at communion table. His father went regularly but never took communion. At home, grace was said before meals, and

> My father would take down the book every Sunday and read chapters, and we would all take turns; and it was a game to see who got the shortest verse. I remember [Neil is speaking in reminiscence and the word rolls out and his face lights with glee]—I remember I managed once to get 'and Jesus wept', and read it triumphantly and my father looked at me as if to say, 'That's not the tone to use.' But that was all.[25]

Neil never belonged to institutional religion—he said he was never inside of Christian orthodoxy—though some of his later books acknowledge the imaginative truth of Christian story: 'Of all the stories man had made,' he wrote in *Bloodhunt*, 'only two were immortal: the story of Cain and the story of Christ.'[26]

In a larger sense, Neil acquired his knowledge and his faith elsewhere, especially up the strath that runs by Dunbeath water to the edge of the moor. The strath was an ideal size for a boy, three miles up and three miles back. The river was lined with birches, rowans, alders and oaks. Surprised rabbits scurried off; a couple of peewits screamed; a curlew joined in. From the hazel tree at the pool a chaffinch gave an angry *spink! spink!* and from the hillside above, a willow wren's song came tumbling down. Nuts were there to be carefully cracked with a stone, and blackberries, pods of wild violet, wild bees' honey. It was sitting one day cracking nuts on a boulder in the stream that he 'came upon himself sitting there'. Climactically, there was the challenge of the salmon pool, 'the brown tinge in the hill water that went black in the depths'.[27]

The episode of the great salmon opens *Highland River*, and is recreated in *The Atom of Delight*. Here the boy is alone. In a more matter of fact newspaper version (c. 1951) he has companions:

> Once when I was about eleven I touched an invisible salmon with the big toe of my right foot. I have never forgotten the peculiar sensation that assailed me then. Three of us around the same age, on an expedition up a glen, came at last, hot and weary as only young hunters can be, to a pool with a convenient ledge on the near side and a dark stretch in the middle. I plunged in last but as I was swimming across the dark place I wondered if I might be able to sound bottom and, if so, what I might touch there. I tried to stand in the water and at

the right moment, tilting my head back a little struck down with the aforementioned toe.

It landed on a soft body which gave perceptibly to what could be no more than a light caress before the water bobbed me off. But I knew it was a salmon and I cried in wonder.[28]

All his life Neil kept that wonder and explored it. Every fishing expedition brought it back, from youth on the Dornoch Firth to his last days fishing the Thurso River with Neil Paterson and that great angler Alec Gunn. But the first pool and the first salmon were best.

How lovely a thing a fishing pool is! It has intimacy and ancestry in it. Old as the blood-stream itself, and as full of intimations and hopes and queer elusive memories. There is an urgency to be at it, and a contrary impulse to take one's time, to do things leisurely and rightly, with a glance up the glen and a glance down, smiling at the flow of the hills or at oneself.[29]

Intimacy and ancestry and a secret smile at oneself—there is the picture of the man and the boy. And 'appropriately enough, this boyhood's paradise had an Almighty Being with an all-seeing eye. We called him the Keeper.' The most profound lesson Neil learned from the strath was the same one he learned from his parents. It pervades *Highland River* and is scrupulously explained in *The Atom of Delight*:

We never saw a god come out of a cloud, but we saw a gamekeeper come out of a clump of trees; and at a crucial moment, had the awful matter of choice been possible, we might have taken a chance on the unknown god.

If only complication stopped there! But the boy's world is contained by the adult world, and to this matter of hunting there was among adults a certain two-faced or ambivalent attitude. From the beginnings of their human history the Highlands have been a hunting ground. With their deer forests, grouse moors and salmon rivers they still are. Until comparatively recent times the Highlander had three freedoms: to take a salmon from the river, to take a deer from the hill, and to distil his drop of whisky from his own barley, without payment or tax. He has never quite forgotten that, hence the ambivalent attitude. The boy has not 'worked all this out'; political, legal and moral aspects are of the adult world; but he knows the attitude at a glance. Just as he knows there is only one final question: 'Did anyone see you?' And if he can answer 'No', then his triumph as a skilful hunter is complete.[30]

It could make a boy proud and famous! Recently in Dunbeath J. B. Caird gave a talk, and he thought he would walk up the strath. He met two old men and spoke with them. They weren't much interested in Neil's literary career, but, they said, 'He was the best poacher in Dunbeath.' Caird repeated the joke to John Gunn, and John replied, 'Not so! I was the best.'[31]

That ambivalent attitude toward 'being seen' by authority must have haunted and amused Neil through all his years as Excise officer.

Some kinds of hunting he had mixed feelings about. As a boy of six or seven he knew a stalker at the lodge up the strath. One morning he found himself there 'amid a bustle of men and dogs and ponies setting out for the grouse moors'. But what he remembers from that morning is standing alone by a lodge window 'and the window went up and a dark-haired lovely Highland girl smiled to me and handed out a slice of brown bread freighted with butter and strawberry jam. It was then I discovered, I think, that the bread of life can not only be the bread of life but also delicious.'[32] As for deer-stalking, Neil tried it and wrote about it, but he remained in troubled awe at the nobility of the stag. 'When a master stag raises his head, lays his antlers along his back and issues his challenge to all comers, the full-throated roar is just about the most fearsome sound in nature I know; perhaps because once, as a boy, I was caught by the twilight of an early October night in a lonely glen when challenge and answering challenge were echoed by the darkening hills as if all the lions in Africa were invisibly closing in. It was possibly the nearest I ever got to doing my mile in four minutes.'[33]

The strath taught by fear as well as by delight, and not just by natural history, but by human history too. He recalled the lessons when, in his last years, he gave one of his three public speeches:

> When you leave Dunbeath Village and go up the strath you come, after half a mile, to the river's main tributary. Above the confluence of the two streams a tongue of land rises steeply and then flattens back to a broch. When I was a small boy the lower part of the broch was still in good shape. You entered through the 12-foot thick wall, past a small guard chamber which I always scanned carefully, to an inner courtyard where over on the left was a low entrance into the wall. Once through this we stood up in a fairly large stone chamber, and here we studied our first problem in architecture, for after the walls had risen vertically for some distance, the flat stones began to overlap, in and in, until the dome overhead was complete, and we wondered how on earth stones managed to stick up. Then in the floor of this chamber we did our first archaeological dig—though I don't suppose we had heard of the word archaeology, unless in our school spellings, but we had heard of buried treasure. Our tools were primitive so we didn't get very deep, but deep enough to come on pieces of shell, of shellfish, and this brought our ancestors near because we thought of them roasting their shellfish before a fire, just as we did. As the shadows drew in they came still nearer, so we stopped and silently filed away.[34]

On another day 'Neilag' and a friend found themselves 'studying the habits of the rabbit', on a ridge across from the broch, a hill full of stones and ruins called 'Chapel Hill'. They 'came upon a circle of flat stones showing above the cropped grass, some three or four paces across. Then another circle, and we thought that these might be the little round houses that we had been told some of the early Christian missionaries built. A short time after that in truly olden times it was called the Hill of Peace, and that set it far back in time. I remember I liked the name and felt some light about it.' The light spread when, years later, Neil read Adamnan's *Life of Columba* and discovered that his Pictish forebears were not the cannibalistic savages of official history.

> And now I should have to tell of a third and terrible force which must have arrived at the Hill of Peace. Briefly, then, down by Dunbeath harbour, there is a long stretch of beach on which a whole flotilla of Viking longships could readily be hauled up. It's the only beach of its kind in the solid rock wall that stretches from Helmsdale to Wick. And that such ships must have landed there we know from the place names. The group of ruined cottages you see on the starboard—the right hand side as you come in from the sea—still bears its Norse name. And there are Norse names on the way to the Hill of Peace. What happened when the armed Vikings arrived there so troubled my imagination that I tried to get rid of the burden by writing an imaginary account of it.[35]

The account was called *Sun Circle*, and it was published in 1933. In his early years as a writer Neil often wrote to 'get rid' of burdens.

But growing up in Dunbeath was not all burdensome lessons, not even the natural history of salmon and rabbits. 'Everyday', said Alec Gunn, 'was as full as the meat of an egg.' And his wife Gretta said, 'It was Heaven.'[36] There were games and sports, and Neil did well at them and was proud of it. His games reputation was perhaps as high as his fame as a poacher. Curling was 'a brotherly game, where the local poacher may be playing against the sheriff who has convicted him of illegally removing deer or salmon from the territory of the chieftain or laird now acting as the sheriff's skip'.[37] And shinty. Neil was 'used to hitting any kind of ball with a stick' by the time he discovered the more genteel pastime of golf in Galloway in his fourteenth year.[38] But the fullest day of all—the 'day of days', Gretta called it—was the Day of the Games. From his sloping garden in Dunbeath village in summer 1978, old Will Bethune pointed to the field downstream from the stone bridge toward the harbour, where the Games were played, and his eyes lit up. The 'games were not an adventure, they were a passion,' wrote Neil.[39]

In a programme preface he wrote for the Hertfordshire Games of 1953 he elaborated:

The Day of the Games was the day of the year, and in every little community there was a field where 'practising' went on for the 'athletic events'. When boys on the way to school had sudden bursts of speed it could be taken that the class-room was not the objective. On the way from school, when they ran anyhow, ditches and bushes were cleared in flying leaps that evoked the names of the more famous athletes who would arrive for the 'open events'. And if ever it happened that a gamekeeper surprised them far from home and they kept on running for a very long distance indeed, they could, in safety at last, say that it was excellent practice for the mile some day whatever.

Then at last the Day dawned. Later, at some celebrated seat of learning, a boy might have to study the philosophic nature of 'dualism', but if so he was already well grounded, for between the events that went on inside the ring and those that went on outside it, where the booths of succulent treasure were with their three balls a penny, he was often most desperately torn. [Ah yes, Gretta remembered, those 'little square gingerbreads with sugar sprinkled on top'.] Interpenetrating all was the scent of crushed green grass, and, perhaps, by way of higher unity, a large silver coin from the Boys' Race. I can remember the feel of such a coin and how I glimpsed it now and then before shutting it tight in my fist, for what magic had given it might take away, not to mention fellow ruffians of whom I was not the least.

'Oh, yes,' Neil told Alastair Reid in the late 1960s, 'and then there'd be all the goings on, the dance at night—we always got to stay up late for it—and the tales we'd collect to tell all week after, for the night of the Games was a rollicking one, all right.'[40]

Dances and concerts were held at the old Dunbeath hall—it burned down in Gretta's time—up on the high road where the police station is now. Local fairs and festivals trained a boy's eye even as they whetted his appetite. Neil remembered 'the old hillmarket at home, the scoffing, the sarcastic witticisms, the derisive toss of the head, the walking away, up to the spitting on palms and clasping of hands, and the withdrawal to the long white tent where healths were drunk with cordiality and mutual esteem'.[41] And the New Year was a gay time when the house was 'not only rich in bottles but also in a massive currant bun and cakes and other seasonal fare . . . Footsteps outside, the rattling of the door—who were coming in from the darkness now?' Perhaps it would be the strath tailor, who would produce his 'one and only song' to 'a sweeping rhythmic action of the right hand that threatened to spill, though it rarely did, the contents of the whisky bottle which it used as a baton'.[42]

The power Neil felt in music should be noted with care. Some say he had no taste for classical music, and when he sang in the car or in front of a shaving mirror the tune carried him more surely than he it. But he came to feel in music the essence of a culture. *Old Music*, a play of the 1930s, conveys it; and the way he always responded to Gaelic folksinging at mods; and the creative nationalism he thought he heard in German folksingers by the Rhine in 1938. In 'Essence of Nationalism', a 1942 essay, he writes: 'Some time ago I listened in to a programme of music by Sibelius . . . the effect upon me was something that I could not have anticipated, for it was as if the whole Northland of forest and loch and legend came alive before me, evoked out of the blood. I am neither musician nor musical critic, and could not have been led away by any technical considerations. All I know is that the music had for me an evocative power, some extraordinary element of intimacy.'[43]

He had once been more than a listener. His wife wrote to Marian McNeill about *The Drinking Well* (in 1947) that 'when he describes an Irishman dancing a jig on the causey stones of the Old Town to a Highland youth playing a fiddle, there may have been more to it than imagination. For as a youth he certainly played jigs and reels on the fiddle himself and even much later surprised his friends by borrowing on the spot a boy's mouth-organ and playing an Irish jig with such verve and precision that he brought Maurice Walsh to his feet, who added to the surprise by dancing a jig with the verve and precision of an Irishman who knew the classic steps.'[44] For the boy in *The Drinking Well*, a fiddle was a farewell present, and homesick in Edinburgh he played the fiddle in his room.

'The apple-tree, the singing, and the gold. The sun and the moon. I can hear now in my childhood's ear a young woman's laughing voice, lifted in farewell. She and two others must have been spending a happy evening in our home, for I distinctly hear her cry as they went into the night: "We'll be back with the new moon!"'[45] There were visitors from afar, and farewells. A boy would scarcely notice, but the old life was going. The fishing was dying. Besides, Neil's mother was quietly determined that her sons would not follow the sea, that they would get away and get on. On a dark night the boys used to count the flashes of Tarbert Ness lighthouse—'and doubtless still do', said Neil—on the Dornoch Firth. It seemed natural to look afar.[46]

His sister Mary was now Dr Keiller's wife and they lived in Galloway with no children of their own. Would Neil come and live with them? He says he wanted to be 'off and away'. But he was not yet thirteen, and if boyhood in Dunbeath was the paradise it seemed, why leave so young? Why Neil? And what was the effect of sending him away from this world of delight and community? We know only that he was finished with school and he went, from one end of Scotland to another, to another pastoral place, St John's

Town of Dalry, with its intimate wooded hills. He went to a different sort of home, of a different social complexion. There were no other children, and Neil was alone in a new way, with a new awareness of where he had come from.

He sometimes rode on rounds with Mary's husband the doctor in a pony cart. He had a black retriever for companion, and his game was golf—the course was just beyond the garden wall. There was no thought of school. Instead, in J.G. Carter, he had a tutor, and a 'literary' one at that, as if someone thought he might go in that direction. His companions were adults, and two older men influenced him markedly.[47]

The tutor published verse and essays as 'Theodore Mayne' and let Neil discover 'that literature could be one man's main preoccupation and delight'.[48] He had been Professor Blackie's assistant in Edinburgh, then lived the life of a tutor in aristocratic Scottish country houses, and came home to Dalry in poor health shortly after Neil's arrival. His verses in the *Kirkcudbrightshire Advertiser* portray a late Victorian romantic dreaming of home, musing on 'The Ideal and the Real', fashioning his own 'In Memoriam' in the melancholy four-line tetrameter of his master Tennyson. The boy from the strath now sat quietly in the tutor's cluttered bachelor study, or summer afternoons by the Ken, while the old man read him Tennyson and Fitz-Gerald's Omar in a quavering voice. But the boy now saw as well through the eyes of a naturalist. 'Mayne's' model was White of Selborne, and his columns 'Notes from the Glenkens', in the elegant ease of late Victorian essay, combine local antiquities and natural history with allusions to Goldsmith and Keats, Hawthorne and Emerson. In his walks round Dalry, Mayne had the company of 'a young friend' who called his attention to the odd behaviour of peewits. The young friend was Neil in his fourteenth and fifteenth years.[49]

The arrangement was informal and intermittent; the tutor was off on literary pilgrimages and European tours, and late in 1906 they said a pathetic farewell near the old walled cemetery. 'Mayne' had guided Neil gently into poetry, art and French (the latter never 'took' much); but Neil worked up geometry on his own, 'flooring' the poor tutor now and then with a 'tiresome problem'. Embarrassed, Neil made the characteristically tactful decision to proceed on his own, and made his own discovery of 'how beautifully neat a game Euclid was'. The fourteen-year-old playing his private game with the beauties of Euclid strikingly foreshadows the man who would astonish friends with rare analytical powers.

For Latin, Neil was sent to the headmaster of the local school. Little is heard of Latin, but this extraordinary man had an effect both wide and deep.[50] He 'met the definition of the solid intelligent Lowland Scot', and he enjoyed Neil's company. Neil remembered him in 'Fishing Lochs of Day and Night', an article of the 1940s:

> I can still remember the faint shock of surprise I got when the headmaster asked me if I would go to fish with him next Saturday on Lochinvar [a four-mile walk from Dalry]. Before my silence, he smiled, his eyes bright with the intelligent humour that distinguished them. 'Yes,' he nodded. 'Young Lochinvar who came out of the west. It's the same loch.' I probably grew embarrassed for I could have been no more than fourteen, and it was the first time I had come in direct contact with that kind of ballad poetry which had hitherto seemed as if not quite belonging to this earth.[51]

There were several day trips with 'rod and basket and lunch' and some stirring fishing. But more things than fish were stirring. The boy was talking with an 'intelligent educated grown-up' who liked to talk with knowledge and exuberance about *everything*: ballad poetry, the names and traditions of wild flowers, the facts of life and the body. He spoke of religious institutions with 'a certain detached, amused criticism', and the boy began to grow into the freethinker of London days, intellectually curious and self-reliant. What seemed most memorable, as he recalled, was the *way* he was learning and the long humane perspective that came with it:

> The boy was not being taught, he was learning by the way from a grown man who knew the traditions of the tribe. And it was this feeling for the people *behind* the wild flowers that was somehow most strongly evoked; not the name of the plant but that *they* should *know*. This was what was new and remained when many names were forgotten. The people *before his time*, in the straths, on the moor, by the sea. The nameless folk who went back into time . . .
>
> These figures of the Strath were nameless and for chime there might be an old bagpipe tune in the darkening in the distance, or a girl's face singing in the firelight in a way that drew all together and drew the hearts out of them, for what was told was the story of some one at some time, and the eye saw destiny last year, or last century, or any time beyond. A thousand years made no difference. Here where all might seem romance there was no romance, or very little. But there was an extraordinary warmth, a profound emotion shared in common, and the boy got the feeling that this profoundly mattered. This is the well from which the human tribe must drink or it will perish.[52]

He would not begin to write for another dozen years, but here was the way his imagination would go. Years later, when Neil said that his greatest male character Old Hector came from two or three older men he had known in youth, he was surely including the Dalry headmaster.

His immediate concern was with other things. He was 'the stranger never quite at home who must pass on'.[53] He wanted to be 'off and away' on his own. The same weekly that printed Mayne's 'Notes' often printed inviting announcements of exams for boys from fifteen to seventeen. They offered 'the most desirable opening into the Civil Service for young lads, and the sure way to future promotion'—which was far from the truth. In fact, the 'young lads' were given four-year terminal appointments as clerks, and at the end a very small percentage would pass the exam into permanent jobs. There would be wearisome work, hard study and gnawing uncertainty.

At fifteen Neil evidently had great confidence. His oldest brother, now in or near London, had led the way. The paper advertised coaching colleges—Skerry's in Glasgow took prospective boy clerks from age fourteen—but it didn't occur to Neil to seek coaching; he had learned to learn for himself. 'A few months later, without any coaching, he set off for Edinburgh and sat the examination.'[54] It took several days, and things went wrong: his penmanship paper slipped off the desk and was smudged, and even his beloved 'arithmetic' gave trouble. Then back to Dalry for a long wait, and finally the results. Sure he had failed, he began reading from the bottom of the list. Only the names of those who had passed were given, and finally near the top his name stared back at him. 'It was the first time he had ever seen it in print and, like first love, it held something he never saw in it again.'[55] We can estimate that he took the exam in the spring of 1907, and in the summer he packed the old gladstone bag, stowed in it a few emergency pounds, and was off and away to London.

3   Unattached Officer

Not surprisingly, the huge spectacle of drab and exotic Edwardian London
made a strong and lasting impression on the stranger aged fifteen from 'the
strath, the corrie, the dizzy cliffs' and idyllic Glenkens. Five chapters in *The
Atom of Delight*[1] are given to the two years he spent there. They almost hide
the sense of strangeness, of fear, of not belonging. 'Though involved he was
forever a spectator,'[2] but one gets the strong impression that he *was*
involved. When later an occasional critic found him ignorant of cities he was
quick to recall that he had known them at first hand for several impres-
sionable years. If, later, he seemed out of place or ill at ease in a city, there is
little hint of that in the London chapters, and none of the solemn Wordsworthian pomp that felt it was not for that place or for that hour.

There is a tell-tale defensiveness in *The Atom of Delight* when he acknowledges that memory has selected the light and the irresponsible. There is
a vague passing reference to experiences excluded: 'There were dreary spells
as dreary as the streets, anxieties and frets and miseries and fears and
conflicts and temptations and illicit desires and obsessive sex and the rest.
The old bundle of faggots . . . And to make light of it in a moment's
lightness is not to forget the moment that was poisoned . . . When the
poisoned moment is gone the world is fresh and wide.'[3] That is all we know
of the darker side of Neil's London adolescence.

We do know the things his memory liked to recall: the competence with
which he did his work; his standing as an athlete; and his ebullient forays
into the cultural adventure of the city. The shy Highlander, who found
silver birches disturbingly out of place on Hampstead Heath, is little in
evidence.

His job was 'hard writing' at full speed dealing with 'warrants', 'acknow-
ledgements' and 'the addressing of envelopes for bundles of bank books'.[4]
He worked at the Post Office Savings Bank at Shepherd's Bush, a long ride
on the twopenny tram or omnibus west of London, beyond Bayswater and
Notting Hill. His brother James found him a place, but soon he was sharing
digs near work with two other boys from Scotland and a landlady who
'stooped slightly, had a thin damp nose-tip, and wore mittens permanently'—petty bourgeois London used to look as if Dickens had created it—in

'one of those innumerable side streets of small houses so drearily alike, one beyond the other beyond the other, that they looked as if they had been arrested, permanently dwarfed, in the class struggle.'[5] Under the pompous surveillance of an elderly civil servant in morning coat, pinstripe trousers, and boutonnière, he learned anxiously to do 'the average' amount of work. He said later that it was the only time in his life he really worked hard.

Hard work continued when, after two years, he won a transfer to Edinburgh, worked on 'the income tax side' and studied for another exam. Hard work continued over the next decade when 'revenue accountancy' required the detailed assessment of crofts all over the north and west of Scotland. Habits of workmanlike efficiency served Neil throughout his life: in keeping books for the Excise, in political management, in writing and revising for deadlines. He came from a background of limited and dwindling resources, and he never forgot the economy which made independence possible.

In London he was paid fifteen shillings a week to start and one shilling annual increment. His lodging (including breakfast and tea) cost twelve. His 'careful arithmetic' told him how much was left for fares and lunches and entertainment, and prudence told him to leave the 'few pounds in the gladstone bag' as long as possible. When he first read of the ill, dying Burns, Burns's was 'the last cry of agony'[6] and he never forgot the terrible importance of having enough money. In days of fame and success, more patrician or bohemian souls might try to make him forget it, and some might even think him tight when he held the 'pounds in the gladstone bag'. But 'careful arithmetic' in the boy clerk, determined not to send home for more help, stayed with Neil all his life. It was part of his real sympathy with the poor, just as hard work made him a lover of idleness.

He was proud, too, of his prowess in athletics. The bold runner of Dunbeath, the shinty player and fearless fighter, had taken up golf in Galloway, was a good player before he left for London, and won a Civil Service tournament a few years later. His games reputation in London earned him a brief introduction to the English game of cricket and one triumphant moment facing that 'lucifer of the sunlight', a fast bowler. But football was his choice, and there was a bold confrontation with a senior boy at the Bank over placement on the team. Last year's players assumed that they would control this year's selection. Neil 'and another fellow didn't think this was right and said so. The debate became heated, and one of the fellows said that if I said that sort of thing again he'd have me out to the cloakroom to settle it, and I told him I was quite prepared to go out to the

cloakroom just *then*!'[7] He won his point and secured a place in the team. It
went further. Neil was asked to play for a west London amateur club. So
Saturday afternoons 'the boy caught his tram and for twopence was hurled
along Uxbridge Road to green fields in the west'.[8]

There were forays into the life of London. 'I recall going by bus with this
fellow Reid [in *Atom* he is called 'Will'] that I had digs with in Shepherd's
Bush to the sixpenny seats in the gallery to see Gilbert and Sullivan. Reid
was very fond of Gilbert and Sullivan.'[9] They went to the Tivoli to see Harry
Lauder (it was embarrassing), spent an early Sunday morning watching for
pickpockets in Petticoat Lane, ran away from an insistent prostitute,
watched the boats in Kensington Gardens, and listened to the atheists,
anarchists, and socialists near Marble Arch.

After the freethought of the Dalry headmaster, this last was especially
exciting. Neil says he took to 'Socialism as a duckling to water'. His
experience, he said, was like Tom's in Glasgow in *The Serpent*.[10] At that
time, 'questions about society and socialism had an eagerness, almost a
bloom, upon them which they have since lost . . . Oh, the excitement in
those days! Impossible for this late age ever to recapture that first fearful
delight, that awful thrill, of Scepticism.' Neil 'knew all the arguments
(Huxley, Darwin, Haeckel and what have you—wasn't it Ernst Haeckel
who wrote *The Riddle of the Universe?*). Anyway, that kind of atmosphere.
And though my reading was very limited, basic statements of doctrine,
etc., were whizzing around among us, or a good few of us. And I did read for
my own information quite a bit of academic pol. econ. I could even give
definitions of Rent, and though all that has vanished from my memory [this
is a letter of the mid-1960s], I can still recall the delight I got from Carlyle's
one (I think I can even repeat it): "A widow is gathering nettles for her
children's dinner. A perfumed seigneur, delicately lounging in the Oeil de
Boeuf (if that's the spelling), has an alchemy whereby he can extract the
third nettle from her and call it rent."[11] It was the sort of image—the poor
widow—that would haunt him for life.

He read Henry George's *Progress and Poverty* and shared London's excitement over Shaw and Wells, 'true and startling innovators'. On the other
side of the fence he read Chesterton and Belloc. Lying on their beds in the
drab digs room, Reid would recite Tennyson aloud—'Airy Fairy Lilian'—
while Neil read Darwin. 'Reid was very strong on Tennyson,' said Neil one
day. 'You were pretty strong on Tennyson yourself,' said his brother John.[12]
And before his youth was over he had read Pater's *Renaissance* three times. In
Huxley's sharply marshalled arguments, Darwin's eye for natural detail,

Pater's vivid impressionism, and Tennyson's delicate orchestration of mood one can see formative influences on what would become Neil's style.

So he took to London with zest, like Tom in *The Serpent*, 'but then he had always had a zest for life, and particularly the outsider's zest. He was not in himself a "character" so much as a "watcher"—something more than a spectator, ready if need be to mix in, and shout, and retreat, doubled up with laughter. Something of the gamin in him from the beginning, beyond doubt.'[13] His age may well have had something to do with it, for his memories of the next two years, back in Edinburgh, from 1909 until 1911, suggest a new degree of refinement and a more sensitive perception of things.

'I lived', he said, 'with medical students in digs near the Meadows. A nice old lady like my housekeeper Isobel at Dalcraig took care of us. There were both sexes in the house, and I'm afraid we were rather wild.'[14] Iain's experience in *The Drinking Well*, while somewhat later in date, recalls Neil's Edinburgh in the years before the First World War. He may have been back for a while in training at the start of the war, for he was on hand when his brother John came to enter the University. When we see Iain the law apprentice showing Angus, his friend from home, around Edinburgh, we glimpse Neil and John. Angus was staying with some 'far out relations on his mother's side'[15] and Neil recalls visiting the Stewarts, playing chess and talking about religion. It was a first exposure to social stratification and cosmopolitan refinement. The exposure was enlarged through the companionship of older civil servants—such as Douglas in *The Drinking Well*.

He recalls the men in two late articles, 'Edinburgh' and 'High on the Haggis'—one a connoisseur in wines, the other in music. 'My earliest introduction to wines', he writes in the second, 'was by an Edinburgh connoisseur whose voice I can still inwardly hear, with its note of reverent gaiety, murmuring that Burgundy was the wine of kings and claret the King of wines'.[16] (Douglas says this in the novel.) And in the first:

Once I saw a friend's face blench with horror at a loud voice demanding 'Scotch and soda'. My God! he muttered and his hand trembled as it added seven drops of water to his 'pure malt' from a Highland still . . . That office man whose legal face grew pale as the stranger drowned his Scotch in soda, had music and cheese for pastimes. In truth, it was an elderly Civil Servant—he played a cracking game of golf—who insisted that my education would not be complete until I knew all about an orchestra, in which he played the viola. Another instructed me in the Continental use of wines. Though perhaps the only real instruction was in laughter. And how they talked!—these quiet reserved fellows who trooped out of their various offices and looked as if enthusiasm would wilt in the air which nevertheless they found it essential to breathe.[17]

The atom of delight hid within the austerities of Edinburgh.

There was another side to the divided social scene: desperate poverty. It was something different from anything he had seen at home, and evidently it had not shown itself in London except as part of exciting radical theory. He explored the narrow wynds of the Old Town where 'the aristocratic area' had become 'a slum of unexcelled pungency, blown on by odours from the breweries and gasworks' near Holyrood. 'I can remember as a boy adventuring down into that region on a Saturday night and taking to my heels when a fight started in an entry (bearing a lordly name) and the police whistles blew.'[18] He was still a good runner. The experience became the start of Iain's surreal night with Douglas in the Royal Mile in *The Drinking Well*:

> The lamps were lit and night stood in the mouths of the wynds and closes. The people were different here from the people in Princes Street, different in their clothes, the movements of their bodies, their features, the way they glanced. Women with shopping satchels, intent or argumentative, forthright or timid, sharp-eyed. Youths in a vennel-mouth. Cat-calls. A figure slipping past, hurried, furtive. A smell that had no name, faint, pervasive, sifting through its age-old blanket. Men going into and coming out of pubs, stopping to argue on the kerb. Oaths—a whipping filthy mouthful. A laughing group, one stout woman swaying, pushing her neighbour away from her in playful emphasis. Two policemen walking along slowly, tall men. A scurry of shrill children. The two policemen stopped, an arguing group dissolved, sucked out of sight up a dark close.
>
> Intensely alert, Iain tried to feel unconcerned—[19]

but he couldn't be. And Neil, though he ran, couldn't be. He had 'the curious childish feeling of human guilt and crime'.

The medical students he lived with could show him both. One of them, doing a midwifery course, went to attend a birth one night in an Edinburgh slum and took Neil with him. The experience was conflated with a similar one—twenty years later in Glasgow with his journalist friend John Macnair Reid—into a nightmarish episode of *Wild Geese Overhead*. There the young mother dies of sheer malnutrition and exhaustion. Neil never forgot this image, but mingled with the horror and desperation he saw the human nobility, too, and he could never accept the harshly naturalistic or grotesque picture of urban poverty drawn by many novelists.[20] In the *Glasgow Herald* of 4 January 1941, he would write:

> During the impressionable years I had got to know in some measure the slums of London and Edinburgh. Accordingly I was not surprised when one gusty

midnight, in what is called 'the worst part' of Glasgow, I stood and questioned a man about his native city and listened to what he had to say . . . I could feel in his voice his hurt contempt for those who had the insufferable conceit and complacency to come and inspect and report on these hard-working women of the tenements as if they were 'some sort of specimens'. Now if this man, who knew his tenements, were to write a novel around the lives of a few normal families who live in them, and write it from the inside, record emotions as experienced in their minds, the result would not be a catalogue of horrors, but a revelation of the higher virtues, of periods of hardship, bravely endured, of the usual human ills, of flashes of irritability, of happy times and good nights, of a whole lot of gossip and not a little sentimentality.

The novel is not one Neil could write, for he did not trust his imagination without a solid grounding in experience. He did, however, carry the revelation of poverty back with him to his own 'grey coast' and it is strongly felt in his early writing.

But when he was eighteen in Edinburgh—a boy clerk on a subsistence wage—the revelation of poverty must have aggravated the anxiety, 'the prospect of being thrown on the scrap-heap'. The time of the exam was approaching, and he had only one small chance for permanency in the Civil Service. To go home a failure to a growingly depressed Dunbeath was a nightmare he would write about more than once. So he studied on his own, and (as in *The Drinking Well*) 'this aspect of the city as a place of study and preparation, as a sort of vast barracks and training ground, was never quite lost by Iain'.[21]

He could not take the exam until he turned nineteen in November 1910, and recalls the exam as 'on the MA level', but only one particular is recorded. The remembered 'loveliness of wooded Loch Ken . . . must have so impressed me that several years later, under what we call "examination hall conditions", I can remember selecting it as my subject for a given English composition on an aspect of Nature and obtaining abnormally high marks, probably because I had aroused the examiner's Wordsworthian interest by introducing "a sense sublime of something far more deeply interfused".'[22] Once more the writer had been recognised, but once more there is no sign of awakened literary ambitions.

He wanted a career in the Customs & Excise that would let him work around the Highlands. It seemed unlikely he would be one of the few who passed. Then, after the waiting time, the lists were sent out. Neil was in bed when the landlady brought him his copy, and there once more was his name. Now there were six weeks of training in Edinburgh, and then would come assignments as an 'unattached officer' to temporary stations, until he had the seniority for a fixed station of his own. It was just right for a man in his early twenties, when many men want the chance to explore options, to 'hang loose' and avoid strong commitments. It is easy to imagine the relief, the exuberant sense of ease, he must have felt.

He could pay a visit home proudly. Brother Alec remembers:

> My first true meeting with Neil was on his arriving home on a motor cycle, a fully fledged Exciseman, when, I fear, my interest in his cycle was greater than my interest in himself; and while my parents were making much ado over their son's homecoming I proceeded to burn my fingers on the cylinder of the motor cycle. A shout brought me inside where presents were being distributed; and on his handing me a large glittering mouth-organ his worth as a brother was considerably enhanced. [23]

There are numerous memories of the young officer burning up remote Highland roads, 'an insignificant buzzing figure on a motor-bike [who] had once nearly broken his neck' on Harris. [24] Or near Drumrunie, where 'a road goes left to Achiltibuie that strings its line of houses before the Summer Isles, with a coast road winding north to Lochinver that has to be travelled to be believed. I first encountered it when a lad on a belt-driven motor-bike, and I have a memory of a back wheel shooting stones like bullets from the loose surface while I ran alongside, for the engine couldn't take us both, the bike and myself, up these sudden reckless gradients.' [25] The whole period in his life has a quality of the reckless against a rapidly changing Highland landscape or of the blissfully idle against a timeless one.

He had time for a holiday to Glenelg on the Sound of Sleat, for here his sister Mary and her husband now lived, and theirs was still his home. Several idyllic boyhood memories seem to belong to this vacation time. They returned when he was 'off in a boat' at the end of his Excise years.

> As a lad I had many a time pulled my row-boat smartly into the current and then laid back to be floated away towards Glenelg. There was a Christmas memory, too, of carrying a pushbike on my back up the hillside through the snow and down the steep slopes to the shores of Loch Duich. But what sticks in the mind most persistently is a boyhood day spent on the moor beyond the stiff climb from Kylerhea . . . It was deep gloaming when we emerged on the moor and followed the road that winds by the little stream towards Broadford. A whole summer day the boy had spent there, guddling yellow trout, looking over the silent moors, seeing no living soul. It had been a day of such curious and intimate loneliness, so withdrawn from all practical ways of being and thought, that I can afford to wonder if it happened to me in this life, or indeed if it happened at all. [26]

It was not, to be sure, always solitary and unearthly.

I had gone across to Raasay with a girl in a row-boat, leaving another couple on shore, and on the way back a growing wind very nearly beat us. Feeling gone from the wrists and arms and pulling with the dead weight of the body, I was lucky at last to beach on Skye . . .

Presently we saw a fishing boat leave Portree. It was now blowing half a gale and getting dark, so she could never be going to sea. At last, three of us got on board her in the shelter of a headland, and I went back along shore to launch our boat to be taken in tow . . .

The exhilaration of a sea-storm turns dull men vivid, dumb men into a shout, and slow men into the leap of a sword. There is no intoxicant to be compared with it.[27]

But he had to get back to the city for assignment, and he was two days late. Appointments had been made. Two other boys had been sent to Ireland— Neil thought if he had been on time he might have gone there too—and he was assigned to Inverness. His training completed, he was appointed an officer on 21 December 1911 and began the decade he recalled as his 'ten years of wandering' as part of boyhood though he was twenty when it began. It was free, vigorous and fun. And the mind of a Highland novelist was being amply stored.

He substituted all over the north and west, coming to know the Highlands and Islands intimately and the crofters who lived there. Once he had to investigate an old couple who lived in a caravan. He asked if they had birth certificates to prove their age. They looked at each other, bewildered. They didn't know that such things existed, and had no clear notion of where they had been born. Well then, did they have a marriage certificate? Here there was a long pause and at last the old man stood up, cleared his throat, and said: 'I am sorry to tell you, sir, that we have been living in sin for fifty years.' They got their pension.[28]

Neil also began to substitute for the Excise officers who supervised whisky distilleries. On Lewis, for instance, was a Customs & Excise station with several officers, and as each was replaced while on holiday, Neil might be there for months at a time.

I remember spending a few evenings in a small hotel in Skye with a famous climber who has left his name among the Coolins (Professor Collie). After wandering in talk from the Rockies to the Himalayas, he told me that he had never seen anything more beautiful in the way of colour than the stretch of moor on the west side of these fantastic mountains . . . I once saw the sun setting amid the ruins of Duntulm Castle, lost Fladdachuain in the twilight, then found myself at a ceilidh where time was forgotten until the sun rose even more remarkably than it had set.

Having mentioned one small island (Eigg), let me add two more. Mostly memory does its work in snatches, in pictures, as those who visit these Isles will find out. I am sitting in the shelter of a boulder on the strand at Pollachar in South Uist waiting for a vessel to take me over to Eriskay. It is a high-flying day, bright and keen, with the wave-top flashing. All at once the eyes focus on a cockleshell of a boat driving fast before the wind, a full belly on the reddish-brown sail, a bush of whisker on the old boy at the tiller, and a pipe sticking out of the whiskers.[29]

On Benbecula he saw a picture of a quiet, slow life:

a picture of great waves on its western strand, a herd girl sheltering against a stook of corn, wild geese on a stubble field, in a grey day of small rain. What virtue there is in that picture I cannot tell, but it has already much of the force of legend . . . It is the mood of human comradeship, quiet and simple, but strong. It is the smile that acknowledges Fate—and no more.[30]

In a small Benbecula hotel he met the odd old English major, who was finally translated into *The Other Landscape* with his trunk of old embassy candles. One night they debated the experiences underlying *The Rubáiyát*, and Neil was knocked into deserts when the old diplomat held him with his eyes and asked, 'Have *you* ever heard *the beating of a distant drum?*' The major never set the hotel afire, but 'he did light all those candles in his room, and I remember going to sleep with a smile for the thought of the place going up in flames and the hope that I might wake up in time if it did.' The small hotels proved grand places for training the ear and eye for characters.[31]

Substituting for a distillery officer was usually pleasant and gave Neil a notion for the future. Shortly before war broke out in 1914 he met one distillery officer who was to become his closest companion in these years and remain a dear friend for half a century.

How Maurice Walsh came from County Kerry to the golden triangle of Moray whiskies is best described by himself (in 1950):

I entered the Excise service, as a boy, in 1901 [he was born in 1879]. I mind well that a week before Christmas I was away down in Valentia Island at the American side of the Kerry Mountains, and looking forward to a pleasant Festival in Tralee, where, at the time, I was coortin' a nice girl—even if she was a Presbyterian. But I spent that snowy Christmas under Ben Nevis, five hundred miles away. That was where they made and matured the famous Long John . . .

I hesitate to tell you that I spent a summer season amongst the breweries of the English Midlands. But look you! After a long, hot July day, to sit over the chimb of a cask in a cool cellar, and draw brown ale from a spigot into a long flagon was a pleasant occupation.

And then I came up to Speyside, and there I bided. But that territory included more than the basin of the Spey; it included the Dev'ron, the Fiddich, the Spey, the Lossie, the Findhorn and the Nairn, from Glenlivet— the real Glenlivet—to Inchgower near Buckie, from Glendronach near Huntly, to Brockla at Cawdor. Into that soberly rolling and chimney-stalked territory three dozen of us young fellows used to gather for the distilling season from October to May: lads from all Scotland, England, Wales and Ireland, the four most quarrelsome nations in the world—but it was not blood that flowed.

We were really a friendly, easy-going, non-conforming community— distillers, brewers, and revenue alike—and we were extraordinarily continent. Continence is the only way between a palate and malt whisky, and we were as continent as a connoisseur with a vintage claret . . .

But when I do get the first whiff of, say, Standfast, I see a vision. I see the long-winding valley with the chimney stalks and kiln-pagodas above the trees; I see the Fiddich and the Dullan running fast and clear over bright gravel, the bald Convals fringed with a hair of pines, big Ben Rinnes with cap atilt over the glen; I smell again the peat, the wash, and the feints, and feel the tightness of carbon-dioxide in my throat; and I see myself getting out of a warm bed in the dark of a Januar' morning. And I see a girl with red hair.[32]

Walsh was at Forres, and Neil was sent to substitute. 'I'd write ahead and say, "Look here! I'm coming to replace you. Kindly see that the books all are in perfect order so that there is absolutely no work to be done".'[33] They became close friends and fellow fishers and hunters all over the north. Indeed, as Neil reported in his wife's letter to Marian McNeill, 'There is even a rumour or myth to the effect that it was only after Walsh had felt it a matter of honour to return to Eire [in 1922] that, in the absence of more exciting preoccupations, they both started writing.'[34] There is a lively sense of the life they shared in Maurice's first novel *The Key Above the Door* (1926), where the narrator Tom King is joined in Moray by one Neil Quinn out of Ireland and one Alistair Munro, a 'rascally Highlandman from the borders of Caithness and the pools of the Dunbeath River knew him but too well'. Munro has Neil's background but Quinn has his name, and it is Quinn who writes from Skye describing Gunn's favourite 'duty': 'I shall be here for a full month [near the Talisker distillery] and shall be able to house you royally. The distillery officer is on leave, and I am doing duty for him. He has loaned me his house, his garden patch, and his motor-boat, so that I—and you— may not suffer as we deserve in the small house they call an inn, where the staple diet is salt herring, fresh whiting, and the flavour of peat. I cook ham and eggs to perfection; the mutton is the best in the islands; and rod and gun yield luxuries galore.'[35] Maurice's visit to Neil on Skye supplied Neil with a favourite story.

'Those few weeks on the southern shore of Loch Harport were just right in every way—the time of year, the weather, and the company.' He had been staying in the small hotel, but with Maurice coming he got an empty house with 'just enough furniture and coal in it to see us through'. He had permission to fish and shoot rabbit, but they weren't fond of rabbit, and they weren't permitted to shoot grouse. And then on the way home one evening they saw a grouse fly up from their feet and not go very far. Surely the bird had been wounded. 'What a shame! The poor bird! . . . Who would leave a wounded bird to die a lingering death, probably in agony? Not us, anyway . . . Let us draw a curtain over the business by saying that humanitarianism triumphed in the end. And, of course, we brought the grouse home. What else could we do with it?' Imagine their moral dismay when they discovered that the bird had not been wounded—before. They had best cook it.

Maurice plucked the grouse while Neil prepared the rabbits. In a roasting tin they surrounded the grouse with bits of rabbit, then covered it with a layer of butter and onions, then more rabbit, more butter and onion, and grouse on top. The next morning they left it slowly roasting and had a long day's fishing. The grouse still troubled their consciences so 'on the way back, we dropped into a place where we got two drams of Talisker whisky, twelve years old, out of a sherry hogshead. We hadn't eaten since morning— we were fending for ourselves and living on two meals a day—and as we floated toward our door we were met by a divine aroma.' It was 'the most memorable dish I ever ate.' Walsh's account of the same recipe will be found in Chapter 15 of *The Key Above the Door*.[36]

The holidays with Maurice were out of time, and the truly memorable for Neil became akin to the 'legendary'. Man the hunter and fisher had been like this before history began. 'This sort of companionship won't disappear in a hurry,' he said later, and he was offering an urgent defence against a modern suspicion of male companionship. His sense of his own manhood was shaped by a culture that idolised 'manliness'. In Maurice's company he found the reassurance of a masculine way of life that was carefree and natural, and throughout his life he cherished the warm reminiscence of times spent sleeping in the heather, telling stories round a campfire. There was a night by Lochindorb in Moray in particular, one of those long twilights of northern summer, when at last it grew too dark to see the flies to fish with.

> The sack is full of peats and some split logs. We take it on board and row over to the ruins of the Wolf of Badenoch's castle which stands on an island in the loch. We build a fire near the great grey wall where a large tree grows (an ash, I

think). The kettle is set to boil and the food laid out. And here is Maurice Walsh to tell us that though we can hardly be said so far to have earned a drink, still, a small one may be necessary, not only to defeat the chills of night, but to keep at a respectful distance the old Wolf 's ghost.

Four of us round the fire: one, our host, who belongs to these parts. No, he answers us solemnly, he has never seen the ghost. Put the flask away, Maurice, because if the Wolf 's ghost is anything like what he was himself, it's as well not to place temptation in the way. We discuss the Wolf. We create the ghostly atmosphere out of the stories, and new stories of modern mediums, and give it all a 'scientific' air by describing some of Crooke's investigations into 'psychic force'. 'Did you hear yon?' someone says. We listen—and laugh—and put more peat on the fire.

Sitting round the bright flame, with night softly prowling through the old ruins; black water and distant moors and our old Scots history. And far back beyond recorded history, men sat thus round the glowing logs that the prowling brute feared, casting a look now and then over their shoulders.[37]

He might have been back in the broch of boyhood.

When Walsh and Gunn began writing novels a few years later, Walsh could use such settings and adventures, with occasional help in plotting from the 'rascally Highlandman', for (as he said himself) his plots were 'wake in the middle'. He liked to boom out 'I write *ro*-mance' and to recite early Yeats; Neil later would imitate him intoning 'Tread softly for you tread upon my dreams'. For Neil, romance was never the thing. But there seems to have been no thought of writing by Loch Harport or Lochindorb.[38]

The first of Neil's writing we know of was done midway through these 'wandering years', during the war, when he worked at Kinlochleven in Argyllshire. The war makes a strange episode, for in a way it seems to have made no difference in his carefree bachelor existence, and yet the war came close and his feelings must have been both deep and mixed. Neil was the brother who did not go.

His recollection is that Excise inspectors were 'ordered to Stirling for the physical exam, but told we wouldn't be called up, and if we enlisted voluntarily we would lose our place. I remember the sergeant chap who did the measuring—he measured me and called out "Six feet!"[39] But I had four brothers fighting and so I decided I had better stay.' Then later John went and was gassed, and Ben was killed, another wounded, another dead of heart disease. Near the war's end even Excise officers with special training were ordered to report. Neil went home to say goodbye to his mother. She looked at him and asked, 'Don't you think we have given enough?' He never forgot that image of the bereft woman left by men going off to fight the historic ego battles of the male. It was the opposite side of his vision of male comrades on the hunt. But he was going. He had reached Inverness on his way when the war ended.

The war had come close at Kinlochleven. He had his work to do for Customs & Excise, but he had received special training. 'I was in charge of shipping and routing ships around minefields—I had been specially trained for work with shipping and mines on the west coast—away from the Minch, which we knew had a German submarine. I got telegrams with instructions from the Admiralty, and sent back reports of all I could learn' from the incoming skippers. He got to know some of the skippers well, and to know the seaways near Kinlochleven almost as well as the pilots. On occasion he even took 'the wheel of a cargo vessel, with steering gear worked by steam, under the eye of a pilot who knew the invisible rocks and currents of some of our own western lochs or fiords. And stemming an eight-knot tidal race in Caolas nan Con with the visible rocks so near that you could nearly spit on them can produce a few anxious minutes in an eight-knot vessel.'[40] Neil had to give each skipper route instructions and a pass stamped on wax. One skipper, a Norwegian, had his reasons for going by way of the Minch rather than Skerryvore, and though it was against regulations Neil got him permission by telegraph from HQ. The skipper wanted to give him a case of chartreuse as a gift, but Neil had to refuse, and received instead a bent threepenny piece for luck. He kept that piece for years. The skipper got through safely but went down later in the war.[41]

Neil was stationed at the pier near the aluminium works. At first he lived in digs, but didn't like them and got himself a bed in the office of the harbourmaster, his friend Captain MacDougall. He was a vegetarian and Neil became one, too, except for fish. In summer Neil would pitch an army tent on a steep hillside near the harbour. The ships would hoot as they passed his tent and he would go out and shake a fist at them. In the morning he would rise and swim round his boat, have breakfast of porridge and eggs, then row to the harbour pier. One wet and gusty night he rowed back to find the tent flat and dishevelled, his bedding soaked, and he had a bad week with chills and lumbago. The tent was pitched on a charcoal-burner's circle and Neil was told that the place was 'not good'. There were queer sounds at night, like a man lying in pain after having fallen off a cliff. Neil could find nothing. Maurice came to visit him for a fortnight in the tent and heard the same sounds. One night something sprang into the tent and knocked over the candle. Neil groped for a torch and it lit up the staring eyes of a cat.

Three vivid and characteristic anecdotes remain from the Kinlochleven years. In Neil's words they are 'odd and adventurous', entertaining in humour, but visionary or frightening as well.

Once on a summer evening on the bleak Moor of Rannoch:

> I had gone with a Glencoe crofter to inspect the village herd (which included three beasts of his own). The one-armed Irishman who looked after the herd, and his lonely hut in the waste of the moor, with bog-candles leaning against its wall. The collie—the whining lean tawny collie—that couldn't believe the miracle of a digestive biscuit. The bog-pine fire that flared at the touch of a match, and the tea. There were one or two miracles in that place. Passing west of Kingshouse in the dead of the summer night and two hulking tramps stopping us to inquire—the time! But we had coolly faced up to them and they had gone on. Then down Glencoe of the massacre with the dawn breaking in bright silver and the birds singing. A riot of loveliness and singing over the graves of the murdered . . . All that caught into time—the murders, the riot, and the singing, and the steadiness in the heart of the pilot like the beacon light.[42]

Here in embryo is Neil's later vision of light breaking through the dark violence of history.

Again, one summer afternoon on his 'long sea-fiord of Argyll' he decided on the spur of the moment to try to beat the sun's shadow as it climbed the high promontory behind his tent. The sun won. Then at the top, near midnight, he saw a herd of stags come over the brow of heather. It was an awesome sight. He came down the slope fast and slid to the promontory verge and right through it into the loch.

Finally, one day on the pier he talked to a man from Tiree who had seen his grandmother evicted from her burning home, had lost his father's croft, gone to sea, and now looked after loading the ships. 'I remember the day he came across to the harbourmaster's office, his face white with wrath.' An order had come from the Works to stow cargo in a way that would save unloading time but was, he knew, unsafe to ship and crew. He had refused.

> When his foreman appeared and publicly reprimanded him, he stood outraged and speechless. Then he found his tongue, gave it to the foreman for a raking minute, and walked off the pier. He came straight over to the harbourmaster and myself who were his friends. His English at such a moment was naturally uncertain. But I remember the culminating sentence: 'I could have broken the pugger in three halves.'[43]

Neil never knew what became of him, but the man from Tiree with his heroic arithmetic remained 'representative of his race, the race that was outraged and beaten and driven forth by the money-lenders of a new age of greed and fear'.

In such episodes the storing of the imagination went on. And Neil was reading a bit. The harbourmaster introduced him one day to 'a grey-haired stranger who had come off the steamer from Ballachulish. He was what they called a colporteur. In time we got round to the subject of books, and more to please my friend the harbourmaster than anything else, I bought three. Two of them I still have [he is speaking on BBC's *Scottish Life and Letters* forty years later], one on Celtic myths and legends [Rolleston had appeared in 1911] and the other a history of economic doctrine, and often in the matter of checking references I have blessed the old colporteur.' Celtic legend and economic history. It is the mixture of which he would make several novels.[44]

He was beginning to write at Kinlochleven, but what he wrote belonged more to the world of 'Theodore Mayne' than to that of the man from Tiree. He identified as his first publication a jolting sonnet out of Omar, Tennyson, and Keats, that is signed 'Nial Guinne' and adorns page one of the first issue of a little magazine *The Apple-Tree*, published by and for members of the Aspirants' Fellowship (Hon. Sec., Esther Hyman, Clapham Road, London). It ought to be preserved here because it came first!

TOAST

Here's to it! The one fine thought that will thrill
The mind of each to some divine desire;
In deeps of mockery and strife and dire
Defeat we'll stumble—but we'll hold to't still.
Come, fill up! We'll drink to it while the wine
Bursts its fragrant bubbles in youth's frail glass,
And pledge ourselves, by this our solemn sign,
To follow our lone quest. And as we pass
Along life's shifting waste, where staring sphinx
And ageless pyramid discuss our dreams
In mocking silence, we'll not halt, but on
And on we'll press, until our dim star sinks
Beyond the desert's rim. Then, if it seems
We have done little—we'll ask Death's pardon.

                                        Nial Guinne[45]

The issue, dated May 1918, holds more promising stuff. It is largely taken up with the report of a Prize Competition. The Committee reports Mr N. M. Gunn to be one of 'the only two competitors of outstanding merit', laments that his short story 'The Divining Rod', while brilliant, humorous, and subtle, 'could by no stretch of imagination be called a story' and quotes his replies to such set questions as, 'What is the artistic value of red geraniums?', 'What is the moral significance of Garden Cities?', 'What are the precise relative values of frivolity and dignity?' and 'What place has a kitten in the general scheme of things?' The reply to this last is priceless early Gunn: 'Women talk, lions stalk, and the gods thunder to gain their ends: a kitten plays endlessly as an end in itself. Consider man "at a loose end": any loose end is good enough for a kitten. The cosmic significance of it!' The prize went to Mr N. M. Gunn, The Pier, Kinlochleven, Argyll, who also won a guinea for an 'almost Chestertonian' comparison of Chesterton and O. Henry, and remarks on Wilde, Meredith, James, Shaw, Stevenson, Walpole, Barrie, Wells, and Galsworthy. The Committee regretted only that neither Mr Gunn nor Mr Wellsted Miller 'seems to have grasped fully the nature of the sonnet'. The Committee also regretted that no story called 'The Divining Rod' was deemed worthy of the prize of two guineas and offered the prize to 'the competitor who submits the best story not exceeding 2,000 words in length, entitled "The Apple Tree", before June 8th.' Mr N. M. Gunn retreated to his tent and got busy. He would always work fast when writing for a deadline. His 'The Apple Tree' won the prize and was printed in the subsequent issue.[46]

It is the romantic-ironic tale of a modern lover on a train, filled with nostalgia for an ecstatic kiss, shuddering with cynicism at his own lack of courage. That strange self-mocking weary smile hangs over the fiction Neil wrote in the earlier 1920s. One brief image from the train window hints at something more to come: 'Stretches of moorland, with lochans, the flight of an occasional bird, and once a lonely cottage on the moor with a woman standing in the doorway. For a long time the vision of the woman lingered in his imagination with inexpressible sadness.' What is this melancholy cynicism in the affable, unattached officer of the pier? In part, no doubt, merely the mannerism of the neophyte brought up on the generation of post-Tennysonians. In part, an awareness in the twenty-six-year-old 'lad' that the idyll could not go on forever. In part, a mood in himself that was always there to be struggled with. And what of the world away from the pier at Kinlochleven?

He seemed about to be called to France—his father dead, his brothers dead or wounded—and he left Kinlochleven. Then the war ended, and the old free life began again. Maurice and his wife Toshon were happy to see him at Forres. One incident took place in their 'country house' near Macbeth's blasted heath that stands out in strange abruptness from these otherwise delightful years. 'After a varied and happy evening,' he recalls,[47] 'I went to bed without a care in the world.' He recounts the same experience in *Off in a Boat*, years earlier:

> Sometime during the night, I awoke, sat up in bed in a room dim with starlight, and saw my door swing noiselessly open. The transition from sleep to sitting up watching the door open must have been almost instantaneous. I immediately went and stared into the long black corridor, but neither saw nor heard anything. Then I closed the door and went back to bed, but could not sleep, for I became aware—or rather I had an apprehension—of what I may tentatively call pure evil. Now strangely though it did not come from inside the house, and not from the ground but from the air, from the vaults of space. It was not a being, a spirit, an imminent presence: it was a force; not a black magic but (if I may be understood) a black electricity. It was quite impersonal, yet not a mere death ray; an emanation from an active principle of evil, as though the old conception of two principles in creation, good and evil, were in fact true, and the evil was at that moment having an undisturbed innings. The method of its operation was disintegration for its own sake, a disintegrating of the mind, the personality, and finally of the body. Its purpose was to break up the tissue of what the good or creative principle had put together, and one had to strive against it with the utmost strength of one's will. This, of course, was something utterly beyond any consideration of social or personal morality, as it was beyond any jugglery of the door, which had conceivably been opened by a current of wind in the long corridor acting on a catch not quite closed.[48]

The account is fuller and more analytic in *The Atom of Delight*. What makes the attack so horrible is that it touches the 'inner circle' that guards the 'second self', the inner core. How much of this is the intervention of later ideas and how much is a fuller realisation of the actual experience we can't say. But the essentials are the same: after a sudden awakening and a somewhat conventional incident of night-time 'haunts' he senses an impersonal energy from space seeking to disintegrate his personality through his body. In neither account does anything lead up to the experience. In neither does he say anything of its aftermath. As if this dreadful Dark Night of the Soul, this sense of imminent disintegration, directed at him from space, simply came uncaused and then departed, leaving behind only a subject for speculation and generalisation, and an episode for *Wild Geese Overhead*. The question for us is what the experience meant for Neil at a certain time in his life. And we can begin only from the sense that it is the polar opposite of the experience of wonder at touching the great salmon with his toe. It is the negation of everything the salmon encounter seems to be.

What more shall we make of it? Shall we see it—he seems to—as purely 'given', as possibly metaphysical in origin? Or was it connected with anything else in his life and personality at this time? We can place it in 1919 or 1920 just after the war. The deaths of Ben and his father, the revelation of John's experience in the trenches—there were enough recent horrors to have their disturbing effect. Shall we see in it a sign that he could no longer be at peace with his carefree unattached life? He was entering a new season expecting a fixed station. Perhaps he was already seriously in love—for in 1920 he was courting the 'golden-haired Norse maiden' (as Maurice described her in *The Key Above the Door*) he would shortly marry. Was it connected with his beginnings as a serious writer? With the Walshes' departure to Ireland in 1922 and his own return to the Caithness coast, he began writing in earnest, and much of what he wrote is filled with pessimism, a darkness of mood, that seems odd coming from the cheerful 'unattached officer' of Neil's memory.

Whatever it was, the disintegrative force of 'black electricity' remained in his imagination, and henceforth living and writing would become ways of fighting against it, ways of opposing this 'ready-made drama of the darkness' with his own drama of the light.[49]

PART TWO

THE YEARS IN INVERNESS

(1921–1937)

4 The Officer Attached

By 1921 Neil had fallen in love. Jessie Dallas Frew was tall and slender, with a wide, warm smile, and golden 'hair down to here'[1] of which she was proud all her life. Her family knew her as Jess, but in later years she was always called Daisy. She was six years older than Neil but her age was never mentioned. The best description of Daisy was written in a letter by her husband after her death in 1963: 'There was a quiet still pool of goodness in her and it turns to light (as it always did) when I think about it; inside but at the same time outside, under the sky, with colour and gaiety in it. She loved flowers and made them grow everywhere and blossom. We were married for over forty-two years, and to look back is to see us wandering over the Highlands, sleeping in our car in lonely spots, in our boat among the Western Isles, times and homes and most of human experience.'[2]

Her father, John Rose Frew, whose grandfather had left County Antrim to fight against Napoleon, was a well-to-do jeweller and watchmaker in Dingwall, the county-town of Ross-shire. He had served for several years as town provost. Her mother was Marjorie Duff Wilkie—related, Neil believed, to Sir David Wilkie the Scottish painter. They had seven daughters (Daisy was the fifth) and all but one married. As her sisters left home for education, careers, or marriage, Daisy remained to help her father with his business in Dingwall. And there, in the shop at 61 High Street, she met the unattached officer in his late twenties.

At least so she told Keith Henderson's wife Helen years later. 'Helen asked Daisy once, "Where did you first meet Neil?" "Oh," said Daisy, "I gave him the glad eye from the door of the shop."'[3]

'You mean,' Pick asked Henderson during their 1978 conversation, 'that Neil went into the shop and bought jewellery just to talk to Daisy?' 'Oh yes,' said Keith. 'Well, at least he went in, and they talked.' 'That was brave of him,' said Pick. 'It was brave for *Neil*,' said Keith. 'It wouldn't have been for anyone else.'

In 1921, the unattached officer awaited his first fixed assignment. He was sitting one idle summer day in a distillery office with Maurice Walsh and others, being teased about the expected assignment. One fellow darkly prophesied that Neil would be sent to Wigan, and the order came, and he was. 'So I wrote Daisy, and she came down here, and we were married in Lancashire'—at the Registry Office in Wigan—'hastily, so that we could have the final six weeks on the lease of my predecessor's house.'

The housing shortage in Wigan was proverbial. Many families were squeezed into wretched caravan colonies. After the six weeks, Neil rented a cottage in a miners' row, with a lavatory at the bottom of the garden. When Daisy, brought up comfortably in Dingwall, was shown through her new home, she said, 'Neil, I can't find the place. Is something missing?' Neil, who had lived for months in a tent in his time, asked, 'What place?' 'Well, *you* know,' said Daisy. 'You come and have a look.' It was a shy marriage. Neil was almost thirty, and Daisy thirty-five.[4]

Neil left few impressions of Wigan. He told Pick that he liked the people, and found them tough, warm, friendly and full of humour. A 1947 letter, written ostensibly by Daisy to help 'Floss' (Marian) McNeill with a profile she was writing of Neil, states: 'When he [Neil] hears eminent Scots talking of the wealth of England and the poverty of Scotland, he suspects that their knowledge is gained from contacts with shooting tenants and the upper strata of London and the "Home Counties". He himself lived in Wigan through one of its longest coal strikes, was in hundreds of miners' homes, and even rented one for a time.'[5]

It was quite a jump from Kinlochleven, Forres, and Skye, to a world of poverty and class warfare. The 1920s had begun in panic. A postwar government had handed the mines, in desperate need of modernising, back to the owners. The owners cut wages, the miners demanded a national policy, the owners ordered a lockout for 1 April 1921. It was a grim honeymoon.

The newly-weds were in Wigan over a year. Neil's work involved investigating household incomes in connection with pensions, and his exposure to grinding poverty was thorough enough to have a lasting effect—he remained a shrewd householder determined to bargain for a fair wage. His strongest reaction was to want to go home to the Highlands, and his transfer application was finally approved. He was sent to Lybster, a small fishing port north of Dunbeath. Here the Gunns were settled by the late spring of 1922, in a house they called Scaraben (local memory places them in the house called Yarrow) on a broad main street stretching from the cliffed coastal road to the narrow, rock-walled harbour. Neil remembered it as a biggish house on a street corner, with rats to cope with, and a room set aside for writing.[6]

From Lybster by motorbike, taking Daisy with him occasionally in the sidecar, Neil toured the impoverished crofting country between Lybster, Wick and Thurso, dealing directly, as he later told Alexander Reid, 'with people and things . . . with the most mundane, practical, factual aspects of Highland life . . . During this period [wrote Reid] Neil Gunn drew up hundreds of balance sheets of individual crofts, and it would have been easy for him, had he wished, to write weighty sociological novels incorporating this factual element. But he was concerned with more important things.' Perhaps so, but he held fiercely to his respect for the 'factual element', and kept his concern for the demoralising effect of poverty.

The shock of Neil's return to Latheron, the boyhood parish he had already begun to idyllicise, was deep. Reid recognised it: 'The Highlands, too, were changed: their economy in ruins; the fishing harbours silted up; the boats that remained rotting on the beaches. Did Gunn expect it to be different? Intellectually he was certainly aware of the situation. Nevertheless, both the extent and the human effects of this Highland poverty seemed to have come as a shock to him—a shock that is reflected in the concern of his first novel, *The Grey Coast*.[7] It is reflected in all his early writings.

At Lybster Neil began to write in earnest. In 1922 the Walshes had transferred back to Ireland, and Maurice and Neil, finding other ploys difficult, challenged each other to write.[8] Neil found some stimulating encouragement—as well as golf—with a local schoolmaster. When Arthur Mowat read *The Grey Coast* in 1926, he wrote, 'The schoolmaster might be myself or any other schoolmaster who has felt the uselessness of 'teaching' poetry. Twelve years ago Starks—your predecessor in Lybster—and myself came to the conclusion that Caithness life would bear only realistic treatment in fiction and that anything in the nature of romantic treatment (of the Scott type) must give an air of unreality. Your *Grey Coast* bears out that conclusion.'[9] Neil would not remain convinced of it, but he was experimenting. And when, in the summer of 1923, Neil was transferred to Inverness, he had written a number of stories and poems to send out, and had been in active correspondence for several months with a young journalist in Montrose named Christopher Grieve.

By late 1923 the Gunns were in Inverness, and Neil began his long appointment as Excise officer at the Glen Mhor distillery. The 'hub of the Highlands' was already a busy town of over 20,000. 'No ancient castle, no ancient church, no ancient bridge,' and yet here, 1,400 years before, King Brude of the Picts had opened his fortress doors to Columba, who had journeyed in peace and safety up from Iona, and, after rational debate, accepted his Christianity. Neil read Adamnan's *Life of Columba* early, and remained fascinated all his life with the peaceable and vulnerable Picts. For all its bustle and traffic, Inverness remained for him the Pictish capital.[10]

Inverness gave Edwin Muir, on his 'Scottish Journey' in 1934, 'the impression . . . of being inconveniently crowded with vehicles of all kinds, most of them stationary'.[11] Years later Neil delighted still in the maze:

> Strangers have remarked that it took the Gaelic mind at its most devious to arrange the central 'No Entry' merry-go-round, but townsfolk are wary of criticism for they know those who are prepared to simplify the arabesque by making it just a little more intricate. For myself, when driving, pedestrian crossings are the gamble. An elderly Inverness lady, walking along the pavement with intent to cross, is far too polite to give you a stern look; on the contrary, she turns her head the other way to indicate that she hasn't seen you approaching, then steps out in front, and you step on the brakes and rock.[12]

Some anxious souls who have been driven by Neil would wonder at the temerity of anyone, young or old, who would step coyly into his path. It is little wonder that when, in the Inverness years, the Gunns bought their black Singer with green upholstery, Daisy was too nervous to learn to drive it. 'The only other capital city I know which maintains an equal order in confusion', continues Neil, 'is Dublin, and there motorists are so mutually courteous that I have heard them wonder what the police are in it for at all. In both, apart from an unpredictable foray, the police have the tolerance of old King Brude.'

But Neil loved to walk, and Inverness is well seen on foot. A guidebook of the time sees it as we see it now at the centre of Neil's world.

> The river divides the town into two parts, and is spanned by four public bridges. The houses stand partly in the valley, and partly on a wooded terrace, 100 feet high, which winds along the glen. The most accessible point of observation is the Castle Hill, a spur of this terrace, crowned by a fine block of county buildings, resembling a baronial castle. The view is extensive and beautiful. In the distance, to the north-west, the most conspicuous object is Ben Wyvis, a mountain in Ross-shire, 3,400 feet in height, and remarkable for its vast breadth and massiveness. It dominates the landscape far and wide.[13]

It would dominate the Gunns' landscape. It hovers over the Heights of Brae where they would live from 1937 to 1949. It climaxes the long western prospect from the shore road below their last home, Dalcraig.

> The eye glances from Ben Wyvis to the sharper crests of Strathconon and Strathglass, which break the distant skyline westward . . .

Neil would often fish the Conon, until, at Kerrow in the 1950s, he had his own fishing river on the Glass near Cannich.

Near at hand are the gleaming waters of the Firth, stretching inland; and on the side of the valley, opposite the Castle Hill, are the rounded heights of Dunain and Craig Phadrick, connected by the Leachkin, a green declivity divided among cottars . . .

When the Gunns built their bungalow Larachan in 1926, it would look across green fields, now filled in with houses, to the craigs.

At the spectator's feet flows the river; a mile away, the line of the Caledonian Canal is shown by masts of yacht or schooner, or by the smoke of a steamer.

Glen Mhor and Glen Albyn, the two distilleries owned in Neil's time by John Birnie, stand at the head of the Canal, and one of Neil's favourite walks was down the Canal from Glen Mhor.[14]

Inverness was expanding uneasily. Small businesses were going under and being amalgamated into large ones. South on the river was the island park, with illuminated fêtes and summer concerts. Winter brought subscription concerts and the Northern Meeting ball. The time was one of Gaelic revival, encouraged by the provost (1925–31) Sir Alexander MacEwen—soon one of Neil's friends—and the scholar D. J. Macleod; the annual Mod, held every few years at Inverness, spawned ceilidhs at hotels and homes. A municipal aerodrome opened in 1933, and the air was filled with controversy over new hydroelectric schemes. It was quite a contrast with the derelict harbours of Lybster and Dunbeath.

On the 'hill' up behind Castle Wynd lived the prosperous merchants and professionals. Across the river the city continued its westward expansion toward Tomnahurich Hill and the canal. Neil and Daisy lived on the west side, a ten-minute walk from the bridges. Turn right off busy Tomnahurich Street into Bruce Gardens and you find a stately brownstone house, Moyness, site of their first (rented) home in Inverness. In 1926, the sale of his first novel encouraged them to build their own bungalow, and the success of *Morning Tide* in 1931 enabled him to pay off the loan.

Dochfour Drive is the first right off Bruce Gardens, and Larachan is a small square bungalow at the north end. There were few other houses then; the rows of council houses would come before the war, and the new High School, built up to the back hedge of Larachan, opened in 1937, the year the Gunns moved away. Larachan had a small lawn and heath garden in front, a garage at the back, and a small caravan in the tiny back yard. Sir Alexander MacEwen's daughters recall the interior: 'To the left of the central front door was a sitting room with a bay window, and to the right was a dining room. Down the hall were the kitchen, the bedroom and a bathroom.' The present owner believes that at the dormer window in front Neil had his writing table, and from here he could look westward toward Craig Phadrick, reputed site of Brude's fortress.[15]

The small house must have been crowded when long-night talking sessions or Gaelic classes squeezed into the sitting room with its two comfortable chairs and book-lined walls. An overnight visitor might be put up—Chris Grieve, J. B. Salmond, or George Blake—but when a trio of Faber partners arrived in 1935, Frank Morley and T. S. Eliot ('Uncle Tom', they called him) had to share the caravan. Others could stay in town. On their 'Skye High' trip of 1937 Hesketh Pearson and Hugh Kingsmill, at Edwin Muir's suggestion, walked across to Larachan, had a talk, a drive to Culloden, a tea, an excellent dram, more talk, and 'It was after midnight when, accompanied by Neil Gunn, they walked back across the bridge, where the river reflected the spire of a church in the still lingering twilight.'[16]

Neil could walk to work and walk home for an afternoon's writing. It is an easy fifteen minutes north two blocks, up Kenneth Street, left into Telford, and north-west a few hundred yards to Glen Mhor distillery by the Muirtown Bridge. Inside the gate on the right is a door with a plaque, 'HM Customs & Excise', and here was Neil's office from late 1923 till the summer of 1937. Neil's office was just behind John Birnie's, and in the old ex-provost he had a superb teacher. Years later Neil reminisced about George Saintsbury's cellar book:

> Many years ago, when I first got interested in this peculiar excellence of a Highland product, I discussed Saintsbury's favourites with the late John Birnie, whose knowledge of whisky distilling was vast, at one of his distilleries—Glen Mhor in Inverness. Mr Birnie was not unduly impressed by Saintsbury's list for he clearly knew other malts that were quite as good in their way (and Glen Mhor still takes a lot of beating), but he added, 'I took Latin from Saintsbury in Elgin,' and I thought how Saintsbury, the Englishman, would have relished this casual blend of malts and the humanities by a Scots distiller.[17]

Saintsbury might also have relished the blend of life undertaken by Glen Mhor's new Excise officer.

Neil was responsible to HM Government for the complex process that took place at Glen Mhor, a process he described with his own fine blend of fact, fancy, and argument in *Whisky and Scotland* (1935). To understand his job, we must observe the process.

First, the distinction between pot-still and patent-still whisky. Pot-still is made of malted barley, yielding single 'malt' whiskies of distinctive flavours. Patent-still uses mostly corn yielding neutral spirit.

> The natural ear of barley, as may be imagined, has to undergo many vicissitudes on its way to the final corked bottle . . . Quite simply, then, the distiller's aim is, first, to ensure that the large mass of starch, held together by proportionately small quantities of albuminous matter, of which all grain is composed, is changed from an insoluble to a soluble condition; second, that this soluble starch is converted into sugar in order that it be fermented or turned into alcohol; and, third, that the alcoholic wash so formed be boiled off into whisky: these three divisions of his labour he calls respectively, malting, brewing, and distilling.[18]

Neil mastered the difficult craft of explaining a complex process in the simplest terms—in his journalism and reports he could do it with politics and economics. But there remained for him 'the graces and refinements of a perfected technique'. He relished the process he supervised as he did fishing and writing.

Barley seeds are moistened, spread and turned on a wide floor, allowed to begin germination, then heated from below. When dry like toast they are stored until needed for brewing. The barley is mixed with hot water into a mash, is cooled, yeast is added, and for thirty-six hours the violent process of fermentation goes on and the wash is locked by the Excise officer. In distilling, the alcohol is separated by heat in a pot-still and tested for specific gravity and purity in a glass box called a 'spirit safe', which is also locked by the officer. The second distillate is stored for maturing in casks in warehouses, locked by distiller and officer together—placed 'in bond'—until both authorise its removal to bottler or blender. 'Long experience', wrote Neil, 'has created an almost perfect system of supervision, interfering so little with practical operations and supplying such figures of liability or accountancy as distillers unhesitatingly accept, that normally the relations between the Excise official and the distiller are pleasant and charged with mutual respect.'

R. J. S. McDowall suggests

> that the Exciseman is a much busier person than sometimes appears if we visit a distillery, but I must confess I have been to a distillery where the warehouse was wide open and the Excise officer was nowhere to be seen. When I remarked on this I was told, 'He trusts us. Maybe he's at the fishing but he keeps wonderful books.' We must remember that the Spey has wonderful fish in September when it is getting near the end of the salmon season. Some Excisemen have had time to become novelists; . . .[19]

Neil had ample time for writing, and time for new friends. One of Neil's earliest Inverness companions, fellow Exciseman Stanley Hill, recalls his first sight of Neil from the days before either was married

> perched up on the saddle of an old Triumph belt-drive motorbike peddling away furiously until the engine fired and then back-heeling away the stand and vanishing down the road to town. He was a striking-looking man—tall, deep-set eyes, cleft chin looking more like a warrior of Clan Gunn with a claymore for sale than a poet or a writer.
>
> We didn't become really intimate until after we both married, which must have been at about the same time—and then I think because Daisy and Jay became warm friends. We lived within a few hundred yards of each other and it was then that we first knew about his writing. . . . I am not sure which periodicals published his verses and stories but I remember advice from the Editor of the *London Mercury*, J. C. Squire, who must at that early time have recognised that something and I remember how touched Neil was by the interest shown by a literary nabob of the day to an unknown unpublished writer. Certainly he received some payments—I think I remember one cheque for £14—which he splashed on some bottles of wine for which he was cultivating a taste, and we had great fun with chat of smell, chiaroscuro, colour and so on.[20]

(To Neil, Stanley Hill wrote in 1963:

> Forty years ago now and I can remember details of events then clearer than things that happened a month ago. You starting a wine cellar and never getting ahead of your drouthy pals; Daisy chalking 'A Merry Christmas' on the sideboard mirror; us looking at the foundations of the new house and thinking the rooms would be pretty small—and then finding them quite big!')

> He was a marvellous talker—I was never capable of debating with him but I think I was an admirable audience. The phrases were carefully composed, giving time for the neat link to be prepared and shaped, with the piercing eye compelling attention. But he was great fun with a wicked sense of humour and delighted with the items of female gossip our wives brought in.

The Excise provided literary companionship as well. A mutual friend of Neil's and Stan Hill's was R. J. McLeish, an unattached officer on distillery duty at Fort William, Tobermory, Oban and, finally, Jedburgh. McLeish wrote short stories, poems, even a detective novel.[21] They argued about Grieve's poetry, Neil playing the ardent advocate.

> I admire you as a critic, [Neil wrote McLeish on 26 November 1930.] I won't attempt to counter what you say about 'Circumjack'. We'd need a night on it, and I think we'd founder pretty well on the same rock. You have a sanity and balance that does my heart good, after the looseness and vapouring it does be

heated to. And your prejudice is ripe as a Christmas pudding, the very currants being themselves and human. For we both know that MacDiarmid's poetry is so much beyond the hellish and intolerable kailyard muck, that we instinctively begin to criticise it on (as he himself would say) the European level. *Sangschaw* and *The Drunk Man* contains the best of him, I think, though I'd hardly admit it to any other, so loyal must one be to the fighter.[22]

They exchanged extensive, well-reasoned, and supportive commentaries on each other's work. McLeish argued with Neil about his beloved Belloc and Chesterton, and sent him the poems of John Davidson and James Joyce to read. It must have been McLeish Neil was recalling in a later BBC interview:

I can remember—I can remember, for example, another writer, then living in the Highlands, and myself being very interested in a magazine produced in Paris called *Transition*. It was all, from the literary standpoint, revolutionary and highbrow and obscure. It was written in English. James Joyce was appearing in its pages under the title 'Work in Progress'. Well, we thought we'd write something for this magazine. I'm a bit hazy now about what actually happened. . . But years later I did come across a draft of what I had actually written. It certainly astonished me, for when I read it over I didn't understand what it was all about.[23]

The reference is to *Transition* from 1927 to 1929, when portions appeared of the book to be published in 1932 as *Finnegans Wake*. The later tone of bewilderment is misleading. For if Neil found few 'modernist' models of direct use in his writing, he certainly was not ignorant of them. Whether or not Grieve, as he later claimed, introduced Neil to Proust and Joyce, Neil knew them.[24] The importance for him of the literary revival in Ireland was considerable, and almost annual visits to the Walshes in Dublin kept him aware of it. Influences for Neil had to be personal, not merely 'literary', and his own world and work in the Highlands offered the literary companionship without which he would not have found writing the delightful ploy it became.

5 Starting to Write

He began in professional earnest when he was thirty. The process was neither quick nor easy, and some starts were false. Poetry certainly was, yet it was natural that he should try it. The tutor in Dalry was a Victorian romantic, and he promoted the line of English poetry from Keats through Tennyson to early Yeats and others of the Celtic Twilight. When young, Neil could recite 'almost half ' of FitzGerald's *Rubáiyát*; and he claimed to have read Pater's *Renaissance* three times—when Neil loved a book he returned to it again and again. Uncongenial critics later charged that he never left the Twilit 1890s. Certainly he carried on a long love-hate affair with 'Fiona Macleod', and the influence of the neo-celts, rather than being rejected outright, was to be transformed through the intervention of more complex moods, more constructive social ideas.[1] But his early work in Excise accountancy had amply stored that part of his mind that would remain doggedly matter-of-fact. And one matter of fact had a strong impact: his return after eighteen years to Caithness.

The reality that met him near Lybster was grimmer than Wigan because it was personal. The remembered boyhood years had in fact been a time of decline, but they were rich when recalled in contrast to post-war depression, economic despair, a fatalistic compulsion among the young to emigrate. The spectacle of his mother, widowed during the war, painfully crippled by a hip fracture improperly treated, obsessed his imagination. No wonder he suddenly saw only a 'grey coast'. No wonder he began to spend hours in the house on Lybster's main street starting to write.

What makes people write? What Neil saw would have driven a sensitive, imaginative person inward, and writing would become an escape, and in the escape he would seek a creative way of responding to a hopeless situation. Then, too, in the face of poverty's spirit-crippling effects, he might well acquire—many children of depression have acquired it—a lifelong sense of the power of money. Freer spirits (Keith Henderson was one) would tutor him in 'aristocratic' values and the unimportance of money. But those who, in future, might find him a bit tight in finance, publishers who teased him as 'Shylock', purists who suggested he had 'sold out', had perhaps known nothing of his long exposure to the depressed crofts of the 1920s. All this, filtered through a youthful addiction to the fatalistic melancholy of Celtic Twilight, made his early writing what it was, and at the same time made him do it with a stubbornly professional determination.

The simplest route was *Chambers' Journal*—respectable, traditional, 'adventurous'. Walsh would go that way, and Neil urged Walsh to stick with *Chambers'*, but he knew that for him it was only a place for short articles of local experience: 'At the Peats' in May 1923; 'Falconry: A Day with the Hawks' in February 1924. But even in this, there is a larger theme—the tyranny of mechanism in hunting with guns. And the innoc-uous-sounding 'White Fishing on the Caithness Coast' (October 1924) hints at the state of mind behind the sport: 'all has gone grey, and the sadness is inexpressible'— the mood is the same in 'A Northern Night'. *Chambers'* was not the place for most of the fiction Neil was beginning to write, grim in subject, heavy in mood.[2]

To sell his stories Neil had to look to England. He never ceased to recall with delight the startling message that reached Scaraben, Lybster, in July 1923, from Odhams Press, London: 'I have read your story "The House on the Moor" and shall be pleased to use this in the *20 Story Magazine* if you will accept £11.11.0 for the first British serial rights.' But a stronger ambition was to break into the *Cornhill Magazine*, then edited by Leonard Huxley. Huxley returned 'Sleeping Bins' on 8 November 1923; he liked the idea, but 'it is treated with a certain over-elaboration which detracts from the crispness of effect'. The author was determined, for twelve days later Huxley accepted its revision! 'Cavern'd Echoes' was returned twice, but Huxley found 'curious interest in the wider current of neo-Celticism which touched your "Half-Light" ' and printed it in November 1925, followed by 'Bird-song at Evening' and 'Musical Doors' in 1926–7.[3] 'Musical Doors' would become 'Hidden Doors' and give its title to Neil's first collection (1929). The collection would also include stories published in 1924-5 in the handsome new *Dublin Magazine*. The other stories chosen for *Hidden Doors* had been published in three journals by two editors who would become crucial supporters in these early years: C. M. Grieve and J. B. Salmond.

When Neil returned from Wigan in 1922, Grieve was working hard in Montrose. He began the *Scottish Chapbook* that year, published the *Scottish Nation* in 1923, and the *Northern Review* in 1924. Grieve was delighted to have Neil's support and willing to print anything Neil sent him—even including five stanzas of four-line trimeters called 'La Madeleine (From a Painting by Henner)', adorned by a Tennysonian gloom of hair and despair. If we also recover 'To A Redbreast' ('Grey thought stood at gloom's

window'), and half-veiled eyes of Samarkand,' and a Petrarchan sonnet 'To
My Gramophone' which rhymes 'woven' with 'Beethoven' and the Keatsian
'dreamily' with 'mimicry' and 'wizardry', and a free-verse imagistic poem
about a black adder—

> Crawling from out the hinterland
> Of earthy gloom,
> Past the cold stones
> Of dreams and old desires,
> Comes my soul to the roses
> Like a black adder—

then we have recalled enough. This late heir to Keats, Tennyson, and the
1890s was not meant for modern poetry.[4] Grieve generously mingled the
worst efforts of new talent in among the lyrics of *Sangschaw* and *Pennywheep*.
He did far better by publishing Neil's stories, 'Down to the Sea' and
'Visioning', 'Between Headlands' and 'The Uncashed Cheque'.

The *Northern Review* was begun to further 'literary devolution', 'rescue
Scottish arts and letters from the slough of Kailyardism', foster Scottish
drama, and promote a nationalist renaissance.[5] The *Scots Magazine* had
begun the same year (1924) to provide 'a high-class literary periodical
devoted entirely to Scotland and things Scottish', to avoid 'the quagmire of
partisan politics' and the disfigurements of 'religious dispute' and to serve as
'the organ of the Scottish societies throughout the world'.[6] The editorship
moved from Glasgow to Dundee in 1927, and the energetic J. B. Salmond
took over. He published a story by Grieve, and Neil Gunn followed. He
published 'Symbolical', 'Blaeberries', 'The Sea' and 'The Moor'; serialised
Neil's second and third novels; published his one-act plays; gave birthplace
to the nationalist essays of one 'Dane M'Neil'; published more stories in the
1930s; and when Neil gave up his Civil Service job to live on writing,
Salmond provided Neil Gunn and 'Dane McNeil' (the spelling purified)
with a periodical outlet. He was a valued adviser on the early novels, and we
shall see him again in that role. But the short story was Neil's major form in
the 1920s.[7]

Elisabeth Bowen wrote once that 'the short story is a young art, a child of
this century'. H. G. Wells recalled that in the 1890s short stories were
reviewed and discussed. Chekhov explained the development simply: 'Maupassant in France, and I in Russia began writing very short stories. There's
your new movement in literature.' Turgenev's saying—'We all came out
from under Gogol's "Overcoat" '—pushes the date back, but Turgenev was

almost unknown in Britain until the 1890s, and Maupassant and Chekhov came late to a culture of Hardy, Stevenson and Kipling. Joyce published *Dubliners* in 1914, and by 1922 the Georgian anthologies could include Katherine Mansfield and D. H. Lawrence as well. When Neil began, the vogue for strong, artistic seriousness was established, and models were numerous.[8]

Neil was never a wide reader of fiction. But his interests and sympathies were strongly drawn to Ireland, where Joyce was shortly followed by O'Flaherty, Bowen, O'Faolain, and others. And there were two traditional influences that mingled strangely with the art-story refinement of the Georgians. First, he came from a traditional culture whose story-telling was an important and elaborate oral art; 'Between Headlands' and 'The Sea' look ahead to the story-telling experience of young Finn in *The Silver Darlings*. Second, the traditional reached him in a highly romanticised—some would say specious—form through the 'legendary' tales of William Sharp ('Fiona Macleod') and the Neil Munro of *The Lost Pibroch*. At the same time, he shared Grieve's commitment to a modern national literature, and his own experience engendered an impulse to socio-economic realism. With such a mixture of examples and impulses, his stories were bound to be extremely various in mode and technique.

He wrote thirty or more in the years prior to *Hidden Doors*. He wrote with the determination to find a market, which meant satisfying various editors. As early as 1925 he was trying to publish a collection: Chatto & Windus rejected one in 1925, and Macmillan in 1927, and Charles Graves of Porpoise Press was hesitant in 1929. The novel seemed more promising. While Neil published short stories off and on for almost forty years, the short story was never his best form.

We can, however, see things about his development if we group the early stories chronologically: those published through 1923; those published in the mid-twenties in *Cornhill Magazine*, *Dublin Magazine*, and *Northern Review*; those published in *Scots Magazine* in the late twenties. Our concern, of course, is not critical but biographical.

The first group is miscellaneous, often mere tricks, exercises, romantic adventures, with few glimpses of things to come. The lover of 'The Apple-Tree' is a cynical romantic defeatist who revisits the window of his sleeping love and departs hopelessly leaving no message. The lover of 'Visioning' fears entrapment in a mundane marriage in a 'grey Scottish port' and follows his vision of a Spanish girl to sea. The 'Braid Scots' friend of the narrator of 'Gentlemen', a sailor in Marseilles, wakes in a prostitute's bed, is

morally shocked to find her child there, and the woman angrily tells off this
'primordial Scot', revealing to him for the first time the naked instincts of a
living woman. 'A Tight Corner' is a poaching adventure that ends with an
odd animism. 'Surfaces', a brief mood-piece about a young painter, an
archaeologist's daughter, and their search for 'essences', hints at motifs to
come. But only 'Down to the Sea' is a clear anticipation: the first of several
pictures of dying old persons on a grey coast.

The more serious efforts of 1924–6 offer a clearer picture. 'Between
Headlands', 'Such Stuff as Dreams' and 'The White Hour' all centre on
dying old persons, their sad thoughts and feelings, their white and solitary
thinness. The old married couple of the first, settled on the Moray Firth to
look across hopelessly at their old Caithness home, are described in words
many would use later to describe Neil and Daisy: no one knew them well;
'the great secret of their life: they belonged to themselves. You could not
think of them apart.' In the second, a delirious old man, seeking to 'get back',
is found drowned in a little water-hole. In the third, a lonely old woman
tells a young man of the terrible whiteness of her foreknowledge of death and
her aloneness. The old bachelor of 'Birdsong at Evening' turns in his
retirement to the company of birds, but becomes involved with a young
librarian, her illegitimate child, her suicide—'the maelstrom of the dark
currents of the blood'; and here is a mood that Neil would try later to
exorcise: 'the darkness has its greatness equally with the light; and in many
ways surpasses it, for there is a mystery and a gathering together of thought
in which the body sits still as a deep pool.' (The situation has its final
transformation in *Bloodhunt*.) Marriage, the artist, the fear of failure, the
growth of divided consciousness are central in 'Adventure in Jealousy' and
'The Uncashed Cheque'.

The key stories, however, are 'Half-Light' and 'Musical Doors'. Their
situations are the same. A Conradian narrator is friend to a doomed hero,
hears of his death (by drowning, on the moor), and seeks to account for it.
Both heroes are victims of an obsession with the dooms of Celtic Twilight.
One has waged a losing battle against 'Fiona', and the other is drawn
through the 'hidden doors' of pibroch to lonely atavism and accidental
death. The first is plagued by a sense of failure on the 'grey coast'; the other is
driven to dissect his own mind—two forms of self-destruction that will
recur throughout Neil's novels. The setting of grey coast, bleak moor,
depression, failure, lonely age is most pronounced. And Neil is seeking to
exorcise the disturbing consolation found in Fiona Macleod and the Twilight.

The last group (1927–9) develop some of these themes. 'Blaeberries' is a passionate, inhibited love story, Lawrence with a difference: generic Man and Woman, he mathematical and precise; she earthy, impulsive, crushing the berries against his mouth. In 'The Moor' a young painter pursues an atavistic past, is mesmerised by a young woman with a mad old mother in a moor cottage, and finds in her the moor personified. 'Symbolical' is the nickname of a crofter with 'disturbing penetration into something beyond'. Neil has now moved into a heavy, visionary symbolism, linked with passionate, fugitive love, desolation, tragic old age and death. But shortly there are signs of other things to come. In the *Scots Magazine* of 1929–32 he published several stories—'The Sea', 'The Man Who Came Back', 'The Mirror' and 'The Dead Seaman'—that would serve as preliminary studies for novels: *Morning Tide, The Drinking Well, Wild Geese Overhead* and *The Key of the Chest*. Much of his later fiction grew out of the slow, gradual elaboration and transformation of early stories.[9]

But what an odd and suggestive contrast between these early stories and Neil's outward existence in the early Inverness years! As yet there was no glimpse of an atom of delight. His first novel, *The Grey Coast*, belongs to the same darkly ironic mood. His second, *The Lost Glen*, written in 1926, compounds it with a desperate anger and a dialectical energy.

The genesis of *The Grey Coast* begins with the return to the north. Neil's mother was still alive in Dunbeath, and, once settled in Inverness, Neil and Daisy would drive back to visit. Alec's later reminiscence recalls that they would spend the morning and afternoon with his mother, then retreat to 'some remote corner'. Gretta Gunn places their campsite at Achnaclyth, eight miles up the Dunbeath river, and here, she believes, Neil met the old retired seaman who told him stories of his father.[10] The figure of the retired seaman living up on the outskirts of the coastal village, harbouring his memories of passion and youth, stands at the beginning and end of Neil's fiction. He is the returned outsider, in but hardly of the community, an anarchic spirit with a secret power he delights in using. Auld Jeems, the sly poacher, has hidden gold. Neil had the power of the transforming imagination. And here he was using the power, as he said years later, 'to get rid of something'.

He was reluctant later to go back to the book, repelled by 'the intensity and complexity which are split open and seem too much now, if not then. . . . As if there is a too muchness that embarrasses.' So he wrote to Hart. And to Pick, 'Nothing much is intensely dealt with.' But there is a good deal in the 'nothing much', and the 'too muchness' is not just style.[11]

The setting is 'a grey strip of crofting coast, flanked seaward by great cliffs, cliffs "flawed" as in a half-sardonic humour of their Creator to permit of the fishing creek', realistically rendered, yet already visionary— 'of this duality of the mind, whereby the colourless, normal life becomes at once a record of the stolidly obvious and of the dream-like unknown'. Four people carry on quiet, intense struggles for love and power: the old seaman Jeems on his poor croft, his niece and housekeeper Maggie, her desperate suitor the young fisherman Ivor, and the despotic, comfortable farmer Tait of Tullach, who is driven by lust for Maggie and enflamed by Jeems's memories of passionate ports. The book portrays the weary routines of croft life and the effects of poverty on the spirit. The effects are fatalistic despair and lust— Jeems's lust for poaching and his gold; Tullach's lust for Maggie.[12]

The schoolmaster, Ivor's friend, has moved over from 'Half-Light'— his name Moffatt only slightly changed from Mowat, Neil's Lybster school-master friend—with his love-hate for Fiona. In him, Neil confronts again his own attraction to Fiona's mystical gloom, and does not succeed, for the young Ivor almost drowns in it. There is a verbose elaboration of self-consciousness:

> One might have an involuntary aversion to this personification of murning gloom, a derisive hatred of it as a wanton, thowless slayer of gaiety and courage; yet there it was—the truth, the unavoidable truth, truest of all in its suffocating atmosphere.[13]

When Neil revised the novel for the 1931 Porpoise edition—making, as W. R. Aitken has observed,[14] noteworthy changes on 168 pages—passages such as this were drastically pruned:

> One might have a derisive hatred of this wanton, thowless slaying of gaiety and courage; yet there it was—the truth, and suffocating.[15]

But the 'something' to 'get rid of' was not merely verbal. The book suggests a man all too ready to respond to the grim spectacle with Ivor's luxury of nihilism: 'The ravelled perversity of his feelings, and self-jeering bitterness that is manhood's dark safeguard, smoothed out into a condition of being as detached from him in a way as the land, as mysterious, as impersonal.' Revealing, too, is the image of old age in this book dedicated 'to my mother' in her final months. Yet Neil has made an interesting transfer, for the pathetic elder is a man, and the central consciousness a young woman.

The character of Maggie struck the publisher to whom Neil sent the novel, and on 11 December 1925, Jonathan Cape responded:

James and Isabella Gunn,
Neil's parents

2 John Gunn, Neil's younger
brother and closest friend

3 Alec Gunn, Neil's youngest
brother

4 The moor north-west of Dunbeath village from the schoolhouse

5 Malcolm Macleod (*right*) and crew. Malcolm was the father of
   Dr Peter John Macleod and sailed with Neil's father

I have read with great interest your story *The Grey Coast* and I should like to publish it. I think you have been very successful indeed in your treatment of the dramatic situation between a woman and two men in a study that seems to me direct from life, and your character drawing is, I think, admirable. You have succeeded in a remarkable way in understanding the feelings of the woman. Personally, I have found it interesting all through; the only criticism I have to make is that now and again there is some 'fine writing' and I think that you would be well advised to tone down . . . Edward Garnett is also pleased, agrees, and will specify.[16]

Garnett 'specified' extensively ten days later. The book was published on 17 June 1926, sold about 700 copies the first year, then dropped to thirty or forty a year. Little Brown published it in the USA, but sales were disappointing and the stock was remaindered in 1928. Cape rejected Neil's next two manuscripts—'We feel that you yourself are perhaps too Gaelic, too "poetic" to write a strong novel'—and Neil had to find a new publisher.

The reception of Neil's first novel was mixed but encouraging. 'I advise you not to buy it,' Neil wrote Mairi Campbell Ireland (7 October 1927)—'folk find it depressing and life is short.'[17] But some reviewers saw its unusual promise, and the message was meaningful: *The Grey Coast* was the best Scottish novel since *The House with the Green Shutters*—another blow at the Kailyard. William Power recalls that, while Eric Linklater's first books didn't 'wring anyone's withers, it was another matter when Neil Gunn and certain other novelists insinuated that Highlanders were subject to like passions with the rest of mankind.'[18] But the most philosophical comments came from the man who had become Neil's staunchest literary comrade in the early 1920s.

Grieve and Gunn had been friends for three years when, in March 1926, Neil sent Christopher a proof copy of *The Grey Coast* and received a long, enthusiastic letter and the essay he would publish that year in *Contemporary Scottish Studies: First Series*. In it he says, Gunn is 'the only Scottish prose-writer of promise, that is to say, in relation to that which is distinctively Scottish'. He is 'our nearest equivalent to the Irish Liam O'Flaherty'. His work 'remains unequal—now almost anonymous in its resemblance to "current fiction" in the mass, now falling into Kailyard rut, now tinged with the Celtic twilight'. But there are 'sudden breakings-through into dimensions in which the editors and readers of popular periodicals of even the best kinds suffer from incontinent agoraphobia' and 'his artistic integrity is bringing him into unmediated relations with Scottish nature, human and otherwise'. There follow long passages from 'Half-Light' and finally this wordy description of what matters in *The Grey Coast*:

> This co-existence of incompatible appearances and realities—the antitheses between what the characters choose to be and ought rather to be—the fact that ostensible character is a subtly manipulated disguise behind which nature seeks to deceive life until, in most cases, it becomes a mere reflex of the disguise—the 'monstrous joy of soiling the ideal'—the algoniac yielding to and fighting with brute circumstance—these and such as these are the themes, subtly developed, of this sincere and searching novel, and it is part and parcel of Mr Gunn's promise that they present themselves with more unanalysable reality and momentum in his dialogues than in his descriptions, intimate and telling as these are.[19]

Grieve has since said, 'In those early days of the twenties, when the ideas of a Scottish Literary Renaissance were first being canvassed, there was no one in Scotland with whom I was in closer touch . . . Gunn and I seemed to have a great deal in common and it was certainly impossible then to imagine that we were to follow very different courses in literature, politics and philosophy of life.' It was a cherished comradeship. Over the years, said old Grieve, 'there is no one I enjoyed meeting more than Neil Gunn',[20] and old Gunn responded with a 'personal tribute out of abundant memories of our joint doings and discussions, of all-night sessions when the speech organs had to be wetted now and then with a drop of old malt', and a fond recall of 'the warm spirit of fellowship in adventure'. Any biography of either man that slights the depth and warmth of that early fellowship is unworthy. Unworthy, too, would be the biography that ignored the years of unhappy, sometimes bitter divisions that followed. We can afford at this distance to acknowledge that both men were imperfect. The story of their later alienation is one of the saddest chapters in modern Scottish biography.

Grieve was just nine months younger than Neil. The son of a postman in Langholm, deep in the Borders, he was educated for teaching, turned to journalism, joined various socialist organisations, served in the RAMC from 1915 to 1918, and in 1919 settled in Montrose with his wife Peggy, working as chief reporter on the weekly paper. In 1922, after two years of anthologising *Northern Numbers*, he announced plans in the *Glasgow Herald* and elsewhere for a new periodical, *Scottish Chapbook*. Neil responded from Lybster and Grieve welcomed his work.

Grieve's letters were strongly supportive. November 1923: 'I follow your own work with keen interest . . . Go ahead! You'll do. And your instinct's right. Chambers and the like are no good to you—except financially. I've a confession to make. I'm Hugh MacDiarmid. Tell it not in Gath.' The next five years brought regular criticism, advice on 'how to make money', letters urging Neil to get busy and write more, even a proposal of collaboration on a novel. December 1927: '*What* about you? What *about* you? What about *you*! Not a cheep! Not a sign! . . . of the novels—not a word . . . Seriously, my dear man, I hope you're not going to let 1927 go to its unhallowed grave in this fashion.' And again: 'Hope you are fit and fine and working like a devil—not at fishing!' Grieve pushed Neil harder than anyone into becoming a novelist; then, suddenly, he was telling Neil that the novel was an unimportant literary form.[21]

The encouragement was mutual. Neil became known as one of Grieve's most vigorous public advocates and sang his praises in the press—'Scotland's Greatest Poet of Today' read the heading in the Glasgow *Daily Record* for 6 February 1929. And Neil's 'Renaissance of Scottish Literature' in a Wick magazine that year prompted a heated debate in the columns of the *Groat*, in which Neil was castigated by 'Norseman' as 'Neil M. Gunn and his brothers of the Renaissance Movement'.[22]

They met probably late in 1924. Grieve was thirty-three, slight in figure, 'his most noticeable feature', Helen Cruickshank recalled, 'being a bush of silky hair above a high forehead and two deep-set eyes. His manner was shy and modest.' By early 1925 there was talk of visits back and forth, and the wives exchanged greetings. The long nights had begun. 'You talk of conversational powers and speculative stamina,' Neil reminisced in 'For Christopher's Cap' when Grieve received his honorary degree in 1957:

> I can assure you there was plenty of both in those early years of the literary movement, which Christopher carried on so valiantly. Wondering if I could fix some sort of date, I looked up my copy of his *Contemporary Scottish Studies*, and beneath his signature on the flyleaf, he wrote: 'Inverness, 3 January 1927, 5.20 a.m.' Not a redundant word: precise, lucid and sober. So that night he must have been staying with me in the Highland capital. Probably there was a good-going foray on. I suspect it had something to do with what we called the Gaelic aristocratic idea, which we were then hunting with all the ardent zeal our ancestors devoted to lifting cattle. Accordingly that Grieve should assume the name of MacDiarmid seemed perfectly natural. That he in particular used the name MacDiarmid when writing in Lallans was merely an instance of that higher logic which embraced all Scotland, and was then prepared to use all Scotland as a starting point for a good-going cattle raid into England, and after that it was the wide, wide world. By five in the morning all this was wonderfully clear. However, my particular pleasure in it was the spirit of adventure. It was not just talk, not merely an indulgence in theories, literary or metaphysical or what you will. A real hunt was on. Should a few English literary cattle of doubtful pedigree show up in the offing, Christopher's

nostrils would quiver in an inspiring way. Anyhow, I have the memory of exhilaration and occasionally a rare delight. And personally I have never found true delight present but the creative spirit was there also—and how richly Christopher has proved that now![23]

In 1927, wrote Helen Cruickshank, 'C. M. Grieve cast his net over literary Scotland, catching big fish and small fry alike in order to found the Scottish Centre of the International PEN movement.'[24] At PEN meetings, Neil met literary people from all over Scotland. In April 1928, Grieve wrote Neil to announce a grand PEN function in Glasgow: Gordon Bottomley would be guest of honour, and Compton Mackenzie, now commencing his own foray into Scottish affairs, would be there. In addition, Grieve's son was to be baptised in Montrose, and Grieve wanted Neil and Mackenzie to be godfathers.

The three converged on Mrs Grieve's church in Montrose, and how the Scottish Episcopal Church must have stretched its small house to include such incongruous mansions! Mackenzie was having a recurrent bout of pain—but let him continue:

> Grieve had been a medical orderly at Salonika in the war, and announced his familiarity with giving injections. Neil Gunn, whose novel *The Grey Coast* I had read with admiration, had just arrived to stay with the Grieves in Montrose, where at the Episcopal church he and I were to be godfathers of the Grieve baby at his baptism. Neil Gunn was standing by when Christopher put the needle into my arm. As it went in, the tall and distinguished figure of Neil Gunn went down on the floor full length in a dead faint caused by the sight of a minute drop of blood. When he became conscious Grieve was able to assure him that lots of men nearly collapsed when being given an injection.[25]

Now, the way the story is told suggests the ill-feelings that soon developed. The two men disliked each other from the early 1930s on. Neil spoke later with puzzlement of Mackenzie's dislike. But he had a way of teasing Mackenzie in public. When that extraordinary marine artist and former Benedictine Peter Anson returned from Barra in 1936, he asked Neil, 'What have you done to make Compton so mad at you?' 'What do you mean?' asked Neil. 'Well, I just mentioned your name and he went up in smoke.'[26] Neil played a somewhat negative role in Mackenzie's erratic career in nationalist politics. In 1934, when Neil received the largest number of votes for election to the new Scottish National Party council, Mackenzie was not elected;[27] and the same year saw publication of Neil's novel of the Clearances, when it was said that Mackenzie was also writing one. When *The Lost Glen* was being widely criticised, Mackenzie sided with the supporters of the new 'rival' Fionn Mac Colla. Someone had circulated the report that Neil's friends were obstructing Mac Colla's career.[28] In short, Mackenzie and Gunn were rivals, antipathetic in personal style. Mackenzie told a mutual friend once that Gunn was the vainest man he had ever met, and Neil thought similarly of him, and each had his reasons. Certainly the sustained hostility is a rare thing in Neil's life. It had a marked impact on his sense of his place among Scottish literati and became an obsession.

But in the late 1920s the new alliance of Grieve and Mackenzie had a more immediate consequence. Mackenzie suggested that the Grieves leave Scotland and settle in London, where Grieve would work on Mackenzie's new radio magazine *Vox*. In September 1929, Neil received this ominous note from Chris: 'I had come to the parting of the ways. Either I must cave in to some extent and "be friends" where I didn't want to be, or clear out. I had absolutely made up my mind to break entirely with almost all of those with whom I had been in any way associated, either actually or in the public mind, alike in the Scottish literary and political movements. And I have now taken that course at the price of expatriation . . . Now I can afford to be absolutely ruthless: and will.' So Neil's literary companion had departed, and at a crucial and discouraging time in Neil's own literary fortunes.[29]

The publication of *The Grey Coast* had been followed at once by the completion of a second novel, *The Lost Glen*. That ill-fated book had been rejected by Cape, and thereafter by Chambers, Ernest Benn, Heinemann, Wishart, and Hodder & Stoughton. The last-named 'do not like the animalism of the Colonel and think that the economic, political and other significance of the decay of Highland life which colours the story so much would not have much appeal to the non-Scottish general reader'. It is characteristic of Neil's tough persistence—some might say his proud obstinacy—that he kept sending the book out. His heated reply to Hodder & Stoughton (19 May 1929) shows his tendency to find in criticism of his books a cultural intolerance:

Those of us who are interested in what is sometimes called the Scottish Renaissance Movement must, I suppose, be sanguine enough to keep looking for the publisher who is prepared to take risks! Though why we should expect him to, heaven knows! for we are aware how comparatively easy—and acceptable—it would be to supply the staple fare of kilts, sporrans, and Romance, in island dawns and Celtic twilights—not omitting a helping of cabbage from the 'Kailyard'! But, amusing as it may seem, we are sufficiently moved by the emergence of new forces in Scottish life to keep blasting away at the new claim. Possibly, after all, it is the only merit of *The Lost Glen* that it stands for the first honest attempt, as far as I know, at introducing the Highlands as they are today.[30]

Having unburdened himself thus, he hints at a willingness to undertake a complete revision. But this he was not to do for another two years.

Meanwhile, the novel, having appeared in serial form in the *Scots Magazine* from April to November 1928, would sit in a drawer. Another serial would follow in the same publication from September 1929 to April 1930—and this one he decided not even to try to publish as a book. The novelist's career had stalled. Had it not been for a literary supporter very different from Grieve, it might never have been continued at all.

James Bell Salmond was born the same year as Neil. He was an easy man to talk to, with a great relish for a good story; a deep-voiced son of Arbroath and an MA of St Andrews, he had a large presence and a strength of body with which, to demonstrate a point in a story, 'he would lift a colleague off his feet and hold him at arm's length'. Once he had taken over editorship of the *Scots Magazine* in 1927, he seemed eager to publish almost everything Neil sent him. In the autumn of 1927 he proposed serialising the new novel; but there were problems: the 'interest is naturally dissipated, and the reader has to wait a month before hearing what comes next'. But all this could be explained and attended to. 'I shall try my best to run up to Inverness to see you.'

Neil understood and was prepared to revise. 'Actually,' he wrote,

> the treatment of the theme is rather curious, being somewhat in the nature of a mosaic which doesn't quite give the picture until you stand back a bit (in other words, until you have read a chapter or two more . . .) . . . what you require, I take it, is the sense of dramatic 'situation' between the characters indicated at an early stage (and at least implied in the first instalment) so that a reader may be tempted to see how it's worked out. But what is important is whether the conception of the novel as a whole, with (to me) its underlying significance, would appeal to you. The theme is really a rather big one, and at this particular crisis in Scottish affairs I think it at least provocative. Whether I have handled it well is entirely another matter![31]

The most profound understanding of *The Lost Glen* on record is that of the American Faber partner Frank Morley, and it echoes the other American partner's (T. S. Eliot's) sense of *Hamlet* (the 1919 essay). Morley wrote it in 1931 for George Blake of the Porpoise Press. *The Lost Glen*, wrote Morley,

> is big with meaning and a blasted harassing book. I can tell you this right now that if Gunn isn't haunted and harassed and touchy as hell about it he's not human. I think it comes from right under his heart, so you be careful. I speak

as a Southerner; I don't mean your British Southerners, but a Confederate Southerner who stands up if you play Dixie, if you could play it. Seems to me the theme is similar; you can say Gunn's is bigger if you like, though that I don't admit. But anyway it's big and hot and I feel actively important . . .

The book bears signs of secret perturbations. When you're not quite sure you try all the harder to seem sure, and that's happening in this book. There's too much protestation, I feel . . . *The Lost Glen* is Gunn's *Hamlet*. The story isn't adequate. It isn't adequate *essentially*. I can't say just why: but there's something too limited and confined about the episodes which are being forced to serve as equivalents for states of mind which they cannot really objectify . . . The wealth of attention he's given to this problem wd be inconceivable to an ordinary bastard . . . *Hamlet* was published. *The Lost Glen* is the most interesting book of Gunn's I've read. It's damnably fascinating and disturbing . . . Why did I despair and leave the South? Because I respect the South. If Gunn does anything unworthy of his theme by God I'll lynch him.[32]

Morley was onto something with his 'objective correlative'. The book tries and fails to give fictional expression to Neil's mind and feelings in the 1920s. Little wonder that the book's adverse reception left wounds never quite healed.

For one thing, it suggests a deep fear of failure. It is one of two stories of the same time centred on the young Highlander who is sent away to 'make good', falls into disgrace, and comes home a failure. The other is 'The Man Who Came Back' or 'Back Home', the story-play later elaborated in *The Drinking Well*. The push to leave the fishing village and 'get on' in the city comes from the mother. The father, a fisherman, is gentler. In *The Lost Glen*, the failed son on his return is responsible for his father's death. His mother is left to suffer, and he must make peace with her.

For another, it presents Neil's first version of the lustful middle-aged English military attaché, retired and living in a small hotel where he can sadistically enjoy his power at the expense of the locals. In *Second Sight* he will take on a different form. Finally, in *The Other Landscape* he will become a comic-pathetic figure, dowsed by cold water. It took Neil almost thirty years to translate the sadistic monster Colonel Hicks into the comic Major, to conquer the power-mad destroyer of delight through satiric laughter.

In the 1920s, that power-lust seemed inseparable from gross lechery. Hicks tries to rape the daughter of Ewan's friend; the physical signs of his lust are given in nightmarish caricature: 'Each fleshy foot fell with a podgy thud on the hearth-rug.' One is astounded by the hatred and disgust with which Neil depicts him and his sexuality. Ewan's characteristic response is a blasting self-irony, its other side a self-conscious Celtic gloom. Highly intellectual, he reflects on the ties of his martyred Gaelicism to Christ and Socrates. When finally revising, Neil would greatly reduce the ideological polemic—Ewan's long tirades on the 'Gael as mental animal'—and the heavy political dialogue. He would make the growing sexual excitement of both the Colonel and Ewan, now ironic counterparts, *more* central and subtle. He would reshape the narrative and prune the style.

A few examples show the artist mastering his verbal craft:

'Something had crept about Colin's astonishment'	(becomes)	'Colin's look hardened'
'Each fleshy foot fell with a podgy thud on the hearth-rug'	(becomes)	'Each foot fell with a thud'
'But that the hectic warfare should carry the full armoury of its conceits to a place like Ardnacloich resulted in a perversion that approached violence'	(becomes)	'But to carry it here was wrong'
'And the strange thing was that her pity had made her words cruel'	(becomes)	'And her pity made her cruel'

Climactically, he would add for Ewan a moment of tragic affirmation just before the catastrophe. If we look at the new passage on the book's last two pages, we see what Neil had essentially missed in the earlier text:

> His spirit rose up in its assurance and mastered the night. His body, the dark storm-centre, swept the cliffs. Nothing negative and suppressed in this vast world. Here freedom was positive and strength superb.[33]

But the assurance doesn't last.

In early 1929, Neil told his friend and ally Salmond of a new serial, and by summer he had sent all the instalments. In September there appeared the first of eight instalments of *The Poaching at Grianan*, a 60,000-word story that reads like a blending-in-pathos of John Buchan and Mackenzie's Highland farces. Here was Neil's reaction to the long frustration of *The Lost Glen*. He would see if he could go Maurice Walsh's route, write popular serials, and still manage to do his own kind of fiction. He decided early that it was not his way, and the serial never became a book.

Grianan is another version of the coast in decay, but comic pathos is the mood. The old laird Macdonald has leased his castle and hunting to a wealthy American and lives in the lodge. To Grianan in autumn comes Callum MacKinnon, Edinburgh shopkeeper, Grianan native, seeking re-creative poaching. With him come journalist Don McAllister and slum radical Finla Gillespie. A love triangle grows—the laird's daughter Eilidh, the American's son, and Don. Don the writer reveals what is Neil's own new dream: 'intensely recreating as an artist the picture of a lost inheritance'. Callum, the loyal retainer, 'the inveterate poacher . . . satyr of woods and river and moor', and the old laird are central. For a moment, Neil recaptures the radical Toryism of Sir Walter Scott and his disciple Buchan.

Now it is the old chief who feels degraded. Macdonald, growing senile, strikes back by poaching on his own land. Callum becomes his protector, and both are besieged in a bothy; the night scene in the bothy is 'not unlike a Landseer composition seen in a nightmare'—and the image captures the book as a whole. The laird is wounded and dies of bloodpoisoning. The loyal Callum inherits the authority of his supplanted chief.

In this intriguing mixture of comic adventure and pathetic violence, self-mockery is now made pleasant by adventure and exhilaration, and a new mood in Neil is struggling for dominance:

> . . . a soft wind on the skin—a sheer bodily delight in life, full of rhythm, of song. The old occupational songs of the Gael—spontaneous beyond a doubt—the rhythmic humming of their unconscious, like the humming of a sleeping wheel. The sense of an infinite past drowsed in him richly; an old sunlight bottled up like laughter . . . The light of life spilled in his eyes in good humour.

The jovial friendliness of the poachers embodies a belief in the primordial goodness of man the hunter with his comrades. And the austere grey coast now seems friendly, as if Neil were groping for promise in his vision of greyness.[34]

So, while *The Poaching at Grianan* was yet another false start for the novelist, it revealed the way the man must go. It suggested a craftsman still searching for his form. The novel seemed a dead-end. The short story had reached a level of modest success with the publication, in mid-1929, of *Hidden Doors* by a small new Edinburgh press, the Porpoise. There was new hope in the drama. In fact, *The Poaching at Grianan* was a narrative reworking of a play to be produced by the Scottish National Players in Glasgow in the autumn of 1929.

6   Detour into Drama

The new direction is signalled in Neil's first letter to a remarkable woman. Nan Shepherd, the Aberdeen poet, novelist, naturalist, and teacher, first wrote to Neil on 19 August 1929 to tell him how much she had enjoyed *Hidden Doors*. Over the years, he derived unusual pleasure from her sensitive and supportive letters about his books. Evidently they met at a PEN dinner in the winter of 1930; for Neil wrote, 'I was disappointed that the PEN function broke up without our having a talk. In talk you can get down to things. And I'm afraid I was prepared for an all-night sitting! Instead of which I was compelled solitarily to go aloft about midnight! It was too bad. Positively without even a good-night to the one or two whom I was really interested in! William Jeffrey said to Cleghorn Thomson (of the BBC) the other day in Glasgow that he would take charge of a certain literary affair if he could hold the meetings in a pub. I homologated heartily!'[1]

> I think [she wrote to us in 1978] he valued my remarks on his books because from the first I had apprehended that inner awareness which his early critics were blind to. He said he never felt a book of his was properly published till I had had my say. But that, you know, was because we felt the same way about life and loved the same things in the world. Since you have read *The Living Mountain* [we had read it and admired it greatly], you will understand why in the last letter he wrote me, he eighty and I not much less, he paid me the lovely compliment—'You are like a lovely day on the hills.' It was an all-sufficient good-bye.
>
> We didn't really meet much—odd occasions like PEN Club dinners or Edinburgh Festivals, or in each other's homes, or in woods or on moors—not putting the world to rights, or even pronouncing on Scotland and her literature, but just enjoying each other's company and the beauty of the earth. He was the sort of man you could be silent with.

But in 1929 he needed more verbal support, and Nan Shepherd offered it. 'May I say', she wrote, 'how sorry I am that your *Lost Glen* has not yet been published in book form. Miss Marian Angus told me some time ago that you were having difficulty in finding a publisher.' 'I'm afraid I'm rather lazy,' Neil replied, adopting the pose he would often assume when writing became a problem or reception was uncertain,

> and haven't, indeed, written a word—beyond reviewing—for some months.

The Lost Glen is still in my drawer—where it will lie for some time. Too political, I'm afraid; a trifle too concerned with the Highlands as they are; not enough romantic tartan. It is so easy to dish up precisely what is wanted! Meantime, my interest has turned to drama. The Scottish Players are putting on a full-dress play of mine in Glasgow in early October. (I'm afraid it won't do them any good!) And the BBC, London, have just written requesting permission to broadcast my one-act play, *The Hawk's Feather* (in current *Scots Mag*) from Aberdeen on 24 Sept. Again, how they are to get it across, I don't know! But it all means that our forces are beginning to make a slight impression. But the real pleasure in the fight comes from an exquisite understanding of what Whitman would call a comrade.

The new movement in Scotland's theatre had begun in the early 1920s. William Power, Glasgow editor, president of PEN and Scotland's 'literary uncle', recalls it in his autobiography:

A new Scotland was trying to come into existence. One of the signs was a meeting convened by my old schoolfellow, David Glen MacKemmie, to form a Scottish National Theatre Society . . . The classic production was 'John Brandane's' comedy *The Glen is Mine*, which has gone round the world . . . Theatrical dynamic diffused itself over Scotland in the Community Drama movement, with nearly four hundred groups, some of them in the most unlikely corners. The soul of the movement is its chairman, Dr Gordon Bottomley, the Yorkshire poet-dramatist, who was drawn to Scotland by his sense of the need for a true national spirit in drama.[2]

Certainly some of the impetus came from Ireland. At any rate, it did for Neil. He recalled the impact from the time of his first visits to the Walshes:

In Dublin, Irish national life was so strong that it created a drama out of itself . . . It said: We will show you your own life translated into drama, and make you sit up, and look at it, and realise it as you have never done before! Here is Ireland, here is Cathleen ni Houlihan, here are your conflicts and your slums, the plough and the stars, and there goes the all-wise Juno . . . I have seen most of the great Abbey plays in the Abbey, and remember vividly still [in 1938, this is] the shock I got when at my first visit many years ago, I heard the Irish voices in *The Shadow of a Gunman* coming over the footlights into the darkened auditorium. I had forgotten, if I had ever known, that contemporary drama could act on one like this.[3]

But the translation of O'Casey into terms of Scottish drama was not simple, and the alternatives commanding attention in Scottish theatre were far from promising. Neil offers a hilarious account of them in *Choosing A Play*, a one-act play written for community production early in the 1930s. Two actors, Don and Flora, argue over what type to pick for local production. She wants serious historic-poetic drama—and he replies scornfully, 'The only people who wear tartan on the stage are Scotch comedians, Scotch coamics. Waggling your stern and thumping wi' a wee bit twisted stick. Flora, ma Scotch bluebell.' He wants a play called 'When the Briar is in Bloom' and Flora adamantly refuses, calls it 'kitchen comedy' and offers her own witty parody—a rare specimen of Neil Gunn exploiting provincial Scots for fun.

> Ay, maybe it is a little early for tea as ye say; but my hardworking son is thinkin' o' goin' to the pictures in the toon an' I was only hopin', just as ye cam' in, that he was no' takin' onybody wi' him! . . . Oh, ay! Ay. The briar is pittin' oot a wee bit flo'er to look at, Mrs MacFadyen, but seemingly tastes differ.[4]

Now these are only extreme parodic versions of what Glasgow took seriously in drama in the 1920s, and both types were written by men Neil came to admire. James Bridie recalls them in his autobiography: 'The Society had some notable achievements to their credit. Among them were Robert Bain's *King James*, Brandane's *The Glen is Mine* and a gloomy play by George Reston Malloch called *Soutarness Water*. The most famous of all was the premier of Gordon Bottomley's *Gruach*.' The revival together of Brandane's *The Glen is Mine* and Bottomley's *Gruach* in 1923–4 illustrates the choice. But Neil was uneasy with both types. He was a determined realist, yet he feared that a superficial realism would degenerate into provincial stereotype. He was a visionary symbolist, yet found little real force in neo-Shakespearian spectacle. He could not follow the Irish playwrights—for he had to be 'Scottish' and 'original'—but what he sought was a socio-economic realism with surreal elements to express a collective unconscious.

He did one-act plays in the 1920s—*Hawk's Feather, Glendaruel, Back Home*—that move unequally in this direction. The last is the bleak farewell conversation of a young shepherd's son with his granny. The first is set in modern times in a bothy on the site of Jacobite Gaeldom's 'last fight'. *Glendaruel* is more impressive. Two journalists argue in a city bar, one a 'fair, keen-faced, abrupt' sceptical Glaswegian; the other a dark, lean, hidden Highlander. As they debate 'historic issues' and matters of 'the racial spirit', a newsboy shouts the grisly details of a story they have just covered. A Cowcaddens prostitute has been murdered. Whimsically, bitterly, the journalists translate the story into a legend of 'the lovely Deirdre'. Outside on a landing the girl's desolate grandmother croons 'Glendaruel', the farewell of Deirdre to Alba, of the Gaelic spirit to the world. One journalist says to the other, 'You've certainly got a bee in your lost pibrok.' It's a good phrase for Neil Gunn, neophyte playwright.[5]

He was working at the drama as early as 1926. Grieve was reading two plays in March and sending sensible advice. He was troubled about them from a producer's or actor's point of view. 'Technically, they won't do—you say too much (drama can dispense with *so* much verbiage . . .)—on the other hand (I'm thinking mainly of the three-act play)—you don't say enough—to clarify the intended action.' He is inclined to recommend sending them to R. F. Pollock, to do for them 'just what some months ago (with tremendous benefit to it and permanent illumination in many directions to myself) he did to a play of mine'.[6]

There is no evidence that Neil went to school to Pollock, but he did to Bridie's mentor, the 'bully, easy-faced man with white hair and a quiet voice', former surgeon, general practitioner, dramatist of whom Bridie would write, 'If anything comes of the Scottish Drama, John Brandane (John MacIntyre) is its begetter. He spent more time driving technique, construction and common sense into raw young dramatists than he spent on work that might have made him famous. He is a most unselfish, great-hearted man, and he loves the theatre as it had been his son.'[7] Brandane wanted Scottish plays from Scottish dramatists. To Brandane, Neil sent a one-act play in late 1928, and Brandane wrote that he would be delighted to see more, and asked Neil why he did not try a 'three-decker' some day.

Neil had one in draft, and Brandane said Hurrah! Let's have it. Neil was eager to do something 'modernist'—this was the time when he and McLeish were reading *Transition*; in December he was reading Joyce's *Exiles*. In January 1929, he sent Brandane *The Ancient Fire*. Brandane found it 'wonderfully good', and enclosed fourteen pages of notes advising simplifications and clarifications. He urged Neil not to publish it in any form before seeing a production (*The Ancient Fire* was becoming *Poaching at Grianan*), and warned him that play-making and writing fiction are as different from one another as sculpture and music. He told Neil to avoid closet-drama, to break up long speeches, to clarify states of mind through dialogue, to avoid puzzling the audience, always to have a character speak as he exits, and not to follow symbolism into minutiae. It appears that Brandane's golden rule was to cut when in doubt.[8]

The Ancient Fire presents a middle-aged Glasgow draper, Lachie Macdonald, seeking the lost freedom 'caged in him' by going north to his old home on a poaching foray. The situation he finds is that of *Poaching at Grianan*: the old laird, the Americans. Lachie shoots his stag, but in Act 2, trying to drag it away, he falls heavily on the antlers, passes out, and: 'A spectral greenish-blue light searches the darkness and finds Lachie rising from the antlers, though the head and shoulders of his real body are still seen huddled amongst the tines.' He talks to his prone body. We are told in a stage direction: 'In dream, the man's unconscious has become incarnate. For the most part, the rest of this scene is played with bare nerves and intense mental life.' The scene—Act 2 Scene 3—becomes a dream-symbol enactment of the essential motives and conflicts of all the characters. Act 3 finds Lachie arriving triumphantly back in Glasgow with his stag. The crush at the shop door forces the antlers into the chest of his gentle friend Angus— seller of caged birds, and Angus is carried off, crying to Lachie to free his birds.[9]

Recalling the play (in 1967), Neil said, 'I was trying a new sort of thing, trying to capture talk—talk in which people never say quite what they *mean*.' So in Act 2 Scene 3 they talk as if from their unconscious, and two ladies in the audience said, 'It must be a dream he's having.' Brandane understood Neil's intention, but was sure the distinction between dream and unconscious would be lost on stage. He was also sceptical of Neil's determination to find a 'national' technique in the mixture of reticence and 'unconscious' dialogue. But Neil held on obstinately; the play went to the reading panel, and was set for production in the autumn of 1929.

It was a time of crisis for the Players. The brilliant young Tyrone Guthrie had been producer-director: Bridie remembers him at this time as a young Irishman of Scottish extraction born at Tunbridge Wells and educated at Oxford, six feet four inches tall, clad in jersey and sandals, with predilections in production running to 'song, mime, and stepladders'. Guthrie had just been forced by a parent's illness to resign and return south, and the actress Elliot Mason had replaced him. Guthrie recalled one meeting with Neil and Elliot Mason, 'having a fish tea behind the Nottingham lace of the Waverley Hotel'.[10] The play was rehearsed for four weeks and opened for five performances at the Lyric in Glasgow on 8 October.

Neil and Daisy could not get down until the weekend, but the faithful friend John Macnair Reid—now a journalist in Glasgow—went to the opening and sent Daisy a running account written on his knees. 'Strange to think that in a few minutes I'll be hearing those rich phrases that I once heard in a dear, quiet room in Larachan . . . The first act has gone down well . . . Lachie is very fair. His *Ach* is passable . . . Oh what a shame that you are not here to see it! But Saturday will come . . . I am afraid that there were some in the audience who failed to grasp the idea. Some were conscious that Lachie was battling against *something*; what, they were not told sufficiently clearly. The cast is very middling and the producing is amateurish. But this is a first night.'[11] The reviewers were less tactful. One admired the courage of the production but found the play 'lacking entirely any semblance of dramatic form'. Another admired Neil's ideas, 'but at present he lacks skill in putting them into dramatic form'. One spectator 'heard a lady next to me say to her companion, "What is it all about?" to which the other replied, "Goodness only knows." ' By mid-October Neil was feeling very badly, feeling that the Players' interest in him was dead, that he had let them down. Even Brandane had to admit that they had 'never been savaged by the Press so badly'.

In the 1930s, Neil retreated to more modest one-act plays for community production. But even here, he had difficulty instructing the actors to avoid the stereotyped gloom in which 'Gaelic' plays were usually steeped. In later decades, he would be better served by skilful directors and actors on BBC radio. Only in the 1950s would he have another three-act play produced; and characteristically, he would return to *The Ancient Fire* and rewrite it as *Beyond the Cage* for the Edinburgh International Festival of 1952.

Perhaps the most lasting advantage gleaned from the whole dismal experience of 1929 was the long and cherished friendship of O. H. Mavor ('James Bridie'). Brandane remained a friendly correspondent for a time. Gentle, sickly Bottomley came to Inverness as president of the Community Drama Association, and the Bottomleys became good friends of the Gunns and remained so until their deaths in the late 1940s, when Bottomley left Neil his Scottish books. But 'dear old Bridie' was special.

He was a Glasgow man, three years older than Neil. He practised medicine until 1938 and served in the RAMC in both wars. At Brandane's urging he wrote a diabolic satire on Glasgow priggery, *The Sunlight Sonata*, and Guthrie produced it in 1928. But he was on the losing side (with Brandane and T. J. Honeyman) of the struggle to build a Scottish drama in Glasgow, lost patience, gave his better plays to England, and won extraordinary success in London. In the 1940s he settled again in Glasgow and joined forces with Honeyman to create the Glasgow Citizens Theatre.

Winifred Bannister sums him up as 'impish . . . He was shy of women, but with old-fashioned courtesy. His politics were liberal humanitarian, but anti-ideological.'[12] For Neil, in the early 1930s, he was the antithesis of Grieve. Linklater finds 'gaiety . . . in almost every convolution of the Bridie riddle: it ruled much of his conversation, it danced in his argument, it shines through the texture of his prose . . . Far away, one thinks, in the depths of that great head, huge thoughts engage in portentous argument— though in fact they may be whittling into shape some new elaborate joke.'[13]

Unlikely as it seems, this impish diabolist became the 'littry gent' Neil loved best. He wrote to Mavor's widow in 1962, 'I saw him fairly often. We were both, for example, members of the British Council, and before a meeting I never failed to tell him he must be there. And he *was* there; which, I rather fancy, never failed to astonish me. After he departed [Mavor died in 1951], I hadn't the heart to attend a meeting for years . . . He was a lovely man, as the Irish say. I really had a great admiration and affection for him. He was the only man who ever made me feel that literature—writing—was a ploy, an adventure in common, like poaching; not a "serious" business but a foray in delight.'

There is the key: a 'foray in delight'. It says much about Neil's growing sense of his vocation. He looked for this kind of literary companionship. Nan Shepherd wrote to him early on that she really wasn't a 'literary person . . . There's a great big bit of me detached, and amused, and quite often cynical, that weighs the wind of the spirit with the weights of corn and potatoes and things.' And Neil agreed (15 April 1931): 'I am not really a literary man. I realise this with striking force when I meet many of my friends (e.g., C. M. Grieve). I play a little bit at it, but I laugh a little too. And I think out of the mixture there comes at odd moments a certain gaiety. For I don't know that one ever wants to have an understanding with anything so much as with life. A certain friendly relationship, mocking occasionally—a certain grimness too for the dumb spot, even the head bloody but unbowed, if without the gesture, even if not without the amusing knowledge of it.' But the traditional Highland male saw the adventure as chiefly a male preserve. And Bridie, after Walsh, was the companion he cherished.

There was another thing. Bridie, like Neil's later close friend Peter John Macleod, was a physician, an earthy humanitarian, with a strong sense of the practical. Neil recalled being in a bar with Bridie once and agreeing with Bridie that the reason for writing was to make money. ' "A writer", Bridie told me, "should be a craftsman—like a cobbler, able to fit shoes to anyone's feet." ' Neil was remembering what he had written to W. L. Renwick at the time of Bridie's death: 'He was as lucid as Shaw and more human. Indeed if we referred to our job it was generally to the craftsman's side. So many couldn't make—hadn't learned how to make—a decent pair of boots. He could let himself go on that.' And he would let himself go, too, on the flaws in Neil's craft; 'you would never mind it,' said Neil, 'whatever he said, whatever the judgements he made.'[14]

It took Neil in his pride some time to get used to a man who could read

6 Neil, the unattached officer, on a 500 cc Rudge Multi in the 1920s

7 Daisy on a camping
holiday in the 1920s

8 Daisy in Germany in 1938
– sporting a Clan Gunn
badge

Hidden Doors and then write: 'If writing is a considerable trade—I don't know, I suppose it is—you are a very considerable writer. I've read no prose writing in recent years that gave me such pleasure in its pure artistry . . . but I still hesitate to put my money on you for the Olympus stakes.'[15] Or one who could speak caustically of Neil's friend Grieve. Or one who could respond to Neil's nationalist evangelising (5 September 1930):

> I am not going to quarrel with you about Scottish Nationalism or about anything else. Only I hate and fear a Gaelic state. I don't believe a single one of the real evils we suffer from would be remedied by a parliament in Edinburgh . . . And I neither understand nor like 'the Gael' though I like all the Gaels I know as individuals . . . I hate government anyway and I don't want any more of it. I believe if the Highlands don't want to be a blood-sport playground they can stop being that tomorrow without a lot of solemn mumbo-jumbo and the wagging of peculiar-looking 'synthetic' flags.[16]

But Neil not only got used to it. He caught some of the same buoyant anarchism.

In those early years Neil could accuse Bridie of being a prig 'with your thin air and your faintly chill manner', and Bridie could fire back: 'as for not being wedded to your muse, you have but gone a whoring with political whores and Guidkens they are as piffle in the wind and the contract stands. She is a complaisant creature as your spooky story in the *Scots Magazine* abundantly shows.'[17] Bridie 'disliked *The Lost Glen* so much that I hadn't the heart to write you about it . . . You couldn't write badly, of course, but you made a damned good try there. God bless you. OH.'[18] The second of his several grouses about *Sun Circle*, which he enjoyed as adventure, was this: 'Though you are one of the best (if not the best) recorders of orgasm in the English language, you do the trick too often for me. You are as much to blame as anyone for the dreary list of Highland fornications that pass for brilliant novels by brilliant young novelists these days.'[19] So no doubt there was truth in his taunt of September 1933, when Neil was having trouble arranging a visit: 'Of course, Hell, the truth of the matter is that you are afraid of me and, by God, you have need to be, totem pole or no totem pole—and what cheek to pretend that yours is a hat stand! And what for the Lord's sake do you intend by the description "intellectual dryness"? Dry, I am at times; intellectual, never. And you know it. Even so, Neil Gunn, come quickly.'[20]

But Bridie had been strongly supportive of Neil's doomed effort at drama. And when at last, not long after *The Ancient Fire* sputtered, Neil became overnight an acclaimed novelist, Bridie was one of the first to send congratulations. 'Great news!' he wrote on 1 November 1930; 'I can only compliment H. Walpole & Co on their remarkable good sense and the Public for being told of a writer from whom they will get real profit and pleasure for a change.'[21] And he followed this up on 25 January 1931: 'I am delighted that you have become a great man because nobody could bear greatness more beautifully than you . . . May I congratulate you most heartily on attaining sweet praise commensurate with your deserts? . . . Anyway, Neil the Second, it's lovely that you've sat yourself so quickly and so modestly on the vacant throne.'[22]

For this, without too much exaggeration, was the impact when, at the end of 1930, the Book Society in London announced as its monthly selection a book called *Morning Tide*.

7 The Novelist Recognised

Here was Neil's situation early in 1930. His short stories had been collected as *Hidden Doors*, had sold about 400 copies, but would soon go out of print. Half a dozen publishers had rejected his second novel. His three-act play had been mauled. The serial novel based on it he would not try to publish as a book. To Mairi Campbell Ireland he wrote on 28 April 1930: 'I'm afraid there's nothing definite fixed, though the question of a novel in the autumn in book form has been put to me. *The Lost Glen* I have been half contemplating recasting. The serial in the *Scots Mag*—just finished—I shall not issue in book form. There the matter rests meantime.'[1] It rested for six months more and then suddenly it changed.

The Porpoise Press was founded in Edinburgh in the mid-1920s 'with the idea of supplying what was sadly lacking in Scotland—a publishing house with imagination and vision'. So Norman Wilson reported to Neil in May 1927. The name was chosen 'because Porpoises are the joyfullest creatures'. It became an agency of Faber & Faber and lasted for ten years. When the founders, George Malcolm Thomson and Watson Kerr, moved south, the press was run in their spare time by Wilson, Lewis Spence, and Charles Graves of the *Scotsman*. Having agreed reluctantly to publish *Hidden Doors*, and having then declined *The Lost Glen*, Graves invited Neil for a talk at 34 Buckingham Terrace, Edinburgh, in January 1930. It was probably a fateful visit. For Graves had wanted to open *Hidden Doors* with a story called 'The Sea', and so the idea of expanding 'The Sea' into a novel may well have been born at their meeting.

In early spring Neil heard from Thomson that he and George Blake were taking over control of Porpoise and would be delighted to see his work. By late May he and Blake were 'deeply impressed by "Under the Sun"'; Blake called it 'a thing of rare and flowing beauty'. But Thomson did not like the title, and 'Under the Sun became *Morning Tide*. Readers' reports went to Neil on 19 June, Neil returned the MS with revisions—working fast as usual—by 1 July, and the book went at once to the printer. On 26 September there arrived at Larachan the following wire: CONGRATULATIONS MORNING TIDE BOOK SOCIETYS CHOICE CONFIDENTIAL MEANTIME UP THE PORPOISE WRITING BLAKE.[2]

Porpoise had made a cautious printing of 1,500 copies before the word from Hugh Walpole of the choice, and now had to 'reprint a big edition', making moulds of the type for future reprints. So Neil ran through the copy, made 'a few small corrections' and bargained vigorously for better terms. In late January the book was out. Neil was honoured by PEN at Helen Cruickshank's Edinburgh flat; the Glasgow publisher D. R. Anderson wired, 'William Power joins with me in wishing to pay tribute to your guest of the evening; we both hope that we are witnessing a morning tide of the Scottish cultural movement and that the temptation of the south is not going to deprive us of the real artist who is now getting his due recognition.' Toshon Walsh wrote from Ireland to 'Daisy Darlin' that Neil was now a great celebrity and her faith had been justified.[3] The triumph must have seemed terribly sudden. Neil received £725 in royalties in 1931 and prudently paid off his loan for Larachan.

Morning Tide is a book of celebration, of memory triumphant and remembered triumphs. Ever after Neil liked to recall how astonished he was that 'a simple story of a few plain people in a remote place' had proven to be so interesting to sophisticates in faraway London. It is, of course, not so simple. But it may have surprised him by being simple to write.

One day on a visit to Dunbeath, Neil and his brother John sat in the unused harbourmaster's hut at the quay wall. While a storm raged outside, they talked of 'the elemental shudder of fear and terror and insecurity', of how a chuckle of security could turn to 'a subtle primal defiance, to something not unlike a snarl of exultation, a shouting back'. Neil recalls the incident in a column in the *Glasgow Herald* of 19 June 1926. John, 'the young Honours graduate', told his older brother, the Excise officer, of the morning when his mother wakened him and he went and stood with the harbourmaster to watch three fishing boats come straight for the small harbour in a winter gale. His brother sailed on one, his father skippered another. 'No,' John concluded, 'it's a morning that I'll never forget; and often, do you know, at moments when I've been up against it—the war and exams, and what not—that morning, with its incommunicable sense of heritage, has had its influence. It is as though one had another life, an elemental life of hidden strength, of which those bred in the towns can surely know nothing.' It happened in 1909 when John was twelve and Neil was away in Edinburgh.

Neil set out to reconstruct imaginatively the memories of his own boyhood in the light of John's experience and its meaning. He would do it again in *Highland River*. One cannot recover the workings of Neil's imagination without the influence of John. In Ben's terrible fate Neil had found the desolate greyness of the coast; in John's strength he found a way of 'shouting back'.

Then, as a novel grew, the 'snarl of exultation' was directed at more than the sea. Other threats follow. In Part Two the brother departs for Australia, driven away by the mother's fear of the sea and by the economic plight of the fishing. The boy Hugh knows nothing of depression; he knows only the emotional threats of fear and loss. In Part Three it is the fear his ill mother will die, and as she recovers, his triumph repeats the first part's victory over death in his father. The survival of father and mother is Neil's triumphant rediscovery—and exultant internalising—of what they were and what they stood for. His imagination is free at last from the grim memories of their painful deaths.

More ambiguous and unresolved is the preoccupation throughout with fear and shame at the sexual threat to his older sisters. His fear turns into a secret shame and then into a reckless pride on their behalf. Inseparable from the boy's growth is a sense of sex as secret, fateful, disloyal. There is no exultant running in response to this threat. There is only a hiding from it and a fierce violence when confronted by it. Neil has come a long way from the gross lusts of *The Grey Coast* and *The Lost Glen*. But not until *Sun Circle* and *Butcher's Broom* would his imagination reach an image of passion that is innocent like the boy's vision of *Morning Tide*.

That vision, by the way, has its literary inspiration. In the very months when Neil was planning his novel, his alter ego 'Dane McNeil' was contributing articles to the *Scots Independent* on the Irish writer-hero Padraic Pearse (see the issues of November and December 1929). Here is his keynote: 'Pearse everywhere finds this delight, this native joyousness of the Gael.' In Pearse's mind, 'all the ends of the Gael have met' and the nobility of Gaelic civilisation is discovered.

> It is with that tradition behind him that Pearse writes his stories and plays and poems. Here he has something not merely worth writing about, but living for and dying for. But he has to go back through the centuries to find its golden age. And to Pearse it is exactly as though he were going back to the swift felt beauties, the inspirations and aspirations of his own boyhood. That, more than anything else, it seems to me, explains Pearse's preoccupation with children, his love of them, their vivid ways, their sudden laughter, their unhesitating acceptance of life as a curious, interesting, continuous adventure, a reality that as yet knows no cynicism and no compromise.[4]

The same is true of the author of *Morning Tide*. And he would cling with obstinacy to his vision of childhood as an archaic link with a golden age.

One enthusiastic reader was shortly to meet Neil and to begin questioning that vision. The artist Keith Henderson read *Morning Tide* and wrote to Neil in September 1931: 'To me you have exactly got that tense quality of the Gaelic Kelts and I know because I'm ore myself with no outside intermixtures. But how the devil am I ever to meet you? There have been distant connections between my father's people (Aberdeen) and yours and between my mother's people (Dunottar) and yours. I swear I'll at least shake you by the hand one of these days whether you will or no.'⁵ Soon he did so. It was the start of a lasting friendship.

Keith Henderson was in his nineties when John Pick went to talk with him in London in 1978, thin and frail but spry and voluble, getting ready for his winter painting trip to Africa. His memory of the first meeting was quite alive —

> as soon as we saw Daisy we knew. We knew instantly that she would be our friend. She was tall, you know, with that golden hair down to *here*, and cut in a fringe. But Neil—he didn't open out. And I thought 'He'll thaw, but I can't talk freely now.' He was shy you know . . . Oh yes, he was proud. He was very proud. I liked that. But you know, at the back of his pride he had a little bit of inferiority complex. And so, sometimes, he could be icy. Did you notice that? . . . Oh yes he was very sensitive. But how did he respond [to direct criticism]? By laughing. We argued a lot you know, but always ended by laughing.

'What did you argue about, mostly?' asked Pick. 'Oh well,' said Henderson, pouring more weak tea into the mugs,

> everything. We talked about everything. But mostly about Neil's notion of the Golden Age. He believed that in the distant past there had been a Golden Age of mankind, at different times in different places. And he really believed that people of his particular upbringing and social level still belonged to the Golden Age and were perfect, but some other classes, the old families, the rich and so on, were wicked.

'Of course he believed in a Golden Age of the Highlands?' prompted Pick.

> Oh yes indeed he did. With no particular date, of course. And sometimes I attacked him on it because of course there was no *possible* date . . . I went to Egypt at the time they were digging up the remains of the people before the ancient Egyptians . . . and I was very interested. Neil wanted to know all about that . . . And he was awfully interested in the Incas of Peru when I told him about them . . . he wanted to go back, and he thought it might all lead back and back slowly to an unrecorded Golden Age. He took to it like a fish to water. But actually he didn't like too much questioning about this Golden

Age and I didn't do it after a while. It was to him as if it had always been there in his spirit-memory. I felt I mustn't smash this idea of his. It would be like smashing someone's religion.

'My impression', said Pick, 'was that he outgrew the need for the Golden Age. Once he had become convinced that each man could awaken in himself and become alive again here and now there wasn't the need for it so much.' 'I think he did,' said Henderson.

The Hendersons helped the process. Keith urged and guided Neil to cultivate immediate perception. Pick writes: 'I remember Neil telling me that Keith showed him his own method of looking at things with such completeness of attention and exactness of observation that a natural object so examined could be brought alive in the mind at any time thereafter. First, swift and full attention to the whole; then careful and precise examination of each detail of colour, shape, texture and structure; then a return to the whole. "Three times, and then he had it," Neil said. The secret lay in emptying the mind of everything other than the object itself. And that is why the saying in the last section of *Zen Flesh, Zen Bones*[6], encountered many years later, so appealed to Neil: "Look lovingly on some object. Do not go onto another object. Here in the middle of this object—the blessing!" Keith tried to persuade Neil that there was no such thing as sin, that it had been invented by the Hebrew prophets. He lectured Neil on the need for physical and mental health. 'The cruelties of existence,' reads one letter, 'seemingly so senseless and—if there were really an outside anthropomorphic deity—so sadistic, must be just brushed aside, MUST, Neil. Sick thoughts are evil.' He read all Neil's books—many before publication—and when he found sick or neurotic characters in them, he protested. 'Oh Neil! Once more. *It's a* COMPLEX. "Sick."' He found in Neil the persistence of negative emotions. 'Does a vague dim pall of violence, of guilt, of remorse really accompany you, Neil? I hope not. I don't hold with a sense of guilt or of remorse at all and have never felt either. So you can't say we ALL have these depressing burdens on our consciousness. Or violence. Do you ever really genuinely want to murder Mr So & So?' But he found also the persistence of wonder and delight. 'Neil was always interested,' he told Pick. 'Well, you know, he was interested in everything. He *enjoyed* everything. That was the great thing about him, he enjoyed everything.' And Henderson cultivated that interest and that enjoyment. His coming on the scene at the time of *Sun Circle* and *Butcher's Broom* helped lighten Neil's imagination as it turned to the Highland past.

The sudden new fame helped. *Morning Tide* brought waves of congratulatory mail. Tyrone Guthrie wrote from Canada. Lawrence Durrell, at work on his first novel, wrote to 'rave'.[7] Old Caithness friends shyly applauded the success of a boyhood friend. There were playful letters about 'best sellers' with Nan Shepherd, and Chris Grieve sent heartiest congratulations and unqualified praise from London. The reviewers were almost as unqualified. The *TLS* thought the 'characters reach a significance beyond themselves' and *Time and Tide* said 'the short book, quickly read, expands, as true fiction will, until the tragedy of the fisher-folk who have lost their livelihood grows and fills the mind long after the book is closed.' John Buchan called it 'one of the most remarkable pieces of literature which in recent years have come out of Scotland' and Compton Mackenzie found in it 'a wonderful sense of that sanctity of manhood which D. H. Lawrence sought all his life to express and never succeeded'.[8]

With such an enthusiastic reception, the question of a follow-up was fraught with peril. We have seen Frank Morley's agonised wish that Neil could 'scrap' *The Lost Glen*, and Blake sent a kindly warning in May 1931: 'Whatever you write and publish now is of vast importance. You will be judged stringently by a large and rather jealous public, to whom you certainly owe a duty, and they will not be content with less than your best.' In July he was trying tactfully to turn Neil's attention to another subject: 'Of *The Lost Glen* I propose to say nothing just now, save that it sticks in my mind powerfully and that I hope to see it some day in print, with or without revision; but that is now a matter between you and your God.'[9] Salmond was consulted and wrote from Fife: 'From my heart of hearts, Neil, and incidentally from what brain and business sense I have, I do firmly believe that *The Lost Glen* in book form will do you no harm commercially. Spiritually I think it is a far greater thing than *Morning Tide*—in fact I think it the very first great *national* book of this generation.'[10] Then came Morley's comment, and 'I'd publish it like a shot, without a question, except for letting the theme down.' Faced with a choice put in these terms, Neil was determined. He did the thorough revision. By late October Morley and Blake had decided that the problems weren't so big, and the book was published the first week in March 1932.

The publisher nervously warned readers of *Morning Tide* that the author 'remains the laureate of the Highlands, but it is a large adult problem he deals with'. Some reviewers understood. L. A. G. Strong in the *Spectator* recognised that 'he has attempted more than in *Morning Tide*; in some ways, he has achieved more; but *The Lost Glen* is technically far less successful.' Gerald Bullett in the *New Statesman*, with great praise for 'an admirable style' and 'a distinguished mind', felt 'the author himself lost his way in it'. The *TLS* spoke in similarly balanced terms. *The Lost Glen* clearly was not the disastrous mistake some had feared, but in this case Neil could not accept balanced appraisals without bitterness. His personal investment in the book was too great.[11]

The bitterness was generated less directly. Fionn Mac Colla's *The Albannach* appeared only weeks later. Mackenzie in the *Daily Mail* found it offered 'a richer promise of something in the future than any novel I have read about Scotland during the past decade' and the *TLS* predicted, 'If Mr Mac Colla fulfils his initial promise, the modern Highlands have found their novelist.' Grieve was now closely associated with Mackenzie, and misguided friends assured Neil that Mac Colla was being used to sabotage him. By August a nasty fight was on. The reciprocal paranoia had reached Neil, for the same day Blake's partner Thomson had to write to Neil, 'Who has been telling you this rot about my denunciation of *The Lost Glen* in Glasgow?' Coterie feuds were undermining serious hopes for Scottish literary development and Neil's own taste for the literary life. The gloomier academic prophets of the time had their excuse to nod and mutter 'Gunn was a one-novel man' and turn to *Sun Circle* for confirmation.

The triumph of *Morning Tide* was, in fact, a sport in Neil's early career. But the trouble came not with *The Lost Glen*, but with *Sun Circle*. Reviewers, booksellers, and readers alike were unsure what to make of it. To understand Neil's career we must recognise that it delayed his full commitment to the vocation of writing for several years. To understand the history of his imagination, we must see it as uniquely important. *Sun Circle* grew directly out of the inspiration for *Morning Tide*.

Having seen his communal past through the innocent eye of the child, he was drawn now to see it in the childlike innocence of its own golden age. He had learned with fascination of the ruins near Dunbeath from his brother-in-law J. G. Sutherland. The reports were coloured by what struck him most in Adamnan's *Life of Columba*: the extraordinary tolerance and peaceableness of the Picts and their druids. He had tried to envision the appearance of Viking ships in the small harbour. How would a community of peace and concili-ation respond to the threat of the power-hungry 'heroes' of History? How could their lack of resistance be interpreted? Leslie Mitchell ('Lewis Grassic Gibbon') was pondering the same questions at the same time with his Neanderthalers and Cro-Magnon people. For Neil, there was no local history to restrain his imagination; there were only, he said once, 'local lore and/or legendary "memories" '. Early in 1932 he was working on the book and telling the enthusiastic Salmond of his ideas.[12]

When we read Salmond's reply, we understand why Neil dedicated *Sun Circle* to him.

> I'm so glad to hear about your 'Glen of Early Days' book. I have forwarded under separate cover *Skara Brae* and *Scotland: The Ancient Kingdom*. Keep them both as long as you need them. I am sorry I have no copy of Mackenzie's *Ancient Man in Britain*, which is the book you should read . . .
>
> I wish, Neil, you would come down to see me. I would get hold of Alan O. Anderson—*the greatest authority on the Picts*, and a man who spends his time translating the old Gaelic MSS for the Irish Universities. An evening with him would be of immense value to you—and he would put you on to everything *that was absolutely exact*. And that's what you want. What about Daisy and you coming for a weekend soon . . . I think the idea absolutely great . . . I'm greatly taken with your Norse-Pict-Celt idea.[13]

A visit with Salmond and probably Anderson provided impetus and material for the book. Neil's notebook of the time contains a long list of standard works on prehistoric Celtic Britain and Viking culture.

As he worked on his 'Glen of Early Days' book in 1932, nationalist politics brought him in touch with another novelist contending with the pressures of success. Eric Linklater had achieved international recognition with his third novel, the picaresque epic-farce *Juan in America*, the same year as *Morning Tide*. Linklater and Gunn, while never intimate friends, remained friendly mutual well-wishers and sometimes neighbours through all the difficult years to follow. In 1932 Linklater was living at Dounby in his ancestral Orkneys, and working, Neil heard, on his own 'Viking' novel. Linklater wrote on 27 July to express concern that his fictional entry into the period might have made Neil shudder and retreat, and his relief that a Gunn novel was in progress. He liked his Viking novel, he said, but the critics wouldn't; they would complain about the gore, never having had the advantage of seeing hockey played in Orkney.[14] In a time when struggling Scottish novelists felt so sensitive about territorial rivalries, this generosity was welcome. And for Neil there must have been comfort in the knowledge of another novelist who was refusing to write a 'sequel' to a big success but going his own way.

The Men of Ness came out later in 1932 and Neil sent Linklater a generous report of his enjoyment. He finished writing *Sun Circle* in late autumn and sent it to Salmond and Blake. Both were enthusiastic.

Blake found it 'a lovely and distinguished piece of work', got from it a sense of 'uplifting and purification', admired the skill 'with which you use the Norse invasion as a tapestry behind the central theme of your poet's development in crisis', but he warned, 'You will realise, I am sure, that it is unlikely to be very popular.' Neil had 'plumbed pretty deep this time' and 'quite often, you have battered words sorely in the effort to catch a velleity'. Blake was 'for publishing as soon as we can get it through'.[15] In late March 1933, Neil wrote to Nan Shepherd, 'Myself, I'm waiting the proofs of an historical (so-called) novel due for about May. No more will it make a fortune than yours you, I suspect. And perhaps I don't like history, as my book may show! But it had its moments of interest.'[16]

It still does, especially for the biographer. *Sun Circle* is not a 'Viking novel'. Nor is it 'historical'. It is a brilliant, sustained improvisation. Aniel is Neil, the hero as young artist, druidic priest, and fugitive from history. The narrative is an act of imaginative projection into prehistoric persons who live chiefly in sensory delight, fear, or ecstasy beyond moral convention. At the heart of Neil's conception of the druid is the power of impersonation: 'The Master—he can enter into human bodies before this body. He can sit down and think and think, back through this morning, last night, the day before, the moon before, the year before, years and years until he is born, back through the life before that in the same way, and back beyond that. But it's very difficult, I've tried it,' says Aniel. He and Neil are learning. Neil is learning, even as we watch, the powers of the imagination when fuelled by a sense of life as archaic, timeless:

> For there is a secret here that neither the lovely dead nor the swift gods know. It is the immortality of life, the young heart against the mother heart, and its music sets a man brooding or walking in defiance, and the memory of it can in a lonely place make him shout with defiance and laugh, for he knows the challenge of his own creation against the immortality of the jealous gods.[17]

He is learning the extraordinary protective power of imagination:

> All that had been spawned out of night, of demon and black magic and gnashing horror, only in the end could they be kept at bay by one who after years of effort won thus within the circle of his own light. As the Sun put a circle round the earth and all that it contained, so a man by his vision put a circle round himself. At the centre of this circle his spirit sat, and at the centre of his spirit was a serenity for ever watchful. Sometimes the watchfulness gave an edged joy in holding at bay the demons and even the vengeful lesser gods, and sometimes it merged with the Sun's light into pure timeless joy.[18]

What the biographer feels in the book is a sense of imaginative liberation, of the triumphant experience of rising into freedom, such as Neil had not felt before. It no longer matters that history repeatedly defeats Pict and Celt, for there is the delight of survival in namelessness, in hiding. Haakon the Viking will win fame and fade into legend. Nessa the golden woman will share his destiny and his doom. Breeta, dark and secret, is the nameless woman of Neil's imagination who survives in spite of history, and with her the circled artist. The Jungian would say that she is his anima, the centre of his secret imagination.

Aniel the impersonative artist can be all these beings without regard to social and moral convention. His experience is filled with elements Neil normally excluded. The juxtaposing of sexual ecstasy (recall Bridie's grouse about orgasms) and brutal violence is especially marked—as when Aniel stabs the Northman about to rape Breeta and then makes love with her by the body. There is ecstasy in hiding and flight and blood sacrifice. Nothing is held back; the book reveals an imagination in all the intensity of amoral defiance. When Aniel had learned what one needs to know to live with the 'jealous gods' of history, then Neil was ready to confront the shame and pain of his historic past. He would do so in *Butcher's Broom*.

But what of his publishers and his public? They were understandably bewildered. A few readers recognised the liberation of power. Gordon Bottomley read it and found 'all your great qualities in it at their greatest height'.[19] Frank Kendon in *John O'London's* made an astute comparison of *Sun Circle* with *The Men of Ness*, 'two such vital (and far from academical) rehabilitations of Northern paganism'. For Linklater 'the thing that mattered was the life of action'. Gunn's book is 'much more subtle . . . inner lives . . . perplexities of youth awakening . . . The task Mr Gunn set himself at the outset was stupendous: to re-create a whole state of society . . . Nobody who reads *Sun Circle* but must stop to admire the unflagging energy of creation involved.' But the *TLS* was 'often uncertain what is happening outside the man' (fair enough, for what matters is inside Aniel) and was put off by style 'often so consciously artistic as to be tiring' (fair, too, for the act of sheer improvisation is essentially an act of style). Other London journals ignored the book, concluding after *The Lost Glen* and now this one that Gunn was a lost cause.[20]

Faber felt this way about the book, too. And when, in May 1934, Blake was readying publication of the next—still called *Dark Mairi*—he confessed: 'These booksellers worry me. There's no use blinking the fact that *Sun Circle*, which they couldn't understand, created a reserve that the travellers are finding it difficult to break down . . . If *Dark Mairi* had come before *Sun Circle* I'd have backed her up to, say, 8,000, but she is really starting off with that load on her weary back.'[21]

There are quite a few reasons, then, why in later years when we argued with Neil about how many novels he had written, *Sun Circle* was the book he always 'forgot'.

It took him a year between the completion of *Sun Circle* and that of *Butcher's Broom*. He had now become extremely busy with other things, chiefly politics. While one Porpoise partner, Thomson, was drawing Neil into ever more political activity, the other, Blake, was already urging Daisy to get Neil out of politics and off to a Hebridean manse where he could do what he was meant to do. She was not in a position to do so, however, and the move was not yet possible. So the busy life continued. And writing *Butcher's Broom* was laborious in itself.

Once more there was 'local lore'. The book is dedicated to Neil's chief authority, his brother-in-law J. G. Sutherland. Neil was already in touch with Archibald Scott at the manse in Helmsdale, minister of the Kildonan region and an expert on the Sutherland Clearances and the Clan Gunn.[22] But there was much reading to do of the kind Neil had always found painful. He wrote of it to Agnes Mure Mackenzie several years later:

> 7 April 1942: I must say that I have found the reading of Scots history at any time difficult. It was either dead uninteresting with no space at all given to real social conditions, the life of the folk, or if really concerned with the truth about Scotland then—*it was difficult to read because of the mental complications engendered in the process*! [emphasis ours]

> 8 January 1951: When I wrote *Butcher's Broom* you will understand how concerned I was to find the real reason for the Highlander's apparent feck-lessness in face of the evictions, for those who had trustfully enlisted (I am thinking of Sutherland) at that time showed themselves to be soldiers of the finest kind. *There was a double betrayal, far ben in the spirit* . . . I still find it difficult to dwell on the sad business, *with its implications reaching to the ends of life*. [emphasis ours][23]

And here is a key. 'Mental complications' indeed! George Bruce asked Neil once why only *one* novel of the Clearances, and Neil replied, 'Because of the shame of the thing.' 'Why should *you* feel ashamed?' asked Bruce. 'Because our own people did it,' Neil answered.[24] To Hart he explained, 'I'd always felt the *need* to write about the Clearances. I hated doing it. Most High-landers hate bringing back that awful recollection, and are not even willing to talk about it.' But actually, he insisted, 'There is very little of the Clearances in *Butcher's Broom*. The tragedy is the destruction of a way of life, and the book is more about what is destroyed.'

Quite so. He had felt compelled to read everything available, but the compulsion was only preparatory. Alexander Mackenzie had published a popular collection, *The History of the Highland Clearances*, in 1883, and it included numerous eyewitness accounts. Neil knew Macleod's *Gloomy Memories*, the recollections of General Stewart of Garth, James Loch's parliamentary sentimentalities, Sage's *Memorabilia*, and the articles collected by Hugh Miller. But of greater importance, because they recorded life in the glens prior to the Clearances, were the extensive notes to Alexander Campbell's 1804 poem *The Grampians Desolate* (on run-rig farming, old land tenure, tacksmen, Highland music and dance, and the problems of re-population). And Carmichael's notes to *Carmina Gadelica* are clearly the source of the long episode of the ceilidh at Angus Sutherland's house. These are the materials for an image of communal life in its wholeness and its natural rhythms.

More important, too, are the personal relations in the book. Once more the women are at the centre of Neil's imagination. *Sun Circle*'s idea of the Gael in history becomes in *Butcher's Broom* the idea of woman in history—women, the 'nameless black knots'. What happened to Neil as he worked his imaginative way through the tragedy is assigned to the girl Elie:

> If all the past had come to her, here in the central place of her heart's growth, as something dead as a corpse, and the future as a dread array of forces, against which, with dull instinct, she would plod and war, then the strife would have been so wretched that even tragedy's self would grow weary and die and any record of the issue had hardly been worth the making.
>
> To Elie now from this world about her, and particularly from the memoried earth and growing things immediately around her, came a mysterious effluence giving her misery so exquisite an edge that she shivered from the cut of it to a hostile happiness.[25]

The 'hostile happiness' of *Butcher's Broom* was born of the 'snarl of exultation' which produced *Morning Tide*.

Butcher's Broom has a less obvious source. The 'Riasgan', the small glen, is situated just off Strath Ullie up Kildonan from Golspie. The main glen had been occupied by Gunns. Neil mentions the Gunns once, in passing, as a sept called the MacHamishes, and this is the single clue that the wild MacHamishes are Gunns. Neil had a literary ploy here, and he enjoyed it. When the book was reissued in the 1960s he re-read it and reported that he had got a kick out of the long curse at the end.[26] The curse is delivered by a wild, learned cattle-drover named Tomas MacHamish who calls himself 'Tomas son of Hamish son of Tomas of St Donan's chair'. St Donan is saint of Kildonan, *anam-caraid* (soul-friend) of Columba and patron saint of the

Gunns. The identification is as sly as the reference to Davie's rebellious friend 'Nial MacHamish of the Heights'; Nial MacHamish is Neil Gunn. But the Gunns had played another role as well. In their MacHamish branch they were the Sutherland's border guards. When they were leaderless after the Napoleonic wars, the Countess of Sutherland found them a chief in George Gunn, and George became factor of Dunrobin, James Loch's successor. Neil's sources referred frequently to 'Factor Gunn'. His statement that 'our own people did it' has specific meaning. The book's dedication to a Sutherland by a Gunn must have been a poignant gesture.

The central figure, however, is the woman Dark Mairi. As Neil drove with the Harts down the coast from Dunbeath and over the Ord to Helmsdale in 1965, he pointed out where the crofters had come down from Kildonan and made their crofts near the shore, and the hills where Mairi had appeared and disappeared. Hart said he had wondered where such a remarkably balanced study of 'primitive' personality had come from. Neil's answer came without hesitation: 'I'll tell you exactly where it came from. I was at a ceilidh of a sort in Inverness one night. Women were doing waulking [beating, shrinking of cloth] songs and so on, and I watched them, but there was a woman there who simply sat forward in her chair—she was in her sixties, but she had straight black hair that was pulled straight back from her forehead, and her cheekbones slanted straight down back below her ears, and a little smile on her face, and this woman's image stayed with me—and became Dark Mairi.' *Dark Mairi* was the book's title when he sent the typescript to Blake in spring 1934.

Early in March Blake was awaiting 'news of Gunn no. 4. Any prospects? And no bloody mysteries, please.' A few weeks later he had read *Dark Mairi* and found it an 'infinitely more sellable book than *Sun Circle*.' 'You have the thing admirably in your grip, and what I admired as much as anything is your scaling down of the actual eviction scene—a grand scene in itself—to a mere episode in the communal tragedy. Perhaps I can put it best by saying that you have got that community just right—which, I take it, was your essential aim.' The title was defective, however. 'I'm really desolate about this title business,' Neil wrote to Frank Morley at the end of May. '*Dark Mairi* is not pronounceable to the average buyer, says George: and besides it has that Celtic twilight flavour!? *The Dark Woman* avoids that. But neither very good. . . . If I could get something that would give the suggestion of a people betrayed or an ancient way of life destroyed, centred on the woman.'[27] But finally: 'I've just thought of a rather terrible title, *Butcher's Broom*. It certainly has nothing Celtic-romantic about it—it is merely the

Sutherland badge! The awful irony does rather stagger me.' *Butcher's Broom* it was, and it was published on 11 October.

Some of the critical hostility persisted. From Glasgow Blake reported that the *Daily Mail* review was outrageous and 'Willie Power [is] about to offer the chieftain of Barra a choice between rapiers and pistols at dawn.'[28] The *TLS* found it a 'notable advance' marred by 'ornate and wordy tiresomeness'. V. S. Pritchett in the *Spectator* was 'baffled by a book which was so confused in movement as a whole and so good in parts' but praised the book as 'a book of atmospheres . . . in which the unconscious ties that bind people and the unconscious impulses they obey are most delicately made clear'. The *Scotsman* found it 'in scope, in quality, in sheer artistic value . . . streets ahead of *Morning Tide*'. The *Modern Scot* judged it Neil's 'finest novel'. *Life and Letters* said, 'Scotland should be proud of Mr Gunn, for he is the best of her present-day writers and his merits are many.' Neil should have been pleased. The public promise of *Morning Tide* had been reinstated.[29]

Evidently he was looking for other things. He wrote to Nan Shepherd (26 December 1934):

> It's odd to have written something that you like and in the same instant to know that you should cut it out (1) if you wish the critics for once to refrain from the word obscure; (2) if you want it 'to sell' . . .
>
> It's different in poetry. It's no doubt the fashion to expect it there. So *you* get off with it. Though of course you don't do it in the way I try to. I'm earthy. You have real light: sometimes all light (as I do maybe sometimes be all dark). I am left with that impression of light: sunlight, icelight, clear water. Have you ever known a coldness so perfect that it took the skin off you, like heat? Then you've never touched the iron of a cartwheel in winter ice. Crying: O cold and cold and wild! With all the red cry behind that. The lapwing cry. The running wheel.[30]

'It's not the praise or the blame,' he wrote to her on 5 June 1937; 'it's that dull opaque eye. In fact, I am never worried by reviews because, I suppose, I know I have had my private fun . . . Then a seeing eye like yours—and all the original warmth comes flooding on a smile—and one has a moment of the sweet embarrassment of understanding. Too much of it might, as I say, be dangerous.'

The imaginative act was so private that critical opacity was almost better than the intimacy of a reader who understood. And yet, the private novelist longed for public company of the right sort. Neil had not yet decided whether the life of imagination was to be a private world or a public vocation. Indeed, by late 1934 both public and private life had become terribly complicated. 'I seem so busy one way or another,' he wrote to 'Floss' McNeill, 'that I'm in danger of losing my identity.'[31]

8 Politics and Society between the Wars

The history of nationalist politics in Scotland has been told from the point of view of the purist militants. It makes a more exciting tale this way. But the truth is exciting enough.

Prior to 1928 nationalist activity was divided among three groups: the old Home Rulers, the Scots National League, and Lewis Spence's 1926 breakaway Scottish Nationalist Movement. Roland Muirhead, modern nationalism's elder statesman, sought to unite them in a National Convention, but a catalyst was needed, and the Glasgow University Scottish Nationalist Association, headed by a young law student named John MacCormick, provided the necessary enthusiasm and the 'capacity for hard lobbying'. In the 1928 rectorial campaign they had radical-romantic old R. B. Cunninghame Graham as their candidate. Grieve and Mackenzie were speakers in the cause, and Graham ran a good second to Stanley Baldwin. With this stimulus T. H. Gibson of the Scots National League proposed a unification. The new National Party of Scotland was inaugurated at Stirling on Bannockburn Day, 23 June 1928, and shortly announced that Muirhead, MacCormick, Spence and Grieve would stand for Parliament.

The party's weakness in early years, writes H. J. Hanham in *Scottish Nationalism* (1969), 'was the lack of experience of most of its members of the day-to-day business of conducting a political party'. Then, too, many Home Rulers found new support in the major parties and remained aloof, helping the impression that the new party was extremist, a somewhat fantastic literary fringe group. Indeed, Spence himself described it in 1929 as a 'maelstrom boiling and bubbling with the cross-currents of rival and frequently fantastic theories, schemes and notions, riotous with tumultuous personality and convulsive with petulant individual predilection'. The purists led by the passionate Gaelic revivalist and Scottish Home Rule campaigner who called himself the Hon. Ruaraidh Erskine of Marr (with Grieve and others) opposed electioneering as a distraction. But Compton Mackenzie's election to the Glasgow Rectorship in 1931 boosted parliamentary hopes. The seats fought, says Hanham, were all urban 'apart from a side-show based on Inverness after 1931'. The 'side-show' was for many, of course, much closer to the centre. Certainly for Neil Gunn it was, and for his friend John MacCormick.

Hanham's history derives from those for whom MacCormick was an ambitious crypto-Liberal who seized control of the party, purged the heroes, treasonably engineered a union with conservative Home Rulers, who, in 1932, had formed their own Scottish Party, and was finally ousted by the followers of Douglas Young in 1942. According to this very partial perspective MacCormick exploited a chaotic conference of delegates in 1933 to expel his opponents and was then free to bring National Party policy in line with Scottish Party aims. MacCormick's sell-out—so goes Hanham's version—led literary nationalists to fight among themselves. Edwin Muir's battle with Grieve in the mid-1930s (Muir was never a nationalist and Grieve was now a Communist self-exiled to Shetland) finally destroyed 'such unity as there had been in the Scottish literary camp'. Muir and MacCormick 'preferred to opt for a purely provincial Scotland managed by local politicians without any sense of a higher national purpose'. The 'Kailyard rejoiced'.

This is effective romantic propaganda. It is hardly careful history. And when, in later years, Neil Gunn was confronted by such propaganda, he was sadly frustrated. For he had spent years working diligently for nationalist unity *and* principle, and he knew well from the inside that the truth was less romantic.[1]

The staunch believer in practical consensus is not glamorous. Neil's political model later was the Labour Secretary of State Tom Johnston of whom he said: 'So [Johnston] propounded his idea thus: on nine out of ten things for the good of their country all Scots agree, but over the tenth they will cut one another's throats, *therefore* let us forget the tenth and come together on the nine.' He admired MacCormick for similar reasons. 'There was [in MacCormick] no air of fanaticism, of an egoism reaching for its own satisfaction, but simply of an assurance that what mattered in our inheritance was of profound value.'[2] He had his differences with MacCormick. When MacCormick spoke in 1936 of negotiating with the Liberals, Neil wrote (2 July) to warn of 'inherent danger in your plan [which] is a subtle dissipation of Nationalist energies and a transference of personal loyalty to another Party'. The Scottish National Party, Neil argued (as he had argued often before), would increase its electoral strength only by adopting a clear, strong economic policy aimed at bettering social conditions.

The coming of war against fascism further dissipated nationalist loyalties. Neil had served for several years on the National Council and was still a

Vice-Chairman when, in 1942, Douglas Young was elected to lead the party, and MacCormick and his followers walked out. After the war MacCormick joined the Liberals, and this (according to Neil's early nationalist ally, the Inverness lawyer Duncan McNeill) was what took the heart out of the SNP cause in the north. When MacCormick almost persuaded Neil's close friend Robin MacEwen to stand as a Liberal, Neil was willing to help. But he remained reluctant for the rest of his life to leave his friends in the SNP and was a contributor to party funds until 1970.

He had joined in 1929. MacCormick came north to hold a first open meeting that autumn. Fewer than thirty attended, but seven joined, and four agreed to found an Inverness branch. Duncan McNeill and Neil Gunn were among them. Within a few months, MacCormick recalled, 'they were able to report the establishment of a branch with over 500 members and money in the bank! . . . From that time Inverness became one of the most active centres of Nationalism and meetings were planned from there all over the north, from Wick to Kyle to Peterhead.'[3] Not bad for a 'side-show' run by political amateurs! And Neil Gunn, as Duncan McNeill recalls, 'was the engine—or the petrol if you like'. He had the drive. He also owned a car.

His position in the Civil Service, combined with (perhaps used to rationalise) his natural shyness at public meetings, led him to work behind the scenes, organising, scheduling, drafting press releases and policy statements. He was 'the ideologue—even the mystagogue', says George Malcolm Thomson; he was skilful at personal persuasion and diplomacy. He wrote for the *Scots Independent* as 'Dane McNeill' but his position was known and naturally MacCormick wanted his name to appear, especially after the success of *Morning Tide*. 'I appreciate, of course, your awkward position,' wrote MacCormick on 11 March 1931, 'but I feel strongly that now is the time when once and for all we must stamp out any vestige of sectarianism and narrow-mindedness in the Party, and I feel that the influence of your name would go a long way towards doing that.' A few months later he was urging Neil to attend a national delegate conference—'surely you could hide yourself in the crowd'.[4]

By May 1932, Neil had joined Compton Mackenzie, Duncan McNeill's sister Marian, and Robin MacEwen on the National Council, and was busy drafting statements of party policy. His chief concern was for a clear and progressive economic policy under the control of an independent Scotland. But political issues were attracting more attention. Would Scotland be a dominion or would it have 'independent national status within the British group of nations' or 'empire' or 'commonwealth'? Would control over foreign policy and defence remain at Westminster? Neil's position was always clear and consistent—nothing about it of the 'mystagogue'. Self-government meant a Scottish Parliament with fiscal control and with authority to determine the nation's future constitution and political status. But first a majority of the Scottish people must support a single unified move toward self-government. To this end the party must broaden its base and avoid splintering. 'Disruption or internal quarrelling', he wrote to a militant nationalist leader, 'has not only been Scotland's curse but has come too perilously near to being her death.'

For a while he enjoyed the frenzy of political activity. In the 1931 general election MacCormick stood as a parliamentary candidate for Inverness and Neil kept a journal of the week leading up to Polling Day.

21 October: Compton Mackenzie called on me at 4 o'clock, and we discussed his recent article in the *Scots Ind*. wherein he said that voting for members of Parliament was no use. After I had explained what damage he had done, he explained that the article had been written before the General Election was declared and that he had left it in the Editor's discretion to print. I made clear how useful to our purpose an Election was . . . C. M. agreed and we went across to Station Hotel where we awaited Cunninghame Graham, who arrived by car about 6 o'clock. White hair, striking profile, thin face, beautiful hands forever moving, a neat braced figure, courteous, charming—or, rather, an aristocratic grace, taut, ever ready. One can see the horseman, the head up, the eyes to the plain—like a seaman's. And the free gesture—adequate and unconscious. Later that night he recalled some of his old friends, including many of the Irish leaders . . . An overflow meeting filled the Central Picture House, where he also spoke . . . C. M. spoke strongly . . .

22 October: Phone message from McNeill in the morning about Kingussie, where hall is booked for Sat. night by Sir M. M. It was amusing my trying to convey my advice quietly so that old Birnie would not overhear, the phone being in his office. Birnie had a few minutes before been talking to his staff strongly on the absolute necessity of voting for Sir M. M. He has no idea that practically all of them will vote for MacCormick. But they have to dissemble to him. Curious power of the master . . . They are all frightened of Birnie . . . Birnie knows from our many arguments that I am a Nationalist, and is avoiding or, at least, ignoring me as far as possible.

On going across this afternoon to discuss plans with McNeill, I found him in a state of anxiety. It appears that no one could trace Robin MacEwen's order to book La Scala Picture House for the night before the Poll. However, the matter was fixed up and the hall arranged—at £20. A huge sum. If Mac-Cormick loses his deposit there will be a pile of debt to wipe off. Daisy came back from Dingwall where her mother is not too well, did a lot of cooking, and caught the 8 o'clock bus for Dingwall . . .

23 October: *Inverness Courier* came out with a tremendous attack on Nationalism and MacCormick . . . Immediately bills were printed and sandwichmen
engaged to go round today . . . MacCormick, McNeill, Macleod and Hugh
Macrae came back with me and spent the night till 3 or 4 a.m. MacCormick,
getting well lit, told us some of his Skye experiences . . .

24 October: I did a rush column for *Highland News* of analysis and rebuttal of
article . . . Have just been across town and learned that Compton has been
elected Lord Rector of Glasgow University. The first Scottish Nationalist
victory. It moves! The boys are excited . . . What fun! . . . MacC. and
McNeill not yet back from Aviemore. Arrived at 1 a.m.

25 October: Boys arrived for evening. . . .

26 October: Had Wendy Wood, MacC. and McNeill to tea. McNeill and
Wendy off to a meeting in my car. Had great difficulty in starting Robin
MacEwen's car and getting MacC. away to country meeting. Went across
town after 7 to find a great queue outside La Scala . . . MacC., McN. and
Wendy came over to house and at 1 a.m. Compton turned up from meeting at
Ft. William. . . .

27 October (Polling Day): Went to the Rooms in the afternoon . . . Found
two young chaps in them. Took one of them back with me and sent him forth
to Clachnaharry area with my two-seater. Returned with car at 7, having
driven many to poll who otherwise would not have voted . . . MacCormick
carried shoulder high into Station and sung away.[5]

Neil's account is a delightful mixture of boyish self-importance, name-
dropping, pleasure in sheer practical activity and an optimistic sense of new
beginnings. Characteristically, too, he was nervous about the cost. The local
people were short of money and doubted until the last minute that they
would save their deposit. Wendy Wood arrived with the missing £30.

In 1932 there began a new phase. Neil received a letter from G. M.
Thomson, now a close political adviser to Beaverbrook, urging him to meet
with a representative of a new Scottish Party, formed that year by a group
that included the Duke of Montrose and Sir Alexander MacEwen. MacEwen
(1875–1941), prominent Liberal and Inverness provost from 1925 to 1931,
shared many interests with Neil in the revival of Gaelic culture in the
Highlands; they even began studying Gaelic at the same time. Neil and
Daisy had become friends and visitors of the MacEwen family in the late
1920s: 'my father', recalled Robin MacEwen, 'admired Neil tremendously.'
'I thought, well damn it, here we are now,' Neil reminisced to Pick, 'both
groups trying to achieve the same end. I said, the only thing is, we will just
have to stop this business of splits. We must meet together and see what can
be done.' But the new Scottish Party was 'more conservative in economics—

less Leftist,' while Neil considered himself a socialist. And when Thomson urged him to meet with the new party's legal theoretician Andrew Dewar Gibb, he resisted and told Thomson that he would not help offer the National Party to a 'horde of vague Home Rulers'.

The threat of splintering, however, was real. Neil's new reputation as a writer, an active nationalist organiser, a skilful personal diplomat, together with his insistence on clear statements of basic principle, combined to single him out as a conciliator. In February 1933, he was drafting agenda for a private NPS meeting to consider policy *vis-à-vis* the Scottish Party. 'Accordingly,' he wrote, 'neither socialism nor any other system can satisfactorily meet the needs of Scotsmen unless first of all Scotland is organised as an economic unit with her own governmental financial centre.'[6] He was bringing MacCormick and MacEwen together. As MacCormick explained in *Flag in the Wind* (his political autobiography), he found Sir Alexander shy and reserved and 'would have found it difficult to talk freely to him had it not been for Neil Gunn who acted as intermediary and for whom the Provost had the highest admiration and affection. With Neil's help the barriers of reserve on one hand and diffidence on the other were soon broken down.' In March MacCormick wanted 'Gunn to draft out more fully, the proposals regarding a constructive Policy which we discussed a week ago.'[7] At the special meeting of the NPS Council at Stirling in late March came five points of agreement with which to approach the new group.

Meanwhile, the more radical segments of the NPS led by the London branch were strongly opposed to such overtures. Once more Neil was called upon by MacCormick, this time to support the efforts of NPS councillor T. H. Gibson, one of the London group, to keep the Londoners from making further divisive statements. Neil's letter of 3 April 1933 to Gibson is one of the fullest statements of his position:

> That extremism in general stands for purity and courage is a species of self-delusion practised by the ego on itself a' for its glory. Division has been Scotland's arch-fiend and has always stood on 'doctrinal purity'. It may be that we are like that and therefore any hope of our ever misgoverning ourselves may mercifully never be realised . . .
>
> At any rate we should by this time have learned from our history that if ever we are going to achieve a national aim it can only be by a major harmony that refuses to be wrecked by a minority discord. Now I maintain that this major harmony can be achieved in Scotland today, but it can be achieved only on a basis of broad principle and will inevitably be wrecked by over-early definition of detail or machinery underlying the principle . . .
>
> It's rather disheartening to think of our efforts resulting in no more than

giving satisfaction to extremists a century hence as they proceed, complete
with sporran, to lay wreaths on Scotland's final Culloden.

At a rowdy national conference in May the Londoners were expelled. In July
came unexpected news that the Scottish Party would offer Gibb as a
candidate for Kilmarnock. Neil wrote Gibb a firm letter warning that he
would oppose him or any other SP candidate and calling the interference of
the SP 'a deliberate and provocative challenge to the NPS'. 'Perhaps,' he
wrote, 'as a people we are unfit to govern ourselves, incapable of rising above
internal dissension. I have struggled to deny that conception. And I should
not like yet to despair.' A meeting of the two leaderships was urgently
necessary. MacCormick, Muirhead, Gibson and Gunn would meet with the
two candidates and Montrose and MacEwen.

But a strong, disinterested and symbolic figure was needed to chair the
meeting. Neil the diplomat was sent to ask Cunninghame Graham to serve.
'He had a big house on the Clyde,' reminisced Neil to Pick and Hart. 'I went
to the door and a maid came. She asked me my name and went away. When
she came back she asked, "What is it about?" I gave a brief message and
eventually I was asked in. Cunninghame Graham had someone with him,
and they were sitting by the fire. He gestured me to a chair by the door.
Then evidently he thought about my name, for he asked, "Are you by any
chance related to Neil Gunn the writer?" "Yes, I am Neil Gunn." He
jumped up, shook hands and showed me to his chair by the fire. I delivered
myself quite simply and clearly of an account of our situation. . . . As we
talked, Graham poked a leaf with his stick, elegantly like a dueller. He
agreed to chair the meeting and walked back with me to my car.'

Caught in traffic, Neil arrived late for the meeting at the St Enoch's hotel
in Glasgow. He was upset and nervous. Graham took him to an ante-
chamber. ' "Now don't worry," he said, "everything will go smoothly.
Here. Can you do this?" and he seized a straight chair and by his powerful
wrists brought it up at arm's length with its back parallel to the floor.' Neil
did the same. 'Keir Hardie couldn't do that,' said Graham. And the shy
diplomat was ready.[8]

Both groups agreed to support MacEwen as the candidate. A few months
later they were united as the Scottish National Party. Late in 1934 Mac-
Cormick wrote to Neil of *Butcher's Broom*: 'It made me realise how much we
waste your time in the less important things. But you're in it now and I
don't see how you're ever going to extricate yourself from the troubles of
Party management.'[9] Neil must have been wondering too. For he was 'top of
the poll' in election to the new party council. In 1935 he was trying to

persuade Montrose not to switch to the Liberals and in 1936 he was doing the same to MacCormick. In a 1936 letter to Gibb he recalled how damned he had been—'how heartily at the last council meeting I attended'—for having engineered the first negotiations of MacCormick and the NPS leaders with the Montrose group. By then it must have seemed time indeed to 'extricate' himself, but if he did so his Inverness friends would think him a deserter. He was damned if he did and damned if he didn't.

One lasting result of his efforts was the further deterioration of his friendship with Christopher Grieve. It was partly a matter of accident—the times and tides of fame in the whirlpool of literary and political Scotland. Partly it was a matter of essential temperamental difference. In the 1920s both men were entering their thirties and struggling for voices and places. Suddenly in the 1930s, called by Duncan Glen 'the most disturbing and disheartening years of MacDiarmid's tumultuous life,' Gunn seemed to move from success to success, while Grieve went through financial disaster, divorce, and poor health, and spent nine years of 'penury and poverty' in a cottage furnished with orange crates on remote Whalsay in the Shetlands. 'In such a position of partially self-imposed siege,' Maurice Lindsay has suggested, 'the seeds of megalomania find fruitful soil.' At such a juncture the blow of Edwin Muir's *Scott and Scotland* (1936)—suggesting that Grieve, while a fine poet, had wasted his time in Lallans—must have seemed cruel indeed. Grieve struck back viciously and frequently. Neil, as he had defended Grieve earlier, now gave Muir a long and devastatingly reasonable critique in the *Scots Magazine* bringing cries of protest from Muir. But the Gunns could never quite forgive Grieve for his subsequent treatment of the Muirs.[10]

Grieve returned, and there were some jovial reunions. But their positions reversed. At the peak of popularity in 1948 Neil was awarded an LLD at Edinburgh and Grieve's disciples ignored the occasion. In the decade that followed, Grieve's world renown was established; he returned as a hero to Scotland. Gunn's book sales and reviews fell off or failed, and feeling increasingly neglected and alone he heard reports of Grieve's solitary eminence in Scottish letters and was informed by thoughtless friends of the remarks Grieve made about him: 'Neil Gunn is wrapped in the cotton wool of bourgeois respectability'; 'Neil Gunn is a writer of the '90s'. Neil was hurt and angry, Chris expressed puzzlement and proposed a reunion, both were called upon for public statements of mutual admiration. It was too late for anything but sad nostalgia and letters from one ill old man to another expressing sympathy.[11]

Let us go back to the 1930s for an extremely interesting correspondence. In London and estranged from his first wife Grieve wrote in financial extremity and Gunn responded promptly with £100 to help secure Grieve a partnership in a small publishing firm. Shortly thereafter Grieve was acclaiming Mac Colla publicly as *the* Highland novelist and suggesting that others had blocked his career. Neil protested and Chris replied on 15 July 1932, explaining that 'no fiction whatever matters a damn in relation to Scotland while any poem whatever above a very low plane matters a great deal', but this 'need not affect our personal friendship'! Their essential difference, he writes,

> boils down to such an opposition—a radical psychological difference; the manifestation of which need not be taken 'personally' nor wound the amour propre of either of us. They are essentially incomparable. I have never done anything—nor do I now—than wish you well in any enterprise no matter how opposed that may be to what I think desirable. Beyond such differences upon which we can agree to differ there are of course further questions—or rather not questions since they are fundamentally undebatable, but rather questions of relative value which only the passage of time can put into proper perspective. I can afford to indulge in all manner of personalities because I proceed from an altogether abnormal basis of impersonality in regard to Scottish matters.

And what must have been Neil's general bewilderment is directly addressed: 'In other words behind all the complex network of my activities there is a definite irrationalism which will not be pinned down and which proceeds from the belief that I personally embody certain forces—I may do nothing of the sort but to construe that belief into a mere aspect of personal vanity or undependability in personal relationships is beside the mark. It is a spiritual phenomenon that lies outwith such considerations all together.'

So speaks the brilliant secular charismatic. It is arguable that without such a conviction Grieve could never have played his unique role in modern Scottish culture. But for the Highlander Gunn, for whom personal loyalties were most real, it was baffling. It was his first lesson in what he came to fear as the 'idealist' personality. That lesson informed his life and work thereafter.

His reply of 20 July 1932 survives in draft (we cannot be sure it was mailed in this form):

> I must say (completely impersonally of course) that you achieve the splendid isolation of yourself as a fundamental thinker or poet over against those whose 'radical psychological difference' (from you) dooms them forever to the plane of strategy or tactics. All of which, forgive me for repeating, is sheer nonsense, so

far as the Rectorial is concerned or my remarks upon it. I said, with regard to the Rectorial, that a certain strategy was necessary . . . You yourself now agree to the need for such a strategy . . . Yet in your public reference to this matter (on which we are agreed) you do continue to make out a fundamental distinction which places you forever with the eternal verities and myself forever with the hole-and-corner of strategy. This is not an illustration of *personal* motive; it ignores even ethical values; but I do say that failing to perceive a frame of reference that was finite (and not infinite or pretending to the realm of pure idea) you misjudged the whole issue and so wrote nonsense. You had no personal motive, I agree; but it might not be an uninteresting speculation to consider how far you have achieved for your readers an immediate *personal* reflection upon the mental processes of your object, namely myself! . . . All I did was to state that your remarks about Mac Colla's having been kept from achieving his destiny by a horde of his intellectual inferiors in the Scot. movement was damned nonsense because, with all its implications, it was more than literally untrue . . . If untrue, then your philosophic (or other) end would have been better served with different illustrations. To manufacture a non-existent attitude in others to illustrate your own Truth is to take yourself into the realm of fantasy. One can be as impersonal as one likes, as irrational as one likes, from day to day and theme to theme, but it is no use talking of fundamentally opposed conceptions of this or that and taking one's stand on *one* of them forever and damning the other fellow for a stand he has never taken at all.[12]

Then Grieve rejected and was rejected by the SNP and Neil was known to be high in its councils. But Neil was not responsible, and he kept in touch, writing to Whalsay to persuade Grieve to play a more conciliatory role. In a firm but friendly reply Grieve urged him and his friends to 'fire ahead and give us even the tiniest instalment of satisfactory results—you have the field pretty well to yourselves, and do not seem to me to be doing anything worth while with it. . . . It's no use trying to tell a modest fellow like me that my single stand in the opposite direction nullifies all your efforts.' He wishes he could get to Larachan for a night's talk on the issues Neil has raised.

The talk had to be postponed until autumn 1937. The Gunns had made their decision and were packing up to leave Inverness. Grieve came to visit and what a leave-taking of Larachan nights it must have been! When Neil took him along to a party of upper middle class Inverness, he said as they walked away, '*These* are the kind of people you belong with, Neil.' The rift could not be healed. Perhaps it was now Neil who was too proud.

He sent Grieve two books at Whalsay—one of them *Highland River*— evidently with the suggestion that Grieve would find them as by one who had 'sold his soul for financial success'. Grieve replied (1 December 1937), 'I think nothing of the kind; what I do in certain connections think is that no mere mercenary motive or submission to the mercenary machinations of others, but much more complicated causes involved in the contemporary organisation of the literary and publishing world and in the agencies that shape our cultural conceptions and predilections have come between you and the maximum services you could have rendered to Scotland and to literature.' In fact—and this is his most suggestive statement—'the elements in your work I question most are not those which have given you such measure of popularity as you have won, but those but for which you would probably have done even better commercially, as well as, in my opinion, artistically.' He cites Neil's 'exemplification of a very general sentimentality'.

Neil's reply is eloquent and irascible, and we will quote it in its place. For it marks Neil's deep uneasiness at a decisive time. He had finally risked a full commitment to a life of writing. He did not give up thirty-one years of Civil Service security quickly or easily. He had to justify the decision in terms of artistic merit and financial feasibility. Could he do the important things expected of him? Could he be 'popular' enough to earn a living? Here was his first enthusiastic promoter saying—in some way he could not fathom—that the two were connected. Was he retreating to his own 'Whalsay'?

There was much to leave behind in Inverness. He had become a local celebrity. Larachan had become what MacCormick called 'the spiritual home' of his group, 'our unofficial headquarters', and 'no matter how late our return from distant parts we would find [Neil] waiting for us, eager for our report and ready to sit up talking with us till all hours.' There, says MacCormick, 'we constantly reaffirmed our faith, not in any narrow and bitter nationalism, but in the capacity of the Scottish people,' and Neil 'inspired us with his clear vision of the Scotland that should be.'[13]

The quieter fun of evenings and holidays with the Stanley Hills gave way to regular Sunday evenings throughout the early thirties when a group would assemble in the sitting room for whisky and talk. Robin MacEwen remembers:

> These were not political meetings. Hugh MacKay, the Gaelic singer who came from Brora and who married Eleanor Elder of the Arts League of Service, used to visit us at Lethington quite often at this time. He had I am sure a warm regard for Neil but he used to refer to him as 'the Grey Coast' and our Sunday evening visits to 'the shrine of Celtic mysticism'. Nobody could have been less malicious than Hugh, and I think this was just his way of reminding us not to take ourselves too seriously. Visitors on the Sunday evenings would as a rule include Duncan McNeill, Hugh Macrae (from Skye and at that time a bus driver with Highland Transport and later Manager of Sutherland Transport at Lairg) and his wife and Stanley Hill (another Excise officer) and his wife. My

own brothers and sisters also used to come to Larachan from time to time and it may be that my brother David and my sister Margaret eventually got rather closer to Neil than I ever did.[14]

Margaret MacEwen recalled: 'Every Sunday night at Larachan it was understood there would be a social gathering, and we felt free to drop in. There were no formal invitations.' But how did all these people fit into that sitting room? 'On Sunday nights it was crowded. There might be as many as ten people, or maybe just three or four. I sat on the floor. Neil would sit in his armchair by the fire. Daisy did not participate much but sat quietly in the background, and then late in the evening she would serve tea.' 'Daisy', said David MacEwen, 'put up with a great deal. Larachan was always filled with people, sometimes until 3 or 4 in the morning, and the noise level was very high.' Neil was a great talker, but he was also very good at drawing others out by 'gentle teasing'.[15]

Larachan saw more than its share of notable visitors. George Blake appeared on occasion with other Faber officials. Salmond came up from Fife to talk about novels and articles and to play golf. The Keith Hendersons came over from Lethington, and no doubt Gordon Bottomley found at Larachan a second 'source of every aspiration of the spirit and cultural aspiration which could serve the Gaeltacht'. Nan Shepherd must have stopped by when she and her mother were travelling north. In 1932 came a postcard from the artist Peter Anson: 'If you are in town and can meet Alexander's bus look out for a reddish bearded man and a black felt hat.' A fisherman's blue jersey matched his eyes, Neil recalled, and 'he brought the sea with him, and surged forward so smartly that the weather broke on our bows.' He came to Larachan to talk with Neil about a book on the fisher-folk of north-east Scotland and to begin the slow process of nudging Neil into a novel that would become *The Silver Darlings*.[16] Pearson and Kingsmill stopped by for tea and whisky on their 'Skye High' foray.

And Neil and Daisy had trips of their own, drives 'over the Ord' to Caithness or up the Berriedale under Morven near the Picts' houses, and forays into the west—'that loop which takes in Contin, Achnasheen, Loch Maree, Gairloch, Poolewe, Gruinard Bay and the Islands in the sea, Dundonnell, and back across the moors to Garve'.[17] There were regular visits to the Walshes in Ireland. On one of these visits, Maurice took them to his native county of Kerry—perhaps to 'drink two or four pints' with his old father (as Maurice would say)—and stopped the car at the Kerry border, got out, shook hands solemnly, and announced in his booming voice, 'I welcome you to my county.'[18]

Neil took a longer trip in pursuit of warmth in 1934. 'I'm going away for a month,' he wrote to Frank Morley. '18 June/17 July—so don't pass then. We'd be infinitely delighted to see you all . . . Three males of us are doing a motoring tour in France. Should be back in London for a couple of days or so about 13–14 July. Can you give me any tips for France? And what's Paris worth anyway? And what about a letter of introduction to a vineyard?'[19]

His companions were Robin and Malcolm MacEwen. Malcolm had had an accident and was in need of a holiday. As Robin explains, 'Neil with Daisy's full approval agreed to come with us. It was a fairly leisurely journey down through England and France mainly visiting English Cathedral towns and similar places in France. Apart from the incident at Zarauz, the holiday was trouble-free and enjoyable.'[20] The incident is recovered in detail many years later in *The Well at the World's End* (1951). And 'it's true in detail,' Neil wrote Naomi Mitchison; 'the only time I have ever copied life exactly in a book—and the Scot who came charging naked down the beach is the fellow to whom I dedicate the book, and the fellow who was nearly away with it was myself.'[21] The book is dedicated to 'R. M. M.'—a printer's error for 'R. R. M.', Robin R. MacEwen, who had saved Neil's life.

The narrative fills eleven pages of the novel, but a few excerpts may convey the outlines:

> It was many years ago, in the inter-war period, when young men had bright ideas of a new world—the brotherhood of man, an internationalism of all the nations . . . We had been warned about the sun, of course, and had been trying to take it in small doses, but when you see a couple of Spanish beauties, with a bare minimum on, taking the sun as if time didn't exist, it's not so easy . . . The combers came curling in as they do on the west side of the Hebrides . . . I waded out a bit, headed through a comber, and while still within my depth turned to swim along the shore. It was good![22]

Then he felt tired, let down his feet, and found no bottom. He was being carried out to sea. He shouted three times, but he heard only the crash of the waves; Robin heard a shout, saw Neil wave, but thought he did so only in greeting.

> When it seemed that drowning couldn't be avoided, my whole past life did not flash by me, but I did have the very distinct thought: how strange that I should have come all this way to die . . . My legs sank; the big toe of my right foot touched something that gave as a great swirl swept me away back. In an instant panic had me and my mouth ripped out a terrific yell. Yet somehow I managed to right myself. And then I saw John [Robin], I saw that he had heard me. I saw him sit up, and then stand up. He was stark naked. Nor did he wait upon the order of his going. He charged. He came down that beach, arms

and legs flying, as only God made him, and not only did the panic fly from me but the Spanish ladies flew from him—or so, at least, I was told afterwards. The naked and unashamed barbarian had emerged.

Robin grabbed Neil like a retriever and dragged him ashore. A Basque cast his shirt to Robin 'like a primitive man casting a net to catch fish' and they were soon drinking French brandy.

> Real life seemed much older that evening than the Old Stone Age . . . When I awoke the dawn was in the window. It was a tall window. Immediately I was wide awake, with a pleasant feeling of lightness. I listened and knew no one else was awake. I could not lie still. I got up and went to the window, and found myself looking out on an old Spanish garden . . . It was now that the odd feeling came over me that the stillness itself was holding something, much as the walls held the garden; and in a moment I realised that what it was holding was time. Time was stopped, not by any kind of magic or enchantment, but actually . . . Quite simply, then, I knew with an absolute conviction as I stood at that window gazing out on the old Spanish garden that there exists an order of things outside our conception of time . . . There was nothing at all in the ordinary sense 'religious' about this experience; but what is astonishing, I think, is that there was nothing personal . . . as I sat down on my bed, looking away towards the garden, I was overcome by a divine, a delicious sense of humour.

The experience centres on five elements: moments of so-called 'illusion'; a state of consciousness akin to 'second sight' in which he has a sharply impersonal vision of himself; 'an order of things outside our conception of time'; a buoyant faith in the reality of brotherhood; and 'a divine, a delicious sense of humour'. The elements are all here of what would become Neil's view of life. And this happened in the summer of 1934.

Back in Inverness the ordinary pace of literary fame increased. Grieve's pioneering efforts for a Scottish PEN, now carried on by Helen Cruickshank, had culminated in the choice of Scotland as the site for the International PEN Conference of 1934. William Power recalls the event:

> H. G. Wells, the international President, was the general chairman. From every country in Europe, except Russia and Turkey, but including Catalonia, where the Congress of 1935 was to be held; from the United States, Canada, Latin-America, Iceland, South Africa, Australia, New Zealand, China, came bands of influential authors. There was a garden party at Holyrood . . . Edinburgh Castle was floodlit. There were receptions by the municipalities, the universities, the RSA, and other bodies. There were tours to the Borders, the Highlands, the Land of Burns . . . In Inverness, where Sir Alexander MacEwen, Neil Gunn, and Dr D. J. Macleod were among the hosts, a Gaelic opera, *Ishbel of the Shealing*, was performed.[23]

At Holyrood Cunninghame Graham introduced Neil to H. G. Wells. How does it feel to realise one has become an international celebrity when one has recently known the miraculous timelessness of a Spanish garden in Zarauz?

'At Inverness,' wrote Power, 'Neil Gunn is the centre of a literary galaxy who are making the town a city in the real sense.' The centre of a galaxy is busy advising smaller suns. Neil was skilful and generous in the attention he gave to other writers. David MacEwen has summed up handsomely: 'Neil Gunn's individual achievement as a novelist is well known. What is less frequently appreciated is the assistance he has given to the whole writing fraternity in Scotland. It has never been Neil's ambition simply to achieve success for himself.' Perhaps David was the 'young and timid poet' of his own story who

> once gathered up his pile of sonnets and walked down the road to visit Mr Neil M. Gunn at his home in Inverness . . . The poet's work was turgid, conventional and imitative. His metaphors were rehashed from the Elizabethans, and he had drunk deep of the romanticism of Keats. All in all it was pretty dreary stuff. If Neil thought so, he did not say so. He read through the painfully written MS with immense care and patience. He criticised gently and with insight. He lent the young man a volume of T. S. Eliot and Roy Campbell's *Adamastor*. He discussed Boswell and Johnson. He embarked on Schopenhauer. He outlined the ideals of Scottish Nationalism and he gave the would-be poet a good dram.[24]

Another beginner, Arthur Ball, had been encouraged by Neil when, a nineteen-year-old at Glasgow University, he published a poem in a Wick magazine. In 1933, he called at Larachan and received like hospitality, a dram and a 'walk along the Caledonian Canal in the summer evening sunshine. I spoke of the experience of living in London and he asked, curious, *"What* experience?" '[25] To Marian McNeill he sent substitute dialogue for the 'tail-end' of a novel of hers too heavy with speech-making. To Nan Shepherd went discriminating commentary on a character in *A Pass in the Grampians* (1933):

> You have realised her not only completely but symbolically (if you'll let the word pass). . . . Indeed you balance her reality by giving the old man not only austerity but kindliness. Otherwise they would have greyed a trifle even before her vulgarity . . . You are surer here than ever before, you are indeed so sure (out of long thought processes) that your detachment at moments may have the air of intricate analysis (i.e., of difficulty) and even almost of coldness as of an exercise. Accordingly a statement of passion in the character (at very odd moments, I mean!) does not carry warm conviction, because the reader (usually spoon-fed or shovel-fed) has not made the subtle intuitive imaginative

effort that leaves him susceptible to the statement as to a stroke on a bell. I cannot see how we can help that.[26]

No wonder his advice was increasingly sought. The wonder is that he found the time to give it.

A triumphant climax to the busy public years of Inverness came in the autumn of 1936. Scottish PEN met in Inverness and the meeting was tied to the National Mod. William Power remembers:

> Inverness in that Mod week was a blaze of Highland costumes; but the costumes were worn by Highlanders of all classes, most of them the sons and daughters of crofters, and all of them Gaelic speakers and singers. The ceilidhs that went on nearly all night in the hotels were communal song feasts in which the chiefs and cotters, magnates and ghillies, Scots Gaels and Irish Gaels, met on the old Celtic ground of soul-brotherhood.[27]

One ceilidh went on at the Station Hotel. To it from Stornoway came Dr Peter John Macleod and his wife Ena. Ena, while a student at Glasgow during the First World War, had come to Inverness to work as summer governess for the MacEwens. At the Station Hotel in 1936 she found Sir Alexander and Lady MacEwen with a large party. Neil and Daisy Gunn were there, and Eric Linklater, and some of the Macmillan sisters, famous Mod singers from Mull. 'Peter and Neil', recalls Ena, 'took to each other from the first moment—they were alike physically as well as in many other ways. About 1 a.m. fourteen of us bundled into cars and went to Neil's house in Inverness (Larachan) to dance to mouth music, to sing and to drink Neil's whisky (he was still in the Customs & Excise then!). I remember being struck by Neil's lightness of foot in the Highland reels, etc.'[28]

Neil wrote of the occasion with delight:

> A few folk gathered in our house for the ceilidh which, like certain rare plants, blooms only after the heat of the day. At that hour, small but measureless, even an adjudicator can sit on the floor and bloom in silence; can drink everything in and expand in the bliss that knows no responsibility and apprehends at last the beautiful folly of adding one mark to another.[29]

And so, Neil seemed to be 'enjoying it all very much' during these last years in Inverness. But surfaces don't tell all. He wrote another reminiscence of the same Mod while packing to leave Larachan a year later:

> While I turn to the Mod and try to see what it is doing for Gaeldom, I find it difficult to be impressed. Despite its concern with the things of the spirit, it is essentially neither a creative body nor an inspiration towards creation. At the core, it stands for the remembrance of things past, and does not envisage a

future in terms of that past. Its most notable leaders or publicists deprecate action of any kind . . . The Mod must remain pure and undefiled . . . And that is why no real Gael, in his heart, believes in the Mod. And when he is a decent man he is troubled, because here in truth are precious things of the spirit, and he knows that the life that bred them is dying.

In his own spirit Neil was troubled. Under the amicable surfaces of his Inverness life all was not well. The future was uncertain. It was time for several decisions. He decided to resign from his public life in Inverness, and to withdraw with his wife to a rented farmhouse in the crofting country west of Dingwall.

9 A Time for Decisions

The episode became in later years a story Neil loved to tell, elaborating as he did so, but coming to focus on the whimsical abruptness with which he bought a boat one night on Skye, sold his house, got Daisy's approval, threw up his pension, and was 'off and away' for a cruise down the west coast. Was it really that abrupt, gay, and reckless? Did Neil ever make critical decisions that way?

Here biographers must speculate with care. They are dealing with profoundly personal matters, with one of the crisis points in a long life, one of the times when much is revealed and more is suggested. They can slip over the surface and simply rehearse Neil's own public account. But if so, they betray the deepest reality of their subject. If on the other hand they try to interpret complex private affairs, they must proceed with caution and tact.

When Hart was writing a biographical essay shortly before Neil died he sent it to Neil for comment and revision. The account of the flitting of 1937 was conventional enough. Neil needed time and freedom to be a full-time writer. Nationalist politics had become an exhausting frustration. Ena Macleod told Hart, 'As his fame as a writer grew . . . he was besieged by the scalp-hunters and though he was trying to combine his distillery work in the morning and writing in the afternoons he found little peace.' He had not published a novel for two and a half years, had finally finished *Highland River*, and was hopeful that it would succeed.

From Neil on 13 April 1972 came one final reaction to Hart's account. He was weak and distracted at the time but certain things were very much on his mind. 'Dear Francis,' he wrote, 'I hope I'm in time for you to insert the attached page, leaving you to cut or adapt p. 25. My doctor was here last night and we had a long talk, and he thought that seeing I had always valued "experience" so much in my writing why leave this concise one out, for it might even be an "enlightenment" for many a reader. I do hope you agree. I feel as if something had been revealed even to myself.' From that time on, his biographers knew that they were bound to give the truth of Neil's *experience* as thoroughly as they could.

Enclosed in Neil's hand was the following addition:

Then suddenly all the thoughts and actions of that period were brought to a focal point, cleansed of their uncertainties, and the bright world of freedom opened before them. It was a remarkable manifestation of a tragic incident in their private lives. It occurred when Daisy was about to have a child and an appalling household incident sent her to hospital and the still-born birth of a male child. They never spoke much of this, if at all. Yet it had the profound effect of drawing them closer together; life became more an affair of intuitions, of final understanding, than of words, and it certainly clarified their uncertain thoughts about their future actions in the outside world now. He sold the house he had built, lost his salary and pension rights and emerged free, leaving him nothing but the old boat he had purchased in Skye.

But the old boat took them to the West Coast, and never had its seas and inlets and islands seemed so vivid, so wonderful.

'Maybe the future is only a beginning,' he said.

Her smile steadied on his face then wandered out over the sea.[1]

Now, like passages in *The Atom of Delight*, this lovely and carefully refined transformation of experience opens more questions than it closes. There is no doubt of the fact. Several people have told us that the tragic incident happened, that little was said of it, that it remained uniquely important to both Neil and Daisy. When Neil lay confused in hospital at the end he spoke often of 'Daisy and her dead child'. Some have suggested that the greatest disappointment of Neil's life was not having a child. Stanley Hill had his own sad reasons for remembering:

Both families suffered tragic losses at this time. Jay and I lost our first child an infant girl and Daisy the little son she could not give life to. What a changed world it would have been for Daisy if only she could have borne a son to her Neil! Thereafter he was her life. She watched him and over him—anticipating every wish and shielding him from all distracting encounters.[2]

But just when was 'this time'? Why did Neil mean to imply that somehow the incident was directly connected to the 1937 decision, that the decision was 'a remarkable manifestation' of it? What were the 'uncertainties', the 'intuitions', the 'final understanding'? What was the 'appalling household incident'? We may never know. As we wonder, we notice how Neil tried to deal with the experience in fiction.

We are haunted now by the still-births in *Butcher's Broom*, by the dead mother and child in the cist in *The Silver Bough*, by the end of *Bloodhunt* when old Sandy watches the betrayed girl give birth in his barn, and perhaps most of all by Aunt Phemie in *The Shadow*, generally supposed to be a portrait of Daisy. We hear that Aunt Phemie lost her husband in a terrible accident with a threshing mill: 'The sight of his body had killed the child in her and an ambulance had taken her to hospital.'[3] When Daisy was given this to type, what would she have thought? Perhaps it is a version of what happened, perhaps the accident that robbed Neil of the sight of one eye, the 'appalling incident' that shocked Daisy into hopeless labour. Perhaps by presenting his surrogate as dead Neil suggested that he condemned himself for the accident. Either way it seems that Neil held himself responsible. One friend has told us that Daisy blamed Neil for it, refused to share her bed with him 'for a long time' and then blamed herself terribly for having done so.

Whatever happened, it seems clear that the later intimacy of Neil and Daisy, so widely and warmly recognised, was achieved only after a time of stress, guilt and blame. Neil was telling us that the move from Inverness marked the hope of a new beginning. Certainly the summer of 1936 was a significantly happy one. Neil and Daisy were off together in the wilderness as he worked on *Highland River*. The decision was made shortly afterwards.

But how long a time of stress was ending? Many knew what had happened but not when. Letters of the late 1920s suggest that Daisy was occasionally in poor health. One of Daisy's cousins thinks Daisy lost her child at the same time one of her sisters had a son, and the son was born in 1931 or 1932. This recollection is consistent with a letter from Neil to the artist William McCance of 27 September 1932 reporting that Daisy had undergone minor surgery, was in a nursing home, would 'have to lie up for a time', and that Neil was left in 'a maidless house'. A letter from George Blake to Neil belongs to the same time: 'My wife and I were grieved to hear of your wife's misfortune, and, while we know that the case was hopeless from the first, we offer our sympathy. Death is death, my son: finish: a terrible thing.'[4]

The important facts are clear. However Daisy felt, she wanted to have a child for Neil, for he wanted one very much. She probably had a series of miscarriages. Finally a child came almost to term and a terrible accident brought about a still-birth. Throughout this period Daisy was in her forties and the prospect of bearing a first child at such an age must have been frightening, but she was always willing to conceal her fear. When the catastrophe came, it is easy to see why she might have blamed Neil and rejected him sexually for 'a long time'. The 'long time' was the later period in Inverness, from the end of 1932 to the happy summer of 1936, the time of Neil's most active public life and the time when Daisy participated least. It seems symbolic that after some years of strain Neil took his long holiday with male friends. It is not surprising what happened to him when he returned.

He found himself in a deep emotional entanglement. He was a shy man in his early forties. Imaginatively, he had moved from a negative, somewhat guilty sense of sexuality in the first novels to the pagan eroticism of the young lovers in *Sun Circle* and *Butcher's Broom*. A sometimes obsessive mind now focused on physical passion; he was like the writer in 'The Mirror'[5] (a short story) who finds himself obsessed with the older of two young sisters, and his strong, thwarted desire for children made the obsession even stronger. It is neither surprising nor shocking that when the temptation presented itself he yielded.

The scrupulously concealed relationship that began in the summer of 1934 continued intermittently until the sixties, and became an important part of his life. Because of its importance, and because the other person has chosen to break a silence of forty-four years, we have decided that this biography would be fundamentally dishonest if it gave no account of the matter.

Doing so is not easy. The many letters Neil wrote to her over thirty years are carefully guarded, written with extraordinary prudence and a peculiar impersonality. Very telling is the complete destruction of hers to him, and we know that several packets of letters were, upon Neil's instructions, destroyed in 1973. Her record of dates and places fits consistently with all we know of the chronology of Neil's life. We have talked with her on several occasions and can set down here our growing admiration of her fairness and honesty. The revelation forces us to reconsider all we know about Neil and his writing and his seemingly idyllic marriage. She has sympathised with us and agrees: 'Even if you were to get it completely right, many people who knew Neil would refuse to believe it.'

Neil was determined to preserve the secret. Hart questioned how he could expect her to carry such a burden for so long, and she staunchly defended him. 'I can't accept the view that Neil put a burden on me or that I accepted it with any particular generosity of spirit. Of course there was a burden, but it was put upon me by whatever strange alchemy makes a girl fall in love.' She had loved him from the time she was thirteen and supposes that her family knew *her* feelings, that perhaps Daisy did too. 'Neil's need for secrecy was not purely selfish, and I'm sure he saw it as equally essential for me and my reputation in a society that was still far from permissive. He thought that it would be better for me to get married to someone else and did, in fact, try to promote marriage . . . in the full knowledge that this would have put an end to our relationship. The only stumbling block was myself—obstinately refusing to transfer my affections.' She never married. Neil never permitted himself to say he loved her, and she never forgot where his first loyalties lay:

> The only choice was between ending the affair or continuing it in secret. Acknowledgement of it was not considered by either of us. For Neil, Daisy always came first, and any knowledge of his relationship with me would have hurt her badly, and perhaps harmed his marriage irreparably. It would have hurt Neil too, and I knew it without any need to discuss it.

We respect the essential truth of this and have no doubt of the deep affection that remained and grew at the centre of Neil's marriage. But we must also recall Neil's delight in secrecy and his secrecy in delight. The two most personal of his novels—the ones he called 'my own peculiar ones of which I'd say nowt'—are those in which his secret life is indirectly revealed, *The Serpent* and *The Shadow*. More will be said of what they reveal in a later section. But here we must quote what is said in *The Serpent* of Tom's inexplicably secret affair with Janet:

> He had much plotting to do, in order to avoid or get rid of the lads, to deceive the village, to do anything and everything that would secretly bring Janet and himself together in the dark night. Why this secrecy? Heaven knew, but it had been part of the run, the delicious essence of their escape into freedom.[6]

> These snatched moments had an intensity of their own, all the greater because in the summer nights someone might be moving about at any hour and it never got black dark . . . There was defiance in it and a secret glory. This mood was rather rare at that time, because the whole circumstances of his life tended to breed a sense of solemnity and youthful purpose, a humourless solemnity . . .[7]

'Be secret and exult!' said Yeats. But she would have it otherwise. Nor would she permit us to cast her in a false role. After our long talk, she wrote to Pick:

> I was a little uneasy on Sunday when you said Neil was a lucky man. I felt that while I'd been trying to avoid the ungrateful role of 'The Other Woman' in a trite West End comedy you were coming dangerously close to casting me as heroine in a dramatic tragedy—which I really didn't feel fit to play! . . . Neil brought out the best in me. He caught me young and helped me to mature both emotionally and intellectually—not least by teasing me and making me laugh at myself when I tended to become pompous. Perhaps he got more in return than I used to think. Looking back, I can see that the relationship couldn't have endured if I hadn't satisfied some deep felt want. Nevertheless I feel the debt was nearly all on my side.
>
> I can see Neil chuckling and giving me a kindly smile—not that I believe in an after-life—at the idea of trying to make an emotional balance-sheet out of something quite simple and natural.

How well she knew him! To Hart she spoke on tape: 'Firstly, please don't feel distressed on my account. I can cry all too easily—I think an inherited weakness of the lachrymose glands—I do it at the silliest sentimental films and books. But I'm pretty resilient and reckon I've had a pretty good life. True, I've perhaps missed some of the best things I might have found in marriage and a family, but equally I've missed some of the worst.'

Having accounted for her presence here, we will let Margaret MacEwen speak for herself.[8] We will interweave portions of Neil's letters with portions of her memoir. The narrative must go somewhat beyond the end of the Inverness years to be seen in proper perspective:

> I still remember my first meeting with Neil—at a Christmas party, I think in 1926. Neil was then in his middle thirties, tall and handsome, and I fell in love with him there and then. Love is perhaps not the right term to use; it was more a teenager's hero-worship. Over the next few years he became an increasingly close friend of my father and of Robin and the family generally, and a common interest in Scottish Nationalism brought him fairly frequently to Lethington. I was only at home during the holidays, and as far as I can remember was usually a silent listener to the talk going on among my elders when Neil came to the house. Gradually, however, I lost my shyness of him, but not my admiration. Some time, I suppose from about the age of seventeen, I started going with Robin to the 'shrine'. This worried my parents a bit, but only on the grounds that Neil gave me whisky. They were certainly aware of my admiration for him. There was a certain amount of teasing from my brothers. It was generally regarded as a harmless schoolgirl crush.
>
> Neil was always kind and friendly to me as I grew up. I remember one beautiful, frosty moonlight evening, when a party of us including Neil went skating near Inverness. I can still remember the exhilaration of being whirled round the ice by him.

In 1934, after she had had a secretarial training and a job in London for a while, she returned to live at home and act as secretary to her father. It was at this time that the relationship with Neil developed. Margaret MacEwen writes:

> I feel hesitant in speculating about other people's feelings—in particular Neil's and Daisy's. But I do think that while he felt guilty, he also believed that there was an intrinsic innocence in our relationship.
>
> We met fairly often over the next two years. The fact that the Gunns didn't have a telephone and my father tended to use me as a messenger helped. Neil was fairly frequently at Lethington in a quite natural way to talk to my father. He would walk up from Larachan and I would drive him home, and we hoped no one would be aware that we'd spent an hour on the way. At other times I would pick him up as he was walking back from the distillery, and we would

manage to fit in half an hour or so together. All this, of course, was very unsatisfactory and frustrating. But even in what I regard as the dark years between 1934 and 1938 there were bright patches. Silly things stick in my mind. I used to sing to him when driving the car—Scots songs, Gaelic songs, dance hits from my schooldays, whatever came into my head. The sillier the words, the more he enjoyed it . . . I had no voice, but then he'd no ear for music either. Attempts to share my love of music with him had no success. [Gene Pick and Lorena Hart recall such demands late in Neil's life. Gene sang to him in his loneliness over the telephone. And while Francis drove the car Lorena had repeated demands for 'Oh, what a beautiful morning!' Neil would gurgle with delight and respond with a booming phrase from 'Frankie and Johnnie'—'She done me wrong!']

I don't think anyone was suspicious. The need for secrecy was tacitly accepted by both of us, and never mentioned by Neil for years until once he said, 'You wouldn't tell anybody about us, would you?' Yet, everyone knew my father and his car. Inverness was a small town; there were few cars. Neil was widely known and many people knew me. I was away for three months in Denmark from April to June 1935, and it has only just occurred to me to wonder whether these absences, which seemed quite natural at the time, had been engineered by my parents . . .

With our move to Kessock in 1936 and later the Gunns' move from Inverness it became more difficult to meet and I became thoroughly miserable. Apart from Neil I was becoming more and more out of sympathy with my father's political work. My brother Malcolm's influence and that of his first wife Barbara, reading of Left Book Club books, and the pressure of national and international events were all pushing me towards becoming a Communist. My subconscious then gave a hand in solving my problems and I became ill—not seriously so, but pale and listless enough for my parents to insist on calling in our doctor. He could find nothing to account for my symptoms and sent me to the medical specialist in Inverness. He was a good doctor and a wise man. I had been feeling that if only I were physically fit I could deal with my emotional problems. The concept of psychosomatic illness was new to me, but he made me realise that I'd have to deal with it the other way round.

Neil's readers may recognise here the germ of *The Shadow*, whose heroine Nan suffers a similar illness and comes from the Left world of wartime London to be healed at a slightly veiled version of Braefarm under the wise and loving care of 'Aunt Phemie'. When she read that novel Margaret failed to make the identification and was puzzled when Neil wrote:

Even you were amused at *The Shadow*. Tut! tut! But I'll try to bear up . . . And anyhow, praise be that you could see I wasn't thinking about yourself, even if it took an intermittent, psychosomatic syndrome to prove it! No, Margaret, hand on my heart, you never came into my head. Odd thing about some of these characters that appear before you as you are writing is that they have a life of their own and to such an extent that if you made them say the wrong thing you would know you were falsifying. A good job, too, when one is dealing with a small watchful Highland community!

'I think', said Margaret, 'that what I probably suggested was that apart from Nan being a member of the Communist Party she tells Ranald near the beginning that she is so angry because she can't remember the statistics but she remembers the *gleam*.' Margaret had said some such thing to Neil in argument. 'We argued a lot about politics and life in general in the early years—sometimes seriously, sometimes both of us with our tongues in our cheeks. I always knew my mind wasn't in the same class as his. But though we argued a lot, we never quarrelled, and I think we recognised in each other a common concern for our fellows.' Years later when Margaret had left the Party Neil asked if she was still a Communist, and when he heard she was not, said he was glad, for otherwise they could not go on. But to return to Margaret's account of her early illness:

> I decided to try and break the vicious circle and go to London and take an unpaid job on the *Daily Worker*. I discussed this with Neil, and he encouraged me to go, putting me in touch with Douglas Muhr, who was then working there, and whom I had once met at Larachan but hardly knew.

> Neil to Margaret, October 1938:
> Not too easy for you, adventuring alone into a new life. Indeed, when we saw you off at Glasgow, the vision of you setting out alone had something rather heroic about it which stuck in my mind for quite a time. My blessings went with you. And I was glad to think that you enjoyed your last few days in Glasgow—and even to learn that you were a trifle sad parting from your 'bourgeois national' friends . . . I like your remark about the perfect antidote to depression and defeatism and the lack of time to cry over spilt milk. Good for you and the *Daily Worker*! When I feel more than usual that I need reinvigorating, I'll know where to come. You could show me round as a specimen and as a warning. Not that I shouldn't have a few things to say for myself, I warn you. And clever as you may become in dialetectics [sic], I should still contrive to throw a few mental arabesques here and there . . . Whiles when I am having my solitary walk away up through the fields, I have a few words with you.

Margaret returned from London to Kessock when the war started in 1939, stayed until her father's death, worked in a war plant in Glasgow until the war ended, then spent eighteen months at Kessock before moving south to Kent in 1947 for four years. After a year in Fife she settled in Edinburgh. 'When I was away from home, Neil used to visit me two or three times a

year, sometimes more often, sometimes less. In the years I was at Kessock
and he was at Brae, I bicycled over fairly often. When I was working in the
south I would come home for holidays. When I was in London, Glasgow or
Edinburgh, Neil liked to make out that he was just a simple country chap
and I was a sophisticated woman of the world and would have to show him
round and keep him right. This was largely a game but all the same he was
not at home in the city and, especially as he grew older, hated noise and
bustle.'

As we re-read *Wild Geese Overhead*, the novel Neil wrote at the time of
Margaret's move to the city, we see his apprehensiveness. The hero-writer,
himself a fugitive from the city, must protect Jenny Baird from the city's
sexual temptations. This anxiety may seem curious unless we recall that
Neil found 'an intrinsic innocence in our relationship, which might be
damaged by knowing looks or snide remarks which could arise if certain
people knew of our relationship'.

Meetings in Glasgow were not easy to arrange. Neil did, however, have
reasons to travel south frequently. At the start of the 1940s he was serving
on a government commission and by the time its work was finished Bridie
had returned to Glasgow and was working to establish the Citizens Theatre.
Occasionally there was a meeting in Glasgow to attend; sometimes Neil
could include a Glasgow visit when in Edinburgh; sometimes he travelled
down when visiting the Macleods in Gleneagles near Perth. His letters often
involve arrangements but always cautiously, and he describes his movements in terms of 'we' and 'us' as if Daisy would be with him.

Neil to Margaret, 5 February 1942:
Your last interesting letter made me smile but not at all cynically. I never did
smile cynically at anything, as you ought to know. Cynicism is usually an
inverted romanticism, and I like my romanticism straight myself. And a smile
straight forbye. So here's me to you, all to yourself . . .

I've never met anything so fair as an Individual at any time, and being a realist
I admit it. And some Individuals are pretty good. And some better than
others. And one now and again—mentioning no names—is more than pretty
good. No? Go away with you! . . .

I'm just back from Edinburgh. But you wouldn't have noticed by the press
that I'm on a Committee of Inquiry? So I'm going to be busy this year rushing
up and down to Edinburgh. Had the meetings been in Glasgow now! . . .

Neil to Margaret, 12 September [1942?]:
I'm off to Edinburgh again on Wed. 16th, arriving that night some time
before 11 p.m. I'll be there for 17th and 18th, staying with friends not far

from your mother's address. If there was any chance of your coming through for either of these nights, I could arrange to see you in the evening. . . . I should enjoy a talk with you about your Parliament work, and we read with the greatest interest your press interview in *Glasgow Herald* about your trip south. Good old Margaret! said I. You're doing grand. I really was pleased, for you have a sound head on you—and a kind heart—and maybe a nature that can hardly be spoiled. And you must admit I'm not good at compliments at the best of times. So you can believe their understatement when they come.

Neil to Margaret, 16 March (postmark 1943):
I had thought you had quite forgotten us. So it's good to know you are still watching the daffodils grow. Keep on watching them, though all the heavens come down in small bits. It's the only real affirmation we can make. The rest is mostly theory. If I were being shot out of hand, I should like to think I'd have the grace to feel none the worse if I knew you were so to speak smiling at something no bigger than a primrose. Which sounds involved, with a smile lost in it somewhere.

Neil to Margaret (postmark September 1944):
Meantime good for you and *The Green Isle*! I'm afraid I didn't think you'd care much for it. . . . You do know what underlies a system or faith, what is needed to humanise a rigid concept. So few do. And the rigid ones are a throttling menace. Out of the goodness of your heart (if nothing else) you call it a great book . . . And all politics apart, how delightful that you like fantasy anyhow! Enough to cheer any old heart. At least it cheers this one!

Neil to Margaret (postmark 21 November 1944):
Sorry I did not manage round the following night. Had lunch with Bridie's party and Bridie asked me to listen to him giving a talk at 7.30 to a literary crowd. I thought that would soon be over and went. It turned out, however, to be a discussion. I got launched into it, and it was about 11 p.m. before anyone moved. I didn't get back to my hotel till about 3 a.m. . . .

One virtue in that literary discussion I've mentioned—it may draw me back to continue it after some weeks.

Now look after yourself and no nonsense—or I'll give you a real row next time. Cheers for yourself.

Neil

These were happier years from 1938 to 1947—'the most important', Margaret calls them. 'Before that I was a worry and a responsibility. He was fond of me and always kind and tender, but I did make a nuisance of myself. In the following years I felt he did love me, though he never said so. I hope I have not failed to convey the essential quality of our relationship. He was nearly always happy and gay, often playful—never boisterously so, more often a chuckle and a smile than loud laughter. He was very responsive to my mood and I was always so happy to see him that we were happy together.'

But 1934 to 1938 were the 'dark years' for them both. Neil was troubled about his marriage, troubled by the certainty he would have no children, by guilt, by this new and importunate responsibility, by the growing frustration of politics—troubled enough about his direction as a novelist to start no new novel for over two years. He had ample reason to tire of the pressures and consider a big move.

Perhaps by the time Daisy describes in the following letter he had already decided. On 7 September 1936 Daisy wrote to her good friend 'Floss' McNeill to invite her to stay at Larachan for the upcoming Mod: 'We had a most glorious holiday all July. We stayed in a little cottage 15 miles from Dunbeath and 8 miles from any habitation. The river Berriedale ran in front of our cottage and the deer came and fed at our door. After that we went to Strathmore to another little cottage in the wilds and had a fishing on the Thurso. Maurice Walsh and his wife were with us. The fishing was great and we were all terribly happy.'[9]

It has all the sound of a new beginning, a reconciliation, with the oldest married friends on hand, and the pressures far away. Who can say that it did not last and grow into the deep and quiet affection of the later years? Who can say that the happy intimacy with Margaret was not an essential condition of that growth?

The Mod and 'Floss's' visit came in late September, and George Blake was on hand too. He left Neil hurriedly in Inverness on the Thursday night at the news that his son was seriously ill and wrote the next day that the boy was recovering. His note pictures a Larachan that was happy: 'The kindness and friendship of your house are now in the weave of our life. Other things come and go; these things—kindness and friendship—rest.'[10] Blake was now back by his beloved Clyde. And there, by his convalescent son's bedside in early November 1936, he had an ample reward. He read the typescript of *Highland River*.

'The Government', he wrote on the 5th, 'has rejected the Forth Road Bridge scheme . . . never mind. No government can touch the validity of *Highland River*.'

As you know, I have lately been sensitised to considerations of the kind, but this, my dear lad, is a great book—and I use my words with deliberation. I call it great in beauty, in scope, in execution, and in its adumbration of a philosophy. You seem to me to speak for all Scotsmen of our generation—and for a great lot of men of every sort. To say that it is your own best is trivial and irrelevant. Quite coldly—though with a special, personal warmth—I assert this to be the biggest Scottish book of my time and a big one in any time.

Now, I can look on it with two sorts of eyes, as you know, and even with the warier sort I can discern its great possibilities of popular (in the best sense) success. It is lucid. Even your most subtle considerations emerge directly from narration of the most attractive sort. . . . My dear Neil, I do lift my hat and slip back to the roadside.[11]

A generous, shrewd spirit had spoken. Now a new commitment could be made.

It had been slow in coming. Following *Butcher's Broom* in the autumn of 1934 another sort of possibility had presented itself. J. Leslie Mitchell had recently completed the third part of his great trilogy *A Scots Quair*. With characteristic energy he had agreed to inaugurate Routledge & Kegan Paul's new Scottish section by compiling and editing 'a series of ten books by ten of the more noteworthy Scottish writers'. He wrote to Neil on 22 October that he had already listed him as author of 'What Whisky Has Meant for Scotland'. Could Neil find the time and inclination to write it? It could be 'in any fashion you consider fit', should be between 35,000 and 40,000 words, and should be delivered by the end of June 1935. Other authors would include Grieve, Mackenzie, both Muirs, Linklater, and Power.[12]

Neil might have felt puzzled. Mitchell was now collaborating with Grieve, and in their joint venture of 1934, *Scottish Scene*, Mitchell had said that Neil was 'the greatest loss to itself Scottish literature has suffered in this century' and was 'merely a brilliantly eccentric Englishman'. Perhaps Neil had not yet seen the words. At any rate, he answered cautiously. 'Before contemplating this Whisky book, I'd better ask about it. In the first place I'm not really a literary person, and know nothing about long essay writing. My knowledge of whisky is severely if copiously practical. One can hardly flog Scots industrialisation, Calvinism and Burns for 40,000 words! I couldn't anyway. Meanwhile I'll think on't. I'm promising nothing—and I hate work.' He sent Mitchell a copy of *Butcher's Broom*.

On 30 October Mitchell wrote: 'I love your coolness and clarity, your charity, and your exquisite English. (All qualities I don't possess myself.) *Butcher's Broom* is Greek and heroic and dreadful in the original meaning of dreadful. But after I finished the book last night I went a walk and thought about it and forgot aesthetic appreciation and was merely filled with anger and pity for those people of yours—detachment in these matters is impossible for me, I'm too close to those folk myself. Great book. I'll send you a copy of *Grey Granite* shortly—it's due out in a week or so.' As for Neil's doubts (this is three days later): ' "Why shouldn't whisky be talked of as a

Frenchman would talk of wine?" Exactly. Why not? Do. Talk of it in any way you please. I've an idea you think of this whisky book being designed by me as propaganda against cant and Calvin. Not a bit! Nonsense to say you're not a "literary person". You write the best English in Scotland; plus that (I'm told from some who heard you at Edinburgh in June) you know everything about whisky and can tell it charmingly. So *do*.'[13]

Neil did. The book let Neil collect his long experience of whisky, its making, its economics, and take a philosophical look at it. It also let him look philosophically at his years in nationalist politics and speak out eloquently for true nationalism at a time when it was under attack from many quarters as fascist or anti-progressive. It let him learn that he could write extensively in the 'essay' form and could work as an essay-journalist in the years ahead. In sum, it allowed him to think of himself more as a 'literary person' and thus to think practically of a full-time commitment.

In this kind of writing he could afford to be more whimsical about critics. When *Whisky and Scotland* came out in 1935, he phoned David MacEwen one day from the distillery and said: 'I have now received the reviews of *Whisky and Scotland*. Would you like to come over to Larachan and see them?' David met him there later. Lining the sitting room walls, fronting the bookcases, were cases of various malt whiskies. Gesturing with a sweep of his arm Neil announced: 'These are the best reviews I have ever had!' One suspects he would never change his mind.[14]

The Faber and Porpoise partners must have been worried. Suddenly here was a new kind of book. For the first time here was another publisher competing for Neil's affections. The future of Porpoise was in doubt. *Highland River* would be Neil's last Porpoise publication (Blake and Neil then agreed that Porpoise as a Faber agency was 'a fraud in the national sense', Blake took his books to Collins, and he almost took Neil's as well). And now (in 1935) Routledge was suggesting that Neil follow up *Whisky and Scotland* with a book about 'salmon and boys'.[15] The Faber partners needed to act.

The big guns arrived in Inverness in April 1935. Morley was there and possibly Blake, and T. S. Eliot (a Faber partner), and Alfred Harcourt of Harcourt Brace in America. Larachan entertained them well; years later Neil recalled the dinner:

> Once we had English and American guests for whom my wife thought she would make a typical meal: broth, roast mutton and a fruit tart—all home produce . . . If the broth was appreciated, the roast mutton drew from the American the comment, 'I have never tasted mutton like this before.' So it was

explained that this was what we call 'hill mutton'. The hill grasses and tender young heather, which deer and grouse know, had for a time been feeding ground for the sheep. Not that what I may call the 'game flavour' was very pronounced, but it was reminiscently there.[16]

One of the Americans sent back some snapshots, including a beauty of himself having just washed some socks, and his warm thanks to the cook: 'Incidentally, your salmon and your mutton, and of course the whisky, have given me standards which will make me permanently dissatisfied with any of those viands as provided in the South. But it is much more the spirit of hospitality that remains a valued memory. I hope that this pilgrimage may continue an annual event.' This was T. S. Eliot to Daisy Gunn, 7 May 1935.[17] Eliot remained an admirer of Daisy for the rest of her life, and a long night's talk led him to report that Neil had perhaps the finest analytic mind he had encountered.

But the visitors weren't there for fun. 'They were unhappy about some book I'd just published,' recalled Neil. 'They told me about a Yorkshire novelist who had just done a novel on his river at home, and suggested I do a book on my own river. They wanted another *Morning Tide*.'[18]

H. R. Jukes's *Loved River*, published by Faber in 1935, is less a novel than a pastoral in the mode of Belloc's *Four Men*. The narrator remakes his river in the image of the boyhood river he recalls: dam-building for fishing pools; making a small lake, a hatchery; 'improving' his river for delightful utility —all mixed in with tales of country neighbours, fishing exploits, and a gipsy camp. The key word is 'charm'. The narrator is an Edwardian Robinson Crusoe delighting in the matter-of-fact of nostalgia.

If this was something of a germ for *Highland River* it was scarcely needed. Neil would find his own way of exploring the elusive relation between 'ideal' and 'real', between past and present selves. His was not a river to be 'made' or 'owned'. It was a river to be rediscovered in a secret poaching foray against the authority of history and society. Morley wrote an encouraging letter in October 1935 and got the following reply:

About your River letter. I'm doing nothing now but politics. Haven't even time to think of a place called the literary world. I am also troubled a bit about your suggestion . . . This idea of yours had already occurred to me and I had thought of its flowering summat in this way: the poaching (salmon) experiences of three boys (one of 'em like Hugh in *Morning Tide*) on this river. Now, out of the memorable moments in their lives, I should like to create a philosophy (appalling word) of sorts. Probably I am getting to that sterile stage where I want to 'say' something. It wouldn't be a novel. It would be

comparatively short. And it would be appallingly difficult to do . . . So we'll
let it slide meantime. But I have the title: *Highland River*. And if ever I did it,
I'd like to do it for you. I suppose it's the old clan loyalty that makes me feel
unhappy away from you.[19]

Eight months later he was still struggling. So he took Daisy off to Caithness
for a month and by October 1936 the book was written.

The actual quest for the river source had a valuable guide. Neil's youngest
brother Alec was asked to come along

to their outpost 14 miles in the heart of our highest hills where the trail ran out
and stopped. At the end of the trail was a well-designed stone built house . . .
used by the Duke of Portland's shooting guests, or as a shooters' shelter in
stormy weather. There, Daisy, Neil, and I arrived in the late evening, and,
after a night-cap, retired, they to their car on the green 10 yards from the door,
and I to the bedroom.
    In the morning the little burn 50 yds from the house was a raging torrent,
the result of a night's incessant rain. 'Should make good fishing when it falls a
bit,' said Neil. I agreed and spent the rest of the day getting our fishing tackle
ready. After breakfast next morning we went down to the first pool, and
scarcely had Neil begun fishing when he hooked and landed a lovely ¾ lb brown
trout. 'Fresh trout for lunch,' he called us excitedly as he hooked another.
    Down at the next pool I tied a salmon fly, and within minutes was well into
a salmon. A wild shout brought Neil at the double. 'Easy with him, boy, easy!
We may not get another chance! The gaff is in the car, so when he is ready, run
him onto the shingle by that sloping stone and I'll take him into my hands.'
The fish tired quickly and I brought him to the landing site where Neil, jacket
off and shirt sleeves rolled up, was in the water, and as his hands closed on the
fish there was a tremendous upheaval. Neil's body lost its equilibrium on the
sloping stone. First his head, then his shoulders, and finally all that remained
of him took to the water. A terrific fight went on below the surface. Then, like
Neptune himself, Neil surfaced, struggled to his knees, then to his feet, water
pouring from every inch of him, and in his arms a beautiful 8 lb salmon. 'Let's
retire and celebrate our first kill,' he said.
    In ten minutes we had a temporary clothes line erected between the house
and the stables. Neil's shirt, underwear, socks, and trousers told their story to
the silent hills.[20]

In such a moment with Alec, Neil the man became one with Neil the boy,
and out of that delightful identification *Highland River* grew. He found the
magic and mystery of coincidence in fishing and saw in it a paradigm of fine
art. To be sure, he wrote later, 'No novelist dare use the kind of coincidences
that happen in real life . . . Great art has joy at its core. Though he may not
proceed at a swallow's pace, he can appreciate the flawless art of that master
sportsman casting perfect arabesques along the air streams.'[21] Neil would

have many good fishing companions after Maurice Walsh. And such companions were ready to vouch for Neil's expertise. But we should recall the judgement of one who fished with Neil and Alec together in later years. Said Neil Paterson: 'Neil was a good fisherman. Alec was a great one.'[22]

On the same occasion, Alec guided Neil to the source of the river.

> The following morning, Neil and I set out to find the source of the river. My bearings from the mountain top proved very accurate, for on rounding the shoulder of a hill, below us was a loch surrounded by sparkling white sand. The suddenness of its appearance and the unexpected white sands held us spell bound for a few seconds: 'a jewel in a brown casket'. Recovering, we did a detour of its banks but found no outlet. Approximately 60 yards below where we thought the outlet should be, water bubbled from a hole 2 feet in diameter. Into the hole Neil thrust his walking-stick, full six feet of it, but found no bottom. 'No doubt about it, that is the visible source,' said Neil. 'But where is the true source? Is it the loch or is some underground current carrying water to the loch?'
>
> Speculate! But at least we were at the visible source.

But when Neil wrote his own reminiscences of the time (in 'Over the Ord of Caithness' and 'Picts' Houses'), he made no reference to Alec. And when the experience had grown by devious imaginative loops into *Highland River*, the brotherly companion had become John.

Dear John [the book's dedication opens]

> This can hardly be the description of our Highland river that you anticipated when, lying on our backs in a green strath, we idly talked the idea over. . . . You will early recognise that though there is no individual biography here, every incident may have had its double. Some of the characters seem to have strayed in from *Morning Tide* under different names. I cannot explain this odd behaviour—apart from the old desire to be in on the hunt in any disguise. However, if only I could get you to see the hunt as a poaching expedition to the source of delight we got from a northern river, I feel that you might not be altogether disappointed should you come back (as we have so often done in our time) with an empty bag.[23]

When towards the end of his life Neil wrote notes for a filmed interview with George Bruce, he had Bruce ask: 'I suppose the boy's battle with a fish as long as himself in the opening pages is really by way of introduction to your strath. It did really happen?' And Neil answered: 'Wherever you find something incredible in a book of mine, you may take it that it did happen. It's too easy to imagine the miraculous. At the same time, I could borrow an incident from my brother just as I could borrow his knife.' Then he added significantly, 'And the presence of authority made the delight all the keener.'[24]

He wanted to clarify the book's view of authority. It was 'the parents' ambiguous attitude' that concerned him. They are frightened for the boy, 'yet they don't have any real moral disapproval of what he's done. Why? Because deep in them there is the knowledge that once upon a time the land and the rivers were the common heritage of the clan . . . But the chief grew dissatisfied with that state of affairs and wanted the whole land, game and all, for himself . . . The supreme poacher was the chief.'

The book was to be a 'poaching expedition' of the mind. Poaching becomes a deep but uneasy and unspoken bond between parent and child. Poaching is the ritual transfer of manhood from brother to brother, from archaic origins to contemporary life. That continuity is cruelly violated when an older brother 'Angus' (Ben Gunn) pales, emigrates, and finally dies in the trenches. Can the secret and anarchic delights of poaching provide a mythic antidote to the terrible ego forces of modern violence? The answer must depend on the powers of vision and understanding that are joined and unleashed in the adventure. More than a fusing of John's and Neil's boyhoods, the book seeks a fusion of the scientist John and the artist Neil and seeks in that fusion a new and healing wholeness of being.

This is too solemn a way of speaking about it. The book has more immediate biographical interest. It is a delightful secret adventure with his brother. It is a sly trick: we are taunted with not knowing what is Neil and what is John. He is hiding even as he reveals himself. The boy's secrecy in *Morning Tide* has become a delight in secrecy that pervades *Highland River*:

> This [curious personal] secretiveness is often full of the slyest laughter. It is laughter out of the corner of the mouth, the corner of the eye, at all that which solemnly in its social toils would deny it. It is the suppressed laughter of a superb, secret joke.[25]

The pleasure of secrecy was at having slipped the 'social toils', evaded society's authority. In Neil's imagination had been born the delightful thought of being a fugitive. The book had grown out of his experiences in the mid-1930s and its direction would guide him away from, in defiance of, much he had been in Inverness.

Apparently he had got away with it. Blake was delighted, and Morley commended him (16 November 1936) for 'such a deep and noble book with so little surface pother'. Even Bridie, who had felt uncomfortable with everything since *Morning Tide*, wrote (22 February 1938), 'Your last book pleased me. It has some of your best work in it and I think you have hit a medium between your subtle, snake-pattern perceptions and those of ordinary mutton-headed Southerners like me. Your next will be Just Right.'[26] It appeared in June 1937. The *TLS* said 'The book must be read as one would listen to music. . . . Mr Gunn's technique has steadily improved, and these scenes . . . are projected with a crystal clarity, sharply defined, with an odd double quality of intense immediacy and a sort of enclosed detachment, like objects seen in a slightly diminishing mirror.' The *Glasgow Herald* did a searching analysis of Neil's personality in the book, and the *Scots Magazine* published a long essay by Neil's German friend and translator Fritz Wölcken that is one of the best articles on his early work. But some critics had reservations, and these made Neil angry.[27]

Grieve had expressed some. In a long and heated reply (perhaps never finished and mailed) Neil lumped Grieve's with those of Day Lewis, Sean O'Faolain, and Muir. The letter is a full and vigorous self-defence and it reveals the confidence Neil now felt:

> Sean O'Faolain, in his critique, says that when he started *Highland River*, he thought it was going to be a 'masterpiece', but then it got lost (I forget his words) in the bog of Celtic Mysticism. Day Lewis runs much on the same line, except that he takes exception also to the preachings and moralisings of Lowland writers (thereby making sure that Scots frae a' the airts get it in the neck). . . .
>
> Take this Celtic mysticism of yours (and the critics). You all detest it. . . . Anyway, take it that such intelligence as I possess has tested the hull of this curious bark with a knife-point fore and aft, and that O'Faolain's shake of the head was not unforeseen nor my own attitude altered thereby . . . pick out any paragraph in *Highland River* and discover for me in it this 'vagueness' of 'Celtic mysticism'. I know it cannot be done. Because any paragraph there I can analyse to elements real to the psyche and designed by me for some artistic or other purpose—precisely as you design your poems. . . . Again, Edwin Muir quoted me to show that I was merely elusive . . . But then I cannot help that. There are thoughts which are devilish elusive. And that elusiveness of the mind is a reality, and any writer with a mind has to do something with it or about it on paper . . .
>
> Now I may be wandering round the central point—and we'll wander a hell of a lot more yet!—of this 'mysticism'. You have got to the point, I fancy, where you are instinctively antipathetic. But that won't do. For mysticism generally has a terrific achievement behind it, both Eastern and Western (religious). However, we don't want vague terms and grandiloquent debate and such nonsense generally. All I am immediately concerned about is the attitude of mind to things (including experience) about it. I achieve, say, a certain relationship to grass and to stones and to folk that make my environ-

ment. This relationship, say, gives me pleasure—and gives me pain, that pleasure be established once more. There are an extraordinary number of psychic constituents. The mystic patterns them in such a fashion that the mind controls the matter, that, at the centre of the whirling constituents, he keeps control. This sort of mysticism is never an escape. It is on the contrary an extremely difficult and prolonged fight to get hold of the whole mortal circumstance and order and dominate it . . . take Yeats in his last book, *The Vision*. Now Yeats deals with all the stuff of 'communications' from 'the other side' (his own experience), Eastern mysticism, and so on . . .[28]

Neil was now set to go his own way. There was much encouragement to do so. Sales of *Highland River* in the early weeks came to almost 4,000. The book would be reprinted frequently, and in the war years a paperback edition of 20,000 copies was all sold. In late April 1938 a letter from Edinburgh University informed him that the book had won the James Tait Black Memorial Prize for 1937, and a cheque for £186 followed in a few days. The recognition became embarrassing, for in September 1938 he had a modest request from Professor John Dover Wilson that he lecture in the English Department on any subject, and he had to beat his customary graceful retreat: 'Had you now been asking me to navigate some small untrustworthy craft into the Arctic, or any trifle of that sort, I should of course have saluted you at once and taken your orders. But a lecture—that requires a courage to which I may not lay claim, and so have resigned myself permanently to my limitations. I can but hope that you will understand.'[29]

Dover Wilson did. But he may have missed the point of the comparison. For by then Neil was also feeling a new confidence as a navigator. He had bought and sailed an old boat from Skye down the west coast and up the great glen and had then navigated his wife and himself all the way from the securities and tensions of fifteen years in Inverness to a rented farmhouse on the braes of Strathpeffer, west of Dingwall.

He had wanted to do something like this for a long time. Early in 1932 Blake was discussing with Faber and Harcourt Brace ways and means of guaranteeing Neil a small annual stipend so that he might leave his job and settle to full-time writing in a Hebridean manse. But then came unsuccessful books and such hopes were delayed. They were further delayed by the political and social involvements of Inverness. The need for a move became more urgent as his personal life grew more complicated. *Highland River* was the test. When Blake and Morley were so enthusiastic, the decision could be made. Markets for European translations were opening up. He had an assured outlet for journalism from Salmond.

His last version of the adventure was noted for George Bruce's final interview:

> I had a friend [Hugh Macrae] who lived next door to me for a while in Inverness. I had been thinking of buying a boat of about 30 feet, and as Hugh was a Skyeman I asked him just as he was leaving our house one night, if he knew of anything suitable in the west. 'Man,' he said, 'I know the very thing for you. She's 30 feet long, has a cabin you can dance in and a lavatory that cost 20 pounds.'
>
> The following morning [about 1 April] we left for Skye in Hugh's 6-cylinder car and as we crossed the watershed and beheld the west, the old familiar feeling came over me, but now with an extra force; for I had lately been dreaming of throwing up my Civil Service job, pension and all, and taking a chance on the wide, wide world. I had mentioned it to my wife, but she hadn't helped me any, for when I asked her point blank if she could run a house on 3 pounds a week she cheerfully answered 'Yes.' At the Kyle ferry Hugh wanted to see a man, and presently after the ferry boat had come and gone a few times, we drank a toast. And so one of the most interesting and intricate days of my life began.[30]

No wonder he had forgotten that Morley, Blake, and 'Uncle Tom' Eliot were expected at Larachan the following afternoon. But he made it back in time. Blake, Morley, and Eliot seemed to know what they had come for—to support the decision. After a 'pleasant and amusing excursion all round', a picnic, and talk of the planned cruise, they promised suitable gifts for the boat. Blake promised and sent Brown's *Nautical Almanac* with information about tides, lights, buoys, and beacons. Morley mentioned a small cannon for the bow with which to pop off German submarines—war seemed close enough to occasion nervous jokes. 'But T. S. Eliot, being a poet, promised a keg of rum.' The keg never came, though it turned up mysteriously seventeen years later in Neil's last novel.[31] But Eliot wrote 'Dear Daisy' a gracious note of thanks on 9 April for 'the most delightful visit to the Highlands that I have yet had. I am so glad that there was the caravan for us to sleep in—I should not have enjoyed my visit half so much if we had had to go to the Hotel.' He said nothing of how much sleep he got or did not get while sharing a small caravan with a large Morley. But it is clear the move had been settled on, for he closed: 'Whether we meet next in the Hebrides or in your wooden house—barring your visit to London, which I hope you will not cancel—here are my thanks and blessing.'[32]

Then 'a man came out of the blue and asked me if I was selling my house.' At the end of May J. A. MacIver offered to buy Larachan for £950 with entry by the end of September.[33] And on 5 June Neil's supervisor received with fatherly consternation Neil's resignation as of the 24th. Its rhetoric is entertaining:

> In recent years I have felt called upon to pursue certain literary work which has resulted in books that have been publicly discussed as of some small value to the literary traditions of my country, and I feel that as this new work [!] might interfere, without my always perceiving it [!], with the proper prosecution of my official duties, the only honourable course open to me is to resign. This decision has been made the more imperative through eye-trouble which has gradually but cumulatively affected my sight.
>
> In these circumstances, and in view of my record of service in this Department of over twenty-five years, I should be glad to know if your Honours could possibly contemplate the grant of a pension, howsoever small. Literary work, when not of a popular or commercial kind, can be uncertain of issue and unremunerative in result, and though I am prepared to take this risk, I would yet ask your Honours to consider my case as a special one based on a long period of faithful service.
>
> I am, Honourable Sirs, your obedient servant,
N. M. Gunn[34]

The skilful rhetoric failed. And 'after these two days' action, our only abode was a boat in doubtful condition, and . . . if we had lost all visible means of support we had at least gained a little control of time.' By the start of July they were off. The officer was once more unattached. The fugitive was at large.

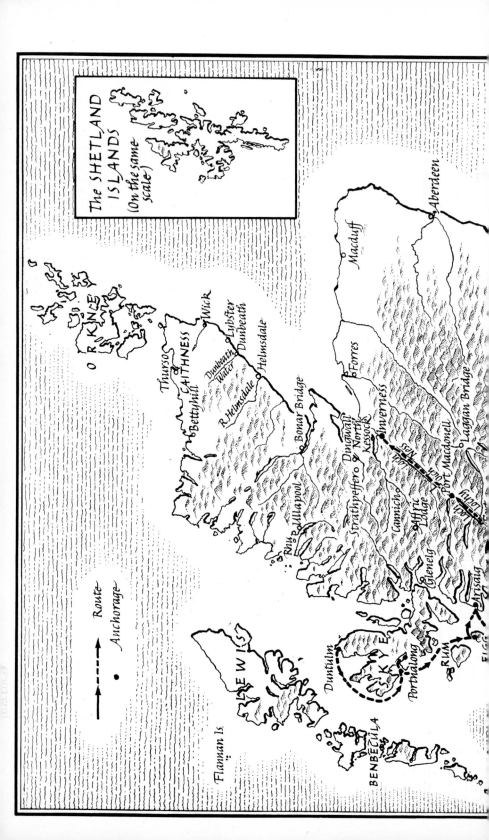

The SHETLAND
ISLANDS
(On the same
scale)

ORKNEY

Thurso
CAITHNESS
Bettyhill
Wick
Dunbeath Water
Lybster
Dunbeath
Helmsdale
R. Helmsdale

Macduff
Aberdeen

Forres

Bonar Bridge

Inverness

Strathpeffer & North Kessock
Dingwall

Port Macdonell
Laggan Bridge

R. Ullapool

Cannich
Affric Lodge
Glenelg

Arisaig

LEWIS

Duntulm

Porthalong

RUM

Flannan Is.

BENBECULA

Route
Anchorage

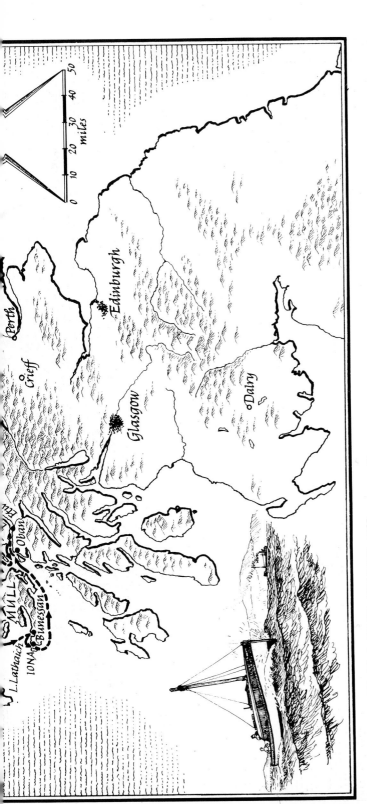

OFF IN A BOAT: SUMMER 1937

Thistle bought at Duntulm, Skye; visit to J. M. Reid and wife on Eigg; at Arisaig picked up Maurice Walsh and wife, who left boat at Tobermory (taking steamer to Oban); John Gunn ('the Mate') came aboard and stayed for anchorages in Loch Lathaich and the Bull Hole on the Ross of Mull, and for the trip to Iona; at Oban, John left Neil and Daisy to navigate Loch Etive by themselves; explored, and then sailed up Loch Linnhe. John rejoined at Kentallen; helped through intricate locks by fishing boats *Invernairne* and *The Gleaners*; anchored at Loch Lochy, Port Macdonell on Loch Oich, and, finally, Inverness.

PART THREE

BRAEFARM: THE WRITER AS PROFESSIONAL

(1937–1949)

10 Off in a Boat

The boat 'in doubtful condition' was the *Thistle*, twenty-seven feet from stem to stern, and seven in beam, built entirely of teak and pitchpine, except for the transom of the square stern, which was oak. A double teak door opened into the cabin; the engine sat on the threshold. Forward against the forecastle was an expensive lavatory with chain locker to port and washbasin to starboard. Under the two skylights 'a simple wooden seat ran down each side of the cabin full-length, about fourteen feet, and the beds were two simple cots, opposite each other as one entered, that folded back against her unlined walls'.[1]

The engine was a poppet-valve Kelvin of uncertain age with a thrawn nature and subject to crotchety fits and tantrums. The emergency sails were a form of insurance against final breakdown.

Maurice Walsh and his wife Toshon, on a roundabout way home to Ireland from a visit to Forres, joined the cruise from Arisaig to Oban, and Maurice sums up the situation in a review of *Off in a Boat* contributed to the *Irish Times* (30 May 1938). Neil, he says, 'started the cruise at a loose end and finished at a looser. His yellow-haired wife was his crew, and she had the courage of a lion or despair; for she had to trust herself to him, body and soul and bones, and she knew that his ideas about navigation were original, and that a man who has those sort of ideas on that very practical subject usually survives just long enough to put the first one into practice. A sea-knowledgeable and daring brother turned up for mate on occasion, and saved one or two difficult situations.'

Certainly the skipper was inexperienced and the crew unskilled but 'what she does not know about internal combustion engines, she makes up on her salads'.

Several people have told us that Daisy's courage was greater than Neil gave her credit for in *Off in a Boat*. According to these witnesses she was intensely frightened all the time they were at sea. 'She said she concealed her fears from Neil because he was so keen to go and she didn't want to be a spoil-sport.' Brother John had already taken his place as the third member of the trio, and there's little doubt that they sorely needed the mate.

There were physical danger, strain, exhilaration, cold hands, wet clothes, a return to the experience of weather in all its vagaries, of the beauty that hides threat, and a series of visions of the west in shifts of light and shade, when mountains become clouds and clouds mountains.

Maurice's account of the trip from Arisaig to Tobermory can be compared with Neil's. Maurice first:

> The two of them, skipper and crew, lured myself and my wife aboard for a week-end from Moidart across Arisaig Sound and round Ardnamurchan to Mull; but that wonderful panorama of mountain islands and mountain land was lost on me, whose eyes could not keep away from the great swells of the sea and the fins of the basking sharks. Coming in to Tobermory harbour I jumped without effort the last twenty-five feet to the shore.[2]

Now Neil:

> The Walshes had to be in Oban in two days, if they were to occupy their berths in the Glasgow-Dublin boat. It looked an impossible job for the *Thistle*, with the wind blowing, as we returned from Mallaig, and we gave up all hope of it. But in the morning there was a calm under heavy skies and I went ashore, roused them out of bed, and got them aboard . . .
>
> This was more like the thing! The previous evening Maurice and I had got the six split-pins and the two holding-down bolts where they should be. I swung the flywheel and off went all fourteen horses to a splendid start . . .
>
> We were gazing all eyes, the engine forgotten, when it missed a beat or two and was obviously going to peter out, but I dived quickly and opened the throttle, which staggered her a bit, until she resumed her beat again. A long black thunder cloud lay out from Eigg. It was any sort of weather next, with the glass perceptibly falling. Southerly wind came freshening the water. Slowly that weather-worn headland with its dark-grey twisted strata fell astern. We could see no bird-life, except for an occasional gull floating like wind-blown thistledown against its immense southern wall. The scene at the height of a winter storm, passing into the dark of night, must be about as near to an inferno as the mind of man can conceive . . .

One other snapshot of the voyage itself:

> The climax came when we ourselves, though making at least seven knots, were actually pooped. I then deserted the engine and with a small fender in one hand and an open clasp-knife in the other, kept my eye on the dinghy ready to cut the painter the moment she filled . . .
>
> I was now facing back on our course and, my eye lifting to the sky, was suddenly dismayed at the sight of clouds massing in darkness beyond the Torridon Rocks, that deep-blue darkness of a thunder-storm . . . Such a storm on top of the seas that were running—better perhaps to cut the painter at once and so get the extra speed to make the head and whatever grace of shelter might be beyond . . .

We rounded Ardalanish Point before the black edge of the storm touched us, and when it passed, we were heading for the Firth of Lorn with the dinghy still in tow and with the wind slackening behind. As if conscious of the blade that so recently had hesitated under the rope, that small craft began to modify her yawing tactics in a shamefaced way, and I got up from my wet, cramped position and had a look round the old engine, which was slogging away in fine form . . .

When I came out, the Mate regarded me challengingly. 'I'd like', he said, 'to try a little bit of sail.' . . .

On hands and knees he got round the mast, took his time, and presently up went the triangle of sail. He drew the lacing taut, and back in the cockpit, pulled with exaggerated effort on the sheet, so that all and sundry might observe this eighth wonder of the world. He turned, nodding humorously, delighted with himself. 'It can snow now,' he said.[3]

That ploy of *Off in a Boat* was intended as a voyage of three weeks, but stretched itself out from a fine June—down the Sound of Sleat to Eigg, by Arisaig and round the Ardnamurchan, to Iona, into Oban, up Loch Linnhe and back to the head of the Caledonian Canal—to a time when 'the corn was turning to gold and the rowan berries were red'.

The trip was for its own sake, but it proved useful to the writer. The sea brought Neil's father strongly back to his mind, and he felt deeply that the demise of the family-boat system of fishing had destroyed 'an ancient way of life with many fine qualities'. The thought was one of those which led to research on the history of Scottish fisheries and eventually to *The Silver Darlings*. But these concerns had been with Neil since long before *Off in a Boat*. Another subject is not in this category. It is dealt with in a passage which seems peripheral to the voyage and yet central to the whole book, as if throughout that period he was pondering the charge that not only the expedition but his future life as a writer were 'mere escapism'.

Have we, in this sense, grown afraid to escape, become dominated by the idea of a social duty that must keep our noses to the human grindstone . . . or has a time come when it may be the better part of courage to withdraw sufficiently far from it to observe with some sense of proportion exactly what is taking place?

Not to mention the purely personal point of view that one has only one life and that, before shuffling off, a little peace may be necessary in which to exercise one's mental attributes and try to get some glimmering of what all the madness is about, or even what is due to oneself, despite all the man-made duties in the world?

For at least nothing seems more certain finally than the loneliness of one's own self which no mass hysteria, or political creed, or religious faith, can save from the last lonely departure which is death.

This defensiveness may seem strange to us now, but in the political atmosphere of the late 1930s, with the clouds of war gathering thickly over Europe (a typical metaphor of the time), the charge of 'escapism' made every literary judge reach for the black cap.

Neil writes in an article of January 1941:

> So drawn together are we in fatality that when the individual breaks free from the concerns of the mass, even for a moment, he is affected by something like a sense of guilt. [And in another of June 1940:] There is much hysterical folly written these days around the word 'escape' and 'escapism'. Indeed there are persons who think it wrong to live outside a vague welter of sensational fear, as if to do so were in some way a betrayal.[4]

His defence in *Off in a Boat* is indirect because he edged away from any claim to a vocation for writing. Sometimes he said he should have been a physicist, at other times a gambler. He was essentially a writer, nevertheless, who could not fulfil himself until he gave his mind to the adventure of exploring in words and legend the meaning and significance of his experience. He wrote in *Off in a Boat*: 'Those who have goodness in them are aware of life in the same way as they are aware of light. Truly, life itself is an inner light.' That is not only an antidote to the contemplation of 'the last lonely departure which is death', but is the theme of his writing life.

In a 1940 essay 'On Looking at Things' he begins with escapism and ends:

> The mind can now almost in any situation achieve a certain detachment. It has fallen into the habit of seeing things with clear eyes . . . with this detachment comes a singular feeling of confidence, of pleasure, and, too, of perpetual wonder. With this as background, one can face up to the desperations of the world with some measure of steadiness and assurance, and, perhaps with that quite solitary sense of humour that is primordial and good.[5]

This is a long step from the occasional unease of *Off in a Boat*. After all, who made the charge of escapism? Neil himself. The voyage may have had something to do with the change.

A careful journal of the cruise was kept, Daisy did her research on some of the islands, and prepared her photographs, and by spring 1938 the publishing qualms and controversies were settled and the book was out. (Angry references to a landlord who appropriated their oars and left a rude note raised such fears of libel that a passage had to be toned down before publication.[6])

11 The Householder

They were back to vacate Larachan in September 1938, and rented a farmhouse where they stayed for twelve years. Braefarm House was the only place except Dalcraig which they left involuntarily, and there Neil did a profusion and variety of writing: short stories, plays, essays, articles, reviews, and eleven of his twenty novels, from *Wild Geese Overhead* (1939) to *The Lost Chart* (1949).

However much he may have preferred to see writing as casual, mysterious, private, intuitive and inconsequential, like whistling a tune while walking the hills in sunshine, Neil was now a professional writer by deliberate choice, dependent for a living not merely upon his creative energy but upon satisfying publisher and public. After the difficulties of *The Lost Glen* and *Sun Circle* he knew what the choice involved.

The storyteller in the Gaelic tradition is anonymous in the sense of being the mouthpiece for a tale already known. A novelist in the late 1930s was an identifiable personality, to be found signing books in Harrods or giving a talk on the radio. From the self-exploitation part of the business Neil recoiled, as from something alien and demeaning.

An example of this withdrawal from personal exposure and public scrutiny is to be found in the convention he adopts in *Off in a Boat* of describing Daisy as 'the Crew' and brother John as 'the Mate'. A forthright Lowland Scots girl, a physiotherapist at Gleneagles when it was a Miners' Rehabilitation Centre during the war, described a visit there by Neil in the company of Dr Peter John Macleod: 'They were actors,' she said. 'Typical Highlanders.'[1]

That would be her reaction, and the reaction of those like her, to the by-play in *Off in a Boat*, to Neil's avoidance of personal definition and directness, to his habitual gallantry to ladies, to the subtleties of *The Atom of Delight*, and to the stylistic arabesques and mazes of the novels.

His friends put it differently. Keith Henderson said that Neil was 'sensitive' and 'shy', but added, 'he was always merry. All our arguments ended in laughter. He laughed a lot.'[2] Robin MacEwen says 'He was a very private and shy person', but talks of his 'friendliness, his good cheer'.[3] A private man with real warmth deployed as courtesy can appear as 'an actor' to a downright, Lowland Scot with her own problems, brought up to see Highlanders as 'silver of tongue and black of heart'.

The 'acting' aspect of the Highland approach is demonstrated in *The Lost Chart*, where there is a description of Dermot (very much the 'Neil' character) visiting his friends.

> 'Bless this house,' he said, 'in the name of the sun and moon.' He bowed to the ladies. 'I place my offering on the throne.' He laid what were obviously two bottles wrapped in brown paper on the model's throne. 'It contains a sup of the sun and a sup of the moon.' He turned to Joe. 'May the light dwell in you and in all you do.' He lifted his face. 'Amen.'[4]

This may be acting but its basis is genuine feeling. A drama, after all, is called a 'play'. It is the sort of high spirits which came from the goodness of Maurice Walsh's heart; it would be native to Peter John Macleod and brother John. Neil's behaviour became balanced and suitable to the company he was in. But such pliable detachment took time to grow into.

There is humour in his evasiveness, but there is deep sensitivity and a strong, wiry and intuitive pride. He felt himself to be emotionally vulnerable, and used adroitly all his tact, courtesy, subtlety and intellectual steel to prevent injury to the quick of life.

Neil would not have described his companions as 'the Crew' and 'the Mate' if he had not been able to see himself as 'the Skipper'. The role of 'Crew' would not have appealed to him. He preferred to be the centre of the circle, and was most at ease when conscious of admiration. There can be an admixture of vanity in pride, but pride is a deeper, more complicated matter, closely bound up in Neil with a sense that his own people had been subtly and terribly betrayed, the values of their community undermined and their history continually and meanly distorted. He did not wish to acknowledge that at some point they had been psychologically defeated. It is as if he asked himself, 'How can such a fine and valuable people come to have given up?' In his novels he was not just celebrating and exploring this people, he was restoring them to life.

Neil Gunn the writer was a professional craftsman seeking a hidden reality, and the way in which craftsman and private individual worked together is fascinatingly described in a letter written in the 1960s to Hart:

> You see, I never worked out the moves ahead in a book . . . I never had any difficulty with invention, never had to wonder where to go next or what was to happen, for I was 'told', if you can follow. And often the telling astonished me. If I had known exactly what was going to happen in a book of mine from the beginning I think I would have been too bored to write it.

This feeling that he was 'guided', that the book just came of itself, was the reason why he could write with so much direct and powerful emotion and still be unaware that he was revealing *himself*. He could always maintain that the story was speaking, and so retain personal essence intact.

In the novels Neil was emotionally committed to a degree that he would not allow in the personal books. In the personal books he is on his guard. Keith Henderson maintains that 'all his novels were autobiographical'. But he transformed and transmuted experience.

The way in which he regarded writing novels as an essentially private activity is well illustrated in a letter to Nan Shepherd. In May 1940 she had written about *Wild Geese Overhead* and *Second Sight*:

> To apprehend things—walking on a hill, seeing the light change, the mist, the dark, being aware, using the whole of one's body to instruct the spirit— yes, that is a secret life one has and knows that others have. But to be able to share it, in and through words—that is what frightens me. . . . It dissolves one's being. I am no longer myself but a part of a life beyond myself when I read pages that are so much an expression of myself. You can take processes of being—no, that's too formal a word—*states* is too static, this is something that moves—*movements* I suppose is best—you can take movements of being and translate them out of themselves into words; that seems to me a gift of a very high and rare order.[5]

This is a kind of intimate praise and admiration which touches the quick more closely when written by a woman to a man, and which would make any writer glow and move with a sudden swift unease; but Neil's response is intriguing:

> You come uncannily at the heart of the matter and . . . when you hesitate before arriving at the word *movements* . . . then it is as if you were surprising me in my very lair. Where, to put it mildly, I hardly expected to see you—or anyone else.[6]

The use of the period after 'lair' is revealing. He had to stop. 'Lair' is the precise and vivid word. There is in the whole paragraph a mingled delight and embarrassment. Writing is an intimate act, but because critics can miss the point you are safe enough. For a reader to 'come upon him' when he imagines himself alone—that is a wonderful, alarming and shameful intrusion upon a solitude of the mind.

At the very times when Neil could be assumed in personal writing to be revealing himself, he withdrew. In fiction he portrayed his own emotion. Emotional truth can only be endured when presented as a story. Neil would not give himself away if he knew he was being watched.

L

Anyway, the certainty that 'making things', whether boats or tables or songs or stories, was fully in accordance with the tradition overcame a dark suspicion in Neil that after all a writer is not an entirely manly thing to be.

There might be something effete, inbred, ambiguous and self-indulgent about Literature and Art as a bohemian, 'Bloomsbury' activity performed before the mirror of a coterie; but experienced as a hunt, a quest, an adventure of the mind as real and vigorous as physical adventures with sea or salmon or stag, it was personally rewarding and provided its own food for the table. ('In fact, the hunting instinct is one of the strongest in my blood.' Journal, 1939.)

More than the need to concentrate on writing and to earn money, more than the need to have a mind clear from preoccupation, sent him first off in a boat and then to Braefarm House. Keith Henderson said that Neil was 'set all the time' on 'discovering the inner meaning of things', 'what is under the surface', 'the hidden reality'.[7] While writing he needed to remember that his readers were concerned not so much with 'inner meanings' as with action and emotion. But if he himself were not able to follow the quest for these 'inner meanings', then his urge to write would leave him. For this quest, solitude and contemplation were necessary.

During his time at Brae he achieved a balance between his own requirements and those of his readers. How he did it is described in a letter to Hart (about 1966):

> And it's often 'the way' (dear old Tao) that holds the lot, and certainly the unexpected insights. Sometimes I was bothered a bit about these insights, because I had a liking for them (like having a drink, a tot, on the way), but the internal thing that did the 'telling' would stand no nonsense. It kept a continuous rein, as it were, on my *way*wardness, in the interest of what I could see it believed in as balance. Sometimes when I got an insight (let the word pass) that might run to two sentences, the 'balance' frowned on what it obviously considered was self-indulgence if not worse (like vanity or whatever). But if I had done a fair amount of straight action, I might have my own way for a whole small paragraph. It was sometimes amusing to look on at this happening . . .

Although determined to work and make a living he was not by nature a hermit and Brae was not the back of beyond. It was in typical crofting country, three miles along the road from Dingwall to Strathpeffer. The house was stone-built, four-square, slate-roofed and solid, not at all forbidding but with a strong friendliness, ready to accept all-comers. It stood on the hillside, facing south, with a garden round it, and about it a gradual ascent through farm and croft land to the open moors and the distant hills.

A couple of miles farther west, at Strathpeffer, lived brother John, Inspector of Schools, with his family. The special relationship between Neil and John was an essential feature of life at Brae. What is more, John's experience had become an integral part of Neil's imaginative life. Alasdair, John's son, has vivid memories of Neil dropping in at Strathpeffer during the Second World War in his Home Guard uniform, wearing a cap Daisy had enlarged for his head by cutting out the back. Indeed, the pictorial history of Neil's life would include a wonderful parade of hats—rakish and floppy, wild and natty, sober and preposterous.

'The farmhouse where we stayed', wrote Neil in 1966, 'is the farmhouse in *The Shadow*.' Nan, the heroine of that novel, describes it as

> really quite a decent farmhouse. All of five bedrooms and an enormous bathroom which may have been another bedroom once . . . The doors and the mantelpieces and the skirtings and the cupboards are all pitch pine, but Aunt Phemie has wallpaper and carpets that tone with it, taking away the grim bareness and giving quite an impression of warmth . . . My bedroom has two windows, one to the south looking across the valley, and the other in the west wall through which I can see the steading and, beyond, the tops of spruce trees that are still in the grey evening . . . and between and beyond them, very far away, a glimpse of blue mountain tops.[8]

Highland Pack (1949) is full of descriptions of Brae country. First, the garden:

> Jibydo is a cock chaffinch who considers it his special duty apparently to treat our house to a regular round of song. 'Round' is the only word, for he starts upon the ancient ash-tree by the north-east window, does a carefree swoop to the aged elm beyond the south-west window, and, when he has exhausted his second urgency of song there, takes a double-swoop to the old plum-tree in the vegetable garden at the back, where he performs with equal vigour.[9]

And now the farmland:

> Today I saw about twenty Highland cattle following a cart of hay across a field. They were drawn out in a line, and with their shaggy dun coats and long horns had a soft wild beauty that held the eye . . . More than once, late at night, with the small burn a solid sheet of ice, I have heard a rustling beyond the hedge, and on peering through have watched them standing there quietly, eating the twigs of some felled trees . . .[10]

> Going up the hill-road this afternoon, I passed three teams ploughing, followed by gulls. The black earth gleamed in the furrow, the horses' heads bent to the powerful shoulders that took the strain, the ploughmen were warm at their peaceful task.[11]

Then the crofting area between farm and moor:

Where there is a crofting area the moors and the mountains are usually not far away; usually also there is a lot of light about and singing larks; and space itself, of which there is more than the eye can readily encompass, is yet as it were parcelled out into smallness and intimacy. The cow is nearly human and the hens lay when they feel like it, which is not often. The dog comes barking and wagging his tail equally furiously; and out of sheer jealousy the dog on the next croft barks back. The child stares. The cat pays no attention. And the cock struts and *kok-koks* with the fine high-stepping action of outraged dignity.[12]

Finally, the moor, taken from *The Shadow*:

In such a waste land the colour was quite incredible. Exotic. The heather had not yet come into bloom, and upon its vast dun space was set down this one acre of glowing colour. You remember the tone of that yellow chartreuse when you held it against the light? That, then . . .

. . . Only the tough hill grass burnt at the tops. Nothing more—except for the spikes, everywhere, rust-coloured rather than withered, of the golden bog asphodel. But when I took one blade of grass, what variety was there, from the fawn-coloured tip, that was the seed, through the brown, the mottled yellow and green, to the green![13]

That is the setting. And the routine of life at Brae fitted closely to it. When there were no visitors, no business commitments, no temptations to go 'off and away', it went like this, as described by Ena Macleod:

After breakfast, and perusing the letters and the daily paper [the *Scotsman*], Neil sat down in a big armchair at the fire with a writing pad and pencil and wrote on his knee till lunch time, always smoking of course. Daisy saw to it that at his right hand side was a very large wide-mouthed copper coal scuttle to catch the cigarette ash that tended to be flicked everywhere but the right place. Daisy brought him a coffee at eleven and retired to type the previous day's script. After lunch they went for a walk up the hill at the back of the house through the crofts and sometimes Neil got a hare or a rabbit for the pot . . . I think most of Neil's reading was done in the evenings.[14]

In fact it was often Neil alone who went for a walk up the hill at the back. It was from these walks that most of the notes which formed *Highland Pack* were drawn.

There was a final rite, described in *Highland Pack*:

The habit of taking a walk round part of the house and out perhaps as far as the gate before going to bed some time around midnight, can become deep-rooted. Often it is so dark that I find myself groping for the door on coming in lest I stub my nose. Even when the weather is all worked up to a slashing rainstorm, at least the door must be opened for a last look . . .

While the roses bloom, whatever the wind may have been up to during the day, it tends to fall away at midnight to a complete silence. There is a hush on the face of the earth and the trees are dark against the sky. For a long period about the height of the year, a livid pallor, a weird afterglow, lingers in the heavens, and the dark tree-tops are a fantastic architecture, utterly still, against the light . . .[15]

At least once a week there was a trip to Dingwall for shopping, where inevitably they would meet someone they knew, and Neil would go one way, Daisy another. Regularly enough they went farther, into Inverness.

And there were ploys of various kinds. Throughout the war years Neil was fishing and curling when he could. And both his concern with curling and his restraint and courtesy under provocation are illustrated by a story. Miss Belle Maltman was a VAD nurse stationed at Elsick House, near Strathpeffer, in 1941. She writes:

> There is a small pond about twenty yards from Elsick House and when it froze we were delighted and begged and borrowed skates which we used that night when we were off duty and though it was dark we enjoyed it and were returning to work next day when we met Neil Gunn. More in sorrow than in anger he pointed out, to our horror, that we had skated over and churned up the local Curling Club's rink. He . . . showed us how to throw a curling stone—I think to let us see how it bumped and went off course thanks to the damage we had done![16]

She adds that as a result of that lesson she became a keen curler herself, and says that he was 'a perfect gentleman in complete control of his feelings, which must have been murderous'.

In these years Neil and Daisy were much together. He described Daisy as she was during the Brae period, as Aunt Phemie in *The Shadow*:

> She is comfortably slim and though well over forty the gold in her hair hasn't faded much . . . She is a tirelessly energetic worker and yet can stand quite still. She is over the average height for women . . . Aunt Phemie does not open her heart, but she can smile and there is a humour in her smile that makes it the most charming self-contained thing you ever saw.[17]

John Pick, who met Daisy at Brae, remembers her expression as she sat smoking, while talk ran on through reaches of the night towards the faint cheeping of the birds:

> It was a reflective, reserved expression containing not so much indulgence as an appreciative and gentle calm as if she were watching all the words fly off among the trees and vanish. For it was not the words she was interested in but the feeling behind the words and the person behind the feeling . . . Her comments on ideas and human beings were perceptive and kindly, and she did

not speak about things of which she was ignorant. She always had an extraordinary quality of youth and freshness, a gleaming humour and a shy yet open
warmth. She was not beautiful in any conventional way—her face was too
strong for that—but something shone from within her which was certainly
beautiful.

The closeness of their relationship from this time on made some old friends
feel left out. It wasn't merely the disappearance to Braefarm House, without
a telephone, and at the end of a long unmade track. More than one insisted
many years afterwards that Neil was not the same man as he had been in his
youth, because Daisy mollycoddled him. But this grievance should be seen
in perspective.

In the Highland tradition woman should be loved, respected, treated
with courtesy—and left in her own place. Neil took great pleasure in the
outdoor and intellectual company of men. He always treated women with a
gallantry which the tradition fosters. Gene Pick recalls: 'He was very gallant
to women, especially when he felt he had been off at length on "men's talk"
and would approach with a twinkle and the hint of a pas de bas and suggest
"Well now, isn't it time for a dram?" '[18] But Daisy was for him a close friend
and companion as well as a woman and a wife—someone who shared his
perceptions while retaining a clarity of her own. Her concentration on his
welfare was absolute. But it did not have the effect of 'reducing' him by
making him dependent. On the contrary it helped the growth of inner being
in them both.

When the hero in *The Well at the World's End* leaves his wife Fand to go off
on his adventures she says, 'I shall wait for you till the end of time.'
And in the next chapter the tale tells:

> To come to himself a man has to get away from a woman, particularly if she is a
> good woman. A good woman is a man's vice. She covers up all the knobs.
>   It was delightful leaving Fand behind. For Fand was both good and
> beautiful. And the truly incredible thing about her beauty was that it
> inhabited her . . . Goodbye, Fand; I'm off! I'm away on my travels! . . .[19]

He was well aware of what might draw him 'away' from Daisy: not his
continuing involvement with Margaret, which was a relationship with a life
of its own which did not reduce or distort companionship with Daisy, but
adventure in the mind, the realm of ideas and speculation and the penetration of his own experience wherever it might lead. But in a sense Fand
herself had become the well at the world's end, and it is the community of
love which enables him to awaken to the meaning of reality.

But they were not limited to their own company at Brae. In *Highland Pack* Neil records conversations with crofters, shepherds, tractor-drivers, cattlemen, mole-catchers, and from every conversation he gained something of value. It is not simply a case of 'all conversation is equally revealing'. Every man rooted in practical life is interesting on a subject which is close to him and which he understands. But more than this, there was occasionally that touch of insight which Neil might himself describe as 'magic'. There are two records of actual conversations of this sort. The first is in *Highland Pack*:

> On the edge of the moor I met the crofter . . . We got talking about deer, for Ben Wyvis was white, and I asked him if the hinds ever invaded his place. 'Oh, yes,' he said. 'Sometimes in the grey of the morning they will be over in the field there, and when they see me they run together and stand still, with their heads up, as if quietly debating which road they would take.'[20] [The same incident is used in *The Shadow*.]

The second appears in *The Well at the World's End* but Neil had been telling the story as his own long before that:

> 'It was last April,' said the shepherd, 'in the middle of the lambing. I was away out on the moor behind. I had had a hefty day and a few difficult births and there were one or two stubborn yeld ewes on the hunt for lambs . . . I sat down, for I was tired. To tell the truth I had forgotten to eat my piece, and I took the bread from my pocket, but somehow I wasn't even hungry . . . There had been a drying wind . . . —not too cold. But now the wind had gone with the sun, and over the moor there was a fine light that went blue in the distance. I never before saw so—so beautiful a sight, so wide and—and beautiful. It came over me . . .
>
> 'I am a married man,' said the shepherd, 'with three of a young family and though I say it myself I know when I'm well off. But—*I didn't want to go home*.'[21]

All the same, Neil did not immediately resign himself to the routine of writing, walking and talking to neighbours, to an existence in which he could not participate fully in life as it was lived. He writes to Naomi Mitchison:

> Here where we are the sea is some little distance away and not a fishing sea at that. We live in the middle of a farm but not our farm . . . The ideal (horrid word) was a small house something a little bigger than a croft, with the sea with a bit of a boat in the offing. But though we scoured the country devil of a place like that was to be had so we had to rent this place where I can't get doing things.[22]

There was no need to trouble himself about the lack of 'things' to do in the early years. His time at Brae started with flights and excursions of a kind which made him aware of the trembling of the world and took him far from the Highlands. They moved to Brae in autumn 1937. In January 1938 he was in Ireland visiting Maurice Walsh. And in summer 1939 there was a jaunt to Lewis, Bernera and the Flannan Isles, the original intention of the trip being to stay with Peter and Ena Macleod, who lived in Stornoway until 1940. The full account of this rich and fruitful voyage among the black rocks and dark seas appeared in February to May 1940 as 'Islands and Seas' in *Chambers' Journal*. The Flannan venture, too, was an essential contribution to the growth of *The Silver Darlings*.

Just as significantly, he was in Germany.[23]

Butcher's Broom, issued in Britain in 1934, had been translated into German and published during 1937 by Langen & Muller. Immediately afterwards Fritz Wölcken translated *Morning Tide*. Fritz became a friend and admirer of Neil while at Edinburgh University. The German edition of *Morning Tide* came out in 1938. Wölcken survived the war to translate *The Green Isle of the Great Deep*, issued in West Germany in 1949.

Neil went twice to Bavaria. In May 1938 Maurice Walsh wrote: 'At this moment Gunn, I understand, is being fêted in Munich on the launching of his *Morning Tide* as the first of a de-luxe edition.'[24] The other visit was in February 1939 when he was taken tobogganing in the mountains. He kept for many years both the photographs of this expedition and the dashing Bavarian hat he bought there, and often teased Daisy by applying superlatives to the charm of a girl he took as passenger down the snow slopes. (Daisy at the time was with her sister in Devon.)

Years later he remembered: 'I was at a fancy-dress ball in the Europa Hotel [Munich] shortly before the war broke out, and learned a lot, from Germans who trusted me, about the ways of dictators.'[25] And in conversation he recalled being with Daisy, during the earlier visit, in a small town on the Rhine. They went for a walk. On the opposite bank they heard boys singing German folk-songs and he recalled 'the delight I received from the thought that someone could belong to a place and a *different* place—and each place could have its own value, its own kind of delight.'

Margaret MacEwen writes:

> Before the Gunns left Larachan, they had given hospitality to a very charming young German whom I met while he was staying with them . . . He was full of enthusiasm for Neil's books, and I thought he was also perhaps a skilful propagandist for the Nazi regime.

Both she and Malcolm MacEwen suspect that Neil's invitations to Germany were connected with a Nazi attempt to use Scottish Nationalism for their own ends. Margaret continues:

> In the summer of 1938 my father had a visit from four young Germans, ostensibly tourists, who were obviously trying to sound him out on this. Neil was very innocent and susceptible of flattery. So, I know, are most of us, but it would never occur to him to doubt the flatterer's sincerity, or wonder whether there was an ulterior motive . . . Neil had been abroad very little, and the mere foreign atmosphere had great charm for him . . . They praised his books and from this he assumed they shared his views . . . Neil would certainly have hated any interference with personal liberty if he had been aware of it, but I don't think he was . . . Neil always regarded cruelty as the one unforgivable sin . . .[26]

Whatever the truth may be about the degree to which he was deceived by his German hosts, they must have come to the conclusion that he was of no use for their purposes. It can safely be said that at the time he failed to realise what monsters moved beneath the surface life of cafés, streets and the Europa Hotel.

Throughout the first years of his life at Braefarm House as a professional writer war was lowering and moving closer, and the sense of its grim, boding approach is ever-present in the journal he kept for a time in 1939. It is tense and erratic in mood. 3 July 1939, for example:

> Dull, heavy day . . . Tide pulling glossy, brimming, in distance. Colour taken out of the fields and all the world a bit sad. Now a puff of air behind the ears—and a few drops of rain . . . This dark shadow over the world is also a shadow on the spirit, which has not the energy to throw it off or to deny it . . . How susceptible the spirit is to small changes! This gloom, by dwelling on it, becomes sinister and hateful.[27]

He was obsessed with the palpable gloom in a nearby crofter's house, where an eighteen-year-old son had left for the Army.

But the most revealing entry comes on 1 September and nowhere else do we find ourselves so close to the workings of his story-telling, legend-building, visualising imagination. He hears wireless reports. 'So it's coming at last. One feels sick a bit, with the mind unable to concentrate on anything.' He looks out on the harvested fields, hears the farmhands talking, recalls the lovely weather, 'almost too much to bear', the suspense between summer and autumn, between peace and war.

> While writing these words out of a mind strangely numb, I had a quite involuntary vision of a woman, over thirty, sitting down on a kitchen stool in a

Highland cottage with a slow movement of the body, a weary drawn-out movement, the tragic side-face and clear bone of the jaw, turning away from me, from the outside world, towards the awful despondency of her mind. And her mind is quivering and tremulous from the numb sickness in her breast. Sickness, nausea, a melting weakness of the flesh. Her mind grows sick. Nothing more matters, nothing more can be borne . . . She could cry out. But nothing matters. He is gone. It is finished.

She is a woman of an earlier age, of the clan days when fighting was not uncommon. Her husband has just answered the summons of his chief to war. There have been bagpipe music and the swing of the tartan . . . The music and the tartan have been drawn away through the little green valleys that gather into the glen. And the woman is left. And this is how she feels about it.

And this is how she has always felt about it. Always and everywhere! . . . That melting sickness of the heart in the breast, the slumping of the vital forces, the numbing of the brain, the gathering sickness in the stomach, until the soul itself can cry no more, can say no more, nothing in the world more, O God, but that he may come back, come back to me.

The writing is full of incantatory repetition of a kind he would not have allowed himself were 'anyone looking', and which he would have pruned away were the piece intended for publication.

He writes on 3 September:

The inarticulate gloom in that farm kitchen.

The woman I can now see (as if I had known her for centuries) in her croft cottage, her man gone.

Behind all the calculations of intellect, behind the megalomania of a leader, behind the religion of an economic system, there is that individual who suffers, who dies, who loves. When we forget to pay tribute, above all things, to the living core and flame of the individual life, at that moment we are heading for the organisation of death.

Another entry shows that as war drew near he was thinking of rejoining the Customs & Excise service. Records prove that he did in fact apply, and that his application was refused. It is difficult now to imagine the degree of pressure which the situation applied to an individual. But Neil felt that he could not stand aside. Conscription took men for the services. They could be directed into work of 'national importance'. The papers were full of news of war preparations and then of approved exhortation. Everyone without exception was in some way involved. How could a man who spent his days in writing private words on paper believe his efforts to be of value to his fellows?

The journal explains:

After all, I have already worked for thirty years, and feel that in the ordinary

way I have made my social contribution. Any extra contribution I had hoped
to make in writing at my own economic risk . . . Yet it is an odd business how
the present unrest gets hold of you so that you feel you should be 'doing
something'.

Fears that the coming of war would reduce his opportunities for earning
proved groundless. Although the shortage of paper prevented books from
being kept in print, it did not prevent them from being published. At no
time in this country have people been more eager to read, to seek, and to
understand than between 1939 and 1945.

Books were printed to austere standards, becoming thinner and less
sumptuous. But not only were they available in the shops, they were
bought.

He did a prodigious amount of work at Brae, and in retrospect his
continual uneasiness about the charge of 'escapism' seems extraordinary.
Humanity escapes from tension into war. During the years in which the
world was convulsed Neil struggled with the causes of such tension and evil,
explored the contribution of his own culture to the understanding of human
community, and showed the way in which an individual can grow into
light. But at a time when everyone joins a mass pouring in a single direction
it is difficult to stay at home and get on with the job. Especially as Neil was
well aware that neither spiritual light nor individual freedom could survive
in Europe if Hitler won.

12   Man at Work

When he settled down to write in autumn 1937 Neil was thoroughly businesslike and practical in his approach to the job. He wasted nothing. He lost nothing. Short stories were published and then turned into novels. When the play *Second Sight* was criticised by Bridie he converted that into a novel, too. Every trip and adventure became an article, and many of the articles were themselves used again as material for novels.

J. B. Salmond of the *Scots Magazine* would print anything he wrote, and Neil supplied essays regularly under his own name. But in 1939, with the advent of the war, Salmond suggested that he should contribute regular notes and comments under the title 'Memories of the Month'. For several years from January 1940 onwards he did so, using the pseudonym Dane McNeill.

He did not simply accept the *Scots Magazine* as insurance and get on with a novel. He was approached by the *Daily Record*, and responded at once. The editor gave him a free hand, with stipulations as general as 'something of interest on Scottish affairs'. He wrote occasionally, too, for the *Glasgow Herald*, and frequently for *Chambers' Journal*. His professionalism is evident. The tone is right, the approach sensible, the material sound.[1]

Those accustomed only to the novelist or the reflective philosopher would find a look at the political and economic articles stimulating and salutory. They move with formidable logic, and their tone is crisp and calm.

A good example of his mode of rational assessment is 'And Then Rebuild It' (*Scots Magazine*, December 1939), where he writes of statistics which show the decline of Scotland:

> And, after all, the Glasgow area, if we take it as a fourth or a fifth of the London area, is in itself a great market, and if the light industries had developed there to a fourth or a fifth of the extent they have developed around London, Scotland would have been relatively flourishing. Whether the Scots are inferior to the English in research, business method and workmanship may be debatable. That Scotland has neither a seat of Government nor an integrated centre of finance is not debatable. Following on that are many supremely important psychological factors, for if nothing succeeds like success, nothing depresses like depression.

He then considers the idea of a Commission for Scotland:

> The trouble is that in Scotland we have historic reason to smile at the idea of
> any London-appointed Commission doing anything of real constructive value.
> We have been disillusioned too often. Granted that a perfectly constituted
> Commission, permanently in session, with adequate finance, could accom-
> plish much; but your Commission in that case would be tantamount to a
> Government, though one of rather an autocratic type, because it would not be
> directly responsible to the people of the country in which it would be
> operating. Let it be responsible to the people concerned through the usual
> democratic channels and you have government without going outside our
> democratic conception of a state; it is difficult to see the matter in any other
> light.

The topic which recurs most often in Neil's journalism is the plight of
Scottish fisheries, and more than once he evokes the contrast between the
prosperity of the herring industry in 1800 and the situation at the time of
writing.[2] And this leads straight into his research for *The Silver Darlings.*

So the journalism was not merely a chore, a grind endured for the sake of
daily bread. It was a field on which he fought the public battles which were
important to him, and a garden in which he sowed seeds which came up as a
crop of novels. Eventually he found it wearing because of his deep need to
immerse himself in the creative, myth-making, legend-making, explora-
tory business of growing fiction in the mind.

Wild Geese Overhead and *Second Sight* are twined closely together in the
early years of his professional writing life. The first work, other than
journalism, which he did at Braefarm House was a play version of *Second
Sight* in the winter of 1937. It was sent to James Bridie for comment.
Bridie's observations made him shelve it. Then, true to his habit of careful
husbandry, he turned to the short story 'Whisky', which had been put aside
because 'Daisy didn't like it', and used that as a basis for the novel, *Wild
Geese Overhead*.[3] Daisy was right. The short story is laden with undigested
emotion. But Neil was never willing to admit failure, and the novel he
wrote from it became a Book Society Choice.

Why did he begin with a subject so uncongenial to him, exploring the
Glasgow slums, in which he could never feel at home? It seems that he was
still wrestling with the charge of escapism. Although he often claimed to be
a socialist, he had little collectivism in him. He was an individualist with a
strong sense of genuine community. In confronting the charge of escapism
he may have felt that he would prove that he could deal with slums,
deprivation and so on as well as the next man. In a way it was his response to

the 'social conscience' critics of the 1930s, in the same way that *The Green Isle of the Great Deep* was his mature answer to the 'social conscience' criticism of 1943. Neil recalled later:

> I knew all these newspaper fellows in Glasgow, and my friend John Macnair Reid, one of them, took me one night through the very worst slums of Glasgow, and up a common stair. There was a woman they wanted to move out to a new council house, and she wouldn't leave because, she said, 'If I need help, I've only to go across the hall to Mrs O'Brien, or step up to Mrs So-and-So, we have a lot of friendliness here.'[4]

But it is not the friendliness which is emphasised in *Wild Geese Overhead*.

The book is an account of how one Glasgow journalist braves the scorn of his fellows in order to put a pastoral distance between himself and the murderous cruelty of city life. In one respect it reverses the early story 'The Mirror',[5] which shows a Glasgow newspaperman renting a room in a crofthouse to write, becoming obsessed with desire for the crofter's daughter, suffering the painful knowledge that he will never write anything of value, and going back defeated to Glasgow.

In the book, by leaving the city Will is seeking that Golden Age which Neil talked about with Keith Henderson. Since the novel is full of arguments about socialism and Will's doubts concerning its effect on individual personality and values, Neil is contrasting his own anarchistic Golden Age with egalitarianism imposed from above by a central State. He is looking for a way in which individual personality can outgrow the need for any Golden Age by realising its own freedom, and awakening to the delight of life. A quotation from the much later *Key of the Chest* is apposite:

> 'The old primordial goodness of the human heart,' said Mr Gwynn.
> 'You believe that's there?'
> 'Always. Basic. And you can measure its strength by its evil opposite, its perversion—and the one hell's broth it brews. The need to feel good must in nature have an outlet. When it doesn't get it—when it gets dammed back for any one reason or another . . . then it bursts through, with mad scaldings and bloody wars.'[6]

There is certainly darkness in *Wild Geese Overhead*. His hero Will fights through to acceptance and understanding, and so does Neil himself. But acceptance is meaningless unless you actually confront what you are accepting. Neil's way forward at this time was the way described in the book. It is an authentic way, not merely a fictional one, and for that reason, despite its uneasy moments, *Wild Geese Overhead* remains healthy and positive.

The review which pleased Neil most was by a young writer named

Alexander Reid, which appeared (unsigned) in *SMT Magazine* for November 1939. He went to the magazine's office, asked to have the reviewer identified, and was introduced to a man who at once became a friend.[7]

Second Sight, which followed *Wild Geese Overhead*, was commercially unsuccessful and remains one of the least satisfactory of his books. He attempts in it what in the later *Key of the Chest* he achieves with confident mastery—the conduct of an investigation into Highland (and human) values at several levels simultaneously, through the association of Highland with non-Highland characters, combining action with intellectual discussion. The book intertwines two separate themes: the quest for the legendary stag, King Brude, and examination of the old Highland phenomenon of second sight.

Nan Shepherd wrote (14 May 1940) about the book: 'Your English folk never really please me—why I didn't like *The Lost Glen*.'[8] Neil replied (17 May 1940):

> More and more you'll find me—gin I go on writing—using cliché and slang and swear. A perversity this, but done, damn it all, with a manner. Isn't that what's wrong with these pleasant English characters whom you don't much care for? How many of us are clichés? And in a shooting lodge, on sporting holiday, well, I mean to say, what?[9]

He has deliberately missed the point, for Nan was saying 'You haven't got it right.' Two things show that he knew this himself—the uneasy jauntiness of his tone, and the fact that far from increasing the use of 'cliché and slang and swear', they largely disappear from his work.

Neil was quite clear what he wanted to do in *Second Sight*. He wrote (20 January 1941) to Naomi Mitchison: 'For that, I'm afraid, very light novel did have its sort of obscure symbolism of the spiritual clearances—following in time the actual physical clearances.'[10] It may well be his personal bitterness against the disintegrating effect of the intruder in Highland life and values which upsets the balance both of *Second Sight* and *The Lost Glen*.

The theme probably took form in his mind as the result of a visit, recorded in *Off in a Boat*, to John Macnair Reid and his doctor wife Josephine, who had flitted from Glasgow and were recently settled on the Isle of Eigg. *Second Sight* is dedicated to them.

The Eigg chapter in *Off in a Boat* focuses on a 'stream where "the washer at the ford" may still be seen, and if you are foolish enough to ask her what she is washing, she will tell you it is your own shroud.'

He recalls several types of occult experience, including second sight and his own 'black electricity' story, described in detail in *The Atom of Delight*, and the prophecies of Kenneth Mackenzie, the seventeenth-century Highlander known as the Brahan seer. He says of his host that he 'finds the place quite eerie and haunted'.[11] There would be long discussions, and at some point during them in Neil's mind the scepticism of the urbane doubter, which he was always able to conjure from his imagination, became related and identified with the equally urbane despotism which kept the Highlander in the servile condition of stalker and gillie. For in the letter to Naomi Mitchison already quoted he continues after mention of 'spiritual clearances', 'And if we discussed something like that at length, we might at last get a slant on the educational and economic problems in the west that you are concerned about.'

It is difficult to decide why the subject first took form as a play, but there is little doubt that the dramatic version of *Second Sight* was one of the first fictional pieces written at Brae.[12] It was then sent to James Bridie. Bridie's comments are as pertinent to the novel as to the drama:

> I think the play is brilliant and would play as it stands; but I am certain you should do something more with it . . . *Second Sight* goes to pieces after page 60 or thereby. You have built up everything with really magnificent power and subtlety for a situation that doesn't happen. After a good first act, as this is, audiences begin to care dreadfully about what is going to happen to one, two or at most three of the characters. The three in your play are Helen, Harry and Alick. Absolutely sweet damn all happens to any of them. It is good observation and good irony for fate to fulfil itself in a casual sort of way, but it is nearly always bad drama unless the very casualness is of cast-iron significance. It isn't here. The practical joke is too, too thin in its motivation and the drug business makes it outrageous. Also although you handle your bright young things with praiseworthy caution in the earlier passages, they get out of hand at the very moment when they become important to the play as you have written it. Slang is a hell of a thing and goes out of date in three years . . .
>
> If you want to make money out of this play—and I don't see why you shouldn't—you should make the tie-up between Helen, Harry and Alick that everybody is expecting and give Geoffrey some nasty designs—pour passer le temps, simply, but very chawing for Harry and Alick. Then kill him (or better still Helen) half or entirely by mistake. You can't kill Geoffrey. He is simply a raisonneur. Raisonneurs are immortal on the stage. I know this is commonplace and will annoy you, but you simply haven't brought off the other thing. And I don't think you can—you or anybody—not after that first act. I should drop the practical joke altogether unless you sketch it in very lightly to heighten the horror; and even then you'll have to be desperately careful that it isn't a hang-up. The one I'd like to see killed would be Joyce. You might prime the others up for murder and then shove a 'wretched rash intruding fool' into the coffin. Do what your spirit moves you to do; only, don't promise the

9 Neil (*second from left*) with Robin MacEwen, Duncan McNeill, John MacCormick and Donald MacCormick at Morar, 1932

10 Picnic at Gairloch, 1932: Neil (*centre*) is seen juggling with hat and teacup; *l–r*: Daisy, a relation of Daisy's, David MacEwen, Malcolm MacEwen, Margaret MacEwen, and two unidentifiable ladies

11 Glen Mhor Distillery, Inverness, to which Neil was attached
as Excise officer from 1923 to 1937

12 Braefarm House, where the Gunns stayed from 1937 to 1949,
the most intensely creative period of Neil's life

audience raw heads and bloody bones and disappoint them. They don't forgive that . . .[13]

And yet—and yet—whatever Neil may have done with the play, the novel retains the form complained of, and the outrageous practical joke is central to the plot.

At any rate, he put the play aside and turned to *Wild Geese Overhead.* Then, aware that *Second Sight* remained within him unfulfilled, he expanded it into a novel, adding all the outdoor episodes and strengthening the King Brude theme. The story of the stag was published separately in the *Scots Magazine* early in 1939—another example of 'waste not, want not'.

But even after publishing the novel he was unwilling to let the play drop. Versions of it exist inscribed with Kincraig and Kerrow addresses, which means that he kept an ambition for it well into the 1950s.

A sidelight is shed on the hunting episodes in *Second Sight* by the entry in Neil's journal for 4 July 1939, which describes his attitude to hunting, of which the novel is so full:

> A world in itself—and a very attractive one, were it not kept up by privilege, and in the end devoted to preserving life in order to kill it . . . At one time I was quite fond of shooting. In fact the hunting instinct is one of the strongest in my blood. I know nothing so exciting, so health-giving, so full of the very glow of life, as stalking game—fish or feather or fur . . . But as a sport it will never be of any use to me now. I don't care to see others shooting. I dislike the distant report of their guns. It sometimes makes me involuntarily shudder . . .

This strong physical reaction is typical both of Neil's experience and of his writing:

> . . . If a man were honestly to face this problem it seems to me he should finally say to himself: 'What I am not prepared to kill myself, I shall not eat.'
> For there is another problem beneath this one. A sensitive soul in war can fire a gun or drop a bomb, whose results in direct human slaughter he cannot see, with comparative calm . . . But that same soul would shrink with horror from having to kill one single body directly with cold steel . . .
> We have raised a mechanism between us and the facts of death by slaughter. When the mechanism becomes so perfect that it operates almost automatically, it will destroy us . . .[14]

Second Sight was not well received, but it had one valuable result. Its publication in 1940 saw the beginning of correspondence with Naomi Mitchison, who wrote that her neighbours in Argyll were uncomfortable about the ending. Daughter and sister of Haldanes, born in Edinburgh in

1897, educated at Oxford, Naomi Mitchison married an influential Labour MP and became actively engaged in public affairs herself. She had recently settled near Campbeltown. At this time she had already written a considerable number of books, among them *The Corn King and the Spring Queen*, for which Neil had a high regard. As a socialist, impatient with individualism, Naomi was forcefully uncomfortable about a great deal in the novels of Neil Gunn. Their correspondence begins at a time when Neil was growing increasingly concerned with threats to the individual not only from totalitarianism but from the analytic materialism which is willing to dissect and plan humanity into a theoretical pattern. The result is a long-running, good-tempered, lively, contumacious debate conducted over several years, of which both *The Serpent* and *The Green Isle of the Great Deep* are in a sense the fruits.

The Silver Darlings was not a matter of controversy at all. This was the book Faber had been hoping for—a solid mainstream novel, rich with emotion, character and incident, without intellectual conversation or philosophising, ideally suited to follow *Morning Tide* and *Highland River*. Neil's reputation was seriously in need of it.

Realisation that this book was just what publisher and public required of him may have been one reason why he was so reluctant to undertake it. He always resisted the obvious. That he *was* reluctant there is no doubt. He had been meditating a story of the Moray Firth fisheries long before *Off in a Boat*. Of course he knew well the huge labour of thought, research and organisation which would be entailed, and it was natural to want to put it off as long as possible. More than this, the history of fishing in the Moray Firth was the story of his own family, and closely identified in his mind with the lives of his father and mother. He would be writing into the tale emotions which ran deep and would be tortuous and exhausting to unravel.

The genesis of *The Silver Darlings* is the story of a book chasing a writer until it gets itself written. Neil says in *The Atom of Delight*, writing of himself, typically, in the third person:

> As his existence had two parents, so it had the earth and the sea . . . In fact he could hardly think of his father without thinking of the sea. Out of the sea came the livelihood of the household. They depended on the sea, and of all the elements in nature it was the least dependable . . . When a storm blew up . . . at sea you had to fight it out, with only an inch of planking between you and what lay beneath . . . Snatches of such fights the boy heard now and then when on a winter's night a half-circle of men hemmed in the kitchen fire . . . telling stories . . .[15]

And of the time in the 1920s when Neil and Daisy were camping at Achnaclyth, Alec Gunn tells us 'For hours he would sit with a select few listening to their tales of storms, calms and great catches, of days of prosperity and adversity, and of the grim uncertainty of the sea.'[16]

During the 1930s an old man in Dunbeath told Neil he remembered Neil's father buying his boat in Sutherland and sailing it home, and told him, too, the story used in *The Silver Darlings* of the first men to sail from Dunbeath through the Pentland Firth to Stornoway, and how they missed the Butt of Lewis in a storm and headed straight for the United States until a ship crossed their bows and put them back on course.

In July 1939, Neil went to visit Peter F. Anson, who kept badgering Neil to get the book done. For years he was like a goblin of conscience haunting the dark, and must have found frustration enough in seeing the project loom and fade in the mist.[17]

That the subject was never far from Neil's thoughts is proved by the fact that he wrote at least four articles on it between 1935 and 1939; the last recording his visit to Anson and describing talks with fishermen along the coast.[18]

The supposedly 'mystical' Gunn had a puritan regard for fact, hard news and historical accuracy. He writes in a foreword to Peter Anson's book *Life on Low Shore* (*Banffshire Journal*, 1939):

> The historical perspective [of *Fishing Boats and Fisher Folk*] crammed with information of every kind gave me the overall picture I had long wanted, while the drawings held a fascination which they have never lost. My own intimate knowledge of this area was confined to the north coast of the Moray Firth, and in these drawings of some of its creeks, which I knew as a boy, Peter Anson could not put a stone wrong . . . The singular thing—and I have never been quite able to follow it—is that his accuracy in representation carries for me an elusive purely aesthetic quality, which would somehow be destroyed if he were to put a stone wrong.

Neil goes on to say that Anson was unimpressed by his complaint about difficulties in research on the herring industry—and when one day he called on the Fishery officer in Helmsdale, he found he was expected! 'When I had studied a register of fish-curers for the year 1815, I was left with no excuse for further dallying.' Time and again in referring to *The Silver Darlings* Neil mentions that register of fish-curers, without which the book might never have been written. What stuck in his mind was the fact that twice as many fish-curers worked the area in 1815 as in 1939.

As soon as he was back from Anson's cottage at Macduff, Neil and Daisy

Illustration by Peter F. Anson from *Fishermen and Fishing Ways* (1932). The books by Anson on fishing boats and fishermen provided Neil with much of the background material for *The Silver Darlings*

left for a visit to Peter and Ena Macleod. At that time Peter was practising medicine in Stornoway. Neil spent every morning with the local fish-curers and east coast fishermen, turning up from his sessions with them, as Ena puts it, 'about an hour late for lunch and full of apologies went to bed for the afternoon to gather strength for the evening session'.

> My father-in-law Malcolm Macleod was still going strong as a fisherman on the island of Bernera . . . He was reckoned to be the best fisherman in Lewis at that time and for many years in his own boat (a half-decked boat that went only by sail) he made the trip twice yearly to the Flannan Isles 30 miles off. In June each year the delicate lambs from his flock were gathered and taken out to graze on the grass of the larger islands. Next year when they went to collect them they had to make two trips—the thirty lambs had grown so enormous that the hold couldn't accommodate them . . .
> . . . Neil met the 'old Man' as everyone called him and discovered to their mutual delight that as a young man Malcolm Macleod went each year to the East Coast fishing in Caithness—he and other Lewis boys sailed across to Ullapool and actually *walked* across Scotland and Malcolm himself was a member of the crew of Neil's father's boat. We took him across to the island of Bernera and there Neil stayed until the local soothsayers declared that everything was propitious for the voyage. Neil has described this saga in three instalments of *Chambers' Journal*.[19]

The essays were later collected in *Highland Pack* and form the basis for the Flannan Isles episode in *The Silver Darlings*. That is not the only episode which owes its background to the Stornoway visit. Ena Macleod relates:

> Neil heard that there was a Religious Revival going on in some of the villages with prayer-meetings being held in the crofters' houses till all hours of the morning. My husband was a bit scathing about it all as he was having to deal with the aftermath of the business—hysteria especially in the younger women and even some of the men, and in quite a number of cases he had to send the patients under escort to the mental hospital in Inverness. Neil was terribly anxious to see this on the spot and two of our local friends, both sensible teachers, volunteered to take Neil to one of the meetings. They sat outside for ages in our car—the guides not having the courage to go inside . . . So poor Neil came back to us unsatisfied.

Other information he needed for *The Silver Darlings* kept tripping him up and falling into his lap. The faces of the fish-gutters of his boyhood – 'happy women' as he said – continually came alive in his mind. He stumbled on a doctor's full record of the plague's assault on Caithness, with prescriptions given, providing all he could need for a graphic account. He discovered the story of a sailor who had acquired a silver plate in his head as the result of being press-ganged for the Navy in his youth. His notebooks show that he

investigated the records of the Herring Fishery Company. They also contain
a bibliography of the north-east coast and extracts from the log-book of the
Maggie of Wick for 1873. It is likely enough that he was making notes for
The Silver Darlings throughout the time that he was writing *Wild Geese
Overhead* and *Second Sight*.

Despite some critics and reviewers, and despite the origins of the book,
The Silver Darlings is not simply 'a story of the Moray Firth herring fisheries'.
It is that, of course. It is a 'folk epic', a 'panoramic chronicle' and all the
other things the critics have agreed it to be. But more interesting from the
biographical point of view, it is a dark, desperate examination of the roots of
male pride, and an account of the way in which Finn arrives at balance
through the swithering of emotions to which it gives rise. Since this pride
was Neil's own, the book is central to his development. And that is what
gives it much of its power.

There is a pride so intense as to grow totally dominant in both Roddie and
Finn. The tale of their conflict over Finn's mother Catrine has a bitter
passion which twists deep into mind and heart. Finn's struggle to live
through to a point where he can make use of pride and self-will instead of
allowing them control was Neil's. And Neil's solution was Finn's, for Finn
grows to be not only a man of action, delighting in the rush of life itself, but
a story-teller, creating legend. An old man in North Uist says to Finn:

> 'You told the story well. You brought us into the far deeps of the sea and we
> were lost with you in the Beyond where no land is, only wind and wave and the
> howling of the darkness. You kept us in suspense on the cliffs, and you had
> some art in the way you referred to our familiars of the other world before you
> told of the figure of the man you felt by the little stone house. There you saw
> no-one and you were anxious to make this clear, smiling at your fancy. It was
> well enough done. It was all well done. It was done, too, with the humour that
> is the play of drift on the wave. And you were modest. Yet—all that is only a
> little—you had something more, my hero, something you will not know—
> until you look at it through your eyes, when they are as old as mine.'
> 'What do you mean by that?' asked Finn.
> But the old man shook his head and turned away. 'Go to your sleep, my boy.
> Many a one may come', he muttered to himself, 'in the guise of the stranger.'[20]

The occupational hazard of the story-teller is self-consciousness. Neil and
Finn were self-conscious enough, and proud enough, already. In the tale
Finn *distances himself* from his own fanatical pride. And this bitter self-
watching is akin to the passionate, withdrawn, self-preserving cruelty of
Aniel in *Sun Circle*, to the secret observing of the boy in *Morning Tide*, and to
the self-tormenting sensitivity of Ewan in *The Lost Glen*.

While Finn's distance often acts as a reinforcement for his own self-identification, Neil's awareness of the 'second self—the existence of which he had discovered as a boy but only gradually came to *realise*—served him here. For the second self is fundamental, it sees without identifying with what it sees. The sense of wonder and delight which this realisation gave him enabled Neil gradually to make use of all the twists and turns of self-consciousness and self-assertion in such a way that the second self speaks through the first, and life can live itself in fiction.

The Silver Darlings was finished by autumn 1940, and when it appeared in 1941 was acclaimed on all sides.

Peter Anson and others tried to persuade Neil to write a sequel. That was what the publishers wanted, too—what Maurice Walsh called a 'dripping roast'. But Neil disliked repeating himself, disliked descriptions of the book as 'an epic', and detested being typecast as a fictional folk-historian. It was as if *The Silver Darlings* (and his father) had been on his conscience as well as on his mind. One character in the book tells Finn, 'Justify your father, and look after your mother.'[21] He had done what conscience told him to do, and now felt delivered of a burden. He was concerned with something else: with the relationship of the individual to a society based upon centralised power, and with the contribution which his tradition could make to creating a proper balance between community and individual. These matters were connected in his mind with some extraordinary events taking place in Scotland.

13 The Man of Affairs

Neil did not sit quietly writing, doing his best to ignore the Second World War. The war was real and terrible to him. It is a brooding background to every piece in *Highland Pack*. At a time when no one could live through a single day without being aware of the atmosphere of war, Neil sought consciously in those notes to give heart by writing of the permanent rhythm of change which moves whether we fight or sleep.

One piece in *Highland Pack* is called 'Visitors' and gives the feel of the war years:

> Now it is quite dark on board and I am talking to a native, skipper of a minesweeper, going home on sick-leave. Two vessels have been sunk under him, blown up. The wind is rising a bit and the night getting very cold. I offer him a cigarette and we light up. Presently there are footsteps coming down from the dark bridge. I cannot see who it is, but the captain's voice says gruffly, 'Put out those cigarettes.' The Lewisman and myself talk for a long time after that in the black-out . . .
>
> A crowded train compartment in daylight, including a Lewis girl and a young Welsh sailor. The girl is asked to sing and does so, straight away, as naturally as she would in a ceilidh at home, though we are all strangers to one another. Her voice is high-pitched and thin, and I think of sea-birds crying above the waves on the western shore we have left behind . . . The Welsh sailor sings a sentimental ballad with such rich, swelling, glorious power that the sheer unexpectedness of it moves us to wonder . . .[1]

He revealed to George Blake in a letter dated 30 October 1943 what part in his moments of fantasy he would like to have played in the war (and this is the temptation Dermot yields to in *The Lost Chart*):

> Though as a full-fledged private in the Home Guard, I whiles indulge in mock battles, though my main job is called 'Intelligence'. I get lessons in the compass—and try to keep my mind from wandering to a very unstable compass on a more unstable boat in western seas and Daisy's mouth dry with excitement. I admit that the only job—alas, this too too human flesh—that I should have cared for in this mortal hunting would have been command of one of these small swift seacraft that go at the rate of countless knots with their engines roaring like the hammers of hell. Man, George, that would have been pretty exciting with a nice bit of sea running.[2]

But life does not work like that. He had to make do with helping to navigate a committee through the shoals of administrative bureaucracy. And he was spared the need for mortal hunting.

In 1939 Tom Johnston, Labour MP for West Stirlingshire, was appointed Regional Commissioner for Scotland to organise and administer Civil Defence. William Ferguson writes in *Scotland: 1689 to the Present*: 'His knowledge of the country and his impatience with red tape marked him out as an administrator of high quality.'[3] Certainly Johnston was all that, but what made him valuable was his ability to enthuse, persuade and hustle others.

In 1941 Churchill urged Johnston to become Secretary of State for Scotland, and Johnston reports (in *Memories*, 1952): 'I was hypnotised into accepting the post.'[4] But if he was hypnotised he showed no signs of it. The conditions he laid down were forthright, uncompromising and Cromwellian. Johnston, together with all living ex-Secretaries of State for Scotland, would constitute a Council of State and when they were unanimous on an issue the Prime Minister would undertake to support their proposals. The result, according to J. G. Kellas in *Modern Scotland*, was that 'Churchill was much too busy fighting the war' and so 'the Scottish Office and the Council of State . . . were virtual rulers of Scotland.'[5] William Ferguson says that 'the supposed propensity [we salute that 'supposed'] of Scots to quarrel among themselves was stilled. Party postures were given up in favour of getting on with the job and on most matters of consequence the council acted with a surprising degree of unanimity.'

The 'matters of consequence' were many. After calling a meeting of Scottish MPs in Edinburgh in October 1941 (the first such meeting for 234 years), Johnston set up thirty-two separate inquiries, and upon receiving reports the Council almost instantly proposed action—on schools, hospitals, fisheries, housing, nutrition, tourism, forestry, hill sheep farming, food and milk prices, juvenile delinquency, rents. The Scottish Council for Industry was formed in 1942, Crown Lands were secured for agriculture, and in 1943 a Bill went through Parliament setting up a non-profit-making organisation for hydro-electric development in Scotland.

The only opposition, according to Johnston, came from a few 'shameless twelfth of August shooting tourists, who took care to live in the electrified south for eleven months of the year'. Obviously he wasn't the man to stand for much argument, and outside war-time this summary rule of the Major-Generals might have run into rough water. All the same, few people now deny that what Johnston achieved was beneficial for Scotland. He himself writes: 'Meanwhile, and emanating from the activities being stirred up under what was the Council of State umbrella, there was arising a new spirit of independence and hope in our national life.'

Neil felt the 'new spirit'. The problems which Johnston chose to attack were those he would have chosen himself. In a sense this ferment of activity was a case of dreams come true. And yet . . . the whole question of collectivism versus individualism now concerned Neil deeply, and after experience of Johnston's benevolent dictatorship he wrote in the *Daily Record* for 5 October 1944:

> Who is to decide when a plan is a good plan and thus will produce more freedom? None but ourselves. It is the essence of our kind of democracy that we make this decision for ourselves. If we don't, tyranny will be clapped on us 'for our good', the tyranny of the super-planner.

A few months earlier he had written (9 June 1944) to Naomi Mitchison expressing reservations about one of Johnston's new programmes:

> And when you accuse me of anarchism, do you mean the anarchism of Kropotkin or just individual chaos? There's a mighty difference. That the herring fishermen should be in a co-operative is anarchism. That they should be run by a State Herring Industry Board is—what? I have always been a socialist all my life, and still am, but I have always been aware of the servile state. I have been supporting Tom Johnston in all his planning schemes. I now hear he is about to bring in a Bill on Herring Report lines, with a strong Herring Board. I am genuinely disappointed at appearing to go against him here. But there is a limit. That doesn't mean that I don't know what such a board could do. Nor does it mean I have any hope of organising a co-operative or union. But certain things have got to be said some time. There's a point where a thing takes the wrong turning. We must have an elementary time sense and look ahead.

With regard to the charge of anarchism it is notable that Neil wrote to Margaret MacEwen on 28 November 1938:

> If you develop your individuality, or rather your individualism, in this way, you may find yourself some fine day doubting the philosophic basis of your creed. And that would be a tragedy! Personally I shouldn't think so, of course, but then I was always an anarchist . . .
> How I should like to see a country like Spain attempt to put anarchism into practice. Abolish leadership . . . and the State.[6]

When the Coalition disintegrated at the end of the war, Tom Johnston left the Secretaryship of State to become Chairman of the new Hydro-Electric Board, the Scottish Committee on Forestry and the Scottish Tourist Board.

On 9 January 1942 Neil and ten others were appointed to the Committee on Post-War Hospital problems in Scotland. He would have preferred fisheries, but did not refuse the job. Their charge was 'to consider and make recommendations within a policy aimed at the post-war development of a comprehensive and co-ordinated hospital service in Scotland on a regional basis'. They were to suggest how to achieve maximum co-operation between voluntary and local authority hospitals; how to finance such a co-ordinated service; and how to administer in peace-time the several new Emergency Medical Service hospitals built for war casualties.[7]

The full committee met thirty-one times between winter 1942 and summer 1943, worked in subcommittee, received evidence, inspected hospitals and reported to the Secretary of State in 1943, proposing Joint Regional Councils, opposing the formation of a National Consultative Committee (in order to preserve local authority), urging the unification of standards, suggesting 'some form of compulsory contribution scheme' for the payment of hospital costs in line with the Beveridge plan for social security, and stating that emergency hospitals should be turned over to local authorities. One result was the Clyde Basin experiment which, according to Johnston, was so successful that by April 1945 'we had wiped out the waiting lists of 34,000 patients on the books of the voluntary hospitals' and 'our scheme had been extended from the Clyde Valley to all Scotland, and blazed a trail for the National Health Scheme of post-war years.'

Neil had no sympathy with the notion of the artist as an impractical man incapable of boiling an egg, or with the self-indulgent bohemian living on his friends, although he would put up with a lot of this in practice. He believed that a writer is necessarily a better writer for becoming a whole man, able to live with balance and resilience no matter the circumstances in which he is placed. For this reason he was very taken in later years with the idea of the 'householder' in Gurdjieff's system. According to that controversial Georgian thinker, unless a man is a 'householder'—that is, capable of leading a solid, practical, effective, ordinary life—then real knowledge and development are impossible to him. Neil was always concerned with practical ability. Pick remembers his look of cold disapproval when inspecting an untidy and inadequate garden fenced off in a field, and on the other hand commending him with remarkable seriousness for doing a simple repair to Neil's car.

We have already seen Neil acting as negotiator, peacemaker, diplomatist. On the Hospitals Committee and later on the Commission of Inquiry into Crofting Conditions, the British Council, and other bodies, he proved himself an efficient committee man, capable not merely of making his points but of choosing the correct time to make them. He could be accommodating on small issues in order to be more effectively unyielding on large. He was courteous but firm, and knew what he wanted.

What did Neil's travelling and public involvement mean to Daisy—and to Margaret? Daisy often went to her sister's or to Peter and Ena Macleod near Perth when Neil was away. She was shy and reserved among strangers, but she liked attention, flattery and friends. Neil's political work was alien to her, and his Committees and Commissions seemed a misuse of his talents. She did not argue against his acceptance of the job, but she took every chance to point him back to the work which both fulfilled him and kept him at home.

The necessary visits to Edinburgh gave him the opportunity occasionally to see Margaret in Glasgow. To Margaret herself they were assurance that she *would* see him. She had struggled to make her life meaningful without him, and had succeeded, but she would be available whenever he came. He told her sometimes he would like to have brought her a present of silk stockings, but daren't go in to ask for them, so brought a bottle of whisky instead. She said she preferred the whisky. Once she carefully saved two eggs from the ration so that he could have one, and he mistook the sugar for salt and ruined it. She writes:

> He was nearly always happy and gay, often playful . . . He was very responsive to my mood and I was always so happy to see him . . . He would soon tease me out of any transient depression or irritation, but once when I was sad over the death of a friend he was very tender and understanding.

And she tells one story about his experience in the black-out:

> He was going to see one of the family—I think David—in Edinburgh, during the war, and was late because he'd lost himself . . . He heard footsteps approaching, someone in high heels, and when the woman seemed near he lifted his hat politely and said 'Excuse me, could you . . .' Before he got further, she gave a little scream and ran off as fast as her high heels would let her. Neil was quite put out. I said she wouldn't have seen the reassuring gesture in the dark, nor his kind face. He supposed not, but was 'quite vexed at frightening the lassie'.[8]

Neil and Margaret argued a lot, but did not quarrel. Not only did they disagree about communism, but Margaret felt that he idealised women, and failed to see them objectively either in life or in fiction.

While engaged with the new role of man of affairs, he not only continued writing, he wrote more than ever. He began the novel which became *The Serpent* and at the same time found himself racing down another track, where the sunshine was brighter and the air full of a bracing fragrance. We know that *The Serpent* and *Young Art and Old Hector* were written almost simultaneously. Although *Young Art and Old Hector* was published in April 1942 Neil reported to Naomi Mitchison that he had completed the proofs of a novel which he did not name, but said the publishers found it very sombre and did not expect it to do anything. 'They're dead right,' he adds. And no one in his senses could call *Young Art and Old Hector* sombre.[9]

Young Art and Old Hector was in fact a beautiful accident. With the publication of *The Silver Darlings* in April 1941 he had become much in demand. At a publisher's party in Edinburgh he met the editor of *Chambers' Journal*, who asked him when he was going to write some stories for the magazine. He indicated that a series would be enthusiastically welcomed.[10]

Neil the literary householder was not one to look a gift-horse in the mouth. But *Chambers' Journal* was a publication with its own peculiarities, of a kind unique to Scotland, insisting on open-air wholesomeness, romance without explicit sex, and the avoidance of dark thoughts. Chambers as a firm were Maurice Walsh's publishers, and often Neil had suggested plots for Maurice. But he wanted to avoid the conscious restraints which writing about adults or adolescents in *Chambers' Journal* would involve, and he wasn't capable of indulging in what Maurice called *ro*mance.

The solution came to him in a flash. In his childhood old men and little boys were often thrown together for the good reason that neither could do a full day's heavy work and they might keep each other out of mischief.

Identifying with a boy always seemed to liberate Neil's writing. He wrote to Tokusaburo Nakamura, Professor of English at Tokyo University, in 1965:

> *Young Art and Old Hector* is about a little boy and an old man in the Celtic Highlands. I confess I patterned the little boy on a nephew of mine who at the time of writing was a very engaging little fellow, full of unexpected attitudes and sayings and questions.[11]

This nephew was Hamish, son of brother Alec and Alec's wife Gretta. Once, in a shop, he saw an engine he very much wanted. The price was 4s 6d. 'Could you possibly let me have it', he asked the girl, looking up, 'for sixpence, as an extreme obligement?'

But Hamish was not the only 'pattern' available to Neil. Brother John was living at Strathpeffer, a few miles down the road, and John's sons Alasdair and Dairmid were comparable in age to Hamish. He watched them all grow up. And it is this 'watching' which differentiates Young Art from the boys portrayed in earlier books. Art's feelings were Neil's, but Art is often seen dramatically from outside as he experiences them.

As for Hector, Neil continues to Nakamura: 'The old man is a composite of two or three old men whom I knew as a little boy.'

The inspiration which saw the old man and the little boy as an ideal pair for *Chambers' Journal* was not sufficient to produce the stories. Something else was needed for that. And here his reading helped him. He was studying the notes to *Carmina Gadelica*, which contain not merely customs and lore and prayers and invocations but proverbs and sayings, and the idea came to him that each story could be based on such a proverb, saying or legend. The notion led him to other collections – he acknowledges J. F. Campbell's *Popular Tales of the West Highlands* in the foreword. He said during the 1960s, 'Whenever I heard or remembered a Gaelic proverb, it led me to visualise a whole story, developing out of the proverb, and I could use Young Art and Old Hector. And I didn't bother to stop for the stories at all, but just went on and finished the book.'

He makes another comment in his letter to Nakamura:

> The talks between the two (Art and Hector), or with others, were as true to life as I could make them. In a certain way, this is a difficult kind of writing, in the sense that, as more than one distinguished poet has pointed out, the most difficult of all characters to depict is a good man. I don't mean that it is difficult nowadays because in recent fiction and drama goodness has gone out of fashion and therefore embarrasses the usual run of readers and spectators . . . I mean quite simply . . . that goodness runs closely parallel to sentiment, to a sentiment that *might* step over into sentimentality, a thing which true goodness never does. A difficult course or parallel to hold, but when naturally successful, how wonderful. There is also, need I add, the final difficulty of making goodness interesting, for in goodness, why, there is nothing to write about . . . The Scottish writer, Naomi Mitchison, an old friend, confessed that she had not come across this kind of relationship in the Highlands; so she thought that, perhaps, I had been exaggerating. Was there here, in other words, something sentimental. This truly astonished me, for such a relationship in our youth was as natural as the flying of birds.

If sentimentality means 'distortion by false feeling or idealisation', then we find none in Young Art and Old Hector. The descriptions of Art's feelings are at once vivid and precise; there are both tenderness and irony discernible, but events are organised by a clear mind, and an objective eye watches everything. In the sense that Art's emotions are Neil's, Keith Henderson is right in saying 'Art is Neil'; and the action of the stories is set in the time of Neil's own childhood. But Art is seen more from outside than is the boy in *Morning Tide*.

Of course Neil's remembered reality includes what Keith called a 'spirit-memory' of a Golden Age. The 'goodness' of Old Hector is in his mind at one with the 'goodness' of the Highland tradition and stems partly from the 'goodness' of his Golden Age. He was contrasting the 'way-opening' wisdom of Hector with the coercive authority of the political state, with the absolutist view of fatherhood, with the hierarchical attitude to human affairs. And in this respect not only were there—and are there—Hectors in the Highlands, and Hectors everywhere, but Neil's descriptions of family life in *Young Art and Old Hector* are accurately realistic.

How far is he justified in holding that the Highland tradition is particularly conducive to the production of 'way-opening' elders? The Highland tradition was directed towards the creation of human beings rather than the creation of things, artefacts, comforts, buildings or works of art, and the proportion of whole human beings it produced is comparatively high. But, of course, Neil is helped by concentrating on the time of his own boyhood; his description of the community demonstrates that it was alive and functioning. Ever since that time it has declined, and one of the reasons for the bitterness evident in his early work is that he saw and recognised its decline. It is true that he does not anywhere deal with the two greatest scourges of the Highlands in its decline—alcoholism and melancholia—but he does deal with the mental atmosphere which produces them. And something of the tradition still survives. Neil's life-work was not directed to reproducing the tradition as it was, but to making the conception of the 'Golden Age' no longer necessary, by experiencing and actualising in fiction the individual way to understanding and wisdom which would in itself help to restore the tradition and recreate community. If the community does survive and grow, then it will be due partly to Neil himself and the experience which his books provide.

Young Art and Old Hector is unique among Neil's novels for the degree of sheer enjoyment he himself got out of writing it. This enjoyment comes through. He has stepped into the light. There is an enchanting freshness and freedom about each episode. What is more, Art and Hector were able to walk straight into a later and greater book in which their meaning as well as their nature is explored.

At a first look we could gain the impression that there is a considerable development in attitude between *Young Art and Old Hector* and *The Green Isle of the Great Deep* in which the young boy and the old man reappear. In *Young Art and Old Hector*, Hector says:

'It is right and fair that the people should have the land back. For untold generations our folk cultivated the Clash, and the Clash was theirs. Whether they made money out of it or not is beside the point. Indeed there wasn't any money to speak of in the old days, and even the laird was content to get such dues as he could in butter or cheese. It's when the greed of money-making started that the lairds got their charters, through laws made by lairds, and cleared our folk off the land . . . And whenever the prime concern in life is money-making, then you have trickery and brutality and wrong. I'm saying that, not from what I have heard, but from what I have observed in a long life among our own folk.'[12]

This might be taken as the socialist argument, that our problem is economic, that once the economic problem is solved, and the capitalist system based upon greed for money is abolished, the human solution inevitably follows. But in *The Green Isle of the Great Deep* the cause of the disease is not money, but power, of which money is only a single form. And that, in effect, is the anarchist argument. In fact, the change of attitude was already taking place before *Young Art and Old Hector* was written, as *The Serpent* makes quite plain.

In *Young Art and Old Hector* there is a conversation about law with reference to that particular law which prevents the Highlander from distilling his own whisky:

'Haven't I proved you the very fount and origin of law-breaking and all that's wrong?' demanded Red Dougal.

'Law-breaking, yes,' said Old Hector. 'But wrong is a difficult word. Many a day I have pondered over it, but I am not sure that I have found the answer. I only have a feeling about the answer and sometimes I go by that feeling. For, you see, laws are necessary, and to break them is wrong. Yet a law can be wrong.'

'And is a law wrong just because *you* find it wrong?' scoffed Red Dougal.

'Yes,' answered Old Hector.

'But the law that's wrong to you is sure to be right to the other fellow, or it wouldn't be in it. How then?' demanded Red Dougal.

'I must still judge for myself, just like the other fellow. That he may have the power to make me suffer does not, of itself, mean that he is right. It just means that he has the power to make me suffer. But it remains with me to judge for myself the outcome of all the elements and to come to a decision on the matter.'[13]

This is a mature and carefully considered individualism, on which it would do us no good to try to pin labels.

After Neil had written and sent to *Chambers' Journal* the first two stories, the characters began to run away with him and he wrote the whole series of

3 George Blake, novelist,
journalist and Director
of the Porpoise Press,
in the 1930s

14 T. S. Eliot relaxing on
a visit of Faber
Directors to Inverness
in 1935

15 Neil and Daisy
'off in a boat',
1937

16 Neil with
Maurice Walsh
at Tobermory,
1937

episodes one after the other until he had completed enough for a book. He outran the ability of a combination of two monthly journals, *Chambers'* and the *Scots Magazine*, to print the chapters before the book came out.[14]

Young Art and Old Hector was finished in October 1941 and Faber rushed it into print by March 1942. They found a variety of reasons for delaying books when they were doubtful of their success, but took one look at *Young Art and Old Hector* and jumped, without worrying about injury to the sales of *The Silver Darlings*.

The fact that Neil read proofs of *The Serpent* only a month after publication of *Young Art and Old Hector* proves one of three things: either Art leapt clear over *The Serpent*'s head into print, or Neil was writing the two turn-about, or—and this alternative seems the most likely—he was well launched into *The Serpent* when he started the stories for *Chambers'* as a sideline, got borne over the hills with Art, and returned to complete *The Serpent*.

Neil had acquired a new correspondent in Agnes Mure Mackenzie—a slight, fragile Lewis woman of 'pertinacity, verve, grit' (to quote Nan Shepherd), who had settled in London, lecturing at Birkbeck College and writing novels, a life of Robert the Bruce, and a series of history textbooks. She became President of the Saltire Society in 1942 and Neil met her in Edinburgh during that year.

He wrote to Agnes on 7 April 1942:

> I am glad you enjoyed *The Silver Darlings*. I am not so sure about *Young Art and Old Hector*, should it come your way. To me here there is a very difficult matter of literary assessment—one on which I am open to any opinion. It's perhaps concerned with a fundamental difference in our (English and Scots) social beginnings. If you like, a difference between the feudal and the primitive communal . . .[15]

As usual the *TLS* tried to confirm his doubts, and the *New Statesman* found the book 'redolent of Celtic charm, which should bring a tear and a twinkle to every Scottish eye. The southerner is likely to think that Art is an unusually slappable child.' The reviewer failed to notice that not only is Art slappable, but he is frequently slapped—by his mother, two sisters, his elder brother and Mary Ann. Neil was too ready to judge English reaction by the tone of the *TLS* and the *New Statesman*.[16]

A letter (14 May 1942) to Nan Shepherd in response to her predictable enthusiasm is revealing in its militant and defensive tone:

> One shouldn't talk of magic, you say? Let me put a circle round, to ward off such heresy. We have listened too long to the clever intellectual climbing out

of the human pit of superstition and him showing off his clever climbing for all to admire and to follow. To think that we never spotted the real truth—that the fellow has no magic in him! With how peculiar a sadism the intellectual witch-doctor has walloped the fun and delight out of the sheer magic of living! Keep an eye on him . . .[17]

Neil is obviously on the verge of beginning *The Green Isle of the Great Deep*, at least in the sense of placing his protagonists Young Art and Old Hector in spiritual opposition to the intellectual witch-doctors who dismiss them as 'sentimental' and who wallop the fun and delight out of living.

In later years he always said that it was Naomi Mitchison's reaction to *Young Art and Old Hector* which provoked *The Green Isle of the Great Deep*. But it's not the whole story. Early in April 1942 Neil met Naomi in Edinburgh and afterwards he writes, about *Young Art and Old Hector:*

> Don't bother thinking about reviewing . . . I was merely anxious that you get the thing before you might go to the trouble of trying to get it for yourself . . . I am inclined to think that personal relations represent about the only final basis on which a poor humanity can conceivably hope to stand on tolerably firm feet. But that would need *a lot of talk.* [18]

If it needed a lot of talk, over the next few years it got it. Naomi Mitchison was always insisting on the need for collective action, and Neil increasingly emphasised the fundamental importance of individual development. In 1943 he wrote to her:

> As to your three ways of changing things profoundly—cheers. There are probably a dozen methods of attack. And we should be beyond revolution in the bloody sense. We have had about enough blood for our lifetime . . . But then I have always been a little repelled by the materialist interpretation of history and all the rest of it when it becomes the new religion. Religion and ideals and what not. Fine. But oh God they do manage to prosecute them to the nth in cruelty. A drunk man with a revolver is a happy child compared with the fellow who has power to convert you. Anyway, if history is to have any meaning at all, surely hundreds of years of understanding of the democratic concept as we have had it in Scotland must count for something . . . After all, take the organisation of the Scottish church, from kirk session or local Soviet up to the General Assembly and you might say it gave Russia its governmental pattern. What a wealth of belief and enthusiasm and shedding of blood went to that foundation! And what do you enlightened revolutionaries think and say of it today? . . . I know what you mean when you say it's no good just altering things so that folk can go twice a week to the films instead of once. But that's precisely what they'll do however you alter things. What could be altered for the better is the community spirit and the kind of flicks. Though here again I am not so sure that the highbrows should have it their

own way. Before you came to Carradale and found what country living really meant, would you have been a sound person to have been placed in charge of their entertainment?

Naomi Mitchison wrote about the need for 'discipline' and about 'not dithering'. Neil replied defensively on 29 June 1943:

> If I put a fellow in a novel who may have any sense of discipline at all, you sicken at the sight of him as a galahad. And accuse me of 'purity' and what not . . . You'll have discipline just where you want it, and that is generally in some idealist, disguised under the name of practical politics. Fine day! If discipline, selection, consistent and sustained action are necessary to achieve anything, perhaps they are necessary in a novelist's character if he wants to bring out summat! . . . So please just step off it and lower somewhat the elevation of your nose as you glance along it at the poor old philosopher . . .
>
> And you making me write all this on a day of such sunshine that it's off after the dead philosopher I am, fair onto the moors, where there's a lost burn, which whiles I fish, and other whiles dip in a pool and sit on the rock to dry. By god, it's good. Peewits, grouse, and the individualism that takes the wandering air on its skin. I never enter that world, but I can look back on other worlds with a certain eye; and if such a picture raises no more than a troubled pity in your attractive eyes, well that's not an unattractive picture either. Or is it a conception too simple and pure—having a couple of worlds to make the best of? Hesitancies and meaninglessnesses and nothing definite and the hours going by—how exasperated a whole afternoon of it would make you!

And one wonders, if there had not been a touch of the flirtatious in the arguments, whether he would have persisted in such lengthy combat?

Young Art and Old Hector and *The Serpent* are both different enough from *The Silver Darlings* to make the immediate efforts to persuade him to a sequel seem short-sighted and ill-advised. And yet there is a sense in which *The Serpent* is itself a sequel to *The Silver Darlings*. *The Silver Darlings* shows the Highlands growing in wealth at the beginning of the nineteenth century, and *The Serpent* shows it in decline at the end. The wise father-figure of Old Hector is replaced by the Calvinist tyrant of *The Serpent*.

Neil had begun to focus his thoughts on intellectual tyranny, on the despotic idealist, on the domination of humanity by arbitrary intellect, and there, looming in the shadows of his own country was the Calvinist fanatic, the authoritarian monster in his known world.

The Serpent is the story of a young man's conflict with the spiritual authority of his father and his father's religion, and of his own movement from turn-of-the-century scepticism to a discovery of the serpent of wisdom. It is the first book in which Neil's philosophical anarchism is overtly stated.

Fundamental to it is a passage which, typically, gives his dream of a future for the Highlands in terms of a vision of the past:

> Once a year the men put on their Sunday suits and went to the place where the Factor was . . . They paid their pound or two, got their dram, and came away. After that each man was his own master, worked his own land, having no boss or bureaucrat over him to drive or direct him. Accordingly in the community as a working or going concern, all were equal in social status . . . The farther back you go the clearer that becomes because you recede more from the power of money. Then almost everything was, as we say, 'in kind' . . . But the crofting country, through long centuries, had reached beyond an active bureaucracy and leaders. True, the chief at intervals stirred up the clansmen to fight for some power-scheme the chiefs had on hand, some dirty business or other, but actually for generations on end whole regions of the country lived in peace, cultivating the land and rearing their cattle and sheep. The individual bits of dirty business are remembered. History has so far been a remembering of the dirty business rather than an understanding of the arts and the way of life of the peaceful generations . . .
>
> They naturally helped one another and at certain times—say, at the peat-cutting—they voluntarily joined forces and worked in squads, and these were usually the happiest times of all. In short, you had a true balance between the maximum freedom of the individual and the common welfare of all, and at the same time . . . they had no bosses, no tyrants, no bureaucrats, no profit-drivers among themselves . . .
>
> Our minds quite naturally take the next step and say: if we could get our society today, *with* the machine, working after the old pattern . . . then once more the life of the folk would be warm and rich and thick . . .[19]

In 1966 Neil wrote to Hart that *The Serpent*

> did absorb me when writing it and I can remember odd moments of what I can only call clairvoyance . . . Of course I have no clear memory of how or why I wrote it, but let me try to reconstruct a possibility . . . When I was a boy there was a man who had gone to Glasgow, to work, then returned, opened a cycle shop, hired cycles, did many kinds of repairs *and* was a freethinker.
>
> A quiet but persistent man, with a sense of humour. Sporadic talks about most things, including socialism and no doubt religion, though I was too young to be more than vague about it. He is not Tom of the book, though the seed of the conception may have been there. But I should say that most communities in the Highlands then would have one sceptic at least. . . .
>
> Next . . . about what you feel is some sort of intrusion in the novel—Janet, her mother, Donald and that side of Tom's life: all that is really made up. But blame Mr Balance, who got the notion that a man like Tom, who was a full man in his fashion, must have had his instinctive or passionate side, and I have little doubt that Mr B . . . linked up this side with the other (freethinking intellectual) by making Donald a son of the manse . . .

Tom's relation to his father: not unnatural, in the context, and without going all Freudian, even if I personally had no such parental experience.

If the Janet affair is 'made up' then it is made up from a deep level of the mind, for its passion, intensity and subtlety make it one of the most intriguing love passages in his fiction. It is in the account of Tom's love for Janet, of his breakdown after betrayal, and of the relationship between Tom and his mother that the burning clairvoyance of which Neil speaks is most evident:

> It was then she [Janet] gave him that strange white look that haunted him for years. There was loneliness in it, something wild and scared. It glistened distantly from him yet came into him and burned him up. It was more than a farewell in its glistening anguish. And from somewhere in the heart of it she smiled at him.
> But the cry, that silent cry of her spirit, remained unuttered.[20]

And then there is that intensity of pride in Tom, as in all Neil's heroes, eventually broken in his acceptance of his mother:

> His mother was moving towards him and speaking, shutting out his vision. 'No!' he screamed at her. To be touched was to be trapped. Premonition of the familiarity of touch revolted him with such fear and hatred that his whole chest felt like vomiting up. But he lived now beyond physical reaction in an unquenchable agony of fear.[21]

> It was an exquisite relief to give in to her, to care no more, to feel her near him. Never had his pride broken like this before anyone; but now that it was broken, his acceptance of his mother was the acceptance of a natural ally who spoke and behaved validly in her own right. That she was not the figure his secret pride and egoism had desired was now all the better. The qualities in her that formerly made him impatient with her were the very qualities of endurance and patience which he now saw were the only ultimates against the cruelties and inexhaustible resource of fate.[22]

The book is sombre, right enough, dark with passion, and the passion runs everywhere through it, burning. It is strange also. Why do Tom and Janet meet secretly? The motivation seems less than convincing. It is taken for granted that they should meet in the dark, in secret, hidden away:

> Once or twice he met her in the village and spoke to her for a few moments. In these moments their lives were brought over the dead days into the living present. 'No chance of seeing you?' 'Tina and myself are going out on Thursday night.' 'I'll wait for you at the back. Don't go in the front door.' 'But I mightn't—' 'Never mind. I'll be there.' Their faces had not lost the innocuous neighbourly smile and they parted at once in a neighbourly way.[23]

This is the only image of Neil's hidden relationship with Margaret which appears in the books—a sense of meeting in the dark, haunted by pain.

The Serpent is itself haunting—it is like a deep, wild night burning with stars. Tom passes through the valley of living death, yet dies at last in peace. 'For if there was no death, then all is life. And if, at the end, there is death only, then here is life's greatness and its beauty.'

In a letter (19 March 1970) Neil corrected Hart for suggesting that Tom the Philosopher had been bitten by the serpent. No, the snake 'touched the wrist innocently with its mouth'. 'But yet I now feel sure that readers will conclude that the serpent did the deed. I should have amplified a little . . . But for some reason I doubt if I could explain I cannot alter that final moment between the serpent and old Tom. That leaves wonder, self forgotten. When the serpent puts its tail in its mouth it's the symbol of eternity.'

Neil and Daisy had a silver biscuit container with a serpent depicted on it, tail in mouth. The serpent as a symbol of wisdom, the serpent in the Garden of Eden and the serpent as a symbol of eternity were all in his mind while writing the book. But these symbols grew naturally as the book grew, and are not schematic.

The Serpent appeared in June 1943 and on 7 August Neil was writing to Nan Shepherd: 'Apart from Edwin Muir they have nearly all said the same. And there is just this compensation—they'll call it "escape". O God, their labels!—that there is a sort of rare freedom in being unnoticed among the damned. It cleanses the mind of ambitions and brings what true delight there may be to the act of catching the unheard melody all for its own sweet sake . . .'

'Unnoticed among the damned' is an odd way of putting it. Many a writer would have given much to receive the praise which Neil received over the years. It seems that he had once more chosen the bad reviews to remember. However, the *Guardian*'s opinion that 'everything is a little dim and wistful in its effect' seems to have been general. Edwin Muir did not share it; in a long essay which appeared in Neil's home from home the *Scots Magazine* he writes:

> *The Serpent* is a mature book, in the sense that we can see in it the free development and use of a mind of rare insight. The effect of imaginative maturity is to make you feel that everything you are shown is in its proper place and on its true scale . . .
>
> That does not mean, of course, that it is made up of a given number of harmonious elements; the harmony resides in the total effect, but the material

out of which it is woven is conflict, disaster, loss, betrayal, and on occasion supernatural horror. The harmony is not achieved by softening or disguising any of these things, but rather by making each ring out with its true note.[24]

In later years Neil always remembered Edwin and Willa Muir with warmth and affection. They had met long before. Letters date from 1931. During the 1930s when Neil was active in the Nationalist movement, Edwin must have distressed him with *Scottish Journey*, which ends with a socialist attack on the Scottish National Party.

And in 1936 Neil in turn upset Edwin by his sharp review of *Scott and Scotland*. Grieve did not like *Scott and Scotland*, either. In fact it is from this time on that, as P. H. Butter puts it (in *Edwin Muir: Man and Poet*), Grieve 'pursued Muir in books and articles with bitter personal attacks which did nothing to advance his cause'.[25] The situation became difficult for Neil: he counted both men as friends. His own review had been measured and impersonal, in contrast to Grieve's vendetta. In fact this vendetta was one reason for Neil's gradual withdrawal from Grieve. When asked in 1967 about the caricatural venom which presented Willa as an aggressive Amazon he said:

> No, that's not fair at all. She may have been a bit positive. She was intellectually self-reliant. Although she treated Edwin like a mother at times, she was a fair, good person, and he in his delicate, quiet way was actually wiry and tough, too. I think Daisy never really forgave Grieve for publishing in that magazine of his a cartoon of Willa as a great big woman, and a little doe licking her fingers that was obviously meant to be Edwin.

When the war came, Willa took a job teaching and Edwin got clerical work in Dundee, commuting from St Andrews. In 1941–2 they were both seriously ill. Then Edwin joined the staff of the British Council in Edinburgh, organising cultural programmes for the international houses set up to accommodate foreign servicemen and refugees. It was a happier time for them both. *The Narrow Place* (1943) gained for Edwin greater recognition than he had ever known before.

Every two or three weeks between February 1942 and late summer 1943 Neil travelled to Edinburgh, and dined often with the Muirs. In congenial company Edwin could be humorous and merry, and they shared a convivial pleasure in various gentle ploys, which didn't always meet with approval. One night they entered the house late for dinner, and singing, to receive a faceful of cooking rice from Willa.

In a letter to Nan Shepherd Neil describes his state in August 1943, seated in limbo between *The Serpent* and *The Green Isle of the Great Deep*. He was waiting for the company which had taken an option on *The Silver Darlings* to begin filming. They did not in fact begin until the war was over. An agreement was reached in 1942 with the Associated British Picture Corporation and Holyrood Film Productions of London. Neil was much impressed by the reputation of the Czech director Karl Grüne. The screenplay was to be prepared by a Glasgow writer, Clarence Elder, and reached Neil in winter 1942. He sent it back noting all sorts of problems in the changes made from the book. He said he saw the need for 'extensive alterations' and proposed to begin 'soaking into the stuff'. Amendments were made and comments received during spring and early summer of 1943, with retyped scripts shuttling back and forth—but difficulties over distribution contracts, office bombing in London and wartime security caused one delay after another. Neil comments 'The script is now finished, so I'm just . . . doing nothing, with not an idea in my head,' and adds 'Though I have a continuation of the adventures of Young Art and Old Hector,' and pretends to be doubtful about whether to publish.[26]

In a letter to Professor Nakamura many years later he gave an account of the genesis of this book, *The Green Isle of the Great Deep*, referring to Naomi's accusation of sentimentality in *Young Art and Old Hector*, and continuing:

> So my mind switched to the intellectual leftish circles that she moved within . . . I realised how provincial, even parochial, not to mention 'simple' to the point of sentimentality, such a book could appear there . . . There was something somewhere at a deeper level. And this was tied up, I could see, with the Celtic culture out of which I had come . . . I now had to ask if that old culture was in fact an anachronism? Had it a meaning for modern living? Was I recording old ways of life beyond possible human interest any more?
>
> So the idea occurred to me to try to let the questions be answered by placing these two characters in the world of today, complete with intellectual arguments on Government, freedom, and all the other pet themes or theories of our time, and just see what happened . . . And what was the end of it all?—that Naomi Mitchison recommended the book strongly to her intellectual and even psychiatric friends! Recently I was having lunch with her in Inverness and told her how it came about that she was the cause of the book's being written.[27]

It is curious that he told Naomi the story only twenty years after the event. Certainly the book grew out of their continuing dialogue, but at the time he offered her quite a different explanation. When her copy reached her she wrote to him making the suggestion that he had in fact written the book for *her*—and Neil denied it!

You are a queer devil, Neil, you're the only writer I know of that never writes the same book twice . . . Who at all would have guessed that this was the next layer to *The Serpent*? . . . Do you ever feel with a book, sometimes by an author you've never met or even heard of before, this book was written for me? I feel that awfully with *The Green Land* [sic] . . . But you've laid down a challenge which I feel bound to take up. I think first, all the same, I ought to say what you no doubt know already, that it's a damn good piece of writing. You are amazingly good at describing the pleasures of the senses, particularly eating. It wouldn't surprise me, though, if you thought eating was slightly wicked . . .

But it is in effect the anarchist case. Now insofar as it is saying power corrupts, that's fine. I think it also says purely intellectual power corrupts, the worst thing is the power of the bureaucrat, the planner at headquarters.[28]

She goes on to insist that since there must be planning, there must be 'something as strong as the Communist Party to stand up to the other side', that the old way is dying in her part of Argyll under the pressure of 'competitive capitalism', that it cannot survive without a revolution, that 'we've got to get capitalism off our backs, and I don't see how we can do it by just being anarchists. The individual may, but what's the good of being free if our neighbours whom we love aren't free?'

Neil fires back (9 June 1943):

Unless we're concerned with life in its vivid living moments, we should take to pamphlets . . . Hell's bells, woman, I've just been listening to the news, and have been told with triumph that we shall soon be able to get dehydrated potato which we can mix with a little water and find indistinguishable from normal mash. And you—even you—acted upon unconsciously by psycho-analytic news, suggest that I—me—think eating wicked, somewhere far ben! Really appalling. When I consider the number of women who don't know how to boil a potato. When I think of the food we have in the Highlands, and how it isn't cooked. Lord, the flavour of a Golden Wonder, steamed in its own jacket, until it bursts its coat in laughter. An oatcake that is really crisp. Butter, real butter on that oatcake. Heather honey. Our berries. Our game. Our prime herring. Hill mutton . . . I refuse to talk to you about it. You'll be calling me a gourmet next. Go away.

How delightful of you to utter the ultimate compliment by saying that you think *The Green Isle* was written for you. That sort of living response would make anyone write a book. In fact I wrote *The Green Isle* right off, just because an old friend of mine in Ireland, who has mostly for company now his little grandson, was so affected by what he considered the inner truth of *Young Art* that he said I mustn't leave them at the River. So I didn't. Can you think of any better reason for writing a book?

Is this remark of Maurice's one of those urgings to a sequel which Neil elsewhere claims to have refused? At any rate his letter to Naomi is disingenuous. Perhaps he won't give her the satisfaction of admitting that he found it necessary to write a novel to counter her arguments. Anyhow, in Neil's last letter to Naomi dated December 1971 he confesses that he has just told a 'critic who is doing an essay on me . . . the story of your finding *Young Art and Old Hector* just a trifle sentimental and how I duly decided to send them to a place I called 'the Green Isle' . . . At that time you and I were about equally leftish, so it seemed a fair joke. I hope you still think so.'

In 1943 he continues:

> Think of what your criticism amounts to. My book is against fascism. You take it as being against communism. Now isn't that a thought! . . . If we take dialectical materialism as the unity of theory and practice, with practice having primacy, isn't it odd that when I leave the theory out and describe only the practice, the actual practice, you assume communism? Yet I described fascism, using its proper word 'corporate' in the Italian fashion and even describing the salute, which is so different from the Russian.

This too is disingenuous, because *The Green Isle of the Great Deep* is closely based on the brainwashing techniques used by the Russians for the Moscow show-trials. The interest he took in these affairs is made evident in a letter to Joseph Macleod dated 10 April 1943:

> One can stand a fair amount of suppression and cruelty and bumping-off, realising the need for force in a transition period, but the purgings of 1937 began to make some of us think. The amazing trial and execution of the old Guard, the attack on Finland, and so on, had a sort of hopeless air from a distance. A book like Louis Fischer's *Men and Politics* was not exactly re-assuring. And the cry that 'the Party is everything, the individual nothing' was tending even here to become suspiciously like one of the slogans of a religious crusade—after the 'Jesus and no quarter' of our covenanters.[29]

Neil knew more about communism than about fascism—he had studied reports, he had read and admired Koestler's *Darkness at Noon,* and he had found the analytical and materialist approach of communism increasingly alien and inhuman. God says to Hector:

> There was a time when the Questioner had wisdom. He used his head and drew on his wisdom. But the more he used his head only, the paler his wisdom became, until at last the elements of wisdom were no longer so but only the ghostly bits he used for making a pattern with his head. He knew in his head that you suffered, but as the head itself does not suffer, he himself was not affected, for what is affected swims deep with the salmon. He has divorced knowledge from wisdom, the head from the heart, the intellect from the spirit . . . and because of the divorce, the taste of life has gone bitter and its hope sterile . . .[30]

In 1945 Pick wrote in an article:

> It may be that Gunn is regarding Nazism as a manifestation of the same
> intellectual and scientific attitude as displayed by the administrators of the
> Green Isle. He deliberately mentions the continent of Europe under German
> domination in the first few pages of the book, to set the stage. This is a
> half-truth. There was science and the use of intellect in Nazism, deliberately
> applied to delude and subdue the people. But the driving-force was not
> intellectual but irrational. It was an appeal to the primitive communal, and
> one of the cries of the Spanish fascists was 'Death to the intellect'.[31]

Neil read this article, and responded warmly to it, but made no comment on
that passage. Did he really believe that he was dealing with fascism and not
communism? Many conversations over many years convince us otherwise.
He was perfectly well aware that the methods he was exposing were the
particular tool of the communist state, but he felt himself to be confronting
totalitarianism in general, mind control in general, the latest threat to the
human spirit.

In an article called 'The Novel at Home', which originally appeared in the
Scots Magazine and was reprinted in the United States, he wrote:

> The notion of testing, as it were, the ways of life of the old man and the little
> boy against the conscious ideology of totalitarianism got a grip of my mind
> that I couldn't shake off . . .[32]

But in fact it is neither Art nor Hector who saves mankind in the Green Isle.
It is the woman, Mary, who clings to the old earth-life, persuades her
husband Robert (so named after Robert Burns) to eat of the real fruit instead
of the de-energised gruel provided by the authorities; it is Mary who hides
Art; it is Mary who resists the Questioner. Can it be that Neil himself came
to forget this?

Naomi complained of the book's anarchism, but a thoroughgoing anarchist might complain about Neil's solution to the problems of the Green
Isle, for administration remains centralised:

> Most of the present Administrators, then, would be removed, and in their
> place would come those who had the urge to serve in an administrative
> capacity and who from time to time would have to consult with the Council of
> the wise men.[33]

But how does the Council of wise men get appointed? And to whom would
they be responsible? It is stated that the wise men will have 'no power'. So
how can they ensure this consultation? And if the administrators, who do
have power, abuse it, how are the wise men to control them? And if in order

to control them, the wise men themselves acquire power, how do they avoid corruption, and how do they retain their wisdom, for it is said 'There was a time when the Questioner had wisdom'?

Naomi reviewed *The Green Isle of the Great Deep* and remained fascinated by the book—proving that it was indeed 'written for her'—and wrote in 1947 that she had read it for the third time: 'I am sure that you don't know half of what is in it yourself. One writes blind.' Here she was underestimating that very conscious and subtle man. Neil knew just what was in it. But on occasion the sheer depth of poetic perception carried him beyond himself. She added: 'I thought I must tell you that I have a friend staying, one of the younger Huxleys, an anthropologist. He says he has read *The Green Isle* three times, getting more out of it every time. I told him it was especially *my* book! But you see, the thrown stone does spread rings, rather oddly sometimes.'

Reviewers in general failed to discern through the lucid waters of the Green Isle the huge salmon swimming in its depth. Neil would not be surprised at that. All the same, they didn't jeer. Even the *TLS* was balanced and appreciative, though a little stuffy.[34]

A first printing of 8,000 compared with the normal 10,000 for a promising Gunn novel and 12,000 for a certainty like *The Silver Darlings* demonstrates Faber's worries. All the same the edition was gone in a few months and they must have reissued, for by June 1948 it had sold just over 18,000 copies.[35]

14 The Mature Writer

Neil was now at the height of his success. *Wild Geese Overhead* and *Second Sight* had been dropped, but a 25,000-run paperback edition of *Highland River* was sold out, *Morning Tide* remained in print, and Faber were struggling to reissue *The Silver Darlings*. Neil was always claiming that many more copies of his books could have been sold if they were available, and this was true, but at the time any reprint of an existing book could mean the refusal of a new one.

After *The Green Isle of the Great Deep* Neil was in general a different writer—more intellectual, more difficult, more complex. He had moved out of the main stream, and as a result his publishers gradually became less and less eager to back him. He had finished with the novel of growing up and was concerned more with the novel of healing. In *The Green Isle of the Great Deep* he had, to his own satisfaction, solved the social problem theoretically, but he must solve it actually, through characters threatened with disintegration. He must lead them through to acceptance and rebirth. Certainly he was still concerned with communal wholeness, but he knew that communal wholeness had become impossible without individual realisation of the wholeness of life itself, through experience of the essential centre of being—which eventually he termed the 'atom of delight'.

In *The Green Isle of the Great Deep* this conversation occurs:

'You see, first of all you get the knowledge. Then you get the wisdom . . . Then . . . you get something else.' And he looked at Old Hector, who looked at him.
'What?' asked Old Hector.
'The magic,' said Art.[1]

In the later books he seeks to complete the knowledge in wisdom and so release the magic. In the sense that he never again achieved the profound lucidity of *The Green Isle of the Great Deep* he did not succeed, but to ask him to return to the writing of *Morning Tide* would be to ask the impossible. He was now in search of the well at the world's end. In *The Key of the Chest* he held the ingredients in such equilibrium that he deceived almost everyone into failing to notice what kind of a book it really was. They did their best to take it for a thriller, and thought themselves safe. But they were not.

Charlie, one of Neil's returned 'failures', rescues a seaman after a wreck. The seaman is clinging onto a chest. The seaman dies. There is suspicion that he did not die naturally, and that Charlie took money from the chest.

Michael at the big house is a photographer and has staying with him the philosopher Gwynn. The doctor acts as a link between the two groups.

As so often, Neil made use of old material to achieve new results. The basis for *The Key of the Chest* is a short story, 'The Dead Seaman', which appeared in the *Scots Magazine* in July 1931. Some passages in the story are simply transferred to the novel with stylistic improvements. But the story does not include the Minister's daughter or Charlie's Edinburgh experiences.

The theme of brotherhood is certainly present in the story, but in the novel it is deepened, widened and elaborated. The 'darkness' which encircles Tearlach's throat—entirely symbolic in the story—becomes real and human and capable of being understood intellectually in the novel. In a very direct and immediate way Dougal in the novel is his brother's keeper.

The novel has two sets of characters—those deeply engaged in the action and the experience; and those who act as watchers: the doctor, the philosopher, the photographer. It is plain that by this time Neil needs an observer half inside and half outside his story, capable of intellectual comment and interpretation, if he is to develop adequately all the levels of his meaning. Often Gwynn represents the author's own abstract ideas while the doctor gives his feelings about the situation. Since the doctor is vital to the book it is right that it should have been dedicated to a real doctor, Peter John Macleod.

The author's consistent approval of the doctor is proof enough that the doctor's feelings are usually Neil's own. He is the only character who is recorded consistently from within. There are times when the doctor, as Highland intellectual, jealous of his tradition, hates the intruding analysts, Michael and Gwynn. When he hates, he grows cold and withdraws, casting them into outer darkness. He never clearly expresses his objection to Michael and Gwynn. But he finds distasteful the way in which they exploit the country and its people for picturesque and illustrative effect, the way in which they pry, probe and explain, no matter how delicate the affairs into which they choose to penetrate. They are altogether too articulate, too knowing, too glib, too self-absorbed, too 'modern'. And the depth and virulence of the doctor's dislike is interesting, since he voluntarily spends so much time in their company, and is not seen socially in anyone else's.

There is a revealing moment in the book when Charlie, 'having come so

far and been defeated, been defeated in his pride, his manhood, his seaman-
ship, it was no longer possible for him to go back', is called urgently by the
girl Flora:

> Charlie came walking down towards them and Michael knew, where the
> marrow crawls inside the bone, that there came a courage, carried lightly,
> without expression, of a kind he had never before encountered.[2]

This is the attitude with which Neil consistently identifies: 'a courage
carried lightly, without expression'. And the key words are 'without expression'. He was a passionate, warm, intellectual, humorous man, ferociously
proud, and very private, who kept his secrets.

At one point Gwynn sums up with impressive clarity the main themes of
Neil's fiction from this time on:

> When intelligence stopped being fused with their belief, it came apart by
> itself, it began to ask questions, to inquire—and so began scientific inquiry.
> So the split in the whole. The spontaneous belief that gave wholeness was
> gone. Now if we could grow a new whole out of scientific inquiry and material
> phenomena alone, then we could see our way ahead. But apparently we can't.
> When a man is happily in love, or listening to a piece of music, or creating
> something, then he has the complete sensation of wholeness. Immediately he
> pauses consciously to inquire into it, he ceases having the sensation itself.[3]

So how can wholeness be restored? Neil's own inquiry was internal, rigorous
and intuitive. It led him to the necessity for the development of the 'second
self ' and to the realisation of the 'atom of delight'.

The book is a remarkable feat of balance, judgement and dexterity, and
brings to a successful conclusion a line of odd, difficult books which begins
with *The Lost Glen* and proceeds through *Second Sight*.

The Key of the Chest was not issued until January 1946. In fact, *The
Drinking Well* was finished by December 1945, although it did not come out
until February 1947.

Delay in issuing both books distressed Neil and on 25 June 1947
he wrote to Morley Kennerley of Faber as the climax of a long saga of inquiry
and response:

> Dear Kennerley,
> It was thoughtful of you to hunt out these income figures of mine. As I got
> some cash for films, the total was even better, so the Income Tax authorities
> had a proper onslaught, against which the £132 for six months proved
> inadequate ammunition. I should, of course, have seen the demand coming,
> but then you cannot blame me altogether as I had expected some cash for
> reprints. Away back a year last January when *The Key of the Chest* had been

over-subscribed, you wrote saying that a reprint of 5,000 was imminent. Nothing ever appeared, and now you do not even mention the book. A year last March, a secretary said that you were expecting a reprint of *The Silver Darlings* any moment. Since then, no word of it. *Young Art* was busily being reprinted over a period when he didn't even exist! And you wondered recently why I smiled when you said you were reprinting *The Drinking Well*! From which—and more of the same—I sort of conclude that news of anything reprinting really means nothing—until possibly some priority machine is set in motion, like the marble in the gambling game, though I'm merely guessing now. Unfortunately, no Income Tax inspector works with marbles, as I know so well, having been a Civil Servant for 25 years and used to instructing the public in the inexorable ways of accountancy. The whole position is wonderfully complicated, too, as the result of a trip which I have just had to one or two of our Scottish cities. One Scots author rather gloated over me by producing his statement from which it was clear that his publisher had managed to get him nearly four times the amount of paper expended on me by mine—in each case, our last book. There seemed to be a sort of general feeling that the firm of Faber is not really interested in the novel and wants paper for other and more expanding business, what are considered more important books. In which respect Faber may be quite right. The trouble with an author, whose first novel appeared over 20 years ago, is that he too may want to go in for more important business, like reading philosophy or contemplating his navel . . . Then again, if an author did make something during the two or three years when the going is good—which seems the sort of position at the moment—he would probably spend it on the wrong things, like buying whisky or a washing machine for his wife, which, as we say in the north, are not in it anyway. So all round this is a very complicated problem, and my heart aches at the thought of all your troubles. But don't blame authors for badgering you, not too much anyway. I rather fancy that they intuitively feel it's now or never—and have it in their bones from history that they are fated to be on the wrong dog. Especially those of them who have been writing for a long time and think that they may have established a faint claim to some kind of priority, particularly when their books do actually sell when they are visible . . . [And then as PS:] Why do you always have to go in for *Morning Tide* and *Highland River* so confidently? I have never heard that you had any difficulty selling other reprints. The sight of something new some time would at least be lightsome.[4]

It was between the publication of *The Key of the Chest* and *The Drinking Well* that Pick met Neil, and he gave this account of the event:

In 1945 I published an article on Neil's work, and sent it to him. His immediate acknowledgement was so courteous, understanding and sincere that I felt curiously indebted to him, as if he had played host to me in a strange country, particularly since the article had contained a number of points of dispute.

Then in January 1946 my wife and I moved from London to the north-west

Highlands. On a spring day in that year I was taking a bath at the eccentric hour of 3 p.m. when a knock sounded on the door, and I paused in the process of dipping my soapy head in the water to grumble a protest. A minute later there was a call 'Can you hurry? Neil Gunn is here to see you.'

I felt like a man arrested in the nude, and arrived with dripping hair, a pattern of surprised awkwardness.

Neil Gunn was at that time fifty-four years old, tall, spare, with a strong-boned face, dressed in a tweed suit of moorland green. One eye had long ago been damaged in an accident and would not move in conjunction with the other. He seemed totally unaware of the disability and within ten minutes I was unaware of it too.

His manner had a quality of objective friendliness which was at the same time non-committal and reassuring. He was willing to accept disagreeable manifestations without comment. Gradually the edgy defensiveness of a young writer fell away as the realisation grew that I was not under critical scrutiny but would be appreciated for any insights I could offer. By the time he left I was convinced that the man was as good as his books.

A few weeks later he called again, accompanied this time by John Macnair Reid and his wife, and they stayed the night. Not long afterwards we went over to Braefarm House on a two-stroke motor-cycle, looking like monsters from outer space, and proved a surprise to Daisy. She said that from the hand-writing of my letter she had expected an academic of fifty with pince-nez instead of a young man with motoring goggles and a hat like a tea-cosy. From then on I typed letters; if I didn't she fled from the room crying 'Spiders! Spiders!'[5]

The Picks did not hesitate to visit Neil and Daisy whenever invited, and they weren't the only ones. During a few months in 1947 as well as the Picks they put up Gordon Bottomley ('We have had Gordon Bottomley staying with us. The poor old fellow lost his wife recently and is a bit wandered.'); Daisy's Devon sister and her husband Bob Bartholomew, a passionate fisherman for whom Neil had a warm, amused affection; an abstract painter named Andrew Taylor Elder; Keith and Helen Henderson; and others. About this time, too, a 'proletarian writer' from Glasgow arrived uninvited and planted himself at Brae, spending his time taking hot baths and telling Neil he was a bourgeois who had sold out to the landlords. Neil recounted this incident with a kind of appreciative awe. It was Daisy who expressed resentment on his behalf.

The household was a warm and peaceful one. Daisy did all the cleaning and was a good plain cook. Neil's favourite meal—not available until rationing ended—was Baxter's Royal Game soup, followed by a roast cooked in its own juices ('We like the flavour of the meat itself, not all these French sauces,' Daisy said), with Golden Wonder potatoes steamed in their jackets, then what Daisy called 'visitor's pudding', which was a lemon mousse. For tea Neil always had a dollop of home-made blackcurrant jam on brown bread; and for breakfast, porridge.

This was the period of *The Drinking Well* and *The Shadow*. *The Drinking Well* harked back to more traditional concerns and methods—'a regional novel of the sheep-farming life'. That it is much more goes without saying.

On 4 February 1946 Neil acknowledged Naomi's kind words about *The Key of the Chest* and describes the new novel:

> It deals with hill sheep farming and is over 170,000 words long! I had a real fight with myself over the end and found how remarkable a hold a theory—socialist theory—can get on one. This was my difficulty. A young fellow wants to follow his father as a sheep farmer. In the end he has to clear out. Normally that would be the end of him. Another emigrant. But I don't want that to happen. So—as there is no one else with money I have to introduce a sound landlord who is prepared to do things to the land by way of reclamation, etc. The inter-war period. In the end you see a young fellow, with plenty of guts and ideas and knowledge prepared to put up a fight, backed by a dear old landlord! And me who knows what the landlords did to the Highlands! How easy to arrange for young fellows forming a kind of glen soviet and all that kind of sweet unreality! But I'm afraid, Naomi, whatever my writing may look like, I'm just a hard-bitten realist . . . Peace and construction be with you, on the County Council and in your writing, now and ever more.
>
> It's at least charming of you to see my books falling into a sort of pattern. There is such a lot of clearing work to be done so that writers coming after us may take a lot for granted and get on with what might be spiritually exciting.[6]

Whether Neil's solution was realistic might well be argued. Hill sheep farming survived, without flourishing, mainly due to Government subsidies. But Neil had moved out of the defeatism of his own early books, and the bitterness was largely overcome—not due to any external change in Scotland but due to development in himself.

The countryside which he had in mind when he started the book was the neighbourhood of Laggan Bridge in Inverness-shire. Neil mentioned in later years that he had visited a friend, Ian, and borrowed from him his shepherd's day book, called in the dedication 'the little black diary'. It is an older Ian who writes in September 1946 to acknowledge the information that *The Drinking Well* will be dedicated to him:

> Strange your letter should have come when it did as only that day I was visiting in a nursing home in town the old Laird of Glentruim now approaching the end of his journey and who persisted in addressing me as 'Blargie'. Both incidents have induced an intense longing to revisit the scenes of my youth—a longing I must shortly indulge.

But what am I to say about your decision to dedicate your latest book to me? That is certainly the source of humble pride—if pride can be humble—and I do indeed fully appreciate it as a wonderful compliment to my old folk and no less wonderful a compliment to my undeserving self . . .[7]

The dedication names him only as 'my old friend Ian'. In fact, 'Ian' was John McKillop, who shared digs with Neil in Inverness around 1913, and later became County Clerk of Inverness. John married a schoolfriend of Daisy.

In his letter McKillop writes:

I think among the archives there are some photographs somewhere of feeding sheep in winter snows, etc. and my mind goes back to my old Dad mixing his dips in an old-fashioned boiler beside the fank—the Crathie crofters arriving with their flocks to use the Blaragie Dipper, old William Campbell complete with shepherd tartan plaid wrapped round his stalwart shoulders and his elder brother Allan on his white horse—with immaculate white linen—clean shaven and with snow-white locks—the headman of them all keeping tally of numbers and generally directing operations—including the issue of the wine of the country (2s 6d a bottle from Drumgask) which became much less sparing as the day proceeded.

These were the days—and the nights too, for it wasn't in reason they'd all go straight home when the dipping was done . . .

Here is the origin for much of the background material of *The Drinking Well*. But the plot is based on a brief, bleak story of the late 1920s when almost all Neil's writing was gloomy and bitter. The young Iain Cattanach returns a failure from the city to a community economically dead and socially desperate. The tale is limited to one tragic scene—a conversation with his grandmother at the end of which his father enters and there is a harsh and acid exchange; Iain leaves for a second time. This incident appeared as *The Man Who Came Back* (Study for a One-Act Play) in the *Scots Magazine*. Later it did take the form of a one-act play, *Back Home*, published by W. Wilson of Glasgow (1932) in a series to provide material for the amateur dramatic movement.

In a way *The Drinking Well* could be regarded as '*The Lost Glen* redeemed', and presumably had the effect of getting out of his system the bitterness of which that book is full, for he did not return to the theme.

The fact that it harked back to an earlier phase of his work pleased the reviewers, who were always looking either for another *Morning Tide* or for another *Silver Darlings*.

But orthodoxy went out of the window again with *The Shadow*. It is an account of Nan's recovery in the Highlands from a breakdown in London. She has a relapse as the result of an encounter with the artist Adam and persistent rumours about a nasty local murder. Her communist lover Ranald and Adam fight. But it is Ranald's analytic approach which has been the main cause of Nan's trouble.

Neil's conversation at the time when he was writing *The Shadow* dealt often with the darkness of contemporary literature, with its concentration on negative attitudes and violence, with the effect of destructive analysis on the human spirit and with the hope for individual integration. During the last year or two of the war there had been a ferment of hope and a burst of new thinking in the country; in the years after the war this gradually dispersed and there was an atmosphere of confusion and doubt.

On 22 October 1946 Neil wrote in reply to Pick's comments on the typescript of *The Shadow*:

> These parentheses—I know. I haven't the heart to cut any more out. Like a mannerism, a pathetic effort at being playfully normal, but hang it, with courage too. What's being perfect, anyway? If a few more flaws would make it easier for her [Nan], wouldn't you shove 'em in? Not to mention making it easier for the chap in *The Times Literary Supplement*.
>
> Ranald and Adam are a bit difficult. They move as it were objectively, males across the female field of vision. And don't confuse Ranald with the nihilist. He represents the theorist in action. I have met many communists like him, for instance, and other theorists, too.
>
> . . . You wonder why Adam cleared out to London. That kind of chap always clears out when he finds that circumstances are enmeshing him. The need to be 'free' is always overpowering. He has his vision of life, but it is personal, not social. The antithesis of the 'responsible' social theorist. He might adorn the perfect anarchical state, which is perhaps why Aunt Phemie was surprised to find that she rather likes him somewhere. There is perversion here, in Adam. The balance—sanity—is in the eyes of the woman. Adam hunts it perversely, because our male has become a perverse social animal.[8]

It would be unwise in the case of a writer as fecund and creative, and a man as reserved and self-protective, as Neil, to suggest any direct transposition of experience into fiction. Life is more subtle and evasive than that.

On the face of it there is a case for seeing the Nan-Ranald situation as arising in Neil's mind from the increasingly difficult relationship of Margaret MacEwen with communism. This may be true. But the differences are more important than the similarities. He writes to Margaret in 1948: 'And anyhow, praise be that you could see that I wasn't thinking about yourself . . .'

Margaret's illness was only a mild one and did not occur during the war as Nan's did, but before the war, and was caused not by her relationship with communism but on the contrary by her relationship with Neil himself. By the time Nan's breakdown took place, Margaret had with extraordinary resilience and courage gained a balance which enabled her to make her own gradual break with communism, to preserve her love for Neil without continual suffering, and to decide by mutual agreement with her friend and colleague Douglas Muhr that they would not marry.

Neil had known Douglas Muhr when Douglas was in Inverness as a young man. He went to London to a job with the *Daily Worker*, and Margaret later worked there too. Douglas was not in any way the analytic Ranald, and far from being a continuing threat to Margaret's growth and balance, actually broke with communism before she did.

Nan's character contains more of Neil himself than it does of Margaret, and Ranald is an abstract lay figure rather than any sort of representation of a known individual.

By an odd chance a letter of Douglas Muhr's to Neil about this very novel survives, and it is obvious that the book appealed deeply to Muhr precisely because he agreed with Neil's analysis rather than with Ranald's. He writes:

> You old wizard you, sitting up there in the Highlands analysing London so well that it's hardly worth the trouble of a poor bloody Sassenach to write a play about the place at all—but he will for all that. *The Shadow* is a book that I have long expected from you, with its message implicit in other words, but here it is itself, and how bravely you tackle it. You have the heart of the matter, as usual, and for the insight which gave you Ranald's reaction to the fight at the burn I have nothing but wonder. I feel myself that perhaps Nan is more typical than you think, Ranald less.[9]

Nan's recovery is due mainly to the love, wisdom and understanding of Aunt Phemie at a farmhouse in the Highlands just like Brae. What does all this mean? Perhaps that Margaret's situation was the root cause of the book being written. That aspect of the material was combined once again with the material of an old short story, and everything suffered a sea-change. We are left with the interesting fact that the core of the book is a relationship between Nan (who is not very like Margaret) and Aunt Phemie (who is a great deal more like Daisy). In fact there was no such warm, close relationship. Margaret said of Daisy: 'I did not dislike her, but would not have sought her out for herself.'

If *The Shadow* is not entirely successful it is because Ranald is essential to the meaning of the book, and he is unreal. Neil dislikes him, and this shows through to such an extent that he becomes an abstraction. Even a cold fish is not a cold fish inside. But Ranald is viewed almost entirely from outside, and despite his handsome exterior and his air of distinction, it is difficult to see how Nan could have fallen in love with him. The first part of the book is in the form of letters from Nan to Ranald. The second part is straight narrative.

On receipt of the book Geoffrey Faber wrote to Neil:

> I made the bad error . . . of beginning to read it somewhere near the middle—a detestable habit of mine, for which I can say absolutely nothing at all. My interest was very strongly taken, and I read on to the end, and then turned back to the beginning! When I read the first part of the book, I must own that I felt a sense of disappointment; and I couldn't determine whether that was your fault or mine. Since then I have had two reports from separate readers; and both of them independent of each other and of me, say that they found it almost impossible to get through the first part of the book; but that, having done so they found their interest gripped by the rest of the novel . . .
>
> This isn't a very helpful letter, I know. If I were you, I think that I would put the novel on one side for a few months and do something else, before going back to it. We have for some time been playing with the idea of a 'Guide to Scotland' . . . we hadn't the conventional guide-book in mind . . . Does this idea appeal to you at all?[10]

Although Neil later wrote articles on aspects of Scotland for American magazines, and was delighted with the money received for them, he didn't take kindly to Faber's suggestion, and wrote to Pick on 15 December 1946:

> I wrote Faber a nice letter, pulling his leg a bit about a distinguished publisher who seemed to revel in 'new' poetry, but when a poor old novelist tried something 'new' or 'difficult' then it was another story. A somewhat lengthy letter, which he assures me he read to his Book Committee who solemnly agreed with the answer he was to make to me. After making it, he says 'That may sound rather cowardly, but even such a master of his craft as you *can* try his readers higher than they wish to be tried!' Which is really very charming of him. So if I don't mind taking the unpopular risk, neither does he, and so he will of course publish the novel as it stands. Plainly, there's to be not even the shadowiest glimpse of a butler in this . . . But then I never have started to make money without promptly cutting my feet from under me. Is this what they call masochism or is it just plain stupid?

The book did not appear until winter 1948, so as not to jeopardise sales expected from the enthusiastic reception of the traditional *Drinking Well*. In fact, on 11 February Kennerley reported that the initial printing of *The Shadow* would be 8,000 and on 12 April told Neil he was pleased with both sales and reviews and that a second printing of 4,000 was doing well!

Nan Shepherd identified strongly with the 'Nan' of the book. She 'read the book straight through' and was 'fascinated' (24 February 1948):

But something nags at the end—something not completed. For, *did* Nan really discover whether or not Ranald was Kronos, and would consume the young of the generation to follow him? . . . What I want to know is what happens to Ranald when he got back to London—how he reacted to himself. Wasn't there a ghost for him to lay? . . . I want to know what he did, and how he lived in his own mind about it . . .

And now you must tell me . . . by giving this girl who loved air and water and light, and who couldn't find all human nature in a formula—by giving her my name, did you wish on me the things that have been happening to me for the last year?[11]

And she described a long period of quiescence prior to major thyroidectomy, during which she made discoveries about the relationship of body and mind, then panicked and lost her sense of identity for days on end. 'And like your Nan I saw a whole earth dominated by an order for which spirit had no reality.'

Neil replied on 23 March 1948:

That was a terrific time you had. I had heard nothing about it. You make it very vivid. I hope you are fine now and taking the sun in. It's a wonderful sun. And the flowers are very vivid. I am getting more and more conscious of the loveliness of things around. But we do depend on the body, I agree. I love shoving the spade right in to the hilt and turning the earth over, just sheer digging, but lord! I started so violently the other day that I found I had a real heart because it got tired. So I sat down and listened to the birds and blessed them, and knew I would bless them though the heart was dying on me! No, I didn't call the girl Nan because of you; at least I don't know why I called her the only name I could call her, because she herself knew it was like a cry. Things are mysterious. Your little poems about the earth had that cry in them. Even the cold spring water on the hillside. The spirit cry out of the peewit body. Ranald will be of no use to her, I'm afraid. In London it would be all right, but when the testing time comes and he answers the call of the head, then Kronos will devour his children. That's the way the world is shaping. The world, ordered by men, will destroy what Nan stands for. I'm thinking of totalitarian man. But we are slipping that way ourselves. Totalitarian or Marxist man, in action, will have no feeling of guilt. And the individual doesn't matter much, and his emotional reactions not at all. That's merely analysis, so don't grow despondent. Not while the sun shines and one can still give the silent cry.[12]

There is some inadequacy of response here, as if Neil felt embarrassed by Nan's real, formidable illness and her intensely personal reaction to the book, or as if he was despondent himself, reflecting that a book can't solve actual problems, but only state them. And why the name Nan? It 'came' to him. There is much of Nan Shepherd in the Nan of the book. Nan *writes* like Nan.

If Neil was self-conscious about the book it is not surprising, because not only is it deeply personal, but his feelings are Nan's. He was quite clear both emotionally and intellectually that our salvation must come through women—from intuitive perception and not from the analytic intellect. He seemed to feel that a woman may arrive at the necessary perceptions as it were 'naturally', while a man cannot attain to them unless he realises the 'second self'. Perhaps only men have completely separated the two selves one from another—and the more women become like men the more they will succeed in arriving in the desert. Of course his refusal to accept a 'new' role for women was one of Margaret's quarrels with him. It is noticeable that his most sensitive and appreciative correspondents were usually women. It was their letters he made sure of keeping. He felt through their reaction to his work a direct personal reaction to *him*, and responded to it.

Agnes Mure Mackenzie wrote (16 February 1948):

> I read it in a gulp, finishing it at 1.30 a.m. And how thankful I was to see someone of your weight hitting out for that particular set of values. I'm old enough to have seen the *trahison des clercs* . . . There is of course a type of mind in all ages with the vindictive hatred of *quality*, in both senses of the word—both the thing that makes one thing different from another, and the thing that makes one thing finer than another . . . I don't know if it has ever been more widespread or more dangerous than today . . . It's a relief to meet Aunt Phemie. How I like that woman! And how solidly she fits into her place. You don't as a rule go in for very specific interiors: one knows they are there, but only the people are fully lit. But I feel that if I walked into her kitchen I could find the towels and the tea-caddy.[13]

There is one more sidelight on *The Shadow* which is worth mentioning. Keith Henderson said in conversation: 'Neil was very fond of Helen . . . When he met her for the second time he kissed her on both cheeks. I thought "Oh hurrah, he's going to like her." He wrote once about Helen, "Helen went outside to light up the moon." '

This occurs in *The Shadow*, told by a very unsuitable character for such a story, Adam MacAlpine. David is a painter.

> People buy David's landscapes occasionally. They buy them, thank heaven. What they really buy is the love between David and Helen, but they don't know that. Neither do the art critics. Never mind. Helen has no theories. She works, looks after David and the house, trims the lamps, puts a box of matches in your candlestick, and sees that light and life go on. Not an interesting job, you may think; too much like God's to be interesting; too full of practical business, boring . . .

And what follows is an account of an actual incident between Keith (as

David), Neil (as Adam) and Helen Henderson. It has nothing to do with MacAlpine at all. The two men go for a stroll:

> It is a lonely landscape with a farm in the distance. The twilight deepens to a fathomless grey dusk . . . Their talk takes on the quietude of the landscape, its illusive distance and height . . . They then come home to Helen's welcoming voice, to friendly movements in and about, slippers and talk of rest, of bed . . . He feels completely stilled, quiescent; bathed, cleansed, and put in a white bed. An owl hoots. The silence follows. And in this silence, just before sleep comes, he has his strange illusion. It seems to him that he is downstairs again and that they are getting ready to go to bed. David, who is stoking the kitchen stove, turns with the small black shovel in his hand, still talking. But Adam is suddenly aware of Helen. She comes carrying a handlamp with a blue glass bowl and has clearly been busy seeing that the house is all secure for the night. The full responsibility of this is hers, unconsciously as it were, and he realises that a day on earth is being brought to a close. She is folding the day up to put it away, when suddenly she remembers she has forgotten something, or could not quite trust someone (like a maid) to have seen to it. She does not want to interfere . . . with our high and important talk, so turns away, murmuring to herself as she is going: *Excuse me! but I'll just go and see that the moon is properly trimmed and not smoking and that all the stars are lit.*[14]

It is a pity for this reason that *The Shadow* was not dedicated to Keith and Helen Henderson. But they had already received the dedication of *The Serpent*.

Long before *The Shadow* came out, Neil was considering *The Silver Bough*. He wrote to Pick on 15 September 1946: 'I seem to have got surrounded by books on prehistory and the last word on atomic physics. Escape literature, I suppose. But I think I could have enjoyed myself as a physicist.' The phrase 'got surrounded' is characteristic, as if somehow these books had arrived about his chair without any volition on his part, and he would be surprised to find himself writing a novel that made use of them.

We know what the books on prehistory were, for a notebook survives headed *The Silver Bough*, containing a pencil sketch of two archaic heads, and extracts from *The Magic Arts Among the Celts* by Lewis Spence; the Report of the Royal Commission on the Ancient and Historical Monuments of Scotland; *Life in Ancient Britain* by Norman Ault; *The Prehistory of Scotland* by V. Gordon Childe; and *The Irish Mythological Cycle* by M. H. d'Arbois de Jubainville translated by R. I. Best. The passage from this book entered into the notebook is the story of Cormac MacArt, Mannanan and the silver bough—which is adapted not too freely by Neil for Anna to tell her daughter in the novel. At the back are notes from the *Iliad,* Sir Arthur Eddington,

Martin Davidson's *The Mid-Twentieth Century Atom* and Bankoff's *The Boon of the Atom*.[15]

Neil would never speak about a novel until it was finished, and so he keeps the reason for the appearance of these books about his chair a mystery.

Before *The Silver Bough* was written the owner of Braefarm House told Neil they would have to leave. They were reprieved and at the same time as the reprieve Neil reported: 'Did I mention that the film studio who had an option on *The Drinking Well* have now exercised their option and paid up like gentlemen? But I am not getting involved. I am not giving up the fields and the wild birds and all the rest of the lovely escapist stuff!'[16] But no film of *The Drinking Well* was made. Neil had little luck with films of his books. *The Silver Darlings,* directed by Karl Grüne and with Helen Shingler in the cast, was misconceived and unsuccessful. *Morning Tide* was bought and never used. And the books which would have made the best films were not taken up.

In *The Silver Bough* an archaeologist, Grant, finds a gold hoard in a cairn, only to have it stolen by his local helper, the 'idiot' Andy. The story of the 'crock of gold' is bound together with the story of Martin of the big house, shattered by war experiences.

Geoffrey Faber read the book when sick in bed at the start of January 1948 and was 'entirely fascinated and held', even though he admits he longed for the rediscovery of the crock. He writes (14 January 1948): 'I know I've missed something essential—the tie-up between the two halves of the story—between the cairn-story and the Donald Martin story. I don't mean the more obvious tie-ups—aren't I right in thinking that there is some deep inner connection?'

In his reply Neil tried to explain:

> I am not really sure what you mean . . . concerning the inadequate 'tie-up' between the cairn story and the Donald Martin story, particularly when you say you see 'the more obvious tie-ups'. It's so easy for a novelist to assume he has made clear to others what is clear to himself! For example, when Grant first mentions to Donald Martin and his sister that he has discovered the skeletons of a young mother and child, discusses the possibility of their unnatural double death, and goes on to make the parallel between the living young mother and child and these skeletons, Donald's sister abruptly gets up and leaves the room. Grant is astonished. And the reader is led to expect some sort of tie-up between the cairn story and the Martins. Only *later* does Grant learn that Martin is the father of the living woman's child and when he does, everything seems clear to him. But I find I haven't written down what he thought was clear and a new paragraph could express it: the sister's jealous care of her

brother, her neurotic desire to save him from an 'impossible' alliance, drenched suddenly with the fear of the effect on her brother should Anna and her child do away with themselves as had the mother and child in the stone cist. No wonder she had abruptly left the room (Grant would conclude).

That's the main human tie-up. There is the more ubiquitous one of Martin to the Neolithic. But actually the book is full of symbols or bits of myths. Accordingly there is nothing that the reader cannot go on thinking or wondering about. The Silver Bough comes in through the child and ultimately links Donald to Anna, and so reconstitutes the family—the father, mother and child. The inner pattern—or plot—is beautifully intricate, like Celtic interweaving—but you can't blame me for that!—*so long* as I the writer am telling a straightforward story about people and their doings. In fact the writer is so practical or realistic that it is not sadism that finally hides the crock of gold but dull history; no archaeologist has ever discovered a gold hoard in Scotland. But if he did, the chances are that it would be like that one in the cairn. Could I be fairer than that? (And if I also give the lovely legend of the crock a further life, would you blame me!)[17]

On 21 August 1948 he writes to Agnes Mure Mackenzie:

I've been correcting proofs of a new novel which the publishers threaten to put out this autumn. This is hardly fair, for when I do a book I sit back and do nothing for six months. Faith, they won't get the typescript of the next one so soon! Though perhaps it doesn't matter so much now, for I feel I have about written enough. But lord, life is a terrible thing, how it will start in biting you over something, when all you want is sweet peace and watching—as I am at this moment—the sheaves being stooked. I have to go to Edinburgh for a British Council meeting next week and we are staying on for a few days to see the Festival.[18]

This was the second trip south that year. On 2 July he had received an honorary LLD from Edinburgh University and Agnes wrote:

The notion of you being smacked upon the head with the relics of George Buchanan's Sabbath breeks and gravely pontificated over by a Dean of Faculty is agreeable, shall I say, in more ways than one . . . And that Edinburgh University of all institutions should honour an open and vigorous Nationalist, let alone a contemporary Scots creative writer suggests a fantastic change in atmosphere. I imagine you felt a little stunned yourself.

Sir Alexander Gray wrote to Neil on 12 August recalling that they 'met at a joyous festival marred by tedious orations', and made 'a provisional date for a glass of sherry and a grilled herring round about Festival time'. He understands that Neil will attend an occasion on which a portrait is to be presented to C. M. Grieve. 'I shall not be at this . . .' Sir Alexander comments that indeed there are few people for whom Grieve has not at some time expressed either antipathy or contempt. Neil was himself hurt that he received no congratulations from the Edinburgh literati on his honorary degree.[19]

The Silver Bough came out late in October 1948 and Faber reported on 4 November that it had subscribed well and the first returns from the trade were encouraging.

The tribute which pleased Neil most came from Edwin Muir. Indeed, Edwin's appreciation justified the book for Neil:

> I add my greetings and my congratulations on such a wonderfully delightful book, a book with a sun of its own (a very old sun—since reading it, Neil, I've got the quite novel feeling that the sun is very old and very experienced and has looked upon us and our fathers and been above us and about us and in us for a very long time.) It's a mature book, steeped in time and your own experience and acceptance of things: it's like a harvest. I feel myself (but you know much more about it) that this last theme of yours fits your intricate and interweaving Celtic imagination wonderfully, and is as if made for it: so many things brought together by such winding and yet natural ways, with the skill and craft and ingenuity of nature. The skeleton of the dead woman and her child repeated in the living woman and her living child gave me an imaginative thrill which I shall never forget: it hints at something which has haunted me vaguely on the very edge of thought, but for which I have never found in any writing before a form. And so much is accepted in the book, and what other real wisdom is there in the imagination? I feel very grateful to you for it and for sending it to us. All good fortune (continuing). With love to you both. Edwin[20]

Having declined in October to stand for Rector in the Edinburgh University election, Neil agreed to produce an article for the student publication *Jabberwock* in autumn 1948, and wrote to its editor, John Graham:

> When I was writing the article for you, it chanced that I had beside me the review of my last novel by *The Times Literary Supplement* and the *Scotsman*. They at once yielded working examples of what we're getting at. For I am not referring, need I say, to any question of quality, but to one of fundamental attitude. Quality is always where we find it, but fundamental attitude is fairly constant. Nor should we really dismiss, as you do, the harassed journeyman reviewer who deals in clichés, for he is precisely the kind of bloke who exposes the 'symptom'. Had they put the really clever critic onto my book he would have concealed the symptom better. I am not having one at the *TLS* which in its time has been very kind to me and even 'chosen' a novel of mine—when it conformed to an accepted 'chronicle novel' pattern.[21]

Neil's bitterness at the mauling received by *The Lost Glen,* about which he was so acutely sensitive, gave him a jaundiced view of critics which he never overcame. But apart from this, he was more and more convinced that criticism had entered a negative phase, and that the disease of which many reviews were a symptom was a dislike for the portrayal of 'goodness' or 'light' and an insistence that 'realism' demanded darkness and violence.

The atmosphere in these years was heavy with foreboding. There was a feeling abroad that war with the Soviet Union would closely follow the end of war with Germany, that the Police State was winning everywhere, and we would never be free of it again. The atom bomb cast its shadow; the mind moved through threatening mist; books with titles like *The Annihilation of Man* and *Crisis in the West* were pouring from the presses; it was the time when Orwell wrote *1984*; and the time when Neil wrote *The Lost Chart*.

Neil sent this 'thriller'—then titled *Behind the Wave*— to Faber on 7 October 1948. And in November Geoffrey Faber and Alan Pringle reported that they were indeed thrilled. In their estimation he had found a commercial alternative to the 'chronicle novel'.

It is the darkest of his books. In it he faced the darkest of his thoughts: the death of the ancient Gaelic civilisation, the death of individuality—fears coming on top of those he had recorded in *The Shadow:*

> Men had gone mad. Aunt Phemie saw quite clearly that men had gone mad. Her vision went all over the earth and saw men in the logical movements of their madness, stalking here and there, into council chambers and out of them, into railway stations and airports, across fields, all the fields of the world, intent and certain, fulfilling the high and urgent law of necessity. Whose necessity? cried her anguished spirit . . .[22]

In *The Lost Chart* Neil makes a naked confession of the emotional significance which Gaelic civilisation held for him, breaks through self-consciousness to leave himself open to that thin, pale, critical face which he always imagined as staring at his work with the eye of destructive indifference. The self-conscious shyness and withdrawal he describes so clearly is his own. Ellen is singing. The telephone rings:

> It had silenced Ellen as it had destroyed the country where they journeyed, that country which he was always a little afraid of, because its beauty, its containing harmony, was sad with the mute cry of the forever lost.[23]

This is close to the cadences of Fiona Macleod. He knows it, and shies away. But then he has the courage to let the true confession through:

> The song—and the singing—had a whole civilisation behind it, an attitude to life and to death over a long time . . . It was the voice of Anna, the face of Anna, when she addressed the young moon, smiling across the black river and

making her curtsey. The sea and the flowers on the machair; youth and the morning. Twilight. To you also I belonged once but I never can again for I am Youth. It was all there. It had manners. It was bright and sharp, and it grew mellow in age. It was sad to a depth that no lead sounded. Beautiful it was . . . [24]

Say it, say it once, say it was a beautiful thing that was murdered; even though they have made you feel a fool when you are saying it, say it. Say it once to your own heart, unashamed, before you grow strong again and ordinary and deny it.[25]

And the song itself:

there was the voice, and there, living and cool and ten thousand years old, note by note, each rounded like a pearl, clear in shape, opaque in colour, lovely and innocent, they came upon him. It was the quiet singing, the remembering within oneself, which Dermot found most difficult of all to bear.

The songs he is describing are the songs the folk singer Helen Macmillan sang to him over many years, and the singer is Helen herself. He said once that she could sing over the telephone in such a way that the song 'ran all the way up your arm'. There is something valedictory about this book.

The darkness is the shadow of totalitarianism, analysis, violence and the threat of final war:

There are folk who think they can make this earth a paradise—and are prepared to blow it up to prove their point.

If men went on living for half a million years in contact with nature, not to mention the millions and millions of years before that when life itself, so to speak, *was* nature—then you can't suddenly divorce men from their immemorial contacts and shut them up in cities without doing them some kind of violence.[26]

The age, the times they lived in, had made personal love, love between a man and a woman, look like some strange and reprehensible passion—old-fashioned, unreal.

I have often told you that the *means* not only conditions the *end*, but that the fellow using the means becomes like what he uses.[27]

Dermot, the hero, is himself caught between police and communist fifth column. At a time of crisis he loses a chart which is of value to the underground, and seeks to get it back. As a result he finds himself working for the secret service. It is a chart of the waters round Cladday, an island he visited during the war, and which means to him the true values of Gaelic civilisation, where the old woman Anna still curtseys to the new moon, saying 'Many a one has crossed over the black river of death since you came here before.' *Carmina Gadelica* is quoted several times:

> Glory to thyself, O god of life,
> For thy lamp of the Ocean,
> Thine own hand at the tiller,
> And thy love behind the wave.

It seems likely enough that *Carmina Gadelica* was a principal inspiration for the book.

When he has caused the arrest of members of the communist underground Dermot is ill, tormented with guilt and confusion, a sense of betrayal, as if Neil himself were tormented by his repudiation of that socialism he claims had been his since he was fifteen. He writes:

> I mean that totalitarianism is a social regress, it's throwing man back thousands of years, back to that tribal age when man the thinker, the individual questioner, had not yet emerged. Now I mightn't mind that. I rather fancy that was the golden age on earth . . . The only trouble is that man cannot go back to an earlier culture pattern. When he tries, he destroys himself.[28]

So much for the Golden Age. Where then is the light? Can the individual retain the light which Gaelic civilisation embodies, and grow through darkness to his own integration? Joe, the painter, represents light and the search for light, as Basil the totalitarian represents darkness—a return to the formal opposition of human beings representing attitudes which had not been used since *Wild Geese Overhead*, another book set in the city. Basil is a more malicious version of Ranald in *The Shadow*—a more bitter version, and less objectively presented.

Joe says of an exhibition of dynamic, disintegrating paintings: 'He uses the light for darkness . . . the betrayal of the light.'[29] Basil continually accuses Dermot of the primitive, of harking back to a lost childhood. And the captured fifth columnist says to Dermot: 'How you can act the police nark, hunt fellows who are trying to bring about a decent state of society, seeing you've got what you *have* got, it beats me . . . Nothing can stop what's coming. Nothing on earth.'[30]

After his illness of guilt Dermot declares himself willing to return to Cladday as a 'responsible' man in charge of a naval vessel, accepting his part in the collective madness, an emissary of those who will in the end fortify Cladday. Is this acting as a 'householder'—or is it unwillingness finally to join Joe in that no-man's-land where you can never be respectable again, but must reject all worldly authority because it distorts the light? To betray communist fifth columnists who hate you is one thing. To betray Cladday by joining those who would turn it into a fortress is quite another.

This is not the only strange unease in the book. There are times when a disquieting self-consciousness steals out of the text through Dermot, an image grows in the mirror, as if the author identifies with Dermot, and looking at Dermot as himself, *approves* of him. Then this image too is drowned in darkness, a darkness produced by the intellect, which should not be a destroyer but the instrument of objective light.

Throughout the book we sense a kind of ambivalence or swithering in the attitude to authority. Dermot sees clearly that Grear, the intelligence man on *his* side, closely resembles the Questioner of the Green Isle. But in the end Dermot acts for authority against would-be authority, so that despite his protestations and doubts, he is on the side of the big battalions, and Cladday will go under. It would go under anyway? Yes. The picture of the world is accurate enough. But *Bloodhunt* and *The Key of the Chest* both come at the matter another way, with authority being in one aspect the community itself, and in another the law imposed on the community. If Sandy in *Bloodhunt* had helped Allan the outcast against Nicol the policeman only because Nicol had gone beyond the law in seeking revenge, and had not helped Allan also against the law of the tribe, then he would have been denying the essential in himself. But he did help Allan in both respects, and his uneasiness at doing so, and the felt necessity to do so, are beautifully and sensitively conveyed. Not only the essence of Sandy but the essence of Neil Gunn speaks here. So there is something unresolved in *The Lost Chart*. It is after that book and not within it that he finds his way.

The basis of the novel was a short story called 'Sun and Moon', published in the *Scots Magazine* in November 1942. (Not only did this story become incorporated into the novel but it was adapted as a radio play *Sun and Moon*, broadcast first in 1944, then again in 1947 and 1956.) The story deals entirely with the Cladday episode, which in the novel is a flashback to wartime from an imagined 1950s setting. A patrol-boat commander causes the body of a Norwegian seaman to be dug up to check its identity. The islanders feel they are not trusted. Old Iain the coast-watcher resigns his position, but then dies rescuing the patrol-boat commander when his vessel is bombed.

Although he had rejected out of hand Faber's 'humiliating' suggestion that he should consider writing a guide to Scotland, he must have meditated on what the nature of a true guide to Scotland would be, and discovered, as he did so, that those short pieces of descriptive and contemplative writing he had produced during the war for the *Scots Magazine*, and those articles which had appeared in *Chambers' Journal*, covered such wide areas of experience and geography that in themselves they constituted something like a guide to Highland life. And once having accepted this, the idea of collecting them together into a book grew in his mind. The result was *Highland Pack* (1949).

His reply to Pick's comments on the typescript of *Highland Pack* show his permanent concern with the practical:

> Your comments on the Rose ['The Rose at the Gable-End', p. 145] I appreciate, but not altogether with agreement. Evidence of a certain kind of old literary-essay style, with mild and even self-satisfied reflections, have blinded you to the fact that I *do* tell not only *how* to smell a rose but all the times *when*. And then I *was* quite naïvely astonished when I turned up those quotations and found that, after traffic with the real rose, they somehow were not enough. That also was an *experience*—and right into the book's barrow.[31]

On 9 February:

> Perhaps I delayed answering in order to tell you that Faber had declined the book. But he hasn't. So I'm writing to Keith Henderson about illustrations. [He goes on:] But we have had bad news which has knocked books out of our head: we have got word to leave Brae. For these last few days we have been far and near on the hunt. Nothing doing.

Keith stayed at Braefarm House, making sketches for the illustrations— Neil holding an umbrella over his head while he stood in blatters of rain on the brown moor drawing the standing stones. And that was the end of their time at Brae. It was also the end of the happiest, most intensely creative period in Neil's life.

PART FOUR

LIGHT AT THE END

(1949–1973)

15   The Well at the World's End

A moment may come in a man's life when he has the uneasy feeling that something indefinable but decisive has happened; nothing will be the same again. This was the case when Neil left Braefarm House. His writing life was never the same, his health and Daisy's were never the same. At Brae he had reached a peak of popular success and esteem. Now a decline began.

It had been difficult to find a house and Kincraig, when found, was awkward to run and too close to the busy Dingwall–Invergordon road. Daisy wrote to 'Floss' McNeill (late in 1950): 'This is a very bonny place, the house is built on a rock, Neil's side window is high up looking on to the sea and the Black Isle across the water. Nineteen swans sailed past the house today, and we see mallard and widgeon and all sorts of birds on the shore. But the house is too small, most of Neil's books are in cupboards and we are just on the edge of the main north road and we just don't like that, but nobody else would notice.'[1]

Ena Macleod describes it as 'a horrid house perched on a cliff overhanging the shores of the Cromarty Firth . . . nothing separating the back of the house from the north road but a white wooden fence.'[2]

But Keith Henderson 'liked Kincraig best. Neil and I used to sit outside and listen to the whooper swans. It was the first time I had ever heard them.'[3]

Kincraig certainly had its peculiarities. Water had to be pumped, a cranky boiler needed continual stoking, and there was no electricity. The Gunns moved there in May 1949. It was over a year before Daisy could write: 'We put in electric light in June, so I have now a press-the-button house, and plenty of hot water and no fires.'

To visit Kincraig was to be received with the same warmth, ease and hospitality as at Brae. But there were ominous signs. Neil loved an evening walk; he was restless without it. At Kincraig you had either to dodge thunderous monsters on the road or find a way down to the shore when the tide was out, wearing stout shoes or wellington boots. The noise of traffic tried the ears of those used to the milder, more congenial farm sounds of Brae.

Symbolic of the atmosphere was the figure on the shore. Neil had given the son of an old acquaintance permission to fish his stretch of the Firth. The young man was tense and taciturn and fished obsessively with great concentration. Whenever you looked out of the window there he was, haunting the tide like a warden.[4]

In mid-January 1950 a refuse dump north of Kincraig began to spread in size and virulence; noisome smells blew down to the house. Neil was not slow in protesting to the County.[5]

He was troubled by another problem: money. Braefarm House had been rented. To buy Kincraig, with no property to sell as a cushion, had eaten into his capital. His investments did not bring in enough to live on comfortably. He needed to earn, and to keep earning. He turned to journalism and to the publication of already available material. In 1949 he wrote to Pick: 'My feeble brain was forced to bestir itself recently by that New York agent of mine. Result: two short stories, both accepted by the two highest-paying magazines in the world—£360 a time. It requires little arithmetic by me, a respectable one-time Civil Servant, to work out a small sum. Four short stories a year and I can look down my nose at you poor fellows swotting at books.'

The invasion of the United States became a ploy, with something gay and piratical about it. There was a quality of innocence, wonder and surprise about such awards of largesse. His New York agent, Brandt & Brandt, seemed wildly enterprising compared with stodgy British counterparts. He felt himself to be sailing uncharted waters with islands of golden sand on the horizon. Over the next few years he followed stories in the *Saturday Evening Post* with a series of commissioned articles for a new glossy travel magazine, *Holiday*, which paid up with the same staggering munificence. He wrote on Scotland, Edinburgh, whisky, Scottish food, deerstalking—a full banquet of traditional tourist fare. And he did it with lively, well-tailored elegance, as to the manner born.[6]

Such a hospitable reception in the new world made him feel confident and wanted. He took to contributing once again to home journals—*Scottish Field*, *Scotland's Magazine* and the *Glasgow Herald*.

All the same he retained determinedly his attitude of independence and wrote in a 1950 letter: 'My back is near broken. All my potatoes down and peas and lettuce. They want another short story from America but I have told them I am too busy. I'll think about one in the autumn, when I'm eating the potatoes.'

He set to work to collect his later stories together with some of those which had appeared in *Hidden Doors* (1929), and made a book of them called

The White Hour. He replied to comments by Pick:

> My first intention was to start with 'The Chariot', but then felt it might be a
> bit tough for a beginning. Now it will be No. 1. The only surprise you spring
> on me is your estimate of 'Pure Chance'. I had thought of having it out! . . .
> Daisy likes 'The Clock'—and still likes it! I'll think over it. The trouble with
> two or three of these 'doubtful' stories is that they are so old, their style dates.
> And that's not so easy a comment as it looks. The way we tell a story now may
> not be the final way. I have read over 'Half Light' again and think it an almost
> perfect period piece. I expect it makes you squirm a bit in places . . . 'The
> Ghost's Story' is just what you say it is—a partisan's story. But it couldn't be
> anything else. What I find interesting in it is a certain rhythm, a sort of very
> remote ballad phrasing. It came on its own and affects me despite myself. No
> detail could be added to it.[7]

Much later he commented on the story 'Montrose Rides By': 'Well, from
some MS source material of the time I was handed the complete picture of
the old woman and her hotel. Note some of the actual detail and the
Inverness bailies of the time—real names of townsmen.'[8]

The White Hour was a form of marking time. Neil had already begun
writing *The Well at the World's End*.

This book is to some extent the expression of a wish to be young again, to
wander with adventurous irresponsibility, making discoveries in freshness
and light. 'It would *happen* to him. All he would have to do was to wait for
it. He would have to forget himself . . . forget his "importance", his notion
of being "somebody".' The book is also an expedition 'to find out if among
ordinary people there were those moments of penetration, the instant when
they went through the boundary, the moment when they saw the crystal
water in the well'.[9] And as the central character Peter says, whisky in hand,
during the course of his travels: '. . . one may discover once one has gone
through the boundary that the boundary . . . is transparent—or even isn't
there.'[10]

The Well at the World's End combines two themes—the spiritual liberation
that each individual has to come to for himself, which proves in the end to be
not a jewel in a lotus but invisible water which when you draw it up, drips
light; and the renewal of marriage.

At the beginning Fand says to Peter:

> 'You have long been wanting to do that.'
>   'Do what?'
>   'Go away and find the well at the world's end.'[11]
> [And Peter says:] 'To come out on the other side of love—and find the well
> there.'

She was silent.

'All right,' he answered her. 'We never come out on the other side.'[12]

[The story ends:] . . . It was the living Fand now . . . He had the fore-knowledge of being with her for a long time and its ease was rare and delectable, like the beauty beyond what was seen of the mortal eye in Fand's face.[13]

Fand is Daisy. The experience of the well with its invisible water had happened to Neil and Daisy. The copy of the book on Daisy's shelf was inscribed: 'This is Fand's own copy, from her husband N. M. G.' And in February 1970 he wrote: 'I have been reading the scripts of *The Well at the World's End* and they've brought vividly back the days when we set off for the wild, for Fand is shaped like Daisy.'[14] An idealised Daisy? No, a Daisy seen in retrospect by an author who wants to pay tribute to her, and to salute the renewal of their marriage.

One extract will be enough to show how the book's essence relates to Daisy's essence. Peter is trying to catch a salmon with his hands:

So Fand had been told there and then to stand in the shallow outlet and, when she saw the salmon coming, to drop a large stone on its head . . .

Fand said nothing, because if she said anything he would think she was stupid and order her about in a peremptory voice . . . [15]

[Peter struggles with the salmon.]

There was a terrific boil under his sunken eyes and lifting his streaming face he yelled, 'Look out!'

When he saw Fand standing in the middle of the outlet with empty hands and drooping shoulders he yelled again with rage and despair like a Fingalian hero in whose fists victory had all but been . . . [16]

But Fand has built a dam of loose stones, and the salmon is caught.

'It was a revelation of another kind of thought, and he knew once again that in all the profound issues of life she could be trusted.'

Neil wrote to Hart years later:

Anyway I began to read—and (I hardly expected this) read on. For it described right off our setting out for a spell at one of our remote places, called 'the Picts' Houses' (an actual place on the map), coming to a cottage, being directed to a well and so on, all as it actually happened. Then the vehicle that wasn't there—I still remember how desperately I looked for a passing place. Then, having arrived, my attack on a salmon and Fand standing so awkward and gauche on the slippery stone with no boulder in her hands . . .

At the end of the book he writes:

Beyond times and accidents and sorrow, graces and vanities, child-death and desolation, beyond the hanging gardens of happiness, he saw in her that which was the immortal fountain, and her face and hair had the brightness of the rainbow.[17]

This is not Peter of Fand, nor Neil of Fand, it is Neil of Daisy. The reference to 'child-death' makes that startlingly clear.

But the book is revealing in other ways. There is a central incident in which Neil writes once again on the nature of pride. Malcolm, the old seaman, takes his crew out when all the other boats stay in harbour. They are caught in a storm and the lifeboat comes to the rescue. Angus, Malcolm's son, thinks it would be wiser to go aboard the lifeboat, but Malcolm refuses:

> And it was then Willie saw that the old man thought his son was afraid. It was a terrible moment. It obliterated all thought inside Willie's head. It would destroy the old man.[18]

Malcolm sails the boat home and the writing grows over-charged with emotion:

> A high sound like a drawn-out sigh rose from those strung along the edge of the quay; here and there a woman's voice broke; and Peter saw that there were no words for the wonder that had come upon them, for the relief and joy, for the gallantry of this old man of their blood who had fought death and conquered.[19]

When they have landed, Malcolm is told that his son wanted to board the lifeboat so as not to offend its skipper, whose daughter he is courting:

> Malcolm stood still for a little; then he sat down as if his legs had weakened; and Willie for the first time in his life saw the forearm that had held the tiller shake.[20]

On first reading, this prompted a number of questions: would it not have required more courage for Malcolm to lay aside his pride, avoid risking the lives of his crew, and go aboard the lifeboat? Must a man never, in any circumstances, fail in courage if he is to be acceptable to his father? Are we to see something admirable in the old man's rejection of his son?

Neil replied to Pick's comments:

> Your other point about old Malcolm the fisherman is interesting and just. And there's no excuse for him. It was just like that—the pride the Spanish anarchists had. But if he didn't shout 'Long live death', at least he faced it. Much the same thing. It was for him a complicated moment. As for the son Angus not being afraid, that too is part of the same pattern, strength and weakness. Reflection would come later. It's more difficult when it concerns Peter's attitude to it . . . Understanding can never be perfect.

And of course it is more difficult again when it concerns the author's attitude, because Neil closely identified with Peter.

There is a very odd and intriguing account of *The Well at the World's End* which appeared in an article contributed to Pick's magazine *Point* in 1968. Neil writes:

> It is very difficult to describe simply, as exceptional conditions of mind have to be evoked. It was also very involved because it was not a direct happening, not a first-hand encounter, but arose while I was engaged in writing a culminating part of a novel. The character involved in the novel had fallen down a cliff . . . and at last set out on a final hopeless crawl. Perhaps it was because I knew the country that I began to identify myself abnormally with my character. I saw what he saw, became as it were the seeing person, improvised his crutch, suffered what he suffered, until in one translated moment, in a look back at the mountain slopes, the swinging footbridge over the gorge, I saw a face, larger than life size, looking down at me with an expression of infinite understanding and compassion, still, not doing anything, not going to do anything, there. The effect upon me was of an intimacy I could never express, for the face was my own face.
>
> Though I have read many psychiatrists' reports on the effect of LSD and other drugs, I have never actually taken any myself. My experience was for me therefore all the more arresting, as it occurred in daylight, on the clear air and not even against a physical background of mountains and birch trees which might have contributed to the creation of an illusory effect. Indeed I forgot, even in the moment of writing this, that the illusion or 'projection' took place in my writing room while my mind was concentrated on its creative task. However, there is no need to complicate the affair but merely to make my point that I had what was for me a clear vision of my second self looking down the few yards of sloping ground at my first self prostrate in the heather and now held by an understanding and compassion that were infinite. Then the infinite itself came elusively in and the second self became a part, a manifestation, of a universal self or essence, a part of, yet individual.[21]

The Well at the World's End is about 'going through the barrier', about flashes of visionary insight, providing 'the tranced moment, the reflective gleam from some realm of rare delight'. The passage describes the author 'going through the barrier' while writing the book. Is this the same type of experience as those described in the story itself: Neil's own vision of the Spanish garden, put into the mouth of Alick the illicit distiller; the shepherd's vision on the hillside; Cocklebuster's paradisal glimpse beyond the wood? In these there is no vision of the 'self', but only of the light.

The experience is used in the article to illustrate the relationship between the 'first self', the everyday ego willing life into patterns, and the objective 'second self' which is free and aware. But compare the account here with that simple, gleaming description in *The Atom of Delight*—Neil as a boy seated cracking a nut on a boulder in the stream:

> Then the next thing happened, and happened, so far as I can remember, for the first time. I have tried hard but can find no simpler way of expressing what happened than by saying: *I came upon myself sitting there.*
>
> Within the mood of content, as I have tried to recreate it, was this self and the self was me.
>
> The state of content deepened wonderfully and everything around was embraced in it . . . And then within this amplitude the self as it were became aware of seeing itself, not as an 'I' or an 'ego' but rather as a stranger it had come upon and was even a little shy of.[22]

The key phrase here is 'a stranger it had come upon', which gives the purest authenticity to an experience of compelling immediacy. The experience described in the *Point* article is at one or two removes from reality. The boy in the stream is saying 'So this is what the world is like—and here *I* am in it!' But the author of the *Point* article is saying 'Here is the character I have created—and here am I gazing upon him in benevolent understanding.' There is no element of pride in the first experience. There is in the second. It would be a mistake to make too much of the matter. We are in difficult country where the shadows of clouds alter shapes with bewildering swiftness; sheep become boulders, and boulders sheep.

Finally, there is a sense in which the book is Neil's *Tempest*, his farewell to fiction—despite the two novels which followed.

> The little fields, coloured with crops, the grazing cattle, a woman walking inside a wooden hoop carrying two buckets of water from a well, a man mending a roof, a boy rushing after a puppy dog, a trundling cart. Then he did a thing which he could never have conceived of his doing before: he blessed that little community.[23]

Which is a fitting thing both for Peter and for the author of so many stories of Highland life to do.

The book was sent to Faber in September 1950. Neil wrote to Pick on 6 December:

> They suggested I should put it aside, as it would be a failure, and suggested I might try something else. I replied. Then they sent me Alan Pringle's full report on it. That winded me. Then they sent me a contract, with a request to make it clear what the novel was all about. To them, apparently, it's a mass of puzzles. I've looked over it—typescript—again and am about to send it back. Not very exciting, what!

A letter of 22 October to Geoffrey Faber is his first effort to explain the book:

> Where most novels of the more ambitious kind today deal with violence and material leading to negation and despair, I thought it might be a change if I got a character who would wander among his fellows looking for the positive aspects of life.
>
> Is it possible to pierce the negative husk, the dark cloud, even for a few moments, and come on the light, the bubbling well at the end of the fairy tale? Do folk still do it, ordinary people? Can this feeling be conveyed, the moment of wonder, of integration? . . . For this, the principal character must appear to have a wide knowledge of life actual and historical, so that the whole may not seem merely naive. And it must be carried through in the spirit of comedy because of a gaiety at the heart of the notion . . .
>
> Now I can quite see that a quest of this kind is very different from the ordinary 'plot' of a novel. But I'm afraid I can't see how this structure can be radically altered in this instance. And in any case the story of a man on a quest is an old and even successful one . . .[24]

On the matter of 'love interest' he says 'here I admit I have also been very—if not shockingly—unorthodox, for the love of a married man for his wife (and them nearly fifty, God help them) permeates the whole book and comes to a life-saving climax at the end.'

Certainly, then, *The Well at the World's End* is the contrary of all that was fashionable at the time.

Fascinatingly, in January 1951, it is evident that Geoffrey Faber has himself recounted an incident of the very kind with which Neil was dealing in *The Well at the World's End,* for Neil writes:

> I was particularly interested in your momentary experience with the Highland cattle which has stayed with you so long. You are exactly right in saying that it's what Peter in my novel is getting at. I have reason to believe that such experiences are more universal than we credit. They have the blessed virtue too of being *actual* experiences, not some sort of concept in a theory . . . If I badgered you a bit about *The Well* it was, I suppose, because I felt I was taking a tentative first step towards seeing the Highland cattle as you saw them, and because such a step may not be unimportant.

Neil was always ready to explore regions where what is said must be less important than what can only be implied, because it is not susceptible to definition:

> . . . Then I saw that the stillness went out beyond the garden; and I held my breath in an effort to catch the suggestion of an utmost sound. But there was no sound. It was now that the odd feeling came over me that the stillness itself

was holding something, much as the walls held the garden; and in a moment I realised that what it was holding was time . . . Quite simply, then, I knew with an absolute conviction as I stood at that window gazing out on the old Spanish garden that there exists an order of things outside our conception of time.[25]

This is an exact account of a real experience, the kind of experience which will mean very little to one who has never known anything similar himself. *The Well at the World's End* is an effort to penetrate the 'something more' which gives a series of real experiences their significance. The book is full of physical adventures but it is the adventures of the mind which are central to it. All of them were either Neil's in life or told to him by people he trusted and understood.

The incident of Peter and the wild man on the bridge happened to brother John. The shepherd's tale has been mentioned before in relation to *Highland Pack*. In November 1951 Neil writes to Naomi Mitchison:

One more point—you wonder what would have happened if Willie didn't recover in the 'ghost' incident. That, too, is based on fact . . . Willie did recover, but the shepherd who helped to frighten the wits out of the three carpenters was in a bad way until he did. He told me about it and how he felt. The house on the West, where it happened, was vacant for years.[26]

And the incident of Cocklebuster and the dog is described as a real event in 'The Peaceful Black Isle', printed in *Scotland's Magazine*.[27]

This authenticity is the key to Neil's writing. He wrote nothing which he did not consider, as the result of experience, to be true. But if his publishers did not know what he was driving at, then it is only too likely that the 'something' they felt they had missed would be missed also by his public.

Yet *The Well at the World's End* found sales, and attracted readers whose devotion was deep, individual and lasting. One of these was Stewart Conn, who produced it for radio. Another was Alex Reid, who adapted it.

16   Goodbye to Books

In 1951 they sold Kincraig and moved to Kerrow in Glen Cannich, with a good stretch of salmon river. Neil said playfully once to Hart: 'I bought a place with a salmon river, so that after being a poacher all my life I could watch out for other poachers.'

The house was a large one standing with mellow dignity in a wide strath, only a hundred yards from the river, which was crossed by a narrow swaying bridge suspended on wires. One way to the house lay from the main road across this bridge, the other down a long drive from a small road on the far side of the glen. You would walk a fair distance along the riverbank with its elms and birches and its cow-rich fields.

Glen Cannich was in the process of change. The Hydro-Electric Board built a high dam to trap Loch Lullardoch and a low one on Benevean. Neil enjoyed and publicised the new domestic conveniences, the flicking of a switch in the sandstone cottages at Cannich, the expanded local school. He saw a future for the Highlands in the carefully sited dams and the minimum of pylons that preserved the wild beauty while fostering human communities. He spoke out in print against the hunting interests and their tourist allies.[1] And he enjoyed some of his neighbours—Robert Wotherspoon at Affric Lodge, a shrewd and practical adviser, and General Angus Collier down the road, a genuine comic poet.

Wotherspoon was an Inverness solicitor, a capable, ambitious business-man with many interests and investments, who supplemented the counsel of brother John on financial matters and became Neil's lawyer. In return Neil wrote speeches for Wotherspoon, who was for a period Provost of Inverness, and helped him in various ventures. After Daisy's death Neil went every Sunday to lunch at the Wotherspoons, where he was treated like the chief of the clan. The companionship gave him comfort.

The settling in at Kerrow took time and patience. A whole gable-end had to be opened to unblock a chimney. Neil and Daisy made frequent oppor-tunities to go 'off and away'. The Picks had moved to a croft house in a small community at Rhu, with a view west to the Summer Isles and east to the mountains at the head of Loch Broom. Neil and Daisy made it a port of call on their way to the far north-west. Each evening Neil would pace up and down in front of the house as the light faded, saluting first the merge of sea and sky, and then the gathered hills. Rhu was a marvellous place for passionate, mysterious sunsets; and sunsets were not the only illumination provided. One night a wild shimmering dance went on for hours in the sky, and the cat grew crazy, rushing up and down a rowan tree in a kind of poetic trance. Neil laughed aloud, applauding both cat and Northern Lights.

The Gunns travelled all over the west, sleeping in the car and watching the light steal through pastel colours into dark as they sank into sleep. Memories of these times with Daisy meant more to Neil than any others. There was magic in them. The west held for him something which his own Caithness could not give.

There were public commitments, too, which took him 'off and away'. Neil was on the Highlands & Islands Film Guild Council for a number of years. And at the same time he was asked to serve on a Commission of Inquiry into Crofting Conditions. No subject except the fishing industry could have suited him better.

Sixty-nine years before, the Napier Report of 1884 had led to the Crofters' Holdings (Scotland) Act, which gave crofters security of tenure. Since then there had been no major changes in number or size of agricultural holdings in the seven crofting counties. Extreme poverty was rare, and security assured, but there remained the problems of part-time holders, low productivity, and holdings too small to provide a livelihood. The drift from the land continued.

On 25 April 1951 the Secretary of State for Scotland, Hector McNeil, announced in the House of Commons that he planned to appoint a Commission. On 10 May he wrote to Neil asking him to serve, and indicating that Principal Thomas Taylor of Aberdeen University had agreed to act as Chairman. Neil accepted at once.[2]

Formally charged to 'review crofting conditions in the Highlands and Islands with special reference to the secure establishment of a small-holding population making full use of agricultural resources and deriving the maximum economic benefit therefrom; and to report', the Commission was appointed on 6 June and held its first meeting in Inverness on the 29th. It invited organisations and individuals to submit evidence, and received it from twenty-seven organisations, and thirty-eight individuals. There were nineteen formal meetings in the next two and a half years. The Commission made advertised visits to the centres of crofting areas and gave ten days of hearings in Inverness and twenty-eight in other places from Shetland and Orkney to Thurso, across Sutherland and Wester Ross to Argyll, Skye and the Outer Isles. They met finally in Aberdeen to consider the draft report on 15 December 1953, and the report was submitted in January of the following year. The Commission found tremendous diversity, a past characterised by wasteful exploitation of resources, unemployment, high cost of transport, poor communications, examples of failure in initiative and co-operation, and communities deserted by the young where the 'old pass their declining years watching the tilled land going back to reeds and rushes'. 'The system, as now organised, is fighting a losing battle against the social and economic forces of the day.'

Yet there was hope and expectancy too, and the Commission unanimously asserted that it was desirable to fight the battle, and possible to win it. It recommended a new Crofters' Commission with increased powers to promote land settlement schemes, reorganise townships, dispossess absentee crofters, supervise and improve croft husbandry, supervise succession of tenancy, take over the functions of the Land Court, and administer land improvement grants. It urged that prompt attention be given to transport costs and services, afforestation policies and price guarantees, and recognised that the problems were not merely economic and administrative, but in the minds of the crofters themselves.[3]

Neil wrote and spoke of his experiences on the Commission in several articles and broadcasts. In *Scottish Field* (1956) he said:

> The main economic problem for the Highlands has still to be faced: how to make a livelihood out of crofts that are too small, with rough hill grazings that need a capital expenditure beyond crofters' means if they are to be fully productive, crippling freight charges, bad side roads, and many other difficulties. Can crofting be kept going, or is the old story of depopulation to complete itself in lands finally left deserted and dead?

And in another place he recalled:

> One Hebridean crofter showed me correspondence with the county authority, the planning authority, the Department of Agriculture and the Forestry Commission. All were sympathetic, for his agreed scheme of improvements was both intelligent and practical, but these bodies had other disposing bodies beyond them, for cash was involved, not to mention legion interpretations of powers. For example, does the Forestry Commission's remit permit them to grow timber belts on Hebridean islands primarily as shelter belts for stock when with the same expense they could grow more timber elsewhere? Anyway, all that grew out of the crofter's efforts was the correspondence, until he was unable to cope with it and the scheme lapsed.[4]

Neil knew that a main problem was the lack of part-time employment and the dearth of larger crofts. But he also knew that the young were leaving because 'in many places life had grown too dull'.[5]

> The Commission travels about the Highlands and Islands. A Shetland crofter gives an impromptu definition of education so precise and profound that the eyes of the scholarly chairman light up with pleasure. For the members do not travel far before finding that what they are investigating is a way of life.

Neil took boyish delight in the excursions and in being a practical man of importance. He wrote to Faber on 18 April 1952:

> I have got to be in Orkney on Monday—I am serving on the Government's Crofting Commission—and, after that, Shetland, and shan't be back for about ten days. In official and authoritative quarters the idea is entertained that I know something about the Highlands!

After the report was received, the Chairman wrote to him: 'In particular I would like to thank you for your sensitive and understanding approach to the whole problem. I think it has been reflected in the Report itself and is the main reason for its favourable reception. I could never have begun to put it down on paper but for the contribution made by yourself and Macleod in particular during all the long discussions we had about it.'[6]

Another member of the Commission, Sir Matthew Campbell, gives us his account of Neil's part in the proceedings:

> On some occasions the Commission split in two in order to be able to cover more townships. [When this happened Principal Taylor took the chair at one series of meetings and Neil at the other.] He took great delight in these tours and in his meetings with crofters. It was a great pleasure . . . to travel with him. He had, of course, the eye to see. It was he who always saw the curtain twitched back in the lonely croft window as the official 'cavalcade' drove by—he who spotted the District Nurse in her car on the west coast road and stopped for a crack (much to the entertainment and enlightenment of the rest of us!) . . . In most bodies of this kind there tend to be two or three members who strike sparks off each other and develop the main arguments on each side while the rest act primarily as a 'jury'. Neil Gunn was one of the 'activists' and contributed much to the recommendations which emerged. He did all this with verve and good humour. I have no doubt whatever that he thoroughly enjoyed himself in the process.[7]

Keith Henderson said of Neil: 'He was always interested. He was interested in everything. He *enjoyed* everything. This was the great thing about him.'[8]

His attitude towards the preservation of crofting as part of the Highland way of life was not merely a conservative insistence upon maintaining what exists. He was concerned with finding a practical economic structure for the

Highlands which would enable those who had been driven out by lack of opportunities to return if they wanted. But he was not interested in the grandiose schemes for establishing large-scale industry which would only have the effect of attracting non-Highland labour. To him the people of the Highlands and Islands were worth preserving for the human values of their culture and tradition. He did not want this culture and tradition destroyed in the name of progress. He was always an advocate of co-operative self-help, of the imaginative development of hill sheep farming, cattle-farming and fishing, and he saw the crofter as a basic ingredient for an independent way of life. The recommendations of the Inquiry were a judicious blend of legal protection and Government encouragement.

The Crofters (Scotland) Act was passed in 1955 and a Crofters' Commission was set up and began its work. Neil retained a lively interest in its doings. Hart recalls spending an evening with Neil in summer 1965 at Ian Grimble's croft-house near Bettyhill:

> Neil had relished the drive up Strathnaver, and the northern air filled him with zestful glee. Ian was a thoughtful host, and while the dram was ordinary, the spirit was high. Ian and his neighbour, a wise and well-informed crofter-carpenter named Robert Mackay, had just made a radio programme criticising Commission policies in taking arable lands for reforestation. Ian's sitting room looked north toward the Orkneys, and as the summer sun dipped for a northwest nap about eleven and reappeared over the islands a couple of drams later, the exuberant debate between Neil and Robert went on. Neil was arguing the human value of reforestation. He had a tough opponent in Robert but held his own. He was elderly now, and rather feeble. But in the dancing arabesques of mind, the keen but kindly shots back and forth, the healthy vision of a land and a people renewed, I had a glimpse of what scintillating things those long and long ago nights at Larachan must have been. Why are public policy discussions so seldom held at this level of intelligence and vitality? A final dram, and Robert went down the field to his wife Babs, and the two tall warriors, Neil and Ian, took a long striding walk over the rocky braes around Newlands. I made no attempt to keep up with them. The next morning early, I heard Neil singing in the bathroom.

After the early 1950s Neil was never again so active in public affairs. Following Bridie's death in 1951 he hadn't the heart to attend British Council meetings with any regularity. In 1952 he served on the Highlands & Islands Film Guild Council, but when asked by Tom Johnston to join the Scottish Tourist Board he declined, and refused also to fill a vacancy among Scottish members of the Forestry Commission in 1956.

He needed part-time jobs which paid. Most of his earlier books were going out of print and only journalism kept butter on his bread. He turned again to the theatre, rewriting *The Ancient Fire* during 1951 and 1952. The new version, *Beyond the Cage*, was produced at the Gateway Theatre, Edinburgh, in 1952, and then dropped out of sight.[9]

The early and mid-fifties saw the BBC beginning to broadcast dramatised segments of the novels for schools. Robin Richardson, Features Producer for BBC Scotland, encouraged him to write dramatic documentaries, and in May 1954 Neil reported to Richardson that he had been working on the script for a sixty-minute programme on whisky, and would next turn to the Clearances. He attended rehearsals in Edinburgh.

In 1952 Margaret had taken a flat there, after working for a year in Fife. Neil would visit her whenever he was in the city. The relationship was now quiet and habitual, without importunate demands on either side. At every opportunity Neil had encouraged Margaret to make her own life apart from him.

Despite increasing difficulties with Faber and their puzzled reluctance to publish each succeeding book, Neil still set out to produce one a year, and *Bloodhunt* is at the farthest remove from the picaresque, episodic, myth-making of *The Well at the World's End*. Surprisingly, at a period when its author was more and more concerned with meditatively exploring the boundaries of thought and experience, *Bloodhunt* is the tightest and most classical of all his novels. A simple retelling of the story would convey theme and meaning; the whole body of the book is a muscular, integrated unit in remorseless and inevitable movement; reflection is cut to a minimum and what reflection there is lies deeply embedded in character and event.

The central figure, Sandy, is a retired sailor who closely resembles Tom the philosopher of *The Serpent*. What's more, the central situation is like an incident in *The Serpent* used as the basis for a new book. In *The Serpent* the minister's son gets Tom's girl pregnant. Tom sets out with intent to kill but fails to find the man. Allan in *Bloodhunt* succeeds in finding and killing the seducer of Liz Murison. The victim is the brother of Nicoll the policeman, and Nicoll is a relentless avenging angel. Again, the continuing friendly argument of Sandy with the minister is a warm firelit reflection of Tom's conflict with his father.

Sandy seeks a way to die in peace:

> It had been one of Sandy's hopes that before the end he would find out if the spirit was immortal.
>
> And then, as simply as a thought might come to him when taking his porridge, he saw that to pass out of his body was in the order of things, now revealed; not an end and not quite a translation, but precisely a passing on and

away. At that moment it would have been easy and pleasant to die. He could have gone.

Not only had death no sting, *it did not matter.*[10]

But Sandy is robbed of his tranquillity. At seventy-four he is faced with a harrowing moral dilemma which strains and tests all his assumptions:

> There were calm stretches of living when a philosophy worked; but when the mind got properly upset, trivial feelings, futile idiotic thoughts would keep invading it, let will and reason do what they liked.

And Neil was himself finding this at Kerrow when conflict with his neighbours began.

Sandy shelters Allan, and his croft becomes Nicoll's trap to catch the murderer. To state this is to challenge any storyteller with the question 'What happens next?' And in *Bloodhunt,* with the locale and characters so tightly limited, a reader will soon find the challenge difficult to meet. But not Neil. With consummate ease and invention he moves the story through simple and acceptable incidents, maintaining the tension without any let-up, clear through to its conclusion—which is only seen as inevitable when it happens.

The light, humour and warmth of which the book is full are not 'dramatic relief ' but an integral part of the story. If Sandy were not *that* sort of man, this would not happen. And if the Widow Macleay is not essential to the story she is essential to its spirit:

> She was very concerned for him now, so ignored him altogether, especially after she saw his eyes were closed. It's rest the poor old man needed and, being only seventy-one herself, she thought of a dozen things from beef tea to soap flakes for a washing.
>
> Her questions were many and he has answers to most of them.

She enters 'cleaving the kitchen with her bows. He felt the draught in the bed.'[11]

Most novelists would not dare to trust their intuition to move the story through its course, for the smallest error, the slightest divergence from the track, and the whole pageant may end in a bog from which it cannot be dragged out. So they plan and summarise and calculate and hope. Neil moves with supple ease, allowing his sense of balance, his grasp of theme, and his subtle instinct for human life to guide him through whatever rough country his story may enter. When he does go astray it is usually the result of identifying too closely with a character very like himself, or of disliking a character too much (the Colonel in *The Lost Glen,* Geoffrey in *Second Sight*).

In *Bloodhunt* the characters are intelligent but not intellectual, and the author remains out of sight. For the first time he explores with sincere understanding the faith of a minister of the Church—and demonstrates how closely he had listened to those with whom he could never entirely agree.

Nan Shepherd went so far as to say that the book was his *Four Quartets*, and Neil replied (13 January 1953): 'I was visited once by the notion of watching innate goodness behave in illegal ways, trying to see if it is innate, and not just Christian . . .'

For the first time he is wondering whether Christianity must be considered *essential*. Somewhere in *Bloodhunt* it is suggested that man has invented only two archetypal stories, those of Cain and Christ. The implication is that if you are to get beyond the first story, you must accept the second. Yet Sandy remains what he always was—a good man without any dogmatic creed, whose perceptions are based upon a recognition of what is permanent in human nature, whether or not this is labelled. For not only did human nature exist before Christianity, so did good men. Neil wrote to Gene Pick on 24 June 1952:

> I suppose I must have been trying, however unconsciously—or half—to get a glimpse of that peculiar quality that we have . . . called 'goodness' . . . It seemed to me finally that it is not a specially Christian quality, not of any particular creed, but, rather literally, primordial.

And later he added to Hart:

> Yes, there's . . . something I had very much in mind, but it never really shows because I didn't *write* it anywhere. When the old sailor finds the policeman's brother's murderer and decides to say nothing, and the girl has her baby in the barn—I thought that the world after the bomb might well be like this—with just a few pockets of life left, and the old man by himself living on the fringes, being forced to decide what laws are to be followed at such a time, and recognising that life must and will go on.[12]

These were the Cold War years.

Geoffrey Faber sent the book straight to production (5 February 1952):

> I finished it yesterday; and am writing at once to say that I think it is one of the very best things you have ever done. It moved me very deeply and the conclusion, which I had been quite unable to imagine for myself while I was reading the story, is perfect.[13]

Neil's travails at Kerrow were by no means as severe as Sandy's in *Bloodhunt*, but he was deeply troubled nonetheless. The garden was too big for Daisy, and an arrangement had been made with a local man to cultivate a section of it for himself in return for keeping the whole clean and spruce. The arrangement did not work. When Neil ended the agreement there was a long guerrilla war over sheds and tools, and the conflict coincided with another. Because of the troubles with the gardener, Daisy could not take pleasure in her gardening, and to Daisy gardening was something necessary and fundamental, like a tree rooting itself.

A farming neighbour considered that he had a right of way for himself and his animals through Neil's ground. Neil did not. Efforts to reach a compromise failed and mysterious animal incursions began: hoofmarks on the lawn, broken fences, a rush of pigs. Such an affair can seem comic and absurd when seen from outside. But the inhabitants of the house felt themselves to be under siege.[14]

Neil's habit of an evening walk must lead him either down by the river or along his drive towards the road. In both directions this was the disputed right of way. It was disturbing for friends to find that he could no longer take the walk without pointing out the signs of damage, and describing the latest incident in the war of nerves. Neil hated the thought that people would be saying 'There's yon writer fellow, Neil Gunn, always showing poachers in his books, and now so set on his own property he's fighting with the neighbours to keep them off his land.' He felt that he had leaned over backwards to accommodate the complainant but that every concession he made was seized upon and used as basis for further demands. His pride would not allow him to surrender. He was prepared to dig in. But to dig in for siege in a place where you had meant to live out your days seemed too miserable a prospect to be tolerated. How intense the worry and frustration became is indicated by this extract from an article written many years later for *Point*. In it Neil places an imaginary friend in his own real predicament:

> The case I have in mind had to do with land ownership, rights, and stealthy encroachments on property and privacy. It grew intolerable, until the younger man, whose rights were being eroded, reached the point of desperation when he discovered one morning that some of his ground beside a lawn had been ploughed up by the enemy's pigs. Illicit sex and other popular entanglements know nothing of the deadly seriousness of the elemental land, decorated with pigs' snouts rooting up fences and ploughing up lawns. Murderous thought and a shot gun go arm in arm, in the twilight, among the birches, along the elms, by the river.
>
> Then in the early hours of one morning, when presumably concentration and meditation could go no further even in nightmare, thought got choked down and the mind rose up and broke through—into the void: and the void lit up. The light was quiet and the only object visible was the brain of the enemy

in the shape of moving plates each about the size of a small story book, but whitish in colour and smooth like damp ice. As the man watched the movement he became aware of every thought in that enemy head. A fine transparency was completely revealing of thought, character, personal idiosyncrasy. The understanding was so complete that the man was touched; and he became aware of himself there, too, a self-awareness that was absolute and pleasant while his vision continued to interpenetrate the smooth easy movements of the plates, of the head around them, and somehow of the man himself, now no longer the enemy. But what needs stressing was not simply the conviction but the absolute certainty that here was revelation, final truth. From now on there would be complete relaxation, easy movements in freedom, and an amused foresight of how to deal successfully with all future events and encounters. And this is exactly what happened. 'I even got, at times, a certain affection for the crafty old devil.' (But he could not tell at what point in this experience he had passed from sleep into full wakefulness.)[15]

That clairvoyant experience reminds one of the imaginary vision of the young woman whose man had gone off to the wars recorded in the journal of 1939. But whereas the 1939 experience is 'myth', the second one is immediate, with direct application in his own life, for a sense of understanding gave him resilience and confidence to deal with the 'adversary'.

It seems probable that the nature and intensity of this vision was due to the type of inner scrutiny and meditation which Neil was increasingly in the habit of practising as the result of his interest in the teaching of Gurdjieff and of Zen. The beginning of his interest in Zen can be precisely dated, but it is misleading to imagine that Zen 'influenced' him. It was of value to him because he recognised it. Zen joined him companionably in the place where he was.

When a man becomes a writer he becomes dedicated to the perception of truth. He cannot help it. To write anything other than truth is meaningless. And to be conscious that there are always visions over the hill is to climb the hill and to go on farther and to reach the well at the world's end.

The deeper Neil penetrated into the Highland landscape of heart and mind, the more his books implied that 'other landscape' which is seen so simply when the 'second self' wakes up and looks at *this* world, alive in all its dimensions, in all its depth and vividness. For the 'other world' is 'this world' seen by one who is fully awake. Once having realised the nature of this 'being fully awake' you look for signs of other people who have experienced it. And Neil saw these signs in Zen, and welcomed them.

For years he had been friendly with the spirit of the ancient Chinese book of wisdom the *Tao Te Ching*, and to meet Zen was to meet the same spirit,

with something added. And this 'something added' was important to Neil.
He would not have responded so promptly to Zen had it not first reached
him through *Zen in the Art of Archery* by Eugen Herrigel. Herrigel was
taught Zen through the practice of archery, and the fact that 'the way'
consisted in actually plunking arrows into the bull's eye delighted Neil,
who always insisted that only what is rooted in practical experience can have
value. As he writes in *The Atom of Delight*:

> The Great Doctrine, or any other doctrine, ideology, or system, remains
> susceptible in thought to any kind of criticism, for example to destructive
> criticism, to the charge that it is illusory or delusory, but the bull's eye
> containing the Master's two arrows was not an illusion. It permitted him to
> talk of 'I' and 'It', of a technique that after rigorous practice could so perfect
> itself that it transcended itself; and if the notion of transcendence were called
> in question, the Master could always bow to the target and plunk his arrow in
> the bull with certainty . . . The Master did not teach in words, he 'showed' the
> way. Theologians or philosophers may dispute; the doer *does*. And it is this
> doing that remains an indisputable *experience*, on whatever level the doing
> takes place. Unless this doing has been experienced, criticism can only be
> irrelevant.[16]

The vision of the adversary's mind as a mass of 'moving plates' which
resulted in certainty concerning the way to deal with him was clearly a form
of 'doing'.

Pick had been writing on sports and games and had become deeply and
practically interested in the phenomenon known as 'being in form'. What
makes the same man play badly on Wednesday and brilliantly on Saturday?
What enables him to move suddenly from mistiming to fluent ease? What is
the secret of being, during a game, at precisely the right place at the right
time?

It was for this reason that a review of *Zen in the Art of Archery* made Pick
buy the book immediately it appeared in 1953. As soon as he had read it he
bought a second copy and sent it to Neil, who wrote: 'I dance my solemn
gratitude before the target, like the Master who didn't believe in words.
Though I'm afraid it wasn't a tap dance he did.'

Once Neil's interest was aroused he read what he could, and meditated on
what he read. Books reached him from many sources and by the time he
wrote *The Atom of Delight* Zen was part of his make-up, an essential feature of
the landscape of his mind.

G. I. Gurdjieff, who, in the late 1920s, had become a cult-figure with a
headquarters at his 'Institute' near Fontainbleau, was quite another matter

and had quite another manner. He was viewed with extreme suspicion by all those sceptical of 'wise men from the East' and 'esoteric systems'. Where Gurdjieff 's 'system' originated from he never said, but anyone who studied it carefully came to realise that its psychological insights—whatever may be said of the 'cosmic' material—were valuable, not personal to Gurdjieff and certainly not invented. He aroused ire in some, adulation in others, and was capable of (and enjoyed) using both reactions for his own purposes. Neil appreciated him with an interested objectivity which he never lost, approaching him first through reading Ouspensky's *In Search of the Miraculous*. He read the book when it first appeared in English in 1950, and gave an account in *Point* of the effect it had on him: 'I was held as by a first-rate novel.'

To Neil the key concept in Gurdjieff's system was 'self-remembering':

> Applying this now to myself I realised that it was the word 'remember' that blocked the line of communication to me. As I read on, however, I found Ouspensky had been familiar with 'moments of self-remembering' since childhood and while travelling in a new place had experienced a momentary sensation of strangeness in finding himself there. This sensation I perfectly understood. Often while on foot in the Highlands, in turning a corner, in opening out a vista, I had been stopped in breathless wonder at the scene before me. But this wonder was pervaded by the wonder of finding myself there. This *I*—this *me*—here! Certainly it had nothing to do with memory. On the contrary it was as if you had found yourself for the first time. Here is not the ordinary self of everyday, but a new self, at once incredibly intimate and utterly undemanding, fresh as the first view of creation. Here at last is the *conscious* self.[17]

Neil recognised with clarity the truth of Ouspensky's observation 'We live and act in deep sleep, not metaphorically but in absolute reality.' But 'we can remember ourselves if we make sufficient effort, we *can* awaken.'

There follows in Neil's *Point* article a most revealing personal passage in which he again removes himself to a distance by recording a real incident as if it has happened to a friend:

> But theorising and imagining are never enough. There must be ever more actual experience that produces this effect of becoming aware of oneself, of becoming *conscious* in this new and illuminating way. And this experience may not be involuntary, a sheer gift from Nature and the Arts; it may come at a profound level only after a fight through darkness with a terrific exercise of the will. One must *do*, as Gurdjieff never forgets to stress. So let me try to illustrate this aspect of becoming *conscious*, of breaking through the mechanical to the conscious self . .

The first concerns a man and his wife who had fallen out. It was a case of the poet's simple disappointment becoming in a few moments a theme for Sophocles, for they had a deep mutual affection. But now the disagreement began to enlarge itself, with ever more and more implications seeping in, until it gave a few 'reasonable' if, on his part, impatient words, a significance that began to clot the very core of life in a dumb and dark way. Finally, before something terrible, unforgiveable, could be said he got up, went out, found his spade and tackled the earth. It was all absurd; it was maddening; still, damn it, there was a limit! . . . The more he tried for an iron control the darker all grew; the darkness began to embody itself . . . he had a dark sight of devil swirls . . . of wrestling with the Devil . . . religious imagery! My God, what next? . . . Because this was getting beyond absurdity it became a struggle within himself, his wife forgotten. But he found he didn't want to win . . . he wanted to enjoy the luxury of letting the devil win . . . So he struggled against the devil with all his might, for he *must* win, to show he could not be beaten, to prove the strength of his will. He would strangle the devil first, before getting back to his wife. He hung on . . . and suddenly the darkness broke, the tension eased, the light came through—and all was calm, simple, delightful. The incredible relief of it! The light itself smiling. He could see in one glance everything that had happened with a wonderful clarity, saw his wife's essential and everlasting nature, loved the very thought of it . . . then saw his own nature, its essence . . . and became *conscious*, as it seemed for the first time, of this permanent self within him, and, in the same moment of realisation, became conscious of his wife's permanent self in the same way. Sheer revelation of what forever endured, however obscured by mechanical happenings, chance moods, in the world of everyday. 'There was a sort of radiant quiet humour in it, too,' he added.

Now this did seem to reinforce G.'s general attitude regarding man's mechanical nature and the tremendous difficulty of recognising it and deliberately dealing with it.'

The idea of 'not expressing negative emotions' and the two lines of man's development, the line of knowledge and the line of being, also confirmed his own experience. He wrote to Hart in 1968 of the invariably 'demonic results from an increasing indulgence in negative emotions'.

He finished the article in *Point:*

So in the end I had to ask myself, among other questions, this question: Was G.'s system never finally realisable, not even by G? The scope of the question precludes any possible answer from me. All I can be sure of is that when Ouspensky had written his book *In Search of the Miraculous*, he gave it for subtitle 'Fragments from an Unknown Teaching'. Fragments, not Unity.

This is correct. We did not know at that time the origin of Gurdjieff's ideas in the esoteric system of the Sufis, which could not conceivably have been presented in its entirety, and its wholeness, to the West. Many of Gurdjieff's formulations were tailored for the West in a way we can only describe as preposterous—no doubt reflecting Gurdjieff's view of our spiritual situation. We have to remember that he was an allegorist, a joker and a consummate carpet salesman.

Neil writes in a letter to Pick dated 11 April 1963:

> I haven't opened *In Search of the Miraculous* since the cat climbed the Rhu rowan tree to have a look at the Merry Dancers . . . But you've brought it back and I feel like a few words. Indeed I feel like a whole lot, for I've been wandering in some odd 'marginal lands' as the farmers say, for a longish while, and fancy I have got a fairly consistent picture of G . . . He wandered from monastery to monastery—or master to master—learning all he could, just as the Zen boys wander to this day . . . The quest for truth—without end . . . As for his charlatanry, it's not quite the word. In his time he acted many parts. Play-acting. Something akin to Yeats's masks. Again, why so wise a fellow should do this is not too difficult to follow—though by follow, of course, I don't mean progression of rational steps so much as getting the *feel* of the doing. His second self could direct the posturings of his first self or ego, and even get some pleasure therefrom in certain company! I'm not unduly worried by this! What's a little more difficult to weigh was his final treatment of Ouspensky. I remember feeling some cruelty in it. Not so much deliberate and malicious cruelty as a total withdrawal of himself from O., and a lack of interest in O.'s hurt feelings. But here we'd have to understand the kind of impact O. was having all the time on G. There was a sort of humourless mathematical integrity in O. that whiles must have become a bit wearing to the versatile G . . .

It is considerations of the kind to which Neil's meditations on Zen, Gurdjieff and his own experiences led which produced *The Other Landscape*, published in 1954.

The Other Landscape was Neil's last novel—complex, rich with humour and aimed at the impossible. Keith Henderson said 'He was always trying to find the truth behind the truth. He rewrote the story of the boy in the stream, he rewrote *Highland River* in *The Atom of Delight*, to get behind it, to get more out of it . . .'

In *The Other Landscape* he rewrote the Colonel in *The Lost Glen*, to understand him, to find some meaning in him, to overcome him in his mind, to achieve a form of reconciliation. The girl in *The Silver Bough* returns in *Bloodhunt* (again bearing an illegitimate child), the cave of *The Silver Bough* reappears in *The Other Landscape*, and Menzies in *The Other Landscape* is a deepening and elaboration of Martin in *The Silver Bough*.

Incidents and situations recur again and again in the novels: the cliff, the storm, the boy and the salmon, the illicit still, the poaching foray, the intellectual intruder, the returning 'failure'. But who would have forecast in 1926 that out of these limited ingredients Neil could have grown books so many in number and so varied in kind? He used and refined and reformed and replenished and restored and recast and deepened and re-imagined his experiences over and over again.

The rewriting of the Colonel (who became a Major in *The Other Landscape*) shows his need to get out of his system a sense that he had not finally overcome the feelings of bitterness and shame which led originally to the writing of *The Lost Glen*:

> The tragedy of the Major was that he couldn't forget himself and I saw this with a certainty that moved me strangely in his favour.
>
> So he would never stop taking it out of me, if only to prevent the indignity, the giveaway, of his own descent into self-pity.
>
> As I brought the two candles from the hall the Major was sitting upright in a deep gloom like Pluto. I had never encountered a scene at once so infernal and classical. Around his glassy, unwinking eyes the candle flickers danced.

The scene in which the Major's room catches fire and Lachlan the gillie gets revenge with a hose for the Major's long baiting is the funniest set-piece Neil ever wrote, and rises to the grotesque rhetorical frenzy of Sir Thomas Urquhart.[18]

But he did not write *The Other Landscape* 'to put the Major in his place'. He wrote it to explore the mysteries of death, evil, misfortune and delight. It is beautiful, sombre, alive and positive, wildly ambitious and strangely youthful.

Whether the choice of first-person narrator was conscious and deliberate cannot now be said. But use of the first person is a way to ensure that the author does not need to know more than his hero. So the central figure in the book, Menzies, can be held to know more than the hero, with the hero groping through darkness towards the 'more'. In these circumstances the author is allowed to do some groping too—to know only in principle what Menzies knows in practice.

An anthropologist goes to the Highlands to find the author of a strange and powerful manuscript. This author is Douglas Menzies, a musician, whose beautiful wife dies in childbirth on a night of storm when a ship is wrecked on the coast. The manuscript proves prophetic. Ideas of 'recurrence' and second sight abound. The musician now lives in isolation with only a savage black dog for company. In the end the dog goes over the cliff accompanied by 'a smell of brimstone'.

Despite the gaiety, the delightful love story, the excitement of storm and rescue, the book is difficult. Its focus is three conversations with Menzies, who seeks for the meaning of that aspect of the deity which wrecks and destroys, and which killed his wife Annabel:

> 'God's ways are non-rational,' he said, 'either non-rational or there is no God. Were it otherwise, did God exist and were he rational, then his doings would be susceptible of a logical exposition. His horrors wouldn't call for faith. So if there is a God—*he must have a different system.*' . . . for Menzies the penetration of the other system was now all that mattered.[19]

The dead girl Annabel is absolutely necessary to this penetration for she already inhabits that 'other landscape' which Menzies strives to enter. There is a moment in the book when Annabel appears to the anthropologist—in reality or projected by Menzies's mind? We don't know, the character doesn't know. There is no need for the author to know. She is simply *there*.

The struggle within the story is a struggle with God—with the nature of that 'other system' which rules the universe and which we are—almost—unable to perceive.

'The Wrecker is God when he wrecks.'

The effort to give an idea of Menzies's mind and conversation without actually providing long swatches of speech runs Neil into a maze of complication from which many a reader will only extricate himself by jumping. Menzies's insight does not express itself in logical argument (he is a musician, after all) but in quick sudden flashing movements among images and symbols and in aphoristic statements of direct vision: 'The atom or the atomic thicket excreted mind.' That is not easy stuff.

Neil comes back to his theme and subject again and again to find ways of presenting Menzies's discoveries:

> I went on about the Wrecker. I explained this particular element of the godhead; and I explained Menzies's quest. It was a hopeless quest, I said, because the Wrecker always had the last word first . . . He was bigger than the Wrecker. And what made him bigger was love, because love was the creative element, not the wrecking element, the creative element that made his music. And that's where Annabel came in. For she was part of the creative element that made him whole.[20]

Menzies goes down the cliff in a wild fierce wind to rescue two men in a small boat. And then, arbitrarily, goes down again to get rum from a cask he has salvaged from the sea—but falls and is killed. On his dead face 'the expression was hardly a smile but rather a characteristic or veiled intensity arrested in quietude . . . from having heard the struck note and knowing what the note meant.'

After having made such a raid into unexplored territory Neil could not return to the ordinary novel, write a 'straight' story, give his publishers comfort. How, indeed, could he return to the novel at all? His last book, which followed *The Other Landscape*, was his direct excursion into this country of the mind:

> It is delightful, and if thought is foolish enough to intrude at all it is to wonder if there may be an order of being to which this delight is natural. And one knows that *there may be*. There may be the other landscape which the delight inhabits.

We are away from the Wrecker now.

Neil wrote to Nan Shepherd in July 1954:

> The critics have sat on me good and hard. They have, and one London critic in particular had only to dip into the book here and there to make a real dog's breakfast of it. So I've been in the wars.[21]

Neil and Daisy had been in the wars in other ways. Accident pursued them relentlessly over these years. In August 1953 a film unit was shooting *The Kidnappers* in Glen Affric. The writer of the story was Neil Paterson. He gives his own account of his call on the Gunns:

> I had gone to Glen Affric to see something of the shooting of one of my films, and, learning that Neil lived close by, I armed myself with a bottle of whisky and ventured to call on him. Neil, a connoisseur of malt, cast a polite but quizzical eye on my indifferent blend, and I wouldn't be surprised to learn that he has the bottle in his cellar to this day. I think he forgave me some years later. Daisy did better. She forgave me on the spot. Despite the fact that she already had guests . . . she insisted on my staying the night . . .[22]

That evening the director and other members of the unit came in and there was gloom, concern and distress because the son of one of the actors had been found dead in a tumbling stream in Glen Affric. There were too many such incidents at Kerrow. One night in November 1953 the Gunns were driving home from Inverness in a snowstorm, and there was an accident with a drunken pedestrian. A police inquiry confirmed that Neil was not at fault, but the incident shocked Neil and Daisy deeply. It made Daisy ill, and Neil was ill already.

In spring 1954 he was suffering from a constant, debilitating buzzing in the ear and from an unusual sense of depression. Just before the move to Kerrow his beloved Bridie had died. Not long afterwards his old, congenial and valued friend Peter John Macleod followed. At the end of 1954 John Macnair Reid, living at Torridon, broke his ankle and died under anaesthesia. He was only fifty-seven.

Neil began to have neuralgic pains in the face and showed symptoms of anaemia. Keith Henderson's letters became a series of jovial, hectoring denunciations, demanding that he ignore his ailments and show what Keith called *'stamina'*. 'The cruelties of existence, seemingly so senseless and—if there were really an outside anthropomorphic deity—so sadistic, must be just brushed aside, *must*, Neil.'[23]

But the victim was sent to the Northern Royal Infirmary in Inverness. On 27 May 1954 he wrote to the Picks:

> I stuck the Northern Infirmary for a full week and then—yesterday—beat it. The intensive treatment wasn't doing any good, so I said to the specialist I'd like a spell off before he started a new treatment. Simple fact is, as he frankly admits, that they don't have any cure. But they have theories! I was feeling so woolly that I misjudged a bloke's bumper by half an inch and tore the back mudguard of my beautiful car.[24] . . . Bad luck has been dogging me so assiduously so long I'll think twice before I'll blow my nose. A big repair is suddenly needed to this house, an expensive business. And so on.

But there were compensations. Neil did not often fish, but the river was there to be visited. 'I recollect Neil,' said George Bruce, 'the tall, thin figure walking easily over the bridge, carrying a fishing rod, then picking his way over stones with an easy balance, to the river and then casting into it and at the same time taking in the whole scene.'[25] He was able to invite his brothers onto the river, too. Pick remembers:

> I took a friend, an aspiring angler, to Kerrow. Neil and brother Alec were on the river. Neil asked him if he would like to fish and said: 'You would do much better with Alec. He's the real expert.' After a few hours with Alec my friend was lost in admiration for his skill and afterwards talked more about Alec than about Neil.
>
> Another time I was with Neil when he got into a fish. A tour bus was passing on the road just beyond the river. The driver stopped and in no time the passengers had poured down to the waterside and were gathered like a crowd watching street theatre. Neil played the salmon until he had it on the stones and then said casually 'Just go in and lift it out', so I walked into the river, lifted the salmon by the tail and carried it ashore. I tried that trick again another time, the fish went through my legs, the line tangled and there was hell to pay. Ignorance is bliss.

Robert Wotherspoon often invited him to Glen Affric. Duncan Maclennan, gamekeeper of the estate, gives an account of one expedition:

> Robert Wotherspoon had another good friend, an American from London, whom he invited once a year for trout fishing on Loch Affric, and Neil Gunn was always in this party too. They called the American C. J. [C. J. Latta was a film company executive and a partner of Wotherspoon and Robert Clark.] . . . C. J. always wanted to cook the trout by the side of the loch . . . On one of these occasions food was still rationed, but C. J. insisted that we take 1 lb of butter (margarine would not do), a pan of mashed potatoes, salt, etc, and we had to have a wood fire. I had to see all these things were put in the boat. When sufficient fish were caught we went ashore and while I got the fire going and the place made as comfortable as possible C. J. was donning his apron, chef 's bonnet, etc, and he then commenced cleaning the fish . . . When the trout were ready for cooking they were put in a large frying pan . . . on the fire, then the mashed potatoes . . . in another large frying pan and what was left of the butter from the trout pan was added to the potatoes. The potatoes were flattened down into the pan and the underside well browned, then the highlight of the whole day was to see C. J. toss the bannock of potatoes into the air and catch it . . . with the opposite side of the potatoes underneath so it could be browned.[26]

When it came to this point in the proceedings Neil would beg C. J. not to toss the potatoes for fear of losing the lot just when his mouth was watering for them. 'But if you insist, take one more dram, and we'll take one ourselves to fortify us against disaster.'

'O.K.,' said C. J., 'another swig of your darn snake-bite!'

And he tossed the potatoes. Duncan Maclennan comments: 'By the way, the meal was truly delicious but it took up the greater part of the day, and very little fishing was done.'

After *The Other Landscape* there were ominous signs. Neil was depressed by the book's reception. His references to giving up writing grew more frequent:

> Even my pen has forgotten how to squeeze out ink, for not a word have I written in many months. Perhaps I am going through some transition period, and have not yet found the new job. I have regretfully eliminated two physical labour jobs. Reading can't be called a job; anyway, I have never really taken to it . . .[27]

But Daisy was quite sure that unless he was writing he was lost and wandering, however much he might choose to disguise or deny the fact. Besides, how could he occupy his time? So Pick found himself being pushed and cajoled into making suggestions. This was a ticklish business. But by the autumn of 1954 Neil was writing to him:

> The part to which I took very great exception in your letter was that which
> suggested (1) I should begin to do some work on (2) of all things, wise insights
> and wisdoms. Apart from destroying my somnolent ease, what on earth do you
> mean? All I know in that way could be shoved down on two pages. And yet
> into me you put that gnawing bug.
>
> I all but killed it by doing an article on 'Deerstalking' for an American
> magazine, with payment now en route of 1,000 dollars. I wouldn't get that
> from Sayings not if I had the wisdom of Aquinas, not to mention Solomon and
> Bertrand Russell, Hume, Kant, Hegel, Spinoza, Plato, Copernicus, and
> Uncle Tom Eliot an' all. So clarify yourself.

But by October he was busy with *The Atom of Delight,* and writes:

> It's some consolation for me to know there's another slave like myself, and
> doubly so when it's the other slave has done it on me. Yes, you've set me
> going, so I hope you're in as many difficulties, incredulities, absurdities,
> nonsensicalities and impossibilities. But no, I couldn't have the heart, not
> even in the case of an enemy . . . For of course I can't write down wisdom, as
> you know only too well. But assuming the thing will have a shape it will be an
> autobiography, a detective story, a Freudian analysis (of Freud), a spoon for
> physics, a critical commentary on Yeats, Proust, Wordsworth, Rilke and
> Uncle Tom Eliot, a high dive and long swim into anthropology, poaching,
> church attendance and sucking eggs, and a way of using these in a sustained,
> convoluting, forward-and-backward search, with a ruthless precision in the
> complexities of expression, into the nature of delight. Now you've got
> it—without the short story which I'm planting in the middle of the plot like a
> flower pot (for something must be plain). And the title, the one and only
> certainty so far, *The Atom of Delight*. I can hear your resigned comment, 'He
> was bound to land among the atoms sometime.' Well, I sure have. Aye, it's
> sad. I shan't be surprised if its half-concealed logic works up into a simple,
> naive philosophic system, and you know how a system chokes the wisdom you
> are always prepared to salute. Though I'll do my best with camouflage. If
> only—if only—I hadn't the vanity which has hitherto made me finish once I
> start! For I *have* started. But I may achieve the sophistry which could well find
> an end anywhere. I don't feel myself in honour bound by nothing.
>
> And now, by God, here's your apparently innocent letter with its talk of
> Ouspensky and G. There's something deep here and damned. Omens around
> and totems. Here is a cunning design to make me include Ouspensky also.
> You can't hoodwink me. Very well. I'll send out a tentacle and haul him in,
> once I've dealt with Rilke, seeing himself as Christ. Anything else? Rags and
> bones!

Obviously, he was enjoying the torture. He probably found more delight
in writing about delight than he found in composing any other book. And

how revealing those phrases are: 'Though I'll do my best with camouflage.'
'I'll send out a tentacle and haul him in.' For Neil knew perfectly well the
nature of his 'naive philosophic system', based with true empiricism on
those personal experiences which had convinced him of their significance,
and to which significance he kept adding as the years went by; but he wasn't
going to set himself up to be shot at by claiming to be a philosopher. He
would approach sideways, under camouflage, and let the perceptions add up
in the reader's mind until they came together suddenly and there was a total
vision of the world.

The book is based on events in his youth but in no real sense is it an
autobiography. You learn less about the emotional life of Neil Miller Gunn
from *The Atom of Delight* than from any one of the novels. And this, of
course, gives the book its peculiar atmosphere. It is based on a series of real
experiences, often vividly described, but with an oddly generalised air: 'A
story is a story with its fascination, and its thrills, irrespective of number,
but that solitary "I" touches the quick . . .' But he goes on: 'To get the full
impact of all the elements, within and without, one had to be alone.' So the
'I' has vanished already and 'one' takes its place! And then follows the
account of 'The Boy and the Salmon' told in the third person, with the
author as 'the boy'. In other words, Neil is no closer to the reader in this
story than he was when he told it in *Highland River*. He is clearly aware of
what he is doing. It's necessary to remember that he was *always* aware. The
device of stepping back into the third person, or the generalised 'one', is not
the result of modesty. Nor does it necessarily increase objectivity, as he
implies. It is essentially protective cover, a way of preventing the hunter
from becoming the hunted.

Even the crucial experience of the book—the boy 'coming upon himself'
as he sits cracking nuts on a stone in the stream—is removed to a timeless
sunniness of contemplation which reduces the sense of that boy being the
author himself, Neil Gunn himself. That is what he aimed at. He wrote to
Pick, on 25 May 1957:

> The Scottish Home Programme is doing an hour from *The Atom of Delight*. The
> salmon story. One bloke speaks for forty solid minutes. An experiment.
> Cedric Thorpe Davie has composed for the lot. I can hardly believe it will come
> off. Awful illustration of N. G. as a small boy wrestling with a salmon in a
> pool, in Scots issue of *Radio Times*. Sort of spot where I want to crawl in under!

Readers would have been willing to digest the philosophy in its dancing
sideways pattern of movement had the author in return opened himself to

them. But he did not. The book is reflective philosophy rather than autobiography. He could only write autobiography in fiction—fictional autobiography at that. Once you accept *The Atom of Delight* on its own terms, and live in its world, it is wise, enlivening, humorous and full of a golden light. It contains nothing that cannot be found in the novels, but it creates a clear vision, a 'system', which the novels do not aim to do, and to return to the novels after reading it is a rewarding experience.

Neil had long distrusted critics and was prepared for misunderstanding. But he was deeply disappointed by the book's reception nonetheless. A writer is not normally affected by adverse reviews provided he feels that at least a few of their authors succeed in discovering what the book is about and recognising its inner nature and value. But the meaning of *The Atom of Delight* was generally missed. If reviewers had shared his enjoyment of the hunt he would have been satisfied. For he enjoyed it hugely: 'Hunting Freud hunting God becomes one of those complications which inevitably attend the pursuit of any living quarry . . .'

Perhaps at this point we should ourselves pursue the quarry a little further in time. Neil Gunn wrote, after all, no more books. In April 1958 Neil heard from Alexander Reid, the dramatist and poet whom he had sought out years before as the most astute reviewer of *Wild Geese Overhead*. Reid had just become editor of the *Saltire Review*. As a keen admirer of Neil's kind of philosophic writing, he wanted more of the same in essay form for the magazine. Neil replied warmly, but indicated that he had no thought of following up *The Atom of Delight* because of its reception. He admired and appreciated Reid, however, and proceeded to do several articles for him, beginning with 'The Heron's Legs' in summer 1958, and ending with 'Landscape Inside' in autumn 1959. (Another, 'Highland Space', appeared after Reid left the editorship.) Had there been more discerning editors such as Reid in Scotland then, Neil might have kept on writing. But readers received the articles with something like embarrassed bewilderment, and the myth grew that Neil Gunn had retreated into esoteric nonsense. In a letter of 22 September, Neil wrote to Pick:

> About reactions to the first article—I had a note from Sydney Goodsir Smith, who did a review of the *Saltire,* apologising for what might seem damaging in that the paragraph he devoted to my article was the only paragraph cut out of his review by the editor! . . . I believe it was reviewed in *Arts Review* on the air. John Grierson said it was on a certain level but that if the author rewrote the whole of the articles after they appeared . . . ! Yet could anything be simpler, more usual, than the first article? What are they going to think of what follows? So you see how it is . . .

In another letter he says:

> But perhaps I am being influenced by what has happened over these articles of mine in the *Saltire Review*. The third one has just been published, and the key paragraph (about Waiting for Godot) has been cut out. I cannot help laughing. I think the editor has made the cut so that the article would end at the bottom of a page. . . . I'm afraid, John, they all think I'm gaga. I blame myself, for I should have had more sense than to let the editor in for it. Unfortunately I cannot help him out, because in the last paragraph of article I say that one more article is coming. And it's the longest and worst of the lot! Reviewers ignore the stuff or are briefly sarcastic. We had George Blake and his wife to dinner in Glasgow. An old good friend. He told me that he had had to review the . . . *Saltire Review* with the first article—but did not mention my article. He did not say why. And I made it easy for him by laughing and passing on.[28]

These essays resemble Menzies's conversation in *The Other Landscape*—sideways, complex, a pattern of Celtic knots, where Neil trusts the reader to concentrate, to smile, to pause, to wait, to follow the movement of the author's mind. And readers tended to demand internally, 'All right, then, come out with it, tell us exactly what you mean!'

But to Neil it was not possible to 'come out with it' in that sense, and to knock in nails with a hammer. He was saying precisely what he meant and they insisted that he was mystifying them. Part of the meaning lay in the hunt, the path through the wood, the sudden illumination by the way. In the novels, passionate emotion and the lure of 'what happens next' carry the reader on. Without that, people who read the novels as it were 'despite themselves' would not follow.

Perhaps Neil now felt that for years he had been deceived into thinking that readers appreciated his books because they appreciated the nature of the mind that made them, only to find that the true 'inwardness' of the novels did not register with them at all—only the surface, the events, the emotional charge.

Another explanation of why he stopped writing was given in conversation with Pick during the late 1960s:

> 'When I finished *The Atom of Delight* I felt that was the end of my youth and now I'd really get down to it.'
>
> 'You mean you had made notes for the flight and now you would take off?'
>
> 'That's it. I would start the real work and have a few years for it. But the energy wasn't there. You need to be able to concentrate. And I couldn't manage it. Otherwise I could have gone far enough, I think, where it matters.'

He did not actually *decide* to stop writing, of course. It just happened. In order to write novels you have to be ready and waiting for a story to grow in the mind. The possibility, the intention, the need, must be present with you always. In Neil's case a combination of circumstances gradually destroyed the intention: lack of enthusiasm from his publishers, lack of attention from the critics, lack of understanding from his readers, illness and loss of energy, worry about Daisy, and concern for matters which he knew quite certainly were beyond the interest of most of his former public.

Not all. He continually received unexpected communications and appreciation from out of the blue, testifying to the value of those very pieces of writing which were generally ignored. Two examples will suffice. He writes on 17 March 1957:

> . . . a letter just received from a lad who goes peddling books on a push bike through the wilds of Scotland. Incredible that such trades should exist today—and wonderful. 'I had among my customers yesterday an ex-radio operator, living far from the sea in Perthshire, who was much impressed by your *Atom of Delight* and who as a fiddler (he plays at the local dances) felt he'd made progress only after studying a book by a professor of a Continental conservatoire, whose methods (or advice, rather) he thought to be about on a par with that of the Master of Zen Archery.' The peddler is now reading Herrigel on the Art.[29]

This is just the sort of thing which pleased Neil most.

Then a publisher's reader and expert on Richard Jefferies, Samuel J. Looker, wrote to him in 1958:

> I have just read your book *The Atom of Delight* and have been greatly moved and uplifted by it. It is not only that some of your thoughts and experiences touch me most nearly in my own life, or your references to that remarkable man L. H. Myers whose novels I have loved so much, but above all it is your atom of longing, of delight, which to me has meant 'the deep power of joy' that has moved me most strongly . . . Amid so much that I find tiresome, trivial, even evil in grain, *The Atom of Delight* rejoices and inspires. How can one say thank you for that?[30]

The 'true inwardness' of his books *was* being recognised.

17 Ploys

Neil found ways other than writing books of occupying his time. In 1954 he wrote:

> And these BBC folk begin to worry me . . . They're bringing a van to this house with a recording box and they want me to talk for several minutes into the bloody box. About Scotland. It's frightful. How can you expect me to drip wisdom under that threat?—I mean, of course, how can I write about atoms? I am really having a shocking time. Me, who was free for over a whole year![1]

Which shows how much he was enjoying being wanted. And later in the same letter:

> Have promised to go to Edinburgh for production of my clearances programme. Being given an informal dinner! Are they drawing me into the toils?

And indeed they were. Robin Richardson, George Bruce and Finlay J. Macdonald, all BBC producers, and all admirers of his books, were after him for one thing and another. Later Stewart Conn and Ian Grimble joined them. In 1955 there began the practice of taking a BBC van to Kerrow to record ten or fifteen minutes for *Scottish Life and Letters* (edited jointly by Maurice Lindsay and George Bruce), the script prepared in advance.

The following year Richardson asked Neil to do a forty-five-minute travel broadcast, 'The Sea to the Isles', to introduce the Queen's tour up the west coast. He was given travel and research funds and he urged Robin Richardson to get Helen Macmillan to sing Gaelic songs.

During 1956–7 he did three scripts for the schools *This is My Country* series. George Bruce became editor of *Arts Review* in 1956 and as a result Neil's involvement increased. The format now consisted of the panel giving short separate talks and then joining in discussion. For the discussions Neil had to go to Edinburgh. George Bruce recalls that Neil was nervous beforehand, but this passed as soon as the programme began and he became interested in what was said. He was sometimes brilliant—as for example when he gave an extended impromptu account of what it felt like to be Hamlet. He always had the faculty of being inside and outside an event or a character at the same time.

The Drinking Well, Bloodhunt, The Green Isle of the Great Deep and *The Well at the World's End* were all dramatised and broadcast.[2]

Ian Grimble, producer of material for the VHF station in the Highlands, gives in a letter of 20 December 1978 a general impression of Neil as a broadcaster:

> He had a curiously throaty delivery, projecting his words from way back . . . Neil would compose a script that was very close to his style of speaking, and read it so that it sounded very much as though he were just talking thoughtfully in that intimate detached way of his. One hardly ever needed to suggest any inversion of word order or other alteration. If it proved advisable, he would spot it first himself. What all this added up to was that a producer didn't 'produce' Neil in the general meaning of that term. He simply recorded. I never recorded him in a studio, only in his own home, and for the first time in Cannich. Fortunately I kept my own copies of the talks he gave to our local VHF station, the first of its kind to be set up in the British Isles which is now full of them. These, on the Moray Firth fishing boom and on Iona, have just been taken for the BBC archives, and are far the best examples of his broadcasting in that collection. The Iona one was subsequently transmitted in the national network and published in the *Listener*. But Neil himself wasn't addressing *Listener* readers or Home Counties intellectuals. If he wasn't talking to himself, he was talking to his neighbours.[3]

Broadcasting was not his only ploy at the time. The renewal of visits to Maurice Walsh in Ireland brought on another one. Association with Maurice always did. He was inveigled into collaborating on a film. A 1957 conversation between Neil and Robert Clark, a Director of Associated British Picture Corporation Ltd, led to the idea of a film about whisky. Maurice reported to Neil that he had been approached with a proposition on this subject by Elstree Studios (owned by ABPC) and he had agreed. He asked Neil to collaborate. He would need a plot. Ever since Maurice started writing Neil had been involved in providing him with plots. Not only did Maurice offer to pay for them, but Neil sometimes took the money.

Neil sent a treatment to Clark in April 1957. Because Maurice was a party to the affair, it was a Walsh plot he invented rather than a Gunn plot. Neil wrote to Pick:

> That film fellow, amid a hubbub of folk and whisky bottles on Saturday, never gave me a chance to say anything, for instead of coming to catch trout, as expected, he suddenly caught a sleeper for London, and left me chewing my cigar with the fairly distinct impression that I had said I would go to London on Monday next (1 July) rather than have a posse of scenario writers up to see me at Cannich. I did say that I couldn't go to London without Daisy. He merely said 'Fine! Excellent! Would you like to go to the Savoy or—.' I thought a change . . . Anyway, I gather that it will be a quiet little place

called the Mayfair . . . However, I did make it clear that this commits me to nothing. The wary Highlander did contrive to make that clear! . . . Roughly, the position is that they are interested in my script and before taking steps about it, they would like me to discuss it with their principal scenario writer and others . . . If after all that I am prepared to play, then things like an agreement and so on would follow. I feel like one of my own fish on the end of my own line, and full of possible evasive actions. But it's sort of complicated because I got Maurice Walsh—and he got me—sort of involved . . .

As it happened, the Picks had left Scotland in October 1956 and were in a London flat for a few months when Neil and Daisy made their film visit. Pick recalls:

> I used to collect Neil and Daisy from the hotel and drive them through the wilds of London. They were very calm and relaxed while being whizzed at high speed round Marble Arch and Hyde Park corner—a daunting change from passing places on the road to Achiltibuie. Neil positively seemed to enjoy the taxis homing in on all sides, the single-minded buses and the hooting Jaguars, and was elegantly unmoved when we ran out of petrol at a traffic light on the Embankment and had to walk to the Army and Navy Stores in the Strand for a petrol tin because the man in the nearest garage was too mean to lend me one.

On 8 August 1957 Neil wrote:

> I have been terribly busy with visitors, salmon, garden, etc. I tumble into bed with the aches of a navvy. In between I have been dashing down stuff for the film, which Daisy has been typing. I am putting it into screenplay shape, all the conversation, complete. I have also signed the agreement. I have been in touch with Maurice, who says that he has lost the kick for work, but also says he won't see me stuck . . .

Neil received £250. Then, when in January 1958 he complained that he had not been paid for his 'treatment', he got another £250. On 31 January he received a third sum. He was to be given a final £250 on acceptance of the screenplay and 5 per cent of the net profits of the film. He wrote in April 1958 expressing displeasure about the delay in deciding to go ahead with the production. In May they offered him a last £250 in settlement, explaining that really they owed him nothing, because the screenplay had not been accepted. Neil immediately replied that this deprived him of his percentage. The film was never made, but one way or another he obtained £1,000 between summer 1957 and spring 1958 for a combination of treatment and screenplay. Not bad going for a 'provincial'![4]

Yet another profitable ploy had got under way, in 1957. He wrote to Pick:

My part-time job? Don't know yet, but when I was writing to you I got a letter from a noble lord . . . asking me if I would be prepared to do some advising on whisky making! It wouldn't take up much time and wouldn't make much use of my name—so he may know some of my peculiarities.

The 'noble lord' was Lord Bracken and his letter is dated 6 March 1957. A new distillery was to be built near Forres. And on 3 April he was asking Neil to spend a day searching for a suitable site. The expedition is described in 'An Affair of Whisky', published in *New Saltire*, December 1962:

We set off for the Moray country to hunt solitary and remote burns and taste their quality.

Lovely as the day was, with a warmth in the air and an inevitable softness in the burn water, I did not depart from my intention to be rigorous and uncompromising in my advice, and accordingly proceeded with the arrangement to test on the spot the effect of the water upon a modicum of old malt whisky . . .

Yet on another day we crossed the watershed and came down into the strath of the Spey, the strath that with its tributaries holds about half of the Highland stills, and more than half of their fables . . .

It was within this rectangle, then, that we found at last a burn, which ran from the Cromdale Hills into the Spey, in quantity enough and in taste admirable. It had its source in a small loch whose Gaelic name meant the loch of gold and, as an extra wonder, it had no distillery on its banks. Its name was Tormore, in the county of Moray . . .

Schenley had acquired Seager Evans & Co in 1956, and the Tormore Distillery was a part of their plans to expand sales. From 1958 into the mid sixties Neil received an annual retainer of £500 for advice on development and promotion. He met John Mackie of Seager Evans, in spring 1958, and they decided on a promotional film to be called *The Tormore Story*. Neil would write script and commentary and H. Forsyth Hardy would produce for Films of Scotland.

A letter to Hardy of 1 May 1958 demonstrates Neil's ability to take in his stride whatever problems might be involved in a piece of writing, and his willingness to accept a challenge:

That 'romantic' word of Mackie's: I have looked again at his letter . . . and find that his only thought is 'that we might extend the romantic interest although this, of course, would not be the predominant feature of the film.' So he means to have romance *in the film*! . . . Items: Highland scene, documentary, whisky making, salmon catching, works construction, history, smugglers, old prints, Highland cattle and Highland depopulation, chemist's lab—to name a few as they come—*and* love interest. All in 15 or 20 minutes? This is so fantastic that I regard it as a challenge worthy of our mettle. Being impossible, it can of course be done . . .

And he proceeds to sketch out 'six shots to cover the love interest and enrich the contrapuntal', with the comment 'All this could be done accidentally, as it were, in the passing. It's the utmost that could be done . . . At the same time it mustn't be touched unless well done.'

On the question of whisky as distinct from films about whisky he writes to Mackie on 8 April 1960:

> I have got the sample of Tormore . . . It is a clear drop, without a trace of that 'guff' which haunts some Speyside stills—it may be for years, if not for ever! For what my opinion is worth, I think it will mature fairly early—and by that I do not imply that it is lacking in body but that it is well bred in the sense of not having objectionable characteristics to be bred out. This, I suppose, means that it will mix in perfectly with your notions of a Long John blend of a light and distinctive character. But I am not thinking of your mere blends at the moment; I am thinking of what a delectable dram this will be, as a single whisky, in eight to ten years' time out of, say, a second fill sherry cask![5]

The distillery was formally opened in October 1960 with Neil in attendance. The promotional film, with Neil's commentary read by Iain Cuthbertson, was well received in London in spring 1961, and in August Neil went to the Edinburgh International Festival to see the Tormore film and another on Skye, for which he had also written the commentary.

He advised Mackie on an elaborate brochure advertising Long John to the trade, correcting historical and technical inaccuracies in the draft material and providing a piece called *The Long John Story*.

Throughout this episode he was half-amused and half-flattered by being swept through the Highland countryside in Lord Bracken's murmuring Rolls-Royce, by being associated with high-powered American business, by being put up at the most extravagant hotels, and by being treated as Somebody not on the grounds that he wrote books, but on the grounds that he knew about whisky. He never overpraised Long John but privately held it to be a good, clean, satisfactory blend without pretension.[6]

It is worth remembering that throughout these years of increasing illness and worry Neil was regarded as a man of affairs to be called on for practical advice by Daisy's family. He had been her father's executor. He gave financial and other counsel to some of her sisters. He helped Jean Robertson, her niece in Aberdeen, until she died in 1957, and did much for a variety of people who were not members of the family at all.[7] He was continually being asked for assistance by writers and artists or by those canvassing on their behalf. He never failed to respond. Here are a few examples. He wrote to Pick sometime during the 1950s (letter undated):

The only writing I have done recently was to the Lord Advocate who wanted my appreciation of the national significance of the work of Marian McNeill (*The Scots Kitchen*) so that he could submit it to Downing Street. Result: Marian has got her Civil List pension. I have recently been moving towards a similar end in the case of Edwin and Willa Muir. But plenty of time for that, for Edwin is still using the cash an American University has given him for work on the Scottish ballads. That is the good and proper end for all true literary ladies and gents. But for the casuals or casualties of the literary fringe like you and me, it's the commercial world and never say die.

He had helped, years before, to obtain C. M. Grieve's Civil List pension, and later worked to get grants and commissions for younger writers. He also gave them practical advice. The technical suggestions he made to Pick over the years would fill a book.

Ronald ('Bingo') Mavor, Bridie's son, first met Neil at North Berwick in about 1947 when Neil came to see Bridie's family at their holiday hotel. Neil and Bingo went for a walk and perched themselves on a sand dune. Neil told Bingo:

> I have discovered that if I work in the mornings for about three months I can finish a novel, and that's all I need. Know how much you need, and do just enough to have it. It's like rounding the shoulder of a hill and coming on a bothy, and finding some wood in it, just enough, that someone has left there so you can have a fire. Maybe a little food, and maybe even a bottle of beer.[8]

And late in the 1950s, when Bingo had become a dramatist and was drama critic of the *Scotsman*, Neil playfully prodded him on contemporary fashions. Bingo had taken on the thankless but entertaining task of introducing Neil to the beat generation, and had sent books. Neil tried some, and wrote back (2 October 1959):

> A provincial who hazards opinion on Lit. must be brought up to date. You are a thoughtful fellow. I got half-way through Kerouac's *On the Road* and stuck. But I'm not of the beat generation, so give me time. I'll make it. Dashing from bed to bed at 80 mph, with pauses for swigs from bottles, is very exciting . . . I think the repetition got too mechanical for me—the very opposite of the spontaneous in which they think they are indulging. I fancy Kerouac has a notion that he is showing Zen in action. I find that very amusing . . . I then tackled *The Catcher in the Rye*, expecting the same, but read right through, laughing and being moved, to the last word. How pleasant to enjoy a thing naturally. Are we getting out of the way o't? He's a skilly lad. But I hope you'll have time for a talk, and I hope you'll look upon it as your duty to continue to further my education.

By late 1958 the Gunns were looking for a new house and trying to sell

Kerrow. With increasing problems of bad health both Neil and Daisy felt that they should be nearer to Inverness. And Kerrow had been heavy with misfortune. On 1 October 1958 Neil wrote to Pick:

> We've decided to cancel the Irish trip, so no chance of meeting you across the Irish sea. I didn't want to take the risk of being a nuisance with this face. When the pain hits, it's really nasty. The worst pain known to medicine, says the doctor. No, don't think it's got anything to do with the buzzing ear: on the other side of the face and in the nerves; facial neuralgia of some sort. Failing all else, they can cut the main nerve to face inside the skull. But I'm not exactly eager for that! Ordinary treatments don't seem much use unfortunately. . . . And Daisy stalks me like a warder, lest I start doing my physical labours. She is quite ruthless, and won't even allow the beginning of an argument. Ironic note: nothing like laughter or chewing for starting pain off!

> Daisy is better [he wrote in January 1959] than she has been for quite a long time, I am glad to say. A month back, I was sort of worried a bit. But up she comes like a prize in a lottery. The only thing that worries me is that I may have to grow a moustache! That ruddy facial pain has concentrated recently in upper lip and nostrils. Haven't blown my nose for a long time!

Daisy's resilience is shown in a letter of June 1959:

> Daisy wasn't too fit some little time back and we got the doctor in, and at the moment we're expecting the result of the medical investigations. But they'll be out of date, for she's fine again. She stopped over in Perth, while I went on to do a theatre, films and a book for *Arts Review,* and having a clear day all to herself she went to shops and bought two pairs of shoes, etc, and these material things must have had vitamins in them in a fashion that would have baffled Ouspensky in his sixth dimension. Then we stayed with Neil Paterson in Crieff and at a dinner party she told stories about having her lunch somewhere and overhearing two old ladies talking about me on Iona on the Third Programme, and said one of the ladies: 'I saw Neil Gunn on the street and he had his wife with him: what a pity she dyes her hair!'

Neil knew that a good price for Kerrow depended on the record of his stretch of river for salmon. He tired himself fishing incessantly, at a time when his strength was fading, to compile an impressive log, calling in the assistance of brother Alec. 'Often when visiting the Gunns,' wrote Pick, 'we lived on salmon, eating it every day, until the sight of those rich and noble steaks, instead of making the mouth water made the gorge rise.'[9]

Farewell to Kerrow was a farewell to salmon. Neil did little fishing afterwards, and what he did was in Caithness.

18   The Greatest Loss

On 10 November 1959 Neil wrote:

> My own news is hot, if non-literary. We've sold Kerrow at a good price. Alone
> I did it, with a charming lady from a manor in Kent (though I suspect she's
> Highland). Having seen over the house she wanted there and then to sign on
> the dotted line. So I sent her to my agents in Inverness. So within a day we
> were homeless—though my native cunning reserved the takeover until 15 May
> next . . . And within two days heard of, and inspected briefly, a house on the
> Black Isle and got my agents to sign on the dotted line for it, with entry on 15
> January. All within the week. Was Daisy at top doh! For the new house is her
> dream come true at last . . . A neat compact cottage of three public rooms,
> five bedrooms, flowers, shrubs and over five acres of woodland, sitting in the
> sun, facing south over the Beauly Firth, about two miles by the shore road
> (quiet) from Kessock Ferry and Inverness. Daisy suggests that 'cottage' is
> perhaps not quite the word. But I insist on calling it a small cottage. After all,
> it's only got one bathroom and one cloakroom. You don't need a bicycle to
> reach the telephone. In fact the telephone in the new place is both downstairs
> and up. You see what I mean? Compact . . . I suspect Daisy of having long
> furnishing schemes in her head, for sometimes she says something about
> something apropos of nothing relevant, if you follow.

The house had a fresh, free atmosphere and was well up the hillside,
catching all the golden light that was going. Behind the house was a hedged
garden beset by rabbits, to the side a wired-in vegetable and strawberry
plot, and in front of the house a curved lawn beset by moss. A steep hill led
down to the shore road; and a steep hill led up through tall pines, rocks and
birches to crofting country and the high moors. That climb was beyond Neil
now, but he loved to walk along the shore, first west towards the mountains
and then turning home to watch the firth open to the sea in the evening
light. Cormorants spread their wings on the old jetty, gulls perched one per
post in the water, oyster-catchers peeped away among the stones, and
sometimes a heron stood in lonely contemplation among the weed. Neil had
marks which he aimed at reaching—the twisted tree, the bend in the road,
the boat-house—and at the turn of the road was a birch with twin trunks
which both Neil and Daisy identified with themselves.[1]

They moved to Dalcraig blithe and full of hope, and for a while things went well. There were more ploys and scurries. No sooner were they settled than Neil was involved with a group chaired by Tom Johnston and including Neil Paterson, John Bannerman, John Grierson and the Earl of Wemyss seeking from the IBA the right to act as programme contractor for North-East Scotland Television. In a letter Neil suggests that he is relieved they were not successful, for success would have meant a visit to Aberdeen every month, and he did not relish that kind of routine travel any more.[2]

The final public effort of his life was in co-operation with Robert Wotherspoon and others, when attempts were made to obtain a University for Inverness. Neil played a major part in drawing up some of the papers. Eventually Stirling was chosen, and his disappointment was more than personal; an opportunity to restore Inverness as a 'capital' city had been lost.

In November 1961 Neil's seventieth birthday was celebrated at a dinner in an Edinburgh hotel organised by Neil Paterson. George Bruce, Stanley Cursiter, Ian Grimble, Finlay Macdonald, Norman McCaig, Bingo Mavor, John Pick, Alex Reid and Robin Richardson were there, and every man jack delivered from the depths of his insobriety a speech the import of which he alone could grasp—and a thing which each had vowed solemnly not to do. And—more unlikely—Neil responded, despite saying in a letter to Bingo Mavor 'Personal tributes have a way of striking me dumb at the wrong time . . .' Daisy at least enjoyed the occasion to the full, particularly her status as the only woman present.[3]

Ian Grimble was a new friend. He had appeared first at Kerrow as a broadcaster, and then, in his dashes north and south he would stop off at Dalcraig whenever opportunity arose. Daisy took a motherly interest in his needs and illnesses, and warmed to his gentle, courtly manner. He did his PhD thesis on Strathnaver and the Mackays in the early sixties, and then had a time as a maverick Labour politician in the far north. Neil relished his fiery, quixotic quality, his extraordinary learning, and his efforts to prove that the Gunns were not Norse but pre-Celt, or Pictish. Neil referred to him as 'the Warrior' and signed himself in letters to Grimble 'Neil Firbolg (remnant of ancient race among mere upstart Gaels and parvenu Norsemen)'. Grimble wrote of his delight at being included in the seventieth birthday party:

> As I sit in my secluded bungalow with no sound but the Dee and no company but some extremely active mice in the roof, and wonder whether those cloud-capped cupolas and gorgeous palaces and eloquent literati are not simply figments of my imagination. But then I remember sitting talking with Daisy in the hotel and that is real: and Neil talking of your adventures in Skye

between huge silver candelabra—and my imagination would never have stretched to that. What a strange and memorable episode it was, and how moved I still am that you invited me to participate in it . . .[4]

But despite such attention Neil felt that he had been forgotten by the literary establishment in Scotland. The suspicion was reinforced by an absurd public discussion on the Scottish novel which took place at the Edinburgh International Festival in 1962. Alex Reid gives an uproarious (and unfortunately unprintable) account of the affair in a letter to Neil, with a description of his own efforts to stem the tide of play-acting and buffoonery:

> Pointed out that Bridie, Edwin Muir, George Blake, Eric Linklater and a dozen other writers of the period were not even mentioned and that the notes about you and Jenkins were both inaccurate factually and critically puerile, and tried . . . to show how your own work was unique in the whole canon of Scottish literature . . .[5]

He ends 'We're in a bad patch, Neil, but never mind: The harder the battle, the greater the honour.'

It was at about this time that the dark thunder clouds began to roll up. In September 1961 Neil wrote:

> Lately . . . Daisy has been getting tireder and tireder so I fetched the doctor. He took a blood test and as a result she has now started on a six weeks' course of injections. After that he'll take another blood count and continue as necessary . . . Yesterday afternoon we were going to do something in the garden, but she had to give in, suffering from pain in the head. When severely questioned she admitted it had been getting worse for some time. So I got doctor to come along. The concealed swelling turned out to be fibrositis. She was so relieved of a deeper fear that she said 'The pain is nothing.'

The struggle continued. Neil and Daisy were always trying to prevent each other from doing 'too much'. Neil himself had been suffering from prostate trouble for more than a year and in January 1962 he went into hospital in Edinburgh. Alex Reid writes (*Scotland's Magazine*, April 1973):

> He and I spent the morning of that day wandering about the centre of the city and talking about everything . . . except the ordeal ahead, which Neil seemed completely to have forgotten. I, too, had been avoiding the subject, but it was much on my mind and when we parted at the corner of Princes Street and Charlotte Street I could not repress a 'Well, here's luck.' For a moment Neil's face became grave as he lifted his eyes and gazed into what was already a long perspective of time. Then the gravity vanished in the mischievous smile of the boy in *Morning Tide*, as he crept into his parents' house with the poached

salmon beneath his jersey, and he brought his hand down on my shoulder. 'Listen, Alex,' he said. 'I'll tell you something. Whatever happens, I've had a wonderful life.'

Daisy wrote to the Picks from her hotel room:

Tomorrow morning he is to have a big operation for prostate gland. He is having all this done privately by one of the best surgeons, who says he should have come long ago. He has a private ward, with one other man in it and there's a bathroom can be entered from the ward. I felt awful leaving him in Hospital and coming back here and when I went up to my bedroom and found it full of the most wonderful carnations I burst into tears which did me a lot of good . . .

I find it terribly cold here not having brought warm enough clothes but maybe I'll get warmer when Neil is smiling again . . .

Later in the year it was Daisy's turn to go into hospital, for an operation to remove an obstruction from the bowel, and Neil wrote:

Dammit, I was full of misery. I am only now realising what Daisy felt when I was enjoying my operations. How much easier to suffer than to look on at suffering in someone. The someone being the rub! I am picking up myself, too, having the strength now of a drowned kitten taken out of a ditch in time!

And he comments about Daisy: 'Those who feel deepest often say least.' In October he reported:

Anyway . . . she is beginning to boss again, and has just told me of some old fellow who got breathless and dizzy, like me, then 'did something extra and popped off dead'. That's her reading the lesson. However, we have made a pact for the moment to behave sensibly and get well and strong together, growing in beauty side by side. In other words, I'll have to do as she says, and she'll do as she says anyhow. Her sister Molly is with us and a treasure.

And in November:

Daisy is definitely and visibly improving, though of course she tires very easily, but the surgeon warned her about it, saying she *must* remember she had a major operation, and won't get working strength back for at least twelve months . . . She uttered a verse of poetry this morning in the real Zen manner, crying it from her room to mine

> Oh, I see a lovely spot in the sky
> Yellow yellow yellow
> On top of the wood.

She doesn't even know she did it yet, for I just growled at her not to get up until I got the house warm. As for myself—though I confess we're getting a bit tired of mentioning illness—the doctor has started a series of ten injections, one a week, to bring up the blood count.

7 Nan Shepherd, poet and
novelist, in the late
1920s – one of the first
to appreciate the true
essence of Neil Gunn's
books

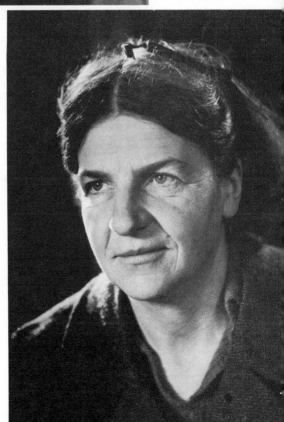

18 Naomi Mitchison in 1949

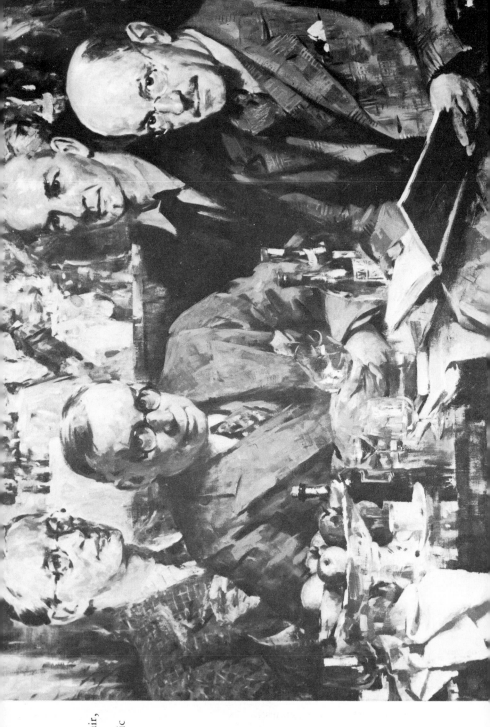

19 *Authors in Session* (1950) by Stanley Cursiter, RSA; *l–r*: Edwin Muir, James Bridie, Neil Gunn, Eric Linklater

There was a burst of joy, gaiety, companionship:

> Off we sallied—I rather think really, Gene, because Daisy has bought a new
> hat (the first for fifty—or fifteen—years) and wanted to wear it. She fair loves
> it, and all she needs is a horse to be a Cossack. She bought it in Inverness—on
> my birthday, so it's in some mysterious way a sort of birthday present and she
> insisted on paying for it. Of course she's quite wealthy now because she cashes
> our National Pensions at local PO and keeps the lot—£6 1s 6d per week . . .

But the clouds came rolling back again—and this time both went down
beneath the storm. Daisy began to develop severe pains, and Neil grew
slowly weaker from a condition of low blood pressure and anaemia. He was
not able to risk even a short walk along the road. On 11 May 1963 he was
writing:

> I haven't read a book for many moons, but am looking forward to G.'s *Meetings*
> *with Remarkable Men*, which should arrive before Daisy and I go into Inverness
> Infirmary on Tuesday. I tried for a private ward with two beds, so that I could
> read G. to her; but when she heard me she chortled, saying my arms would all
> be bound up or fixed to receive blood transfusions so I couldn't read.
> However we've just heard from Infirmary that two private wards are reserved,
> with consultants laid on. I was very pleased at being able to motor Daisy to
> Inverness on Wednesday last for consultation. She's been suffering continuous
> pain. Surgeon diagnosed kidney infection, but X-ray pictures needed yet. My
> iron injections have done no good and getting steadily weaker.
>
> They think Daisy's ferocious pains come from arthritis in spinal disc, felt
> elsewhere. I'm sort of sub all round and they're giving me more tablets (I
> already have to take a daily nine for duration) . . . After returning from
> hospital Daisy promptly took a sort of flu dysentery and she's only now
> thinking of getting up. She has to take tablets indefinitely to deaden pains. If
> you want to know just how a boxer feels when he's groggy, ask me.

A few months later she was back in hospital and Neil was distracted, his
letters jerky and disjointed:

> I go for a short spell in afternoon and her sister Molly in evening. She gets very
> exhausted. Yesterday she had to confess to houseman that she was utterly
> exhausted and he took some blood for test. Nothing but fruit juice, but some
> of it does stay down. The dietician tries many liquid foods, and Daisy knows
> by first sip of it if it will make her sick. Sickness—retching—leaves her clean
> done.

Events moved painfully, wretchedly, inevitably after that. They are recorded in even shorter, more agonised notes from Neil:

> I'm afraid the last weeks are a bit hazy, with one crisis after another, and Daisy

getting weaker. She is fighting hard. The exhausting sickness continues . . .
She had four long days of X-raying . . . But I can hardly think about it all.
Terrible.

11 September 1963:

Alas, I hate to tell you she has now got jaundice, and an affection of the liver is
something I won't think about—until I meet the surgeon in two or three days.
I can only live from day to day. She was very tired, and couldn't find any
resting place for legs or body. The jaundice does help to explain her nausea and
dislike of food.

A few days later:

When I saw Daisy yesterday, she got sick and after a little asked me to leave.
But she doesn't get sick quite so often though the paroxysm drains her so much
that I don't know . . . John my brother may be here tomorrow for a spell. Neil
Paterson, on flying back from Los Angeles, phoned he was coming up to see
us, so he and Rose were here for three hours on Saturday . . .

Then:

Last Sunday surgeon told me that there was no hope. Yesterday her words
came through to me still. John my brother is with me . . . I have just heard
from sister in hospital that she is very weak this morning. I cannot write.

Daisy died in October. Pick wrote:

The cemetery in Dingwall is on top of a high windy hill overlooking the
town—bumpy, fresh, and alive with trees. It was a crisp, cold autumn day.
Everyone was there. People used to flatter Daisy for Neil's sake, but they loved
her for her own. Neil was frail but calm. Brother John was always with him.
Afterwards I went home to Dalcraig with Neil, John and Alec. Once, for a
moment, the brothers were both out of the room and Neil said suddenly, with
the air of asking only a general question: 'Do you think there is survival after
death?'

I knew that no 'comforting' answer would do. I had to speak from the
depths. I think I said: 'The first self goes out like a candle, but Daisy was all
essence, and if essence survives, she must.' I still believe that.

The night after I got home, very tired, I woke suddenly from a dream and it
seemed to me that Daisy was laughing, as if telling me something. I wish I had
told Neil this, but I don't think I did.

Stanley Cursiter wrote to Neil: 'You and Daisy had achieved such a complete
"oneness" that it spread like a radiance to all your friends.' That wasn't
achieved easily. Gradually from the Brae years onwards the relationship
deepened and grew intimate on the level where intuitions and perceptions
were shared. The marriage might have foundered over the death of the child.

But it changed and deepened because of that. What happens depends not merely on time and accident, but on the inner nature of the individuals concerned. Neil and Daisy were continually aware of the possibilities in one another, they recognised one another, and grew into an atmosphere of warm acceptance.

Some people thought that Daisy was 'snobbish'. She was not that. She was proud that Neil was a well-known writer, and proud to be his wife, and proud to be recognised as his wife, and she wanted Neil's worth to be acknowledged everywhere. But she was always simple, straightforward and sensitive. She liked people, and responded to people.

It was a long time before Neil recovered from Daisy's death—if he ever did.

19 Alone

Neil's companionship with Daisy had become so deep and necessary to him that he and Margaret had moved apart. She herself says:

> From the time I went to Kent in 1947, we saw less of each other, but I had become a habit, a comfortable and pleasant one which gave him something he still needed, perhaps. There remained strong affection between us to the end, but looking back I see that at least on my part my love, which might have grown and deepened in a life with Neil, was wilting a little from lack of nourishment.
>
> Neil was becoming more and more preoccupied with what he called 'all this esoteric Eastern stuff '. I was glad in that it seemed to help him to a greater serenity and peace of mind. But insofar as I could understand it, it was wholly alien to my temperament.

Kerrow was hard to visit, and Margaret only went once or twice. She still saw Neil occasionally in Edinburgh and visited them both at Dalcraig at least twice a year, but she was now 'pretty absorbed in my work and enjoyed a social life in which he played no part', and as her mother needed help and care she had obligations of her own.

Then came Daisy's illness and death.

> At that time I felt I was the last person to be able to help him. Later I thought he badly needed someone living in the house who could look after him. I knew his brothers and other friends helped him as much as they could and that he had Isobel and Kate to look after him for much of the day, but he was still alone a good deal of the time and was not really fit to be so. So in 1964 I wrote and offered to go and look after him. I explained my own problems concerning my mother, but said that if he wanted me to come I was sure we could work out some solution.

Neil's reply was curiously cautious, muted and formal:

> I do appreciate your letter with its kindness and understanding and desire to help, but the simple truth is I am not fit to do as you suggest. I have been suffering for a long time from various ills, including in particular physical exhaustion and as I am over seventy-three I realise there is no hope of real improvement. Where there is exhaustion there is no energy, and so no desire for anything, except the desire to be left alone and so carry on for a little longer on a sort of marginal energy . . . I dislike talking about my ailments like this (it's the only sort of thing that depresses me) but sometimes I may say I've been

pretty low, so low that I arranged my affairs under my brother's care . . .

But I must see my surgeon in Edinburgh some time soon—he was abroad when I was last in Edinburgh—so I hope we'll meet then, and it would be luck if I felt well enough to ignore temperature and similar environmental factors! Anyway it would be a pleasure to see you and spend all the attention I had.[1]

None of this could have done much to reassure Margaret. But she accepted it:

I never raised the question again. Nor did he. My mother's death in 1969 would have made it easier for me, but I didn't want to press him when I wasn't sure if he really wanted me. We continued to see each other from time to time—the last occasion the summer before his death. We talked fairly frequently on the telephone. On two occasions after my last visit, he asked me when I was due to retire. I told him not until the end of 1973. He seemed quite cheerful and admitted to nothing more than feeling tired. In retrospect I have wondered if perhaps it was a call for help, which he couldn't make more directly, but felt he might be able to make when I had retired. I just don't know. Of course I felt deeply distressed by his death, and did feel, and still do, that perhaps I failed him at the end.

Not so. No one failed Neil at the end, least of all Margaret. It is a rare individual who inspires the degree of loyalty which Neil enjoyed from his friends.

Immediately after Daisy's death he went to Edinburgh with brother John. On 30 October 1963 Neil wrote to Pick:

We have got back from the south, John and I, and I must now begin on the pile of letters on my desk, for they say such lovely and true things about Daisy that I must acknowledge them with my own hand . . . I am being a bit pampered here. Finlay Macdonald will arrive today and whirl me to Glasgow, where I hope to have a few words with a suitable doctor. Then back here for week-end and off on Monday for north—with brother John, if his wife well enough. I'll spend a week with Alec, probably. But I still live from day to day.

I have no complaints, though Daisy's absence gets the better of me whiles.

It's sad that I'll have no one to sing to but myself. Alas for those transcendental moments when I called her a complete ass and she me an utter idjot.

He is re-reading *The Key of the Chest:*

Daisy (it's her copy) has three marked passages. But one of them is doubly marked: and though one would need to read the previous page to get it properly, here it is: 'But at least once each one turns away from a grave, and the sunlight is on the face or the soft rain and lo! that which is buried is not buried, but is the sunlight and the rain, for love knows no burial but remains everywhere.'

Memories and impressions seem to sharpen rather than grow dim. And all I'd
add to that is—for your personal application—that I'd destroy all I ever made
for one glimpse of her sitting out on the patio in front of me, weeding.'

For a writer of more than twenty books, that is tribute enough.

His brothers and friends were assiduous in their efforts to look after him
and keep his mind off his loss. In February 1964 Neil and Rose Paterson
took him to Gran Canaria. Before he left Neil wrote to the oldest and dearest
of all his friends, Maurice Walsh, who was very ill:

> I hear you are back in dear old Ard-na-glaise, where we spent many a good day,
> and I am delighted to think of you among your own folk. Indeed I have been
> thinking a lot about you and about the past these last days, and I must say that
> the whole area from Lochindorb via Forres to the whole Laigh o' Moray has a
> golden glow over it. And no wonder, for through golden autumn weather
> we—and a keeper or two—must have wandered over every square yard of it. I
> like to think, too, of the amount of work I did for you and your station when
> both were in my charge. Good good times and I am grateful for them. For
> there's one thing I know and it's this—and you may as well compose yourself
> and listen—a proceeding you may not be unacquainted with—it's this, I say,
> that whatever you may privately think about the Fates and the bitterness they
> can inflict upon us, still and on, and in their teeth if you like, man has created a
> golden time of his own. You and I had a share of such a time and those who
> were near to us helped to sustain it; bless them forever more. Unless you are
> feeling too tired, there will be a powerful urge of speech upon you now, and
> you can see me prepared to listen with all my customary patience.
>
> I have been feeling very tired myself for a while—a sort of sheer physical
> exhaustion—and the medicine men don't seem to do much good, with their
> iron injections and what not, but I'm still hanging on to the idea of setting off
> next week for the Canary Islands, arranged by the writer Neil Paterson (from
> about Banff) and under his care. Do you remember an old idea of buying a
> couple of donkeys in Seville and doing a loop around that southern part of
> Spain? It's just about the only thing we didn't bring off. Perhaps the sun will
> do some good. I'll be telling you. Perhaps it will make me tough enough to
> come over and see you on my own. Here's to hoping. All the best, bless you.
> Neil[2]

Two weeks later Maurice was dead.

On his return from the Canaries Neil comments on how well Isobel
Welch, his housekeeper, is looking after him: 'Like a hen with an outsize
chicken. Some day, no doubt, I'll have to get a whole-time housekeeper, but
that's a bit of a gamble, for simple friendly relations make life agreeable, and
anyhow when the time is ripe, the fruit will no doubt fall.'

Isobel was a nervous, taciturn woman, but fiercely and generously loyal
to Neil. She lived three miles away and although in her sixties, cycled over

every day bringing supplies. Neil tended to take her for granted, as he took Kate for granted, and as later he took Molly Hendry, Chrystine Frew and Gretta Gunn for granted.

In 1966 he reports: 'Isobel threw a tantrum this morning and told me I should have to get someone else . . . She says that between me and Sammy (the crofter whose house etc. she runs and whom she brought up) she'll land in Craig Dunain (previously known as the Asylum) . . . One koan in a paperback begins: "What is the path?" Master: "Everyday life is the path." You see what I mean?'

But in 1968 he was writing 'I want to get this off with Isobel, who has been looking after me positively anxiously.' 'Isa and Kate seem to like looking after me.' And 'At which point Kate came in to cook my Sunday lunch. Isa and Kate spoil me a bit . . .'

Kate Sharpe had for many years helped in the garden, and when Isobel found the work too much and came less regularly Kate took over the household duties. Sammy grew ill and Isobel had to leave at last. Then Kate was wholly in charge. She had a fund of common sense and a warm heart. Chrystine Frew (a young relation of Daisy) and Molly Hendry (Daisy's sister) were also regular providers of practical help.

Ian Grimble, writing in 1976, gives this picture of Neil in the last years:

> During the remaining decade of his life Neil saw no collected edition of his works published, and few of his novels even remained in print. While a flotsam of politicians and planners filled the newsprint, and the usual pulp literature covered the northern bookstalls that tall, spare, lonely man would wander in the garden that his wife had created at Dalcraig, delighted the relatives and friends who visited him with his hospitality and conversation, immersed himself in eastern philosophy.[3]

It was not quite like that. Although his publishers and the established critics ignored him, he was not only continually in demand from the Scottish BBC, but discerning people were writing to him from all over the world.

During 1955 and 1956 Nakamura and Hart were browsing in bookshops to discover second-hand copies of Neil Gunn novels, and Robin Lorimer at Oliver & Boyd was editing for publication Kurt Wittig's solid, perceptive book *The Scottish Tradition in Literature*. Wittig's volume was published in 1958 and Neil read with astonishment and delight the sober and unequivocal praise that it contained.

Nakamura first wrote to Neil in May 1955 with a truly Oriental reverence: 'It is with an ineffable sense of awe that I am writing this letter. The sense of awe comparable with that of Kenn when he first beheld the salmon trout in the cool Highland river.' Over the next seventeen years he wrote Neil more than 130 letters, all couched in the same tone of admiring obeisance, sending expensive volumes of art reproductions, flower prints, a wonderful painting of a heron by Tanan (Neil's prize possession), and gramophone records of Noh plays. Neil in return sent him copies of those novels which Nakamura could not find, called in the polymath Ian Grimble for advice and aid, and sent long, patient replies to all his questions. On occasions he found that being so thoroughly outdone in Highland courtesy could prove a strain.[4]

Nakamura published, in Japanese, a treatise on Neil's work in 1962, and in 1965 sent to him for editing an equivalent English manuscript. The language was elaborate and fulsome, often straying into flower gardens instead of hitting a nail on the head. Neil worried for months about how to suggest suitable and delicate changes. He could not bear the thought of offending such goodness, friendship and generosity. Eventually he explained to Nakamura that he simply could not manage the task.

At the same time Neil was receiving requests for information from students in France and from Hart in the United States. Neil wrote to Pick in 1961:

> By the way, another literary gent has got interested in *The Green Isle.* An American—assistant professor in English Department at University. He really bowled me out. Asked to read a paper 'at next December's national convention of the Modern Language Association of America, in the literature and society colloquium on modern Utopian literature', he adds that 'I immediately expressed a desire to concentrate on one of the most profoundly exciting books I have ever read (three readings haven't shaken this)—*The Green Isle of the Great Deep.* ' He encloses a twenty-page typed thesis on the subject, which he hopes to get published in one of the 'scholarly or critical quarterlies'—and asked permission to go ahead. But his real aim is 'a critical appraisal' of my whole box of tricks. Dear me and well well![5]

And a letter of 1963 showed the gratitude he felt to those who were writing and thinking about his books:

> Same with Francis Hart's article, though here it did please me that he dealt with some of my later books and on a level which took a certain achievement for granted. I have never had such understanding from Scots critics . . . but abroad—Japan, USA, Germany . . . it's different, and it gives a certain warmth to have such friendship . . . Perhaps all literature does is to give you a few friends.

A letter on 17 November 1964 (to Pick) shows how important to Neil was the sense of being surrounded by friends, and how necessary it became for him to feel central to their lives and contributing to the world, so that he could retain a hand in whatever was being created for delight and profit:

> In Edinburgh talked to relays in small pubs. George Bruce was, as usual, crammed with business so we had to step up the rate of our exchanges . . . Norman McCaig was in good form for half of a Saturday, so was Alex Reid for another half day, and Stanley Cursiter invited me to be his guest in Orkney for a week next year. Neil Paterson is working on a short novel. I told him about you and David Lindsay and he was very pleased. The young American professor [Hart] has just finished a book on Walter Scott and is coming over to see me next June. So all my friends are busy, and I'll be seeing their efforts presently. Which also cheers me. Naomi Mitchison had me to lunch yesterday and tried to inveigle me into writing again. Some hope!

After four years of increasingly informal correspondence Hart paid his first visit to Neil in the summer of 1965, concerned to elicit details of the writer's career and development. Neil was flattered but at the same time determined to widen the scope of discussion to infinity and beyond. He evaded many a specific query with koans about wild geese and passing clouds.

Once Hart grew able to accept the relationship with the same lack of self-consciousness as Neil himself, and the whole family entered in, there was a joyousness and verve about every hour of it. Neil talked often of the state of his 'bloody corpuscles' and said that it might not be long before he 'went to the fairies'. It was always a joke. He wrote to Lorena Hart:

> The fairies have been after me for the last ten days, riding high temperatures, but you must have said a few words to them at critical point, for now I am declared free of infection, and tomorrow I may be permitted to go downstairs. I went to Edinburgh (a cold bitter windy place it was) early part of last month to be with my brother (whose wife underwent operations; she is still pretty exhausted). After about three weeks (during which I caught a bronchial cold from poets barking at me in pubs: I ought to have more sense but nevah mind) I came north and on to Caithness, taking my younger brother and his wife back here to bring in New Year. For two or three days I felt even more delightfully light-headed than usual, but it was the deceitful work of those I had shut in the ring of toadstools. But you knocked them off their stools finally. Many thanks.

Neil's letters were full of laughter, encouraging Hart's insights, and gently easing him into reliance upon them. In 1968 Neil was almost persuaded into a trip to the United States, but his health betrayed him. In a letter to the Harts of 14 September 1972 he was still playing with the idea of a visit. But he knew it was not to be, and closed:

But enough. On your part you might help understanding if you got your secretary to pick out 'd' and 'p' on your typewriter! And how's the Witch herself? Speechless I watch her in her speechless ways. Dear me, that I should have to be silent. Fare thee both well. Neil

They would not hear from him again.

Of the other younger men, Neil particularly appreciated Alex Reid and Ian Grimble, and they in turn never hid their devotion and gratitude to him. Here, too, is a letter from another Reid—Alastair Reid the poet—written on 16 April 1962 which shows clearly the feelings which many held for him:

My dear Neil,
Somewhere in the recesses of my mind, there always lurks a letter to be written to you; and I decided today that it should be written, in case it just blows away.

I have always wanted to say to you something unsayable, and perhaps now I am old enough and remote enough to get it said, although you more than anyone will know how difficult it is. It's just that, from the time life dawned on me, I have felt such a debt to you as you can have no idea of. When my eyes were opening, you opened them in such a way as to let me see clearly right through to the very heart of things; and when I was first struggling to say things, you wrote me a letter which gave me heart enough to go on without question. I came here recently for a brief spell, and decided to re-read all those books of yours which struck me with the first awe. And indeed, they filled me again with it, and I marvelled, and found that all the delight and all the joy were there, tangible, as if I could move through time.

Encouragement is rare, and oh so golden, it makes a boy's heart turn over. But I am not writing you as a boy now—I am just wanting to thank you for the peculiar wavelength of understanding and awareness you have, which has given strength and substance to all I have tried to do.

Since I saw you and Daisy last I have been living in Spain, and writing steadily—my first novel will come out soon, and I have been writing a good lot for the *New Yorker*. Poems come more rarely, but more truly; and they always search for that elusive atom of yours, and try to be instances of it. I am on my way back to Spain now; but perhaps later on, I can find you.

If anyone were ever to ask me about my writing, I should be able to say, very simply, that you showed me how intricate, subtle, simple and miraculous a thing it is to be alive. I might have found this out for myself—and in a sense I did. But you have been so much a part of my seeing, that, graceless as it may seem, I have at least once to thank you for your being. And Daisy too, since she is so much a part of it.

There now. I send you both a blessing.[6]

All his friends spoke of the 'special atmosphere' he created during this time. According to Pick:

He could achieve it anywhere, but particularly in the warm ambience of his own home. He was at once courteous, humorous, lively and relaxed. I have a vision of him resting in his armchair on the small of his back, with his slippered feet up on a stool, twirling those pliable gold spectacles in a loosely dangling hand, his white hair ruffled, listening with an expression of reserved, appreciative tolerance, or talking in that slow, lilting voice full of pauses and variations in light and shade. Or throwing up his hands with a rich chuckling laugh in abandonment of all resistance when some quirk of fancy tickled him, or wearing an expression of a man at once suffering and relishing the flavour of a lemon as he refrained from a comment which would be too devastating. I can see him, too, at a time when he was ill, striding out with exaggerated vigour and a grandiloquent swing of the stick, to demonstrate his rude health. The atmosphere he created was inspiriting because he *accepted* whoever was with him.

Neil was of benefit to younger writers because he was concerned with encouragement, shaping and leading people towards wholeness. He could be tough, but never destructive.

Sometimes he talked of the necessity for a 'school'; of passing on systematically and deliberately what he had learned; of making a solid contribution to the development of others. He wrote to Pick:

G. and Ousp. go on insisting that nothing can be done without a *school*.

I do wish you would get a full novel on the go. It would somehow help me a lot if you brought it off and became famous . . . When Gurdjieff talked somewhere of the need for a master having one behind him on the upward steps if he himself hoped to reach the higher levels, there was more than summat in it.

He still saw Keith Henderson and Naomi Mitchison, lunching with her occasionally in Inverness, being most impressed on the last occasion by her robust lack of inhibition in reading him a poem in the public lounge of a hotel.[7]

His best friend remained until the last his brother John. John and Alec were devotedly attentive. Indeed, in a seemingly casual and accidental manner they took it in turns to look after him. Every letter of Neil's from 1963 onwards seems to mention the coming or going of one brother or the other:

Brother John has been with me these last two weeks and before him brother Alec and Gretta were here for a spell. I fancy they think they're keeping an eye on me.

Brother Alec and his wife . . . have pushed off to Caithness, but they'll be back on Monday for another week to tidy up the garden . . .

Pick remembers making a flying visit, walking the two miles from the 8 a.m. ferry to be plied with porridge and bacon-and-eggs by Gretta Gunn with Neil looking on in benevolent approval.

Almost to his last year he enjoyed being in Caithness with Alec and Gretta, as if they had finally reconciled him to the past.

At this time a growing friendship with his general practitioner Dr Munro began to mean a lot to him. Special cakes and sandwiches were always prepared for the doctor, who made sure of arriving at the time necessary to appreciate them. On occasion the afternoon entertainment of tea moved imperceptibly into the evening entertainment of a dram, while the talk went on. As Neil said: 'The only thing we forget to mention is our state of health.'

Apart from companionship, correspondence and 'being interested in everything' he found other ways of fighting off the demons of illness and melancholy. He planned his days to preserve energy, taking up to bed a tray laid for the morning and enjoying his breakfast with great deliberation. Pick remembers: 'When we were there we took him porridge to add to the feast and he made a great ploy of relishing it, uttering loud cries of appreciation as he spooned it in. We could hear them downstairs.'

Often he could not sleep, and lay awake practising his own form of meditation. The book beside his bed was *Zen Flesh, Zen Bones*,[8] and his favourite saying there was 'Look lovingly upon some object. Do not go on to another object. Here in the middle of the object—the blessing.' He would read a paragraph before lying down to sleep and if he could not sleep would let his mind move with the words until they carried him away from dependence upon that inconvenient body in the bed. He had no formal training in 'meditation'. His pride would never have allowed him to become anyone's 'disciple', or sit at the feet of any 'Master' or enter any 'school'. He had by concentrated attention, intuitive perception, practice and the analysis of what he read, developed his own method of focusing the mind; and it was this lonely struggle which helped him through the nights of pain and loneliness. He wrote to Pick:

> In the middle of the night I awoke and began thinking of the koan about Joshu's 'mu', and got into some rare regions of light, where the light not only lightened but enlightened, never precisely, logically or in such nonsensical wise, but expanding into freedom, formless as being itself, which has its own form, before it goes beyond it.

Even in his debilitated condition, with facial pains, a buzzing in the ear, continually smarting eyes, anaemia, loss of energy and so on, he wanted only to be 'joyous' and to concentrate on the light. After describing his symptoms in a letter he wrote: 'But let me talk of something else . . . Anything—like the numbered sayings at the end of the book of 101 short stories [*Zen Flesh, Zen Bones*], to the effect "Cast attachment to the body aside, realising you are free. To be free is joyous." ' And in 1965: 'I have just read in a book of haiku "The real nature of man's mind is delight." '

A letter dated 16 January 1966 gives the quality of the delight which he sought everywhere:

> But the heavy words are beginning so I shan't start tonight to go through the thicket and dance out on the other side. Think of me trying to dance anyhow! Without thinking I did a step or two to a Highland reel on the radio the other night while my bacon was sizzling—and had to sit down. (The body—that the gay psyche had forgotten). To have some sort of immortal body to match an immortal soul: what a dance would be there! To shout hooch! once in paradise would be something. The word 'squeeze', beloved of financial vipers, had a different connotation when I was young. It sure had.
>
> A lady phoned me last night, from the Glasgow region I think (phone indistinct), introducing herself as Miss or Mrs Yum-yums, asking me if I would act as a judge, at some sort of old folk's gathering, of a clothes or dress competition (I rather gathered, at third repetition) embracing Scotland (I feel sure), and when I again asked for her name she said Mrs Yum-yums, though it may have been Williams, or thereby.
>
> . . . It was Isobel who solved the riddle of this, saying: 'It's that photograph of you in the *Glasgow Herald*, over the article about your birthday.' In this photo I stand poised, or posed, one hand grasping a bunch of flowering viburnum and the other disposing of a walking stick which supported me aft in an elegant manner, thus exhibiting to advantage a well-tailored suiting and a new rather modish hat . . .

A number of events gave Neil pleasure at this time and should have assured him that he was still alive and flourishing in the communal mind. There was a modest programme of reprinting when Cedric Chivers issued *The Grey Coast* and *Butcher's Broom* for the London & Home Counties Libraries' Association. Other books followed. In 1967–8 Neil finally made an agreement (too late) with Faber & Faber that copyright of out-of-print books should revert to him, and when Club Leabhar (Highland Book Club) was formed in Inverness he allowed them to reissue *The Serpent*, receiving no royalties until publishing expenses were cleared. Finally, the Scottish Arts Council set up the Neil Gunn International Fellowship to promote understanding and friendship by bringing a novelist of international distinction and achievement to Scotland every second year. As Neil Paterson said: 'Neil was very proud of it, and took delight in the word "Fellowship".'

Then there was the last ploy of all—to produce an idea for a film. The proposition was manufactured in autumn 1966 to allow Neil to get more than the limit of £50 for his winter holiday in Majorca with brother John. Robert Clark had arranged for him through the Bank of England £100 in Spanish money as a return for producing an idea for a film with a Majorcan setting. To Neil the hunt for an idea 'became at times a positive obsession, but amusing, pleasant, tantalising, in which my brother joined heartily, and certainly earned the pesetas I was able to distribute'.

He wrote in February 1967:

> I have just finished and posted no less than thirteen pages of type (my greatest typing feat for thirteen years) full of boggles of the imagination for an 'idea' for a film.[9]

The Majorca visit included a call on Alastair Reid:

> We had marvellous weather, the best winter . . . for sixty years it was said. The second week I shed some clothes and the third week we actually dipped in the sea and then sat on the sand in the sun. Once or twice I heard a voice murmuring: 'This is divine.' It was mine own.

During 1967 Hart was in Scotland and Neil in top form. 'I am coming down to Edinburgh', he said, 'in search of the elixir. I'm sure there must be a magic elixir *somewhere*, such as the one given to Maggie the tinker, who was so weary she couldn't lift up her two hands.' And he pantomimed Maggie with great enthusiasm. He chose at that time to believe in the miracles of science, and was determined to throw away all fears of pain and inhibiting doubt. He walked strongly and refused to allow any day to end. He wouldn't let Hart go to bed (a trait known to all his friends), and said: 'If I could just find the bone-marrow stuff—the elixir—for fatigue and breathlessness and something to help my eyes, I would be busy reading and writing, perhaps.'[10]

In 1968 he went with the Picks for a holiday in Cornwall. Pick writes:

> It was a disaster. He suffered facial pains and a foot injury; he found great difficulty in breathing; the weather was damp and airless, thunder rolled continually among the hills, the house lay at the bottom of a deep dell thick with green foliage, our youngest son was very sick, and the first week I had (inadequately) to do the cooking. Eventually we called in the doctor, a forthright Yorkshireman who denounced Neil's medicines, the Health Service and the general condition of man with such vigour that after he left we had to restore morale with a hefty dram.

His last fling abroad in November 1969 was altogether more successful.

He went to Portugal with brothers John and Alec, Alec's wife Gretta, and
Ena Macleod. Rus and Lorena Hart joined them later. At first the weather
was stormy, Neil frail and listless. But when the sun came out he blos-
somed. 'My ancestors were sun-worshippers,' he said.

With the help of an arm from Hart and a flow of conversation he managed
along the side of the lagoon at Vila Nova de Milfontes, over the dunes to the
beach and a boisterous Atlantic. Hart took his picture there, standing
jauntily in a floppy hat. Neil sat down on a dune top, his face glowing with
delight at having made it to the shore. They talked about those he called 'the
few great companionable chaps' in literature. He had written to Hart of
Hesse's *Siddhartha* once, 'It was companionable. It was and is where some of
us belong. From the end of time, I can only say that that is what literature is
for, the literature that matters.' And now on the dunes near Milfontes he
remembered: 'There was some fellow a few years ago who asked a lot of
people to write and say what they thought was the most important thing in
the world—and that fellow you mentioned yesterday, E. M. Forster, who
did the Indian novel I liked, said "human relations". And when you look
back from the end of your life, down the long corridors, that's all there is in
it.' 'Ah, those sands of Milfontes,' he wrote afterwards, 'where I walked at
creation's dawn before clothes were invented!' And of the photograph: 'And
indeed another wonder, for there I stand against the Western Ocean—and
suddenly I remember my moments of Immortal Youth.' In March when he
was feeling the neuralgia: 'Alas that I hadn't just stayed on at Milfontes . . .
I feel myself walking along the edge of the tide, with no human in sight and
America on my left hand, swinging my dry bikini on my forefinger after my
plunge. Wonderful it was, and is.'[11]

For after the Harts left, Neil had not only managed down to the beach
once more, but had gone naked into the ocean, no doubt with his usual yell
of triumph and agony at the cold. An immortal hour indeed!

The preparations for his eightieth birthday in 1971 were too much for
him: an exhibition at the National Library of Scotland; a Blackwood's
commemorative volume (which he never saw completed); a television
programme and a film, *A Light in the North*, produced in his honour by
Educational Films of Scotland with financial support from the Scottish Arts
Council. He grew exhausted by the demands on him, and fainted during
the shooting of the film.

Neil Paterson writes (in the Blackwood's volume):

I went to see Neil on his eightieth birthday. I hadn't seen him for some months, although I had spoken to him regularly on the telephone. I knew that he was not at his strongest, and I intended to stay only a few minutes. I got to the Black Isle just after lunch. Neil was in fine fettle. John was with him, and the floor around them was heaped with letters and telegrams of congratulation. Neil poured us a wee dram. (Willie Birnie's, of course.) Nobody pours whisky as Neil does. The act of pouring and the offering of the glass are themselves ritual celebrations. It is almost unnecessary to drink the whisky, although we always do. We talked for half an hour, John leaving us every few minutes to take another telegram from the telephone. Neil was relaxed, physically at ease, marvelling at the interest his birthday had aroused, full of a kind of joy that is wholly innocent and wholly his, and of course, contemplating ploys. . . . How about going back to Gran Canaria in the early spring? . . .[12]

The trigeminal facial neuralgia returned. He went into the Western General Hospital in Edinburgh during September to have a facial nerve cut, but was released without surgery. John Gunn wrote: 'Meantime, Neil is bright and confident that all will be well in the not-too-distant future.' That is the extraordinary thing: he always *was* bright and confident about the 'not-too-distant future', as if time could flow full circle and he grow young again.

But by the end of November he was in and out of hospital once more, and early in 1972 began to complain of memory lapses and a muddled mind. He wrote to Pick: 'At the moment am deep in study of how to go to sleep without tabletic aid (Zen, of course, and I'll report progress).' So he was still fighting, still resilient, and clear enough in the head to know what weapons to use and how to use them.

Gene Pick writes of this time:

A telephone call came one evening. It was Neil's voice, frail and muffled. I had a vivid picture of him in his bedroom, green curtains drawn back from the big window overlooking the Firth, his breakfast tray set for the morning on a cabinet at the side, his electric over-blanket on for comfort, and his utter terrible loneliness.

'Oh, Neil, I'm afraid John is out,' I said, and wished he could come to us and be cared for, and knew it was too late for that. He was phoning to hear another human voice, so I sang him 'I know two bright eyes smiling for me' to remind him of his early days.

John and Alec were with him throughout the winter. He hardly realised the sacrifices they made. Alec's wife Gretta had undergone an operation; Alec had heart-trouble. The continual travelling, either from Edinburgh or Caithness, was a sore trial to them both. But it never occurred to either brother to complain.

Late in summer 1972 there was another period in hospital. He managed

20 Neil with James Bridie on Calton Hill, Edinburgh, August 1949

21 Indian summer: Neil on holiday in Portugal, 1969

an eighty-first birthday party in November, attended by Kate the house-keeper, by his friend the doctor, by Chrystine Frew who had been a continual source of aid and comfort over the past few years, and by J. B. Caird and his wife. Caird wrote: 'We always returned from a visit [to Neil] elated and conscious of being privileged in some way . . . He reinforced one's intuitions and taught one not to despise them.'[13]

For a time then Neil was much alone. John and Alec were both unwell, and twice Chrystine had been unable to come over when asked because she could not get her car out in the frost. Once he fell and cut his head. A few days afterwards Neil went into the kitchen, looking vague and troubled, and told Kate he must go to hospital. He had telephoned Chrystine the night before, asking her to collect him at nine in the morning. She found him distracted and bewildered, trying to pack a case. As they drove to the Infirmary they met the doctor, who wondered where they were going; he was on his way to tell Neil that a bed had been arranged for him. On arrival at the Infirmary Neil was asked for his name and could not remember it.[14]

During the final weeks he was sometimes lucid, sometimes confused, sometimes restless and sometimes violent—a tragic irony for a man who had never in his life been violent. This was so harrowing a spectacle that only the family were allowed to visit. He kept talking about Daisy and her dead child, and struggling for light and air. Alec Gunn told Pick: 'You would not have liked to see him. He was not himself.' Neil Gunn died on 15 January 1973.

Dairmid Gunn, John's son and Neil's nephew, wrote to Hart after the funeral:

> The day of the funeral was one of those perfect northern days . . . The sky was cloudless and there was no wind. The ground was white with hoar frost. At the cemetery high above Dingwall one could see through the leafless trees to the hill and moor country near Braefarm House, where he had written so many of his books. We buried him to the cries of rooks in the bare branches. The mourners were all good friends. They included people like John Pick, Neil Paterson, Ronald Mavor, Finlay Macdonald and Ian Grimble. The Gunns present were able to treat them to a lunch in the National Hotel at Dingwall . . . The atmosphere was relaxed and happy but inevitably there was an undertone of sadness. We all felt we had to be cheerful in honour of him. He would have wanted it that way. Neil Paterson and John Pick returned with members of the family to Dalcraig for a farewell dram out of respect for him and the happy times they had had there.

John Gunn couldn't find the key to the house. He looked distressingly like Neil as he stood, grey and spare, groping amiably in all his pockets. When

Alex Reid telephoned John at Dalcraig to apologise for being unable to attend the funeral, John said: 'It went off very well. There was an air of quiet happiness around. Neil would have been pleased.'

'I think Neil *was* pleased,' said Alex. 'He was a tall man . . . but he was never contained between his hat and his bootlaces. I think there is still a lot of him around.'[15]

John Gunn wrote:

> Dalcraig seems different without Neil, not perhaps so much during the day when I am kept very much on the move, but during the evening when peace prevails and I am all alone. It was during this latter type of period that Neil could set a discussion going which tended to make the evening pass all too quickly. The recollection can, however, have a charm of its own.[16]

A man survives through the influence he has had on others, who grow because of him. In Neil's case this influence spread to all corners of the world through his books, which reflect him truly. When young we expect a writer to be as good as his books. Often, in the event, he doesn't seem to be. But whatever the complexities of his life, Neil Gunn *was*. That may restore some faith both in literature and in humanity, for those who need it. A good enough reason for ending this record with the toast: 'Here's to the light!'

Notes on Sources

The principal sources for this biography are Neil Gunn's twenty-eight books, thirty-three boxes of his papers and photographs on deposit in the National Library of Scotland, his letters to numerous friends (also in NLS) and to us, the reminiscences of those who knew him, and our own reminiscences of visits to and conversations with him over the years. For a more detailed listing, see Selected Bibliography. Assuming that most readers would prefer as little interruption as possible to the narrative we have kept documentation to a minimum. In copying manuscripts we have taken such minor liberties as to spell out abbreviations for the sake of clarity, since this is not a scholarly edition of letters.

I YOUTH (1891–1921)

1 THE GUNNS OF CAITHNESS

1   The initial descriptions of Caithness by NMG himself are from 'Caithness', a ts in NLS Dep. 209, Box 8, sent to *Country Fair,* 20 March 1956. Many of NMG's travel essays are drawn upon in this section, and often, in the absence of a complete bibliography of his journalism, we must cite merely his own copies (in Boxes 8 and 9 of Dep. 209), often either in ts or clipped without identifying title or page or date.

2   From John R. Allan, *North-East Lowlands of Scotland* (London: Hale, 1974), pp. 61, 63.

3   NMG from an essay, 'Caithness and Sutherland', in *Scottish Country*, ed. G. Scott Moncrieff (London: Wishart, 1935), pp. 59–76.

4   *The Atom of Delight* (London: Faber & Faber, 1956), p. 101.

5   The road is described in 'The Dornoch Firth' (ts for *Scotland's Mag.*, Oct. 1960), 'My Bit of Britain' (*The Field,* 2 Aug. 1941), and 'Over the Ord to Caithness', printed copy in Box 9.

   The glens and straths are described in 'The Straths and Sea roads of the North-East', printed copy from *SMT Mag.* (n.d.) in Box 9.

   Sources other than NMG (and our own observation) include *The Caithness Book*, ed. D. Omand (intro. by NMG) (Inverness: Highland Printers, 1972); David Keir, *The Desolation of the Highlands* (Fact No. 17, 15 Aug. 1938); Cuthbert Graham, *Portrait of the Moray Firth* (London: Hale, 1977).

6   Mark Rudd Gunn, *History of the Clan Gunn* (Glasgow: Maclaren, n.d., but *c*. 1965).

7   Ian Grimble, *Scottish Clans and Tartans* (London: Hamlyn, 1973), pp. 101–2.

8   NMG in 'Caithness' for *Country Fair,* Spring or Summer 1956.

9   M. R. Gunn, *History of the Clan Gunn,* p. 214.

10 NMG for *Radio Times,* 24 Nov. 1954, quoted from ts in Box 8.

11 For the 'boom century', see *Caithness Book* and *New Statistical Account of Scotland*.

12 NMG, from 'Over the Ord to Caithness', printed copy in Dep. 209, Box 9.

13 'The Fishermen of the North-East', printed copy (1938) in Dep. 209, Box 8.

14 Information for this section was also obtained from public records in New Register

House, Edinburgh, and from conversations with NMG, with John W. M. Gunn, and Mrs Gretta Gunn.

15 NMG, *Atom,* p. 103.
16 *Atom,* pp. 103, 104.
17 The young cousin is recalled in NMG's address to Caithness County Council, on the presentation of his portrait by D. M. Sutherland, October 1965.
18 *Caithness Book*, ed. Omand, p. 147.

2 THE BOY AT HOME

1 On the two selves, see *Atom,* pp. 83, 85, 97, 153, 158.
2 *Atom*, p. 124.
3 *Atom*, p. 155.
4 NMG as 'Dane McNeil', 'My Best Day's Fishing', *Scots Mag.,* Jan. 1929, pp. 260–1.
5 *Atom,* p. 114.
6 *Highland River* (Edinburgh: Porpoise, 1937), p. 98.
7 *Highland River*, p. 157.
8 *Highland River*, p. 73. For NMG on food, see *Holiday Mag.*, Nov. 1959, p. 130, and cf. *Medical World*, 8 Nov. 1955. Margaret MacEwen recalls his 'connoisseurship in the matter of potatoes', and Pick his advocacy of the Golden Wonder.
9 *Atom*, p. 34.
10 William Mowat's letter is in NLS Dep. 209, Box. 21.
11 W. A. Sutherland's letter is in NLS Dep. 209, Box 22.
12 *The Serpent* (London: Faber & Faber, 1943), p. 28.
13 *Atom*, p. 123.
14 *Highland River*, p. 31.
15 *Off in a Boat* (London: Faber & Faber, 1938), p. 179.
16 *Butcher's Broom* (Edinburgh: Porpoise, 1934), p. 321.
17 *Atom*, pp. 123–4.
18 The 'old school jotter' is identified by NMG in a brief autobiographical sketch dated 30 Aug. 1965 (NLS Dep. 209).
19 Alexander Gunn, in a letter to Lorena Hart, 20 Feb. 1972.
20 *Atom*, p. 92.
21 *Whisky and Scotland* (London: Routledge, 1935), p. 72, recalls the minister; Gretta Gunn supplied his name.
22 *Atom*, pp. 96, 111.
23 John Gunn described his parents' religion in conversation with Hart.
24 *Highland River*, pp. 101–2.
25 NMG anecdote in conversation with Hart.
26 *Bloodhunt* (London: Faber & Faber, 1952), p. 233.
27 On the river, see *Atom*, pp. 24–9, 37–9.
28 NMG from 'Living in the Free Sunlight', probably *Glasgow Herald, c.* 1951, cutting in NLS Dep. 209, Box 9.
29 NMG, 'The First Salmon', *Scots Mag.*, April 1938, p. 18.
30 *Atom*, p. 33.
31 J. B. Caird told his anecdote to Hart in Jan. 1979.
32 The morning on the grouse moor is recalled by NMG in an early version of 'Beautiful Balmoral' for *Holiday*, ts in Box 8.
33 NMG in 'Deer Stalking in the Highlands', 1955, ts in Box 8.
34 'Portrait Address' (1965).

35 'Portrait Address'.
36 A. and G. Gunn from conversations with Hart.
37 NMG from 'Curling', ts in Box 8.
38 *Atom*, p. 185.
39 *Atom*, p. 128.
40 See Alastair Reid, 'The Sporting Scene', *New Yorker*, 29 Aug. 1970, p. 64.
41 *Off in a Boat*, p. 33.
42 *Atom*, p. 174.
43 NMG's earliest recollections of traditional music are in 'The Gathering of the Camerons' and 'The County Behind the Camerons' in Box 8. 'Essence of Nationalism' appeared in *Scots Mag.*, June 1942.
44 The biographical letter from Daisy Gunn to F. Marian McNeill (evidently dictated by Neil) is dated 11 May 1947 and is to be found in NLS Acc. 5453.
45 *Highland Pack* (London: Faber & Faber, 1949), pp. 65–6.
46 The flashing lighthouse is recalled in 'The Dornoch Firth', ts in Box 8.
47 For Galloway memories, see *Atom*, especially pp. 165–71 and 184–6.
48 *Atom*, pp. 165–9.
49 The poetry and essays of 'Theodore Mayne' appeared in *Kirkcudbrightshire Advertiser and Galloway News*, published weekly in Castle Douglas. 'Notes from the Glenkens' appears first on 6 Jan. 1905; on 3 Feb. the 'young friend' reports to him on peewits, and again 11 Aug. 1905; 2 June 1905 has a good example of the Gilbert White manner. For literary matters, see 8 Sept. and 22 Sept. 1905. From 27 April to 24 Aug. 1906, Mayne was away. 23 Nov. 1906 (shortly after Neil's fifteenth birthday) is the last record of walks with the young friend.
50 *Atom*, pp. 181–4.
51 NMG from 'Fishing Lochs of Day and Night', clipping with no title of journal, *c.* 1942.
52 *Atom*, pp. 182–3.
53 *Atom*, p. 187.
54 *Atom*, p. 188.
55 *Atom*, p. 190.

3 UNATTACHED OFFICER

1 *Atom*, pp. 191–222.
2 *Atom*, p. 219.
3 *Atom*, pp. 215–16.
4 *Atom*, p. 192.
5 *Atom*, p. 199.
6 *Atom*, pp. 195–6. Other than *The Atom of Delight*, our only sources for the London years are our own conversations with Neil. Quotes otherwise unidentified (such as NMG's reminiscences of theatre visit) are from those conversations.
7 NMG in conversation with Hart.
8 *Atom*, p. 195.
9 NMG in conversation with Hart.
10 *The Serpent* (London: Faber & Faber, 1943), p. 8.
11 NMG in a letter to Hart, *c.* 1966.
12 NMG in conversation with Hart.
13 *The Serpent*, p. 9.
14 NMG in conversation with Hart.
15 *The Drinking Well* (London: Faber & Faber, 1946), pp. 162–3.

16 'High on the Haggis', *Holiday*, Nov. 1959, p. 96.

17 'Edinburgh', *Holiday*, Aug. 1947, pp. 95, 101.

18 NMG in ts of 'Edinburgh' (NLS Dep. 209, Box 8); these words do not appear in *Holiday* itself.

19 *The Drinking Well*, p. 134.

20 NMG gave an account of the midwifery episode in a letter to Hart, 19 March 1970, and in *Wild Geese Overhead* (London: Faber & Faber, 1939), pp. 86 ff.

21 *The Drinking Well*, p. 171.

22 NMG in 'Fishing Lochs of Day and Night', Box 8.

23 Alexander Gunn in a letter to Lorena Hart, 20 Feb. 1972.

24 *Off in a Boat*, p. 73.

25 The road to Achiltibuie and Lochinver is described in 'Across Kylescue', ts in Box 8. The surface has improved, but the coast road still has to be travelled to be believed.

26 *Off in a Boat*, pp. 46–7.

27 *Off in a Boat*, pp. 16–17.

28 NMG's story about the would-be pensioners was told to Pick.

29 'The Western Isles', ts in Box 9.

30 *Off in a Boat*, p. 207.

31 The Major is referred to in *Off in a Boat*, and was described in conversation with both Hart and Pick.

32 Maurice Walsh's reminiscence is to be found in his Foreword to J. Marshall Robb, *Scotch Whisky: A Guide* (Edinburgh: Chambers, n.d., but the Foreword is dated 3 May 1950).

33 NMG in conversation with Hart.

34 The letter from Daisy Gunn to F. Marian McNeill is in NLS Acc. 5453.

35 Maurice Walsh, *The Key Above the Door* (London: Penguin, 1958), p. 100.

36 Neil's account is given in 'More Fishing Lochs—and a Feast', *c.* 1942, in Box 9; and in 'High on the Haggis', *Holiday*, Nov. 1959, p. 94. Maurice's in *The Key Above the Door*, pp. 110–11.

37 'Fishing Lochs of Day and Night', printed copy in Box 8.

38 Reminiscences of Walsh from conversation with Pick.

39 The physical examination at Stirling was recalled in conversation with Hart, as were the visit to his mother and his duties at Kinlochleven. In fact, NMG was an inch or two *over* six feet.

40 *Highland Pack*, p. 211.

41 NMG tells of the Norwegian skipper and the threepenny bit in 'I've Got my Threepenny Bit Yet . . .', *Daily Express* clipping, undated, in Box 9.

42 *Off in a Boat*, pp. 318–19.

43 *Off in a Boat*, pp. 25–6. The story of the man from Tiree remained one of Neil's favourites for telling aloud.

44 The 'colporteur' is recalled in a radio script for *Life and Letters*, Feb. 1957, in Box 10. In general, pictures of life at Kinlochleven are from conversations with Pick, unless attributed elsewhere.

45 The first issue of *The Apple Tree*, 1918, can be quoted passim because Neil gave his copy to Hart in 1967: 'Here is my first publication.'

46 NMG's story in the second issue, 'Apple-Tree', was kindly provided for us in xerox by C. J. L. Stokoe.

47 *Atom*, p. 257.

48 *Off in a Boat*, pp. 142–3. See also *Wild Geese Overhead* (London: Faber, 1939), pp. 115–16.

49 Pick responded to Hart's first draft as follows (23 May 1979): 'Are you being

psychological about it because you feel that is expected, or because you yourself have doubts? I have none. The experience was a real experience of an actual outside force. Neil would never confuse a subjective with an objective experience. That is what gives his writing its quality. He knows, and can distinguish. And I say this as one who would prefer not to believe in a separate evil power in the universe, and whose philosophy hardly accommodates it. Also, I have a feeling that Neil told me once the room concerned *had* produced strange experiences for other people who had slept there.' Hart replied: 'I have no doubt about the reality of the experience, and my own philosophy amply allows for the reality of a separate evil power (though it is less secure about your distinction between "subjective" and "objective"—old Coleridge). Your questions are directed at my speculating about mechanical "causes" in Neil's life, causes of the event's happening *when* it did and *how* it did. I see no necessary contradiction. I do not mean that he simply "imagined" the event. What matters is the significance he attached to it. Let's leave the evidence all there and let the reader ponder it.'

Footnote by Pick: 'No, what matters is the reality of the event itself. As for "separateness", I have never been convinced by the idea of a separate evil force in the universe in continual conflict with the good, and since writing that letter have more fully appreciated Neil's own aphoristic resolution of the matter in *The Other Landscape*—'The Wrecker is God when he wrecks.'

II THE YEARS IN INVERNESS (1921–1937)

4 THE OFFICER ATTACHED

1 A phrase used by Keith Henderson in conversation with Pick.
2 NMG's description is given in a letter to Hart, 12 Dec. 1963.
3 Keith Henderson's account, 25 Oct. 1978.
4 Anecdotes about the 'idle summer day' and 'finding the place' in Wigan from conversations with Hart and Pick.
5 Daisy's letter to F. Marian McNeill in NLS Acc. 5453.
6 Recollections of the house in Lybster, and of Daisy in the sidecar, were given in conversation with Pick.
7 See Alexander Reid, 'The Theme is Man', *Scotland's Mag.*, July 1958, and 'Neil Gunn's Mysticism' in *Neil Gunn: The Man and the Writer,* ed. Scott and Gifford (Edinburgh: Blackwood, 1973), p. 348.
8 The story of Maurice and Neil challenging each other to write is given in Daisy's letter to F. Marian McNeill.
9 Arthur Mowat's letter, dated 23 July 1926, is in Dep. 209, Box 21.
10 Descriptions of Inverness from *Inverness Courier Guide,* 1939, and 'The Hub of the Highlands', *The Book of Inverness and District* (Inverness Field Club, 1975).
11 Edwin Muir, *Scottish Journey* (London: Heinemann, 1935), p. 191.
12 TS, 'Inverness', for *Weekend Mag.*, n.d., in Dep. 209, Box 9.
13 *Inverness Courier Guide,* 1939.
14 Information on Glen Mhor distillery supplied to Hart by Mrs Rena Wilson, together with a fine dram.
15 Much material about Inverness and Larachan was provided by Molly and Margaret MacEwen, 19 Nov. 1978.
16 Hugh Kingsmill and Hesketh Pearson, *Skye High* (London: Hamish Hamilton, 1937), pp. 98–100.
17 NMG on Saintsbury is in 'Malt Whiskies', ts Dep. 209, Box 9.

18 *Whisky and Scotland: A Practical and Spiritual Survey* (London: Routledge, 1935) and (London: Souvenir, 1977) p. 130.

19 Our chief source on whisky other than NMG is R. J. S. McDowall, *The Whiskies of Scotland* (London: Murray, 1975) 3rd edn., especially pp. 101–19 and 130.

20 Stanley Hill's reminiscences were sent to Hart in late Sept. 1978. His letter to NMG is in Dep. 209, Box 27.

21 McLeish's letters to NMG are in Dep. 209, Box 21.

22 NMG's letters to McLeish, courtesy of Mrs Fionna Macleod of Ullapool.

23 Undated ts of interview with John Wilson of BBC in Dep. 209, Box 10.

24 Grieve's claim was reported in lecture on NMG by J. B. Caird, ts from NMG to Hart.

5 STARTING TO WRITE

1 NMG's recollections of Pater and the *Rubáiyát* in conversations with Hart. The love-hate relationship with 'Fiona' is described in several NMG letters to Hart, and is evident in *The Grey Coast* and several short stories.

2 See also 'The Romance of the Reel' and 'Strath Ruins', *Chambers' Journal*, 15 Aug. 1925 and 3 Sept. 1927.

3 Letters from Odhams Press and *Cornhill* in NLS Dep. 209, Box 12.

4 For the poems, see *Scottish Chapbook*, Feb. 1923; *Scottish Nation*, May and June 1923.

5 The aims of *Northern Review* appear in 'Causerie', May 1924.

6 *Scots Magazine*, April 1924, Foreword by 'C. S. B.'

7 'Symbolical' is in *Scots Mag.*, Dec. 1927; 'Blaeberries' in Feb. 1928; 'The Sea' in Jan. 1929; 'The Moor' in April 1929.

8 For general comments on the short story, see T. O. Beachcroft, *The Modest Art* (London, 1968), especially pp. 1–4, 119–49; Frank O'Connor, *The Lonely Voice* (London, 1963), pp. 14–16, 170; Sean O'Faolain, *The Short Story* (London, 1948), especially pp. 36–7.

9 The first group of stories appeared as follows: 'Apple-Tree' in *The Apple Tree*, June 1918; 'Visioning', *Scottish Nation*, July 1923; 'Gentlemen' (see *Hidden Doors*, original unlocated); 'The Clock' (see *Hidden Doors*); 'The Hind', *Scottish Nation*, Dec. 1923; 'The Hat-Box', *Glasgow Herald*, 13 Oct. 1923; 'A Tight Corner', *Glasgow Herald*, 20 Oct. 1923; 'Surfaces', *Scottish Nation*, Aug. 1923; 'Down to the Sea', *Scottish Nation*, Sept. 1923. The second group: 'Between Headlands', *Northern Review*, Sept. 1924; 'Such Stuff as Dreams', *Dublin Magazine*, Feb. 1925; 'The White Hour', *Dublin Magazine*, March 1924; 'Birdsong at Evening', *Cornhill*, Sept. 1926; 'Adventure in Jealousy', *Northern Review*, Aug. 1924; 'Uncashed Cheque', *Northern Review*, Aug. 1924; 'Half-Light', *Cornhill*, Nov. 1925; 'Musical Doors' (later 'Hidden Doors'), *Cornhill*, March 1927. The third group: 'Blaeberries', *Scots Mag.*, Feb. 1928; 'Black Woollen Gloves', *Scots Mag.*, Jan. 1928; 'The Moor', *Scots Mag.*, April 1929; 'Symbolical', *Scots Mag.*, Dec. 1927; 'The Sea', *Scots Mag.*, Jan. 1929; 'The Man Who Came Back', *Scots Mag.*, March 1928; 'The Mirror', *Scots Mag.*, May 1929; 'The Dead Seaman', *Scots Mag.*, July 1931.

10 On *Grey Coast*, see Alexander Gunn's letter to L. L. Hart, 20 Feb. 1972; Gretta Gunn's conversation with Hart, Sept. 1978.

11 NMG letters to Hart, 23 Aug. 1965; and to Pick, June 1965.

12 References to the text of *Grey Coast* are to the 1st edn. of 1926; the setting is given on p. 14.

13 *The Grey Coast* (London: Jonathan Cape, 1926), p. 218.

14 W. R. Aitken, 'Neil Gunn's Revision of his first novel', *Bibliothek*, VI (1972) pp. 114–17.

15 *The Grey Coast* (Edinburgh: Porpoise, 1931).
16 For corresp. with Cape, see Dep. 209, Box 11, and for publishing details, corresp. with Faber in Box 11 and with Porpoise Press, Box 12.
17 NMG letters to Mairi Campbell Ireland are in NLS Acc. 4559, Box 2.
18 William Power, *Literature and Oatmeal* (London: Routledge, 1935), p. 191.
19 *Contemporary Scottish Studies*, First Series (London: Leonard Parsons, 1926) p. 273.
20 Grieve on Gunn, see *Neil M. Gunn: The Man and the Writer* (Edinburgh: Blackwood, 1973) pp. 360–1; the BBC 'Tribute' of 1961 for NMG's seventieth birthday (copy in possession of Hart); and *The Company I've Kept* (London: Hutchinson, 1966), pp. 72–3, on all-night talk.
21 Grieve's letters to NMG are in NLS Dep. 209, Box 17, quoted by courtesy of Mrs Valda Grieve.
22 NMG in *Wick Mercantile Debating Society Magazine*, early 1929.
23 'For Christopher's Cap', ts in Dep. 209, Box 8.
24 Helen Cruickshank's reminiscences appear in *Hugh MacDiarmid: a Festschrift*, ed. K.D. Duval and S.G. Smith (Edinburgh: Duval, 1962), especially p. 189; *Saltire Review*, Winter 1968, p. 34; *Octobiography* (London: Standard Press, 1976), Ch. 9.
25 *My Life and Times, Octave 6* (London: Chatto & Windus, 1967), p. 134.
26 Peter F. Anson's visit to Mackenzie on Barra, the return from which NMG recalled in conversation with Hart, is recorded in Anson's *Harbour Head: Maritime Memories* (London: Gifford, 1944).
27 The result of the SNP Council poll was reported by John MacCormick, 11 April 1934.
28 The brawl over *The Lost Glen* was reported by George Blake, Dep. 209, Boxes 15, 17.
29 Information about Grieve is taken from Duncan Glen, *Hugh MacDiarmid and the Scottish Renaissance* (Edinburgh: Chambers, 1964).
30 Correspondence with publishers is in Dep. 209, Boxes 11 and 12.
31 Information about Salmond comes from an obituary, *Scots Mag.*, LXVIII (1957–8). Gunn-Salmond corresp. is in Dep. 209, Box 14.
32 MS letter from Frank Morley, late 1931 (addressed initially to George Blake), in NLS Dep. 209, Box 17.
33 The earlier version of *The Lost Glen* appeared in *Scots Mag.* (eight instalments) from April to November 1928; comparisons are with the first book edn. of 1932.
34 *The Poaching at Grianan* appeared (eight instalments) in *Scots Mag.* from Sept. 1929 to April 1930. For quoted passages, see Oct. p. 39 and Dec. p. 209.

6 Detour into Drama

1 NMG corresp. with Nan Shepherd is in NLS Dep. 209, Box 19 and in NLS Acc. 5449 and Acc. 6118.
2 For the movement in Scottish drama, see Power, *Should Auld Acquaintance* (London: Harrap, 1937), pp. 114–15.
3 NMG on the Abbey Theatre, *Scots Mag.*, Nov. 1938.
4 *Choosing a Play: A Comedy of Community Drama* (Edinburgh: Porpoise, 1938), reissue of *Scottish One-Act Plays*, ed. J. M. Reid (Edinburgh: Porpoise, 1935), pp. 117–40.
5 'Hawk's Feather', *Scots Mag.*, Aug. 1929; 'Glendaruel', *Scots Mag.* Dec. 1929; 'Back Home', *Scottish National Plays* Series, 9 (Glasgow: W. Wilson, 1932).
6 NLS Dep. 209, Box 17.
7 James Bridie, *One Way of Living* (London: Constable, 1939), pp. 260–2.
8 Letters from 'John Brandane' (John MacIntyre) in NLS Dep. 209, Box 18—late 1928, Oct. 1929.

9   'The Ancient Fire' survives in three corrected tss in Dep. 209, Box 5.
10 Letters from Tyrone Guthrie, NLS Dep. 209, Box 17.
11 Letter from J. M. Reid, in NLS Dep. 209, Box 21.
12 On Bridie, see Winifred Bannister, *James Bridie and his Theatre*, (London: Rockliff, 1955).
13 Eric Linklater, Foreword to Bannister, and *The Art of Adventure* (London: Macmillan, 1948), pp. 32–3.
14 NMG letters to Bridie and his widow, and to W. L. Renwick, courtesy of Ronald Mavor. Comments on Bridie were made in conversation with Hart.
15 Letter, 16 Aug. 1929, in possession of Pick, to whom it was given by NMG.
16 NLS, Dep. 209, Box 18.
17 9 Jan. 1932, in possession of Pick.
18 22 July 1933, Pick.
19 7 Aug. 1933, Pick.
20 16 Sept. 1933, Pick.
21 1 Nov. 1930, NLS Dep. 209, Box 18.
22 25 Jan. 1931, NLS Dep. 209, Box 18.

7 THE NOVELIST RECOGNISED

1   NMG to Mairi Campbell Ireland in NLS Acc. 4559, Box 2.
2   Corresp. with Porpoise and with George Blake, Dep. 209, Boxes 12 and 17. Corresp. with G. M. Thomson, Box 20.
3   Toshon Walsh to Daisy Gunn, Dep. 209, Box 21.
4   'Dane McNeil' on Pearse appears in *Scots Independent*, Nov. 1929, pp. 9–10; Dec. 1929, p. 21; Jan. 1930, p. 33.
5   Henderson letters to NMG are in NLS Dep. 209, Box 18.
6   See section called 'Centreing', *Zen Flesh, Zen Bones*, ed. Paul Reps (London: Penguin, 1971), p. 156.
7   Letters from Guthrie and Durrell are in Boxes 17 and 18.
8   Reviews of *Morning Tide* are preserved in Box 3. *TLS*, 26 Feb. 1931; *Time and Tide*, 24 Jan. 1931. Buchan and Mackenzie are quoted in advertisement, *Spectator*, 14 Feb. 1931, p. 233.
9   NLS Dep. 209, Box 17, May 1931. On *The Lost Glen*, Box 17, July 1931.
10 Letters from J. B. Salmond are in NLS Dep. 209, Box 14.
11 Reviews of *The Lost Glen: Spectator*, 26 March 1932; *NS*, 19 Mar. 1932; *TLS*, 14 April 1932.
12 The genesis of *Sun Circle* is described by NMG in pencilled notes for a late interview with George Bruce, Dep. 209, Box 10.
13 Early 1932, in Dep. 209, Box 14.
14 Letter from Linklater to NMG in NLS Dep. 209, Box 17, 27 July 1932.
15 Late autumn 1932, NLS Dep. 209, Box 17.
16 To Nan Shepherd, NLS Acc. 6118.
17 *Sun Circle* (Edinburgh: Porpoise, 1933), p. 234.
18 *Sun Circle*, pp. 365–6.
19 Letter from Bottomley, NLS Dep. 209, Box 17.
20 *John O'London's Weekly*, 3 June 1933; *TLS*, 22 June 1933.
21 May 1934, NLS Dep. 209, Box 17.
22 Corresp. with Archibald Scott is in Dep. 209, Box 21, and NLS Acc. 5504.
23 Corresp. with A. M. Mackenzie is in NLS MS 9222.

24 George Bruce recollections reported to Hart.
25 *Butcher's Broom* (Edinburgh: Porpoise, 1934), pp. 193–4.
26 NMG's reactions to the re-reading thirty years later were reported to Hart in conversations and letters.
27 NMG to Morley, NLS Acc. 5412.
28 NLS Dep. 209, Box 17, Oct. 1934.
29 Reviews: *TLS*, 1 Nov. 1934; *Spectator*, 30 Nov. 1934; *Modern Scot*, Autumn 1934; *Life and Letters*, Nov. 1934.
30 NLS Acc. 6118.
31 NMG to F. Marian McNeill, NLS Acc. 5453.

8 POLITICS AND SOCIETY BETWEEN THE WARS

1   Chief sources for the summary of politics are H. J. Hanham, *Scottish Nationalism* (London: Faber & Faber, 1969) and J. M. MacCormick, *The Flag in the Wind* (London, 1955); and also NMG correspondence with MacCormick, Grieve, G. M. Thomson, A. Dewar Gibb, T. H. Gibson, et al., and documents preserved by him, in Dep. 209, Boxes 15, 17, 18, 20, 21, and conversations of JBP with Duncan McNeill and G. M. Thomson. Hart received advice and counsel from R. R. MacEwen. Specific quotes from Hanham, pp. 153, 154, 161–2.
2   NMG's remarks on MacCormick are quoted from his obituary, copy provided by NMG.
3   *The Flag in the Wind* (London, 1955), p. 45.
4   MacCormick's letters to NMG are in NLS Dep. 209, Box 15. This one was dated 11 March 1931.
5   NMG's 1931 journal is in NLS Dep. 209, Box 1.
6   NMG kept copies of letters to SNP leaders; in quoting from them we must assume they are true copies of letters actually sent.
7   Quote from *The Flag in the Wind*, pp. 65–6. The letter from John MacCormick is to Duncan McNeill, March 1933.
8   Anecdotes of R. B. Cunninghame Graham were given by NMG in conversation with Pick and Hart.
9   21 Oct. 1934, Dep. 209, Box 15.
10 On Grieve, see Glen, *Hugh MacDiarmid*, esp. Ch. 5; Lindsay, *By Yon Bonnie Banks* (London: Hutchinson, 1961) esp. pp. 162–3; P. H. Butter, *Edwin Muir* (Edinburgh: Oliver & Boyd, 1966); Power, *Should Auld Acquaintance*, pp. 210–12.
11 Reports of what Grieve said about NMG come from NMG at third hand, and must be taken accordingly.
12 Grieve's letters to Gunn and copies of NMG letters to Grieve, in Dep. 209, Box 17.
13 *The Flag in the Wind*, pp. 45–6.
14 MS reminiscences of NMG by Robin MacEwen were provided to Hart in autumn 1978.
15 Reminiscences of Margaret MacEwen and her other brothers, David and Malcolm, given in conversation with Hart, winter 1978, and in letters to JBP.
16 On Anson, see NMG foreword to Anson's *Life on Low Shore* (Banff, 1969).
17 On the trips with Daisy, see especially (in addition to NMG's reminiscences in conversation) 'Wayfaring Memories of 1938', *SMT Magazine*, Jan. 1939, p. 67; 'Edinburgh', ts in Dep. 209, Box 8; 'Off in the Car', ts in Box 9; 'Picts' Houses' in the same.
18 NMG reminiscences of Walsh on entering Kerry, in conversation with Hart.

19 NMG letter to Morley about 1934 trip, NLS Acc. 5412.
20 Robin MacEwen's reminiscences in MS cited above.
21 Letter to Naomi Mitchison, NLS Acc. 5813.
22 *The Well at the World's End* (London: Faber & Faber, 1951), pp. 139–48.
23 William Power, *Should Auld Acquaintance*, pp. 175, 207.
24 David MacEwen's anonymous sketch appeared in *Scots Review*, Feb. 1948, p. 150.
25 Arthur Ball's reminiscences sent to Pick, 6 Feb. 1979.
26 NMG to Nan Shepherd, NLS Acc. 6118, dated 24 March 1933.
27 *Should Auld Acquaintance*, p. 196.
28 Ena Macleod provided reminiscences of NMG to Hart in Feb. 1972.
29 NMG in 'The One Who Will Come', ts in Dep. 209, Box 9, and in 'The Ferry of the Dead', *Scots Mag.*, Oct. 1937.

9 A TIME FOR DECISIONS

1 Hart's essay appears as 'Neil M. Gunn: A Brief Memoir', in *Neil M. Gunn: The Man and the Writer* (Edinburgh: Blackwood, 1973). The passage as revised by Hart is on pp. 43–4.
2 Recollections of the lost child come from family visitors to Neil in hospital, from David MacEwen in conversation with Hart, Jan. 1979, and from Stanley Hill, in MS reminiscences of 1973, sent to Hart in Sept. 1978.
3 *The Shadow* (London: Faber & Faber, 1948), p. 98.
4 References to Daisy's poor health come from MacEwen family reminiscences, Chrystine Frew, corresp. with Grieve, Blake (Dep. 209, Box 17). NMG letter to William McCance, courtesy of Mrs Margaret McCance.
5 'The Mirror' was collected in *The White Hour* (London: Faber & Faber, 1950), pp. 158–66.
6 *The Serpent* (London: Faber & Faber, 1943), p. 67.
7 *The Serpent*, p. 122.
8 Letters of NMG to Margaret MacEwen, copies courtesy of M. MacEwen. Her reminiscences are taken from an extensive taped memoir made for us in Dec. 1978, and several letters to us of the same time. The account given here is selective.
9 Daisy Gunn to F. M. McNeill in NLS Acc. 5453.
10 NLS Dep. 209, Box 17.
11 As above.
12 Correspondence of L. G. Gibbon with NMG in Dep. 209, Box 17. *Scottish Scene* (London: Jarrold, 1934), p. 200.
13 Ian S. Munro, *Leslie Mitchell: Lewis Grassic Gibbon* (Edinburgh: Oliver & Boyd, 1966), p. 188. Text here is taken, rather, from NLS Dep. 209, Box 17 MS, which differs somewhat.
14 David MacEwen reminiscence of *Whisky and Scotland* in conversation with Hart, Jan. 1979.
15 Corresp. of NMG with Routledge & Kegan Paul, NLS Dep. 209, Box 12.
16 'High on the Haggis', *Holiday*, Nov. 1959, p. 96.
17 T. S. Eliot letters are in Dep. 209, Box 17.
18 NMG reminiscences of the visit in conversation with Hart.
19 NMG to Morley in NLS Acc. 5412.
20 Alexander Gunn's reminiscences in letter to Lorena Hart, Feb. 1972.
21 NMG in 'Reaches of the Conon', printed copy in Dep. 209, Box 9.
22 Neil Paterson's judgement on anglers, in conversation with Hart, Nov. 1978.

23 Dedication to *Highland River* (Edinburgh: Porpoise, 1937), p. 5.
24 Pencilled notes on *Highland River* for interview with George Bruce, Dep. 209, Box 10.
25 *Highland River*, p. 121.
26 Morley, NLS Dep. 209, Box 17. Bridie, Box 18.
27 Reviews: *TLS*, 12 June 1937; *Glasgow Herald*, 3 June 1937; *Scots Mag.*, June 1937.
28 Draft letter to Grieve in Dep. 209, Box 17.
29 Dover Wilson's request (19 Sept.) and draft reply from NMG in Dep. 209, Box 21.
30 Cancelled pencilled note on Macrae for Bruce interview, Dep. 209, Box 10.
31 The visit of Faber partners was recalled in conversation with Hart.
32 T. S. Eliot to Daisy in Box 17.
33 The offer to buy Larachan was recalled in conversation with Hart, and documented in Box 27.
34 NMG's letter of resignation from H.M. Customs & Excise by permission of the Controller of HMSO.

III BRAEFARM: THE WRITER AS PROFESSIONAL (1937–1949)

10 OFF IN A BOAT

1 *Off in a Boat* (London: Faber & Faber, 1938).
2 Walsh, review of *Off in a Boat*, *Irish Times*, 30 May 1938.
3 *Off in a Boat*, pp. 243–5.
4 'A Balance Sheet', *Scots Mag.*, Jan. 1941.
5 'On Looking at Things', *Scots Mag.*, June 1940.
6 Daisy's notebook is in NLS Dep. 209, Box 1, and her photographs are in Boxes 29–33.

11 THE HOUSEHOLDER

1 The physiotherapist's reminiscence was provided to Pick.
2 Henderson's description from conversation with Pick, autumn 1978.
3 R. MacEwen's recollections from MS memoir sent to Hart.
4 *The Lost Chart* (London: Faber & Faber, 1949), pp. 208–9.
5 Nan Shepherd to NMG Dep. 209, Box 19.
6 NMG to Nan Shepherd NLS Acc. 6118.
7 Keith Henderson in letter to Pick, autumn 1978.
8 *The Shadow* (London: Faber & Faber, 1948), pp. 32–3.
9 *Highland Pack* (London: Faber & Faber, 1949), p. 68.
10 *Highland Pack*, p. 56.
11 *Highland Pack*, p. 199.
12 *Highland Pack*, p. 32.
13 *The Shadow*, p. 20.
14 Ena Macleod's recollections are from MS memoir provided to Hart in 1972.
15 *Highland Pack*, p. 146.
16 Belle Maltman sent her reminiscence to Pick in winter 1978.
17 Description of Aunt Phemie, *The Shadow*, pp. 35–6.
18 Gene Pick's description was written for Hart in 1972.
19 Daisy as Fand, *The Well at the World's End* (London: Faber & Faber, 1951), p. 34.
20 *Highland Pack*, p. 61.
21 *The Well at the World's End*, p. 62.

22 NMG letters to Naomi Mitchison are in NLS Acc. 5813 and 5869.
23 The German trips are recounted in 'As Drunk as a Bavarian', *Scots Mag.*, April 1939.
24 Review of *Off in a Boat*, *Irish Times*, 30 May 1938.
25 The fancy dress ball is recalled in a letter to Hart, 11 Aug. 1964.
26 Margaret and Malcolm MacEwen gave their views to Pick in letters, 1979.
27 The 1939 journal is in NLS Dep. 209, Box 1.

12 MAN AT WORK

1 Working without a complete bibliography of NMG's occasional writing we have had to depend on the large collection of clipped articles preserved by Daisy and now in Dep. 209, Boxes 8 and 9. *Daily Record* arrangement is reported in a letter to Naomi Mitchison, 25 Oct. 1942.
2 See, for example, 'The Family Boat', *Scots Mag.*, June 1937, and 'The Herring Industry', *Glasgow Herald*, 7 May 1940.
3 The short story 'Whisky' we have only seen in ts in Dep. 209, Box 4.
4 NMG's late recollection about *Wild Geese Overhead* was given in conversation with Hart, 1967.
5 'The Mirror', see *The White Hour*, p. 161.
6 *The Key of the Chest* (London: Faber & Faber, 1945), p. 207.
7 Alexander Reid recalls the meeting in *Scotland's Mag.*, April 1973.
8 Nan Shepherd to NMG, NLS Dep. 209, Box 19.
·9 NMG to Nan Shepherd, NLS Acc. 6118.
10 NMG to Naomi Mitchison, NLS Acc. 5813.
11 On the genesis of the 'second sight' stories, see *Off in a Boat*, pp. 137–43.
12 Two ts copies of the play 'Second Sight' survive in Dep. 209, Box 6.
13 Bridie's comments, dated 5 March 1938, are in Dep. 209, Box 18.
14 1939 journal is in NLS Dep. 209, Box 1.
15 *Atom*, p. 101.
16 Alexander Gunn's recollection is in a Feb. 1972 letter to Lorena Hart.
17 On Anson's influence, see NMG foreword to *Life on Low Shore* (Banff, 1969).
18 'Doom in the Moray Firth' and 'The Family Boat' were in *Scots Mag.*; 'Fishermen in the Northwest', in *Scotland*.
19 Ena Macleod's memoir, written for Hart, was dated Jan. 1972. The account of the Flannan Isles trip was published initially in four parts in *Chambers' Journal*, Feb. to May 1940, with a follow-up on the ship they passed in *Scots Mag.*, Aug. 1940.
20 *The Silver Darlings* (London: Faber & Faber, 1941), p. 540.
21 *The Silver Darlings*, p. 456.

13 THE MAN OF AFFAIRS

1 *Highland Pack*, pp. 203–4.
2 NMG to George Blake, courtesy of Mrs Ellie Blake.
3 William Ferguson, *Scotland: 1689 to the Present* (Edinburgh: Oliver & Boyd, 1968), p. 383.
4 Tom Johnston, *Memories* (London: Collins, 1952), p. 150.
5 J. G. Kellas, *Modern Scotland* (London: Pall Mall, 1968), p. 139.
6 NMG to Margaret MacEwen, courtesy of M. MacEwen.

7   Information on the Hospitals Commission from the Report of 1943 (Dep. 209, Box 24).

8   Reminiscences from Margaret MacEwen written to Pick in winter 1978.

9   NMG reported to Naomi Mitchison in April that he was completing the proofs of a novel that is obviously *The Serpent*, but Faber hesitated to bring out the new and sombre book for another fourteen months, reporting wartime problems with paper supplies.

10   The 'beautiful accident' is reconstructed from conversations with Pick and Hart.

11   This letter is taken from NMG's carbon, n.d., provided to Hart, 1965.

12   *Young Art and Old Hector* (London: Faber & Faber, 1942), p. 173.

13   *Young Art and Old Hector*, p. 190.

14   The parts appeared as follows: 'The First Run of Grilse' (*Chambers'*, June 1941); 'The Birdbeast and the Seven Puppies' – renamed 'Machinery' (*Chambers'*, Sept. 1941); 'Under the Old Gooseberry Bush' (*Scots Mag.*, Nov. 1941); 'First and Second Childhood' (*Scots Mag.*, Dec. 1941); 'The Knife, the Glass Ball and the Penny' (*Chambers'*, Jan. 1942); 'The New Jersey', 'Art Runs a Great Race' and 'Nowhere and Somewhere' (all *SM* Jan., Feb., March 1942). The book appeared in March. (Note the switch to *Scots Mag.* NMG evidently felt that he owed some stories to Salmond.)

15   Corresp. with A. M. Mackenzie is in Dep. 209, Box 21 and NLS MS 9222.

16   Reviews: *TLS*, 14 March 1942; *NS&N*, 9 May 1942.

17   Corresp. with Nan Shepherd, NLS Acc. 6118.

18   Corresp. with Naomi Mitchison, NLS Acc. 5813 and 5869. NM to NMG in Dep. 209, Box 18.

19   *The Serpent* (London: Faber & Faber, 1943), pp. 175–6.

20   *The Serpent*, p. 218.

21   *The Serpent*, p. 181.

22   *The Serpent*, p. 187.

23   *The Serpent*, p. 122.

24   Reviews: *Guardian*, 25 June 1943; Muir in *Scots Mag.*, Aug. 1943.

25   P. H. Butter, *Edwin Muir: Man and Poet* (Edinburgh: Oliver & Boyd, 1966) and *Selected Letters of Edwin Muir*, ed. Butter (London: Hogarth, 1974), pp. 151–2.

26   NMG corresp. about films and film-companies is in Dep. 209, Box 14.

27   The letter to Nakamura is the same one quoted regarding *Young Art and Old Hector*, taken from NMG's carbon of 1965.

28   NMG-Mitchison corresp., Dep. 209, Box 18 and NLS Acc. 5813 and 5869.

29   NMG to Joseph Macleod, courtesy of Joseph Macleod.

30   *The Green Isle of the Great Deep* (London: Faber & Faber, 1944), p. 242.

31   Pick article, see *Gangrel*, no. 2, 1945.

32   'The Novel at Home' appeared in *SM*, April 1946 and later in *The Writer*, June 1946.

33   *The Green Isle of the Great Deep*, p. 245.

34   *TLS* review, 24 June 1944.

35   Sales figures as reported to NMG, NLS Dep. 209, Box 11.

14 THE MATURE WRITER

1   *The Green Isle of the Great Deep*, p. 226.

2   *The Key of the Chest* (London: Faber & Faber, 1945), p. 228.

3   *The Key of the Chest*, p. 206.

4   For NMG corresp. with Kennerley of Faber, see Dep. 209, Box 11, and NLS Acc. 5412.

5 A version of this account is given in 'Memories of Neil Gunn', *Studies in Scottish Literature,* vol. XIV, 1979.
6 NMG to Naomi Mitchison, NLS Acc. 5813 and 5869.
7 Ian McKillop's letter to NMG is in Dep. 209, Box 21.
8 Letter to Pick.
9 Douglas Muhr corresp. in Dep. 209, Box 21. Quoted by kind permission of Mrs Mary Muhr.
10 Faber corresp. is in Box 11 and in NLS Acc. 5412.
11 NLS Dep. 209, Box 19.
12 Letters to Nan Shepherd in NLS Acc. 6118. Neil is more hopeful in a letter to Gene Pick: 'You wonder if Nan can help Ranald in London. The way it struck me is that she would help by *being* rather than by *doing*, whatever she might actually do. That's about all that can be said. Ranald will go his own way, quite remorselessly, but Nan's *being* will affect him in the deep place, until at last he will question what is missing in his theory, and this will lead to doubt.'
13 A. M. Mackenzie corresp. Dep. 209, Box 21.
14 *The Shadow,* pp. 74–5.
15 *The Silver Bough* notebook is in NLS Dep. 209, Box 1.
16 Letter to Pick, n.d.
17 NLS Acc. 5412.
18 NMG to A. M. Mackenzie in NLS MS. 9222.
19 Sir Alexander Gray to NMG is in NLS Dep. 209, Box 21.
20 The letter from Edwin Muir appears in *Selected Letters of Edwin Muir,* ed. Butter, p. 150.
21 NMG letters declining to stand for Rector and agreeing to write the *Jabberwock* article ('Calvinism and Critics') are taken from carbons kept by Neil.
22 *The Shadow,* p. 207.
23 *The Lost Chart* (London: Faber & Faber, 1949) p. 157.
24 *The Lost Chart,* p. 306.
25 *The Lost Chart,* p. 307.
26 *The Lost Chart,* pp. 100, 110–11.
27 *The Lost Chart,* pp. 319, 325.
28 *The Lost Chart,* p. 122.
29 *The Lost Chart,* p. 107.
30 *The Lost Chart,* p. 277.
31 Cf 'The Rose at the Gable-End', *Highland Pack,* p. 145.

IV LIGHT AT THE END (1949–1973)

15 THE WELL AT THE WORLD'S END

1 Daisy to 'Floss' McNeill in NLS Acc. 5453, dated by internal evidence as late 1950.
2 Ena Macleod's reminiscence is in MS memoir of Jan. 1972.
3 Keith Henderson's view from conversation with Pick.
4 Descriptions of Kincraig from recollection of Pick.
5 Dep. 209, Box 27 contains domestic records and complaints about the dump.
6 *Holiday* articles (from 1947 to 1959) have been drawn upon for Part I. Corresp. with U.S. agent Brandt & Brandt is in Box 11 of Dep. 209.
7 Unless otherwise indicated, NMG's letters to Pick were not dated.
8 To Gene Pick.
9 *The Well at the World's End* (London: Faber & Faber, 1951), pp. 20, 27.

10 *WAWE*, p. 133.
11 *WAWE*, p. 10.
12 *WAWE*, p. 19.
13 *WAWE*, p. 295.
14 To Pick.
15 *WAWE*, p. 22.
16 *WAWE*, p. 23.
17 *WAWE*, p. 292.
18 *WAWE*, p. 251.
19 *WAWE*, p. 256.
20 *WAWE*, p. 258.
21 *Point*, no. 4, 1968–9, p. 25.
22 *Atom*, p. 29.
23 *WAWE*, p. 262.
24 NMG corresp. with Faber in NLS Acc. 5412.
25 *WAWE*, pp. 147–8.
26 Correspondence with Naomi Mitchison in NLS Acc. 5813.
27 'The Peaceful Black Isle', an example of the kind of local travel essay which NMG did so often during the Kincraig and Kerrow years, appeared in *Scotland's Mag.*. Oct. 1961. For the origin of the 'Well' episode, see 'The Pursuit of Light' (*SMT Mag.?*) in Dep. 209, Box 9.

16 GOODBYE TO BOOKS

1   On Glen Cannich in the process of change, see NMG 'Giants and Distant Bells', *Glasgow Herald*, 18 Feb. 1950 and 'Living in Scotland Today', *Scottish Field*, Feb. 1956.
2   Information on the Crofting Inquiry comes chiefly from *Report of the Commission of Inquiry into Crofting Conditions*, April 1954 (Edinburgh: HMSO: Dept. of Agriculture for Scotland).
3   NLS Dep. 209, Box 16 contains NMG corresp. and reports and minutes relative to his role in the inquiry.
4   'Highlands and Islands', a ts by NMG, n.d., in NLS Dep. 209, Box 8.
5   'Life in the Highlands', script for Maurice Lindsay's BBC Overseas programme in Dep. 209, Box 10.
6   We are indebted to Lady Taylor for permission to quote Sir Thomas Taylor's letter.
7   Sir Matthew Campbell's letter was sent to Pick in 1979.
8   Keith Henderson in conversation with Pick, 1978.
9   Corresp. relating to 'Beyond the Cage' is in NLS Dep. 209, Boxes 5 and 12. Box 12 also contains corresp. concerning Neil's work for BBC.
10 *Bloodhunt* (London: Faber & Faber, 1952), pp. 30, 57–8.
11 *Bloodhunt*, pp. 111, 129, 133.
12 NMG in conversation: see *Neil M. Gunn: The Man and the Writer*, pp. 50–1.
13 Letter from Faber, NLS Dep. 209, Box 11.
14 The troubles at Kerrow are described in a letter to Robert Wotherspoon (20 July 1952) in Dep. 209, Box 27, and otherwise are from the recollections of Pick.
15 'Light' in *Point*, no. 3, Summer 1968.
16 *Atom*, pp. 143–4.
17 'The Miraculous', *Point*, no. 4, Winter 1968–9, p. 23.

18 For the Major, see *The Other Landscape* (London: Faber & Faber, 1954), pp. 203, 195, 200.
19 *The Other Landscape*, p. 70.
20 *The Other Landscape*, p. 258.
21 NMG to Nan Shepherd in NLS Acc. 6118.
22 Neil Paterson's reminiscence of Kerrow is in *Neil M. Gunn: The Man and the Writer*, pp. 61–2.
23 Keith Henderson's letters to NMG are in Dep. 209, Box 18.
24 Neil had sold the Singer with its special let-down seats after many years and bought a new Austin A40.
25 George Bruce's recollections of NMG at Kerrow were written to Hart in 1972 (see *Neil M. Gunn: The Man and the Writer*, p. 54).
26 Duncan Maclennan's recollections in a letter to Pick, 1979.
27 To Pick, n.d.
28 *Saltire Review* articles unnamed in the text appeared as follows: 'The Flash', Autumn 1958; 'Eight Times Up', Winter 1957; 'Remember Yourself', Spring 1959. NMG's (17 April 1958) letter to Reid (Dep. 209, Box 19, carbon copy) provides the autobiographical basis for Reid's account in 'The Theme is Man'.
29 To Pick.
30 The S. J. Looker letter to NMG is in the possession of Pick to whom Neil sent it with a request to call on Mr Looker. Quoted by courtesy of Joan Looker.

17 PLOYS

1 Unless otherwise identified, letters quoted are to Pick.
2 Scripts of NMG's broadcast talks and dramatic programmes are in NLS Dep. 209, Box 10; correspondence with BBC people is in Box 12; letters from Bruce and Grimble are in Box 17; and NMG letters to Grimble are in NLS Acc. 5416.
3 Grimble's description of NMG as a broadcaster, in letter to Hart, 20 Dec. 1978. Other information regarding NMG and broadcasting from George Bruce in conversation with Hart, Jan. 1979.
4 Corresp. about the film script *The Water of Life* is in NLS Dep. 209, Box 14; four copies of script and 'treatment' are in Box 7, with the contract.
5 NMG was right: The Tormore *is* a delectable dram.
6 Corresp. and other items concerning the Tormore distillery and NMG's work for Long John are in Box 13. Copies of many NMG letters to H. Forsyth Hardy and Films of Scotland by courtesy of Neil Paterson.
7 NMG family papers are in Dep. 209, Boxes 27 and 28. From 1953 to 1970 Neil made drafts of letters, articles and addresses for Robert Wotherspoon in seven notebooks, now in Box 1, and much information in this chapter comes from them.
8 Ronald Mavor in conversation with Hart, Dec. 1978. Mavor generously gave access to his files of James Bridie corresp., containing letters from NMG to Bridie and himself.
9 'Memories of Neil Gunn', *Studies in Scottish Literature*, XIV.

18 THE GREATEST LOSS

1 Recollections of Dalcraig are from numerous visits by Pick and Hart. Letters of NMG are to Pick unless otherwise identified.

2 Accounts of the Grampian TV venture from conversations with NMG, Neil Paterson, Ian Grimble.
3 Account of seventieth birthday party from Mavor, Paterson, Pick.
4 Letter from Grimble to NMG in Dep. 209, Box 17.
5 Letter from Reid to NMG in Dep. 209, Box 19.

19 ALONE

1 Letters of NMG to Margaret MacEwen, courtesy of M. MacEwen.
2 NMG letter to Maurice Walsh is from NLS Acc. 5461.
3 Ian Grimble's reminiscence is in *Leopard Mag.* (Aberdeen), Autumn 1976.
4 Letters from T. Nakamura are in Dep. 209, Box 18.
5 Letters from F. R. Hart in Dep. 209, Box 19.
6 This letter to NMG is in Dep. 209, Box 22, and is printed here by courtesy of Alastair Reid.
7 NMG's own reminiscence, in conversation with Pick.
8 *Zen Flesh, Zen Bones,* compiled by Paul Reps (London: Penguin, 1971), particularly the section called 'Centreing' at the end of the book.
9 The thirteen-page film idea survives in a letter to Robert Clark, Dep. 209, Box 14.
10 Hart reminiscences are from journals of visits to NMG, kept 1965–71.
11 From letters to Hart, in his possession.
12 Neil Paterson in *Neil M. Gunn: The Man and the Writer,* pp. 65–6.
13 Recollections of eighty-first birthday party from J. B. Caird in a letter to, and conversation with, Hart.
14 Account of NMG's last hours in Dalcraig, Kate Sharpe in conversation with JBP, and Chrystine Frew in a letter.
15 Alex Reid's account is in his 'Appreciation' of NMG, *Scotland's Mag.,* April 1973.
16 John Gunn to Hart, late Feb. 1973.

Selected Bibliography

The complete bibliography of Neil Gunn's published work prepared by C. J. L. Stokoe has not yet been published, nor have we seen it; we have made no attempt to duplicate his years of work. The following lists Neil's books (based on W.R. Aitken's bibliography in *Neil M. Gunn: The Man and the Writer*, pp. 392–7), the locations of principal manuscripts used in this study, and other works cited by us. Detailed references are found in our Notes on Sources.

I BOOKS BY NEIL M. GUNN

The Atom of Delight (London: Faber & Faber, 1956). Autobiography.

Bloodhunt (London: Faber & Faber, 1952).

Butcher's Broom (Edinburgh: Porpoise, 1934; repr. Bath: Chivers, for London & Home Counties Branch of the Library Association, 1965; repr. London: Souvenir, 1977).

The Drinking Well (London: Faber & Faber, 1946—actually pub. early 1947; repr. London: Souvenir, 1978).

The Green Isle of the Great Deep (London: Faber & Faber, 1944; repr. London: Souvenir, 1975).

The Grey Coast (London: Cape, 1926; Edinburgh: Porpoise, 1931; repr. London: Souvenir, 1976).

Hidden Doors (Edinburgh: Porpoise, 1929). Short stories.

Highland Pack (London: Faber & Faber, 1949). Essays.

Highland River (Edinburgh: Porpoise, 1937; London: Faber & Faber, 1942, 1943; repr. in Arrow Books, 1960).

The Key of the Chest (London: Faber & Faber, 1945; repr. Bath: Chivers, for Library Assoc., 1966).

The Lost Chart (London: Faber & Faber, 1949).

The Lost Glen (serialised *Scots Mag.*, Apr.–Nov., 1928; Edinburgh: Porpoise, 1932).

Morning Tide (Edinburgh: Porpoise, 1930, 1931; London: Faber & Faber, 1953; repr. London: Souvenir, 1975).

Off in a Boat (London: Faber & Faber, 1938). Travel & autobiography.

The Other Landscape (London: Faber & Faber, 1954).

The Poaching at Grianan (serialised *Scots Mag.*, Sept. 1929–Apr. 1930).

Second Sight (London: Faber & Faber, 1940).

The Serpent (London: Faber & Faber, 1943; repr. Inverness: Club Leabhar, 1969; London: Souvenir, 1978).

The Shadow (London: Faber & Faber, 1948).

The Silver Bough (London: Faber & Faber, 1948).

The Silver Darlings (London: Faber & Faber, 1941, 1969).

Storm and Precipice (London: Faber & Faber, 1942). Anthology of extracts.

Sun Circle (Edinburgh: Porpoise, 1933).

The Well at the World's End (London: Faber & Faber, 1951; repr. Bath: Chivers, for Library Assoc., 1968).

Wild Geese Overhead (London: Faber & Faber, 1939).

Whisky and Scotland (London: Routledge, 1935; repr. London: Souvenir, 1977). Essay.

The White Hour (London: Faber & Faber, 1950). Short stories.

Young Art and Old Hector (London: Faber & Faber, 1942; repr. London: Souvenir, 1976).

II PRINCIPAL MANUSCRIPTS

A   National Library of Scotland, Deposit 209 (N. M. Gunn Papers, deposited by J. W. M. Gunn, 1973). Thirty-three boxes containing notebooks; typescripts of *The Atom of Delight*, plays, stories, articles, interviews, addresses, broadcast talks; clipped printed copies of short stories and articles (sometimes without date or source); reviews and articles about NMG; corresp. to NMG and numerous copies and drafts of NMG's replies; poems by NMG; government papers regarding NMG's public service activities; adaptations of novels by NMG; family papers and photographs. Detailed references appear in the Notes on Sources.

B   Letters of NMG in the NLS: to George Bruce (Acc. 5471 & 6154); Faber & Faber (Acc. 5412); Ian Grimble (Acc. 5416); Mairi C. Ireland (Acc. 4559); Agnes M. Mackenzie (MS 9222); Ena Macleod (Acc. 5457); F. Marian McNeill (Acc. 5453); Ronald Mavor (Acc. 5472); Naomi Mitchison (Acc. 5813, 5869, & 5885); Alastair Reid (Acc. 5799); Robin Richardson (Acc. 5310); Nan Shepherd (Acc. 5449 & 6118); Maurice Walsh (Acc. 5461); Kurt Wittig (Acc. 5450).

C   Other Principal Manuscript Sources (additional items are identified in Notes on Sources): MS Memoir from Alexander Gunn to L. L. Hart (Feb. 1972) possession of Harts. NMG letters to H. Forsyth Hardy (copies courtesy of Neil Paterson). Letters of NMG to F. R. & L. L. Hart, 1961–72 (approx. 100, possession of Harts).

Conversations of NMG with Harts (1965–71), notes possession of Harts.

MS memoir of Stanley Hill (copy from S. Hill).

Letters of NMG to Margaret MacEwen (copies courtesy of M. MacEwen).

Memoir of Margaret MacEwen (tape in possession of Hart).

MS memoir of Robin R. MacEwen (possession of Hart).

MS memoir from Ena Macleod to F. R. Hart, Jan. 1972 (possession of Hart).

NMG letters to O. H. Mavor ('James Bridie') and Ronald Mavor (possession of R. Mavor).

NMG letters to J. B. Pick and Gene Pick (1946–72, approx. 150, possession of Picks).

Conversations of NMG with J. B. Pick (notes possession of Pick).

III OTHER PUBLISHED SOURCES

Aitken, W. R., 'Neil M. Gunn: A Bibliography', in *Neil M. Gunn: The Man and the Writer,* ed. A. Scott and D. Gifford (Edinburgh: Blackwood, 1973), pp. 389–97.

'Neil Gunn's revision of his first novel', *Bibliotheck*, VI (1972), pp. 114–17.

Allan, John R., *North-East Lowlands of Scotland.* London: Robert Hale, 1974.

Anson, Peter F., *Harbour Head: Maritime Memories.* London: Gifford, 1944.

Life on Low Shore (Foreword by N. M. Gunn). Banff: *Banffshire Journal*, 1969.

A Roving Recluse. Cork: Mercier, 1946.

Bannister, Winifred, *James Bridie and His Theatre.* London: Rockliff, 1955.

Beachcroft, T. O., *The Modest Art.* London: Oxford U.P., 1968.

Bridie, James (O. H. Mavor), *One Way of Living.* London: Constable, 1939.

Butter, P. H. *Edwin Muir: Man and Poet.* Edinburgh: Oliver & Boyd, 1966.

Campbell, Alexander, *The Grampians Desolate.* Edinburgh: John Moir, 1804.

Carmichael, Alexander, *Carmina Gadelica* (in Gaelic and English, six vols.). Edinburgh: Scottish Academic Press, 1971–2.

Cruickshank, Helen B., *Octobiography.* Standard Press, 1976.

Duncan, Jane, *A Letter from Reachfar.* London: Macmillan, 1975.

Duval, K. D., & Smith, S. G. (ed.), *Hugh MacDiarmid: A Festschrift.* Edinburgh: Duval, 1962.

Ferguson, William, *Scotland: 1689 to the Present.* Edinburgh: Oliver & Boyd, 1968.

Gibbon, Lewis Grassic (J. Leslie Mitchell), & MacDiarmid, Hugh (Grieve, C.M.), *Scottish Scene.* London: Jarrolds, 1934.

Glen, Duncan, *Hugh MacDiarmid and the Scottish Renaissance.* Edinburgh: Chambers, 1964.

Graham, Cuthbert, *Portrait of the Moray Firth.* London: Robert Hale, 1977.

Grieve, C.M., *Contemporary Scottish Studies: First Series.* London: Leonard Parsons, 1926.

The Company I've Kept. London: Hutchinson, 1966.

Grimble, Ian, 'Neil M. Gunn', *Leopard* (Aberdeen), Autumn 1976.

Scottish Clans and Tartans. London: Hamlyn, 1973.

Gunn, Mark Rudd, *History of the Clan Gunn.* Glasgow: Maclaren, n.d. [*c.* 1965].

Hanham, H. J., *Scottish Nationalism*. London: Faber & Faber, 1969.

Hart, Francis R., 'Neil M. Gunn: A Brief Memoir', in *Neil M. Gunn: The Man and the Writer*, ed. A. Scott & D. Gifford.

The Hub of the Highlands: The Book of Inverness and District. Inverness Field Club, 1975.

Inverness Courier Guide, 1939.

Johnston, Thomas, *Memories*. London: Collins, 1952.

Jukes, H. R., *The Loved River*. London: Faber & Faber, 1935.

Keir, David, *The Desolation of the Highlands*. Fact No. 17, 15 Aug. 1938.

Kellas, J. G., *Modern Scotland*. London: Pall Mall, 1968.

Kingsmill, Hugh, & Pearson, Hesketh, *Skye High*. London: Hamish Hamilton 1937.

Kirkcudbrightshire Advertiser and Galloway News, 1904–6.

Lindsay, Maurice, *By Yon Bonnie Banks*. London: Hutchinson, 1961.

Linklater, Eric, *The Art of Adventure*. London: Macmillan, 1947.

MacCormick, John M., *The Flag in the Wind*. London: Gollancz, 1955.

McDowall, R. J. S. *The Whiskies of Scotland*. 3rd edn., London: John Murray, 1975.

[MacEwen, David], 'Neil M. Gunn', *Scots Review*, Feb. 1948.

Mackenzie, Alexander, *History of the Highland Clearances*. Melven Press, 1979 [reprint].

Mackenzie, Compton, *My Life and Times. Octave Six*. London: Chatto & Windus, 1967.

Morrison, David (ed.), *Essays on Neil M. Gunn*. Thurso: Humphries, 1971.

Muir, Edwin, *Scott and Scotland*. London: Routledge, 1936.

  Selected Letters, ed. P. H. Butter. London: Hogarth Press, 1974.

Northern Review, August and September 1924.

O'Connor, Frank, *The Lonely Voice*. London: Macmillan, 1963.

O'Faolain, Sean, *The Short Story*. London: Collins, 1948.

Omand, D. (ed.), *The Caithness Book* (Foreword by N. M. Gunn). Inverness: Highland Printers, 1972.

Paterson, Neil, 'A Friendship', *Neil M. Gunn: The Man and the Writer*, ed. A. Scott & D. Gifford.

Pick, J. B., 'Memories of Neil Gunn', *Studies in Scottish Literature*, XIV (1979).
  'The Work of Neil M. Gunn', *Gangrel*, 2 (1944).
  (ed.) *Point*, Summer 1968; Winter 1968–9.

Power, William, *Literature and Oatmeal*. London: Routledge, 1935.
  Should Auld Acquaintance. London: Harrap, 1937.

Reid, Alastair, 'The Sporting Scene', *New Yorker*, 29 Aug. 1970.

Reid, Alexander, 'Neil M. Gunn: An Appreciation', *Scotland's Magazine*, April 1973. (See also 'Neil Gunn's Mysticism', *Neil M. Gunn: The Man and the Writer*.)

'The Theme is Man', *Scotland's Magazine,* July 1958.

Robb, J. Marshall, *Scotch Whisky: A Guide* (Foreword by Maurice Walsh, dated 3 May 1950). London & Edinburgh: Chambers, n.d.

Saltire Review, 1957–9.

Scots Independent, 1929–30.

Scott, A., & Gifford, D. (ed.), *Neil M. Gunn: The Man and the Writer.* Edinburgh: Blackwood, 1973.

Scott Moncrieff, George (ed.) *Scottish Country* (Includes 'Caithness and Sutherland' by N.M.G.). London: Wishart, 1935.

Scottish Chapbook. Feb. 1923.

Scottish Nation. May and June 1923.

Walsh, Maurice, *The Key Above the Door.* Harmondsworth: Penguin, 1958 (orig. pub., Chambers, 1926).

Index

314

Index